Part 1

2000: Key News and Turning Points

2000
Table of Contents

PART 1 2000: Key News and Turning Points
Publishing Overview, Children's Books Take the Lead   7
Market Overview, Magazines & the Millennium   25
Timeline, 1999 Marched On   37

PART 2 Market Perspectives
PreK Nonfiction, Across the Street or Across the Millennium 51
Middle-Grade Fiction, Intense & Funny, Safe & Searching   59
Poetry, Voices of Verse   69

PART 3 Submissions & Style
Submissions, Win the Day with Queries, Cover Letters,
    & Other Correspondence   79
Biography & Characters, Real Lives, Real Stories   109
Language, At the Service of Story: Dialect, Slang, & Accents 119
Focus in Nonfiction, Follow the Thread   127

PART 4 The Business Side
Networking, How to Connect the Publishing Dots   137
The Making of a Magazine, Set the Tempo   145
Distribution, Getting Books to Readers   153
Special Sales & Niche Marketing, Reach an Expanding Marketplace 161
Book Fairs & Clubs, The Right Book in the Right Place   169
Career Concerns, Insurance for Freelancers   177
Agents, Forecast: Sunny, a Few Clouds on the Horizon   183

PART 5 Reference & Research
Resources, The Wondrous & Complex World of
    Five Research Libraries   195
Sports Research & Writing, All About Stats?   211
Online Research, Lost & Found on the Internet   223
Online Research, In Search of Photos on the Web   229

Part 6 Profiles

Mary Azarian, Picture the Moment	239
Marilyn Edwards, Values-Added Publishing	243
Frances Foster, Open to Story	249
Nancy Gruver & Joe Kelly, Girl Power & Media	255
Mary Heaton, When Words Call	259
Jacqueline Briggs Martin, To Bear the Weight of Story	263
J.K. Rowling, A Magical First	267
Louis Sachar, Writing for the Fun of It	271
Stella Sands, Honest Work	277
Judith Woodburn, A Bookshelf to Be Filled	281

Part 7 Idea Generation

Idea Generators, 52 Exercises for the Year 2000	287
Ideas Online, Alive with Inspiration	299
Sparks for Ideas, Feasts & Celebrations	305
Sparks for Ideas, Anniversaries in History, Science, & Culture	313

Part 8 Award, Contest, & Conference Listings

Writers' Contests & Awards	331
Writers' Conferences	383
Conferences Devoted to Writing for Children, General Conferences	383
Conferences Devoted to Writing for Children, SCBWI	387
Conferences with Sessions on Writing for Children,	
University or Regional Conferences	391
Conferences with Sessions on Writing for Children,	
Religious Writing Conferences	401

Index   403

CHILDREN'S WRITER®
Guide to 2000

Editor: Susan M. Tierney

Contributing writers:
Elaine Marie Alphin
Marilyn D. Anderson
Joan Broerman
Kim Childress
Pat Conway
Donna Freedman
Vicki Hambleton
Mark Haverstock
Veda Boyd Jones
Jean Lewis
Catherine Frey Murphy
Julianne Papp
Patricia Curtis Pfitsch
Pegi Deitz Shea
Margaret Springer
Carolyn Yoder

Cover art & illustrations: Catherine Frey Murphy
Profile portraits: Joanna Schorling

Copy Editor: Cheryl de la Guéronnière

Editorial & Research Assistants:
Pat Conway
Marni McNiff
Joanna Schorling

Publisher: Prescott V. Kelly

Copyright © Institute of Children's Literature® 2000. All rights reserved. The material contained herein is protected by copyright. Quotations up to 40 words are permitted when *Children's Writer Guide to 2000* is clearly identified as the source. Otherwise, no part of *Children's Writer Guide to 2000* may be republished, copied, reproduced, or adapted without the express written permission of the Institute of Children's Literature, 93 Long Ridge Road, West Redding, CT 06896-0811.
1-800-443-6068. www.writersbookstore.com
e-mail: services@writersbookstore.com

Printed and bound in Canada.

Publishing Overview
Children's Books Leap Ahead

By Catherine Frey Murphy

"I think we're living in fortunate times," says Rick Richter, President of Simon & Schuster Children's Publishing. "Send the word out: It's a terrific time to be in the book business!" As children's publishing advances into the new millennium, many publishers and editors share Richter's optimism.

"We're bullish on the children's market. Our sales have been going up at least 10 percent a year," says Susan Katz, President and Publisher of the HarperCollins Children's Book Group. One reason for her optimism, Katz says, is the high number of children born to baby-boomer parents in the last couple of decades. "The children's population from birth to age 18 or 19, is nice and beefy," she explains. "There's a steady supply of children, and there seems to be a willingness in the marketplace to spend money on books for kids. Of course, you should never get over-confident, but things look good."

"I am dead opposed to those in my business who claim doom and gloom. We grew by 23 percent last year, and the rate is similar in 1999," says Richter, who finds another reason for confidence in the proliferation of new consumer outlets where books are sold. Today's readers, he says, can find children's books in new, more accessible places, like Wal-Mart and Target. "I don't see people giving up books. I see people who didn't buy books before taking them up. Now, you can buy books at Stop 'n' Shop! So what's all the doom about?"

Market Fuel

Although not all publishers are experiencing growth figures as impressive as those of HarperCollins or Simon & Schuster, sales of children's books have been increasing across-the-board, and the growth is expected to continue. The Book Industry Study Group projected 1999 children's book sales would rise 5.7 percent over 1998 sales, reaching a total increase of 17.5 percent by 2002. Unit sales during the same period were expected to grow by 10 percent.

Analysts say the expansion is fueled by an increase in school and library funding and increasing sales outlets. Online book sales are the fastest growing segment of these new sales outlets. According to the Book Industry Study Group, bookselling through Internet sites like Amazon.com rose 300 percent in a single year.

More and more often, publishers grow not just by boosting sales, but also by merging with one another or with larger companies. German conglomerate Bertelsmann AG, one of the world's largest media companies, purchased Random House, acquiring Bantam Doubleday Dell Books for Young Readers, Knopf, and Crown as part of the deal. HarperCollins announced plans to purchase William Morrow and Company, including Morrow Junior Books, Lothrop, Lee & Shepard, Greenwillow Books, Avon, and other imprints. Added to the united houses of Penguin Putnam and the acquisition of Macmillan by Simon & Schuster several years ago, the result is a small number of large, powerful trade publishers who lead the children's marketplace in numbers and often in direction.

When HarperCollins acquired Morrow, the company underwent a dramatic reorganization. In the autumn of 1999, 74 employees in editorial, marketing, and operations lost their jobs, and publishing imprints at both houses closed their doors. From a combined total of 17 children's imprints at the two companies, the restructured HarperCollins Children's Book Group emerged with only eight lists: Greenwillow Books, Joanna Cotler Books, Laura Geringer Books, HarperCollins, HarperFestival, HarperTrophy, Avon, and Tempest. Closed imprints included, among others, Michael di Capua Books, Morrow Junior Books, Lothrop Lee & Shepard, Beech Tree, and Mulberry.

Melanie Donovan joined the editing staff at HarperCollins after Lothrop, Lee & Shepard, where she was Executive Editor, was closed by the merger. "There's been a great deal of consolidation," she says, adding that she doesn't believe the trend toward mergers and consolidations has ended. "Random House/Bertelsmann is just getting under way. There's a shaking out, a wave of the future."

While many observers express concern that the trend toward fewer and larger publishers will reduce individuality in publishing lists, Donovan says the mergers are "not necessarily a bad thing. It's only just happened that we've got these three giant publishing companies," Simon & Schuster, Random House/Bertelsmann, and HarperCollins/Morrow, "in the last five years. It's not fair to make a judgment in that period of time. Some of these businesses were floundering, and now they have a healthy bottom line."

Under the ownership of large corporations, Donovan points out, some publishers have flourished while retaining a large measure of independence. "Henry Holt and Farrar, Straus & Giroux are owned by the same company but have been left to their own devices," she says. The owner is Verlagsgruppe Georg von Holtzbrinck of Stuttgart, Germany. "Orchard Books is owned by Grolier, but you rarely hear about it," Donovan adds. For companies like these, corporate ownership can offer financial security that allows editors to take risks by publishing new, unknown authors, or unusual books.

Donovan admits the merger and acquisition trend has altered the focus of the children's book industry. "It does make a more merchandise-oriented business. Merchandising is still the big thing." By merchandising, Donovan means "a picture book *and* something—a book you can sell with a toy or a kit or that can be tied to a TV series. Sometimes we forget we are a business. Most editors don't come from a business perspective, but they do have to think about it."

Successful mass-market merchandising can support the publication of new authors and risky literary titles, Donovan says. She likes to quote Robert Graves, who wrote commercially successful books like *I, Claudius*. "He was really a poet, and he said his novels were the dogs he bred to feed his cat."

Better and Better

Richter admits that publishing's recent mergers and consolidations have lowered the number of books published each year. As he points out, in 1995, when Simon & Schuster acquired Macmillan, the combined list went from 900 books a year to 400. But he says quantity is not the most important issue.

"We're making better and better books every year, promoting them better, using more craftsmanship." For Richter, the secret is to do less, but do it well. Although he agrees with Donovan that merchandising is more important in today's children's marketplace, Richter does not believe that high-quality children's literature will suffer. "Will there always be a place for a wonderful picture book or a wonderful first novel? Yes. That's our business at the end of the day and it's a great business."

When publishers merge, they look for ways to accentuate their own strengths while making up for perceived weaknesses. In HarperCollins's acquisition of Morrow, Katz explains, "Morrow's strengths are similar to Harper's. They have strong educational sales, and the quality is very high." She adds that because some well-known authors are published by both houses, the merger offered the chance to bring the two backlists together into one stronger one. Avon's strength in paperbacks was another attraction. "It's a nice mass-market list, where Harper's mass-market paperback list was not quite as strong."

Explaining a successful Harper's season, for instance, Katz says, "More than anything, it was driven by a great list," including four picture books that each sold more than half a million copies: *Today I Feel Silly and Other Moods That Make My Day*, by Jamie Lee Curtis, *If You Give a Pig a Pancake*, by Laura Joffe Numeroff, *Swine Lake*, by James Marshall and Maurice Sendak, and *Why Do You Love Me?* by radio personality Dr. Laura Schlessinger. Two recent novels, both Newbery Honor winners, were also strong sellers: *Ella Enchanted*, by Gail Carson Levine, and *Wringer*, by Jerry Spinelli.

As the range of authors and types of books in this list suggests, Katz says part of Harper's success comes from carefully planned diversity. "We decided that we would have a strong segment of the list articulated for each segment of the market we serve," she explains, such as retail, school and library, price clubs and discount stores, and special markets. "Basically, we went market segment by market segment, determined what that segment wanted to buy, and made sure we had books that would do well."

Of course, Katz adds, the creative process cannot be governed by business planning. "You never know until the book comes in if it's going to be what you, the author, and the illustrator envisioned. You can't make a best-seller the way you'd cut out fabric and make a dress. The part that is luck is when it all comes together—the author, the illustrator, and the creative process—and the market agrees with you!"

Harper's long tradition of literary excellence fuels its sales. "Part of our success has been based on looking at our backlist and cultivating it, issuing refreshed versions of the books. Backlist sales have been very strong, and in some cases even gone up."

The depth of Harper's backlist began, Katz says, with legendary editor Ursula Nordstrom, who nurtured the careers of Shel Silverstein, Maurice Sendak, and Margaret Wise Brown along with many others from her office at Harper Books for Boys and Girls, as it was then known. "We owe her a tremendous debt of gratitude," Katz says.

All observers of children's publishing, writers as much as most, should take heart that the high quality cultivated by such editors half a century ago continues to produce such companies and writing, despite erratic numbers and a much changed business environment.

Smaller but Bigger

Not every successful publisher is enormous. Many smaller children's publishers thrive in today's market, often by marketing to specific niches. One relatively small and notably successful press is Charlesbridge Publishing, which has celebrated its tenth birthday. Charlesbridge—a children's-books-only house—publishes 20 to 25 books a year, primarily picture books suitable for the trade and educational markets. During each year of life, the press's sales have grown in double digits.

Vice President and Associate Publisher Mary Ann Sabia explains that Charlesbridge created its own niche by intentionally moving its nonfiction list away from the plain, factual texts illustrated with photographs that once dominated the institutional market. Instead, she says, the company finds an "entertaining text that's factual and pairs it with spectacular art, to create four-color illustrated nonfiction books that really pique a child's interest." That strategy has paid off, as Charlesbridge has grown from its initial list of five alphabet books by Jerry Palotta, which have since sold more than a million copies.

The company's growth has been helped by the increasing use of trade children's books in classrooms. The wave of whole language education has passed in some ways, but the best of the theory remains and has had a lasting effect on children's publishing. Whole language education rests on the principle that children learn to read more successfully by reading, not text books but "real," trade publishing, books with exciting stories and genuine literary quality. Schools subscribing to the whole language philosophy purchase children's books with budget funds that used to go for textbooks.

Sabia is not discouraged that some school districts have returned to teach-

The Giants

BERTELSMANN AG
Random House; Bantam Doubleday Dell; Crown Books; Alfred A. Knopf.

Random House has become the largest children's book publisher in the U.S. Sales were approximately $197 million last year, according to *Publishers Weekly (PW)*, up 9.4 percent. Recent best-sellers: *The Watsons Go to Birmingham—1963*, Christopher Paul Curtis (a 1995 book that still made an appearance on the 1999 bestseller list); *A Mouse Called Wolf*, Dick King-Smith; *Star Wars* books; Arthur books, Marc Brown.

PENGUIN PUTNAM
Dial Books; Dutton; Puffin; Viking; Philomel; Grosset & Dunlap; G.P. Putnam & Sons.

Penguin Putnam is the second largest children's book publisher with sales of $156 million, estimates *PW*, up 5.4 percent. Recent best-seller: Philomel's *The Very Clumsy Click Beetle*, Eric Carle.

GOLDEN BOOKS
Once the largest publisher of children's books, after several years of difficulty, Golden is now number three, with sales down 13 percent last year to about $141 million, says *PW*. Recent best-seller: *What's Heaven?*, Maria Shriver.

SIMON & SCHUSTER
Aladdin; Richard Jackson imprint; Atheneum Books; Little Simon; Margaret K. McElderry; Pocket Pulse; Simon Spotlight.

The fourth largest children's publisher, Simon & Schuster experienced one of the highest growth rates in the last year, with sales up 30.5 percent to $124 million, according to *PW* estimates. Recent best-sellers: *Eloise in Paris*, Kay Thompson; *The Dance*, Richard Paul Evans; *Frindle*, Andrew Clements; the Blue's Clues series.

HARPERCOLLINS/MORROW
HarperCollins Book Group; Avon Books; Greenwillow Books; Joanna Cotler Books; Laura Geringer Books; HarperFestival; HarperCollins; HarperTrophy; Tempest. *Now closed:* Morrow Junior; Michael di Capua Books; Lothrop, Lee & Shepard; Beech Tree; Mulberry.

The fifth largest children's publisher before its merger with Morrow, but expect the company to move up in rank. HarperCollins sales were $116 million and Hearst's Morrow/Avon sales were $46 million, according to *PW*, which also reported that combined HarperCollins and Hearst revenues were estimated at $162 million. Recent best-sellers: *Today I Feel Silly & Other Moods That Make My Day*, Jamie Lee Curtis; *Ramona's World*, Beverly Cleary; *Ella Enchanted*, Gail Carson Levine; *Ophelia Speaks: Adolescent Girls Write About Their Search for Self*, Sara Shandler.

2000

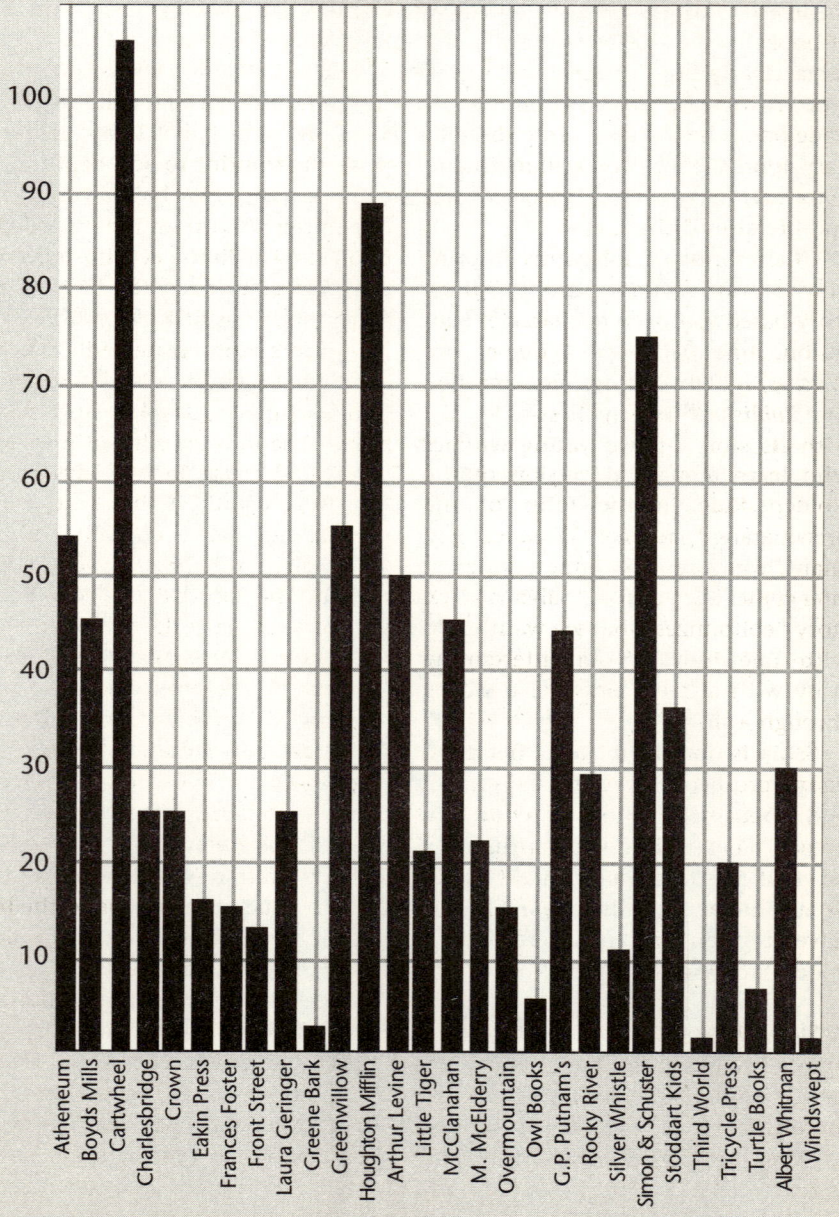

ing reading through phonics. She acknowledges that the whole language approach "as the only method" of teaching "is gone in many areas." But she insists, "What's not gone is the use of books in the classroom." By *books*, Sabia clearly doesn't mean *texts*. She sees an increase in classroom use of trade books that offer an interdisciplinary approach. "Now it's all math and literature, or science or social studies and literature," she says.

Charlesbridge's Talewinds imprint moved away from nonfiction to offer a story-based approach to character education. *Alice and Greta: A Tale of Two Witches,* by Steve Simmonds, reached the *Publishers Weekly* best-seller list with its story of two young witches who learn a magical version of the Golden Rule in the form of the Brewmerang Principle: "Whatever you chant, whatever you brew, sooner or later comes back to you!" Sabia says the story "epitomizes what we want to do with Talewinds. It's an entertaining story with a good message, teaching through a story."

Sabia is optimistic about her company's prospects for continued growth and about the future of children's books. "There still is, and continues to be, that need for good quality children's literature," she says. "People haven't given up, and there's still a good market for quality."

A Slow Burn

Across the children's book landscape, new imprints are springing up. At Simon & Schuster, an as-yet-untitled new imprint will be headed by Richard Jackson, whom Richter describes as "something of a legend in the children's book business. Not only has he established some of the biggest names in the business, like Judy Blume and Gary Paulsen, but he's also brilliant at finding new authors."

The fall 2000 list is the first of Jackson's imprint, which will reach full strength by the fall of 2001. Richter expects the imprint to add depth to the company's list. "We have a very serious commitment to traditional hardcover publishing at Simon & Schuster, as one of the largest, if not the largest, publisher of serious fiction for kids."

Authors who create serious fiction need what Richter calls a "slow burn," that is, time to develop over several books. A serious imprint within a large, diversified house, Richter says, can afford to give authors that time, and financial reward eventually follows. "You might not find a Dick Jackson book on the Barnes & Noble best-seller list, but it'll make the same money in the long run, by weaving itself into the children's book culture."

Dial, part of the Penguin Putnam group, recently launched another new imprint in Phyllis Fogelman Books. Fogelman explains, "From my point of view, it was a way to give up some of my corporate responsibilities and get back to what attracted me to the business in the first place, which was working with authors and artists."

Fogelman's distinguished editing career has encompassed books by Jerry Pinkney, Jean Van Leeuwen, and Mildred Taylor, along with Rosemary Wells's Max and Ruby books, the first board books to tell picture-book-like stories. She says her new list will reflect

The Middle-Grade—and Publishing—Story of the Year: Harry Potter

Like their older brothers and sisters, middle-grade kids want to have fun when they read, and they've proved it with their joyful response to the transatlantic publishing sensation, the Harry Potter books. First published in England in 1997, the middle-grade novel *Harry Potter and the Sorcerer's Stone,* by J. K. Rowling, won the British Book Award and the Smarties Prize, and swiftly conquered legions of readers in America. The book has so much appeal for adults as well as kids that a second version had to be published with more grown-up looking jacket art, so adults could read it without embarrassment.

An exuberant, brilliantly imaginative tale about a boy who discovers he's a wizard and enrolls at Hogwarts, a wizard school where sports are played on broomsticks and the people in portraits leave their frames to visit each other, the Harry Potter books are the talk of every playground in America. In the spring of 1999, the first novel rose to the top of the *New York Times* best-seller list and stayed there for months, soon followed by its sequels, *Harry Potter and the Chamber of Secrets* and *Harry Potter and the Prisoner of Azkaban.* No other children's book had appeared on the *Times* list since 1952, when E.B. White published *Charlotte's Web.*

"We all realized what we had when the book was first launched at a sales meeting," says Michael Jacobs, Senior Vice President, Trade, at Scholastic. "We realized that the book had a chance to break out of the children's publishing world." As a result, Scholastic marketed the book carefully. "The author's story was very interesting and promotable. It was a very goal-directed marketing campaign. We asked, 'If there were 10 great things that could happen to this book, what would they be?' They all happened, and then some."

Jacobs is a Harry fan himself; he has read the first book 10 or 15 times. But *(continued on next page)*

---

her interests. "I've always been interested in books for the very young, and I will continue to publish preschool books." Fogelman's list will also include older picture books and middle-grade fiction.

"I think that the area with the most growth is still preschool, the very young books, up to age six," Fogelman says. "What I think is that more people buy books for younger children. More parents and groups purchase books for loved children to own when they're young. As children get older, maybe they're less sure what to buy. All of us, whether we're professionals or parents, when we look at a picture book, we know right away whether we like the look of a book, the feel of it, the design. You can tell if it's a book

The Middle-Grade—and Publishing— Story of the Year: Harry Potter

(continued from preceding page)
he says nobody at Scholastic expected the tremendous reception the Harry Potter books have received. "Kids have embraced these books," he says. "It's hard to attribute it to anything in particular. As marketers, you want to feel that you've created the buzz, but I think it's the story."

In the newly wired world of online bookselling, Harry Potter's popularity posed an unexpected problem for Scholastic. The second book did not appear in the United States for a year after its British publication, and in the interim, impatient American readers used Amazon.com.uk and other British bookselling sites to purchase the sequel directly. To protect its U.S. sales from electronic attrition, Scholastic, owner of the U.S. distribution rights, moved up the publication of the third book in the series, *Harry Potter and the Prisoner of Azkaban*, so that it appeared in the U.S. in September 1999, only three months after its British debut. Even so, many copies crossed the Atlantic into the U.S. before the American book was published. As a result, the fourth book was set to appear in both countries simultaneously, in mid-2000.

Scholastic's experience has caused some observers to predict that future contracts may no longer allocate rights according to territorial boundaries, moving perhaps to English language rights, which may more effectively acknowledge the electronic global village today's world has become.

Even though Scholastic lost some sales to electronic buyers, Jacobs has no complaints about its success. "It's Harry Potter's world, and we're just lucky to live in it," says Jacobs, who says the company's marketing strategy now consists primarily of trying to get out of the books' way. "Don't be Muggles! That's our motto," he says, referring to the nonmagical and sometimes clueless inhabitants of Harry Potter's world. "Our job is just to continue to believe in the book."

---

you'd like to own. It's harder to know with books for older children." Fogelman would like to find ways to extend that appeal into books for older kids, because, as she puts it, "the non-book-owning children become non-book-reading adults."

New imprints at Pleasant Company include American Girl Fiction and History Mysteries. The new imprints, says Vice President of Editorial Development Judith Woodburn, are "for older readers, 10 and up, rather than our core group of readers in the past." The original series, the American Girl Collection of historical fiction, targeted girls aged seven and up, featuring characters like Kirsten, a Scandinavian pioneer girl in the Midwest and Addie, who escaped slavery in the mid-1800s. Girls who fall in love with the books and their accompanying dolls, Woodburn says, want their books to grow up along with them. "We were getting many requests from readers who'd read everything we published and were looking for something more challenging."

The History Mysteries respond to that need by continuing the original list's focus on history and adding a mystery-story component. Woodburn says the books won't be "Nancy Drew in bonnets! The stories are more complex, have more of an emotional component and more character development, set in a historical framework."

American Girl Fiction, Woodburn says, will be "only in the loosest sense a series. It's a grouping of books that all have appeal to girl readers in the 10-and-up age group." The American Girl Fiction imprint also offers the Pleasant T. Rowland Prize, a prestigious award offering publication and a $10,000 advance.

Woodburn says, "We're always optimistic about books!" After the startling success of the original American Girl Collection, she says, "We saw that the same group of readers had an interest in contemporary themes as well." Responding to that interest, the company launched *American Girl* magazine, followed by a group of nonfiction books offering tips and instruction on crafts, friendship, parties, and other subjects girls requested. "With each succeeding imprint, we saw that there were areas we hadn't yet tapped into. We're responding to what we see of the readers that we have a relationship with." The company, Woodburn says, will continue to respond to the needs of its young female readers by publishing "books that take their interests and concerns seriously."

An unusual new children's imprint comes from an academic publisher, the University of Pittsburgh Press. Golden Triangle Books will offer historical fiction in the form of re-issued classic novels for children 9 to 14. Part of the imprint's goal is to benefit from the thriving educational publishing market by relating its books to a website offering additional resources to parents, teachers, and librarians.

"There really are some great books that fell out of print," explains Jennifer Flannigan, University of Pittsburgh Press Marketing Director, such as *Three Golden Rivers,* by Oliver Price, and *Duffy's Rocks,* by Edward Fenton. The books, often written in the historical periods they describe, offer a regional and historical emphasis useful to schools that are following the recent educational trend to use trade books in the classroom. "They're really nice books. There's not much violence or profanity, so we can recommend them without reservation," says Flannigan.

The press's website offers extension activities that help teachers find creative ways to use the books with kids. Since glassmaking figures in *Three Golden Rivers,* for example, the site provides activities related to making fudge, which has a viscosity similar to glass. Using a website is less expensive than teachers' guides, Flannigan explains, and it increases the attractiveness of the books in the school marketplace. "Teachers are very enthusiastic. They really thought this was great; it's a market that they can't seem to get enough of."

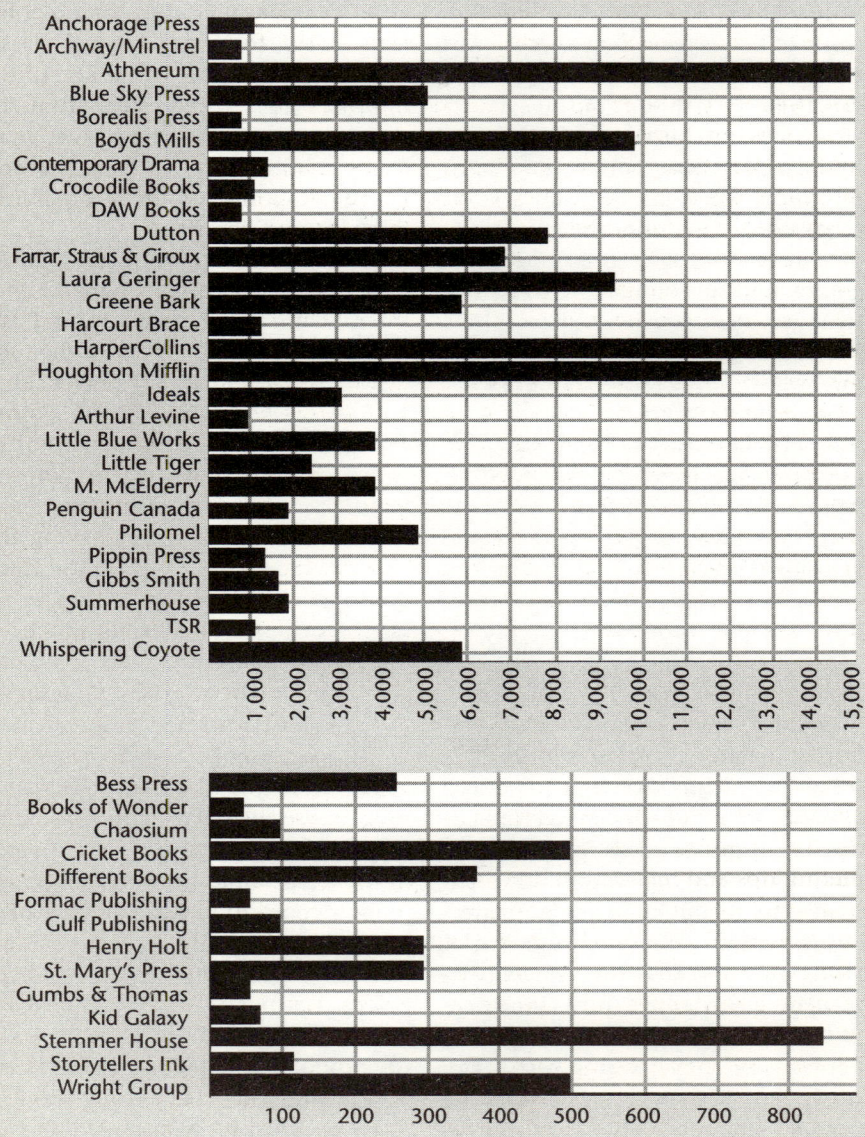

Bigger, Wealthier Market

Pocket Pulse, a new imprint from Pocket Books, markets young adult fiction and nonfiction directly to teenagers, not to schools or parents. Nancy Pines, Vice President and Publisher of Books for Young Readers, says the current teen market is "bigger and wealthier than all previous teen generations. There are 31 million teens in this country now, with another 30 million growing into it even as we speak. They also have more personal freedom, and adult responsibility, than we did as teens—and more pocket money."

According to Pines, it's a challenge to market books to teens amid the distractions of today's advertising-soaked, computer-connected popular culture. "These days, having a brand name is more important than ever, because brands seem to be the only things Americans have time to notice," Pines says. "That's why our editorial direction leans towards projects that have some other, noisy, aspect to them, such as television tie-in books. Current or upcoming examples from Pocket Pulse include *Dawson's Creek, Buffy the Vampire Slayer, Angel,* and *Charmed.*"

Sometimes, Pines adds, the process happens the other way around, as a book inspires a television project. "We actively seek book properties that we believe will lend themselves to other media." Responding to the thriving teen culture on the Web, Pulse also links book releases to Internet sites, as with *DEAL WITH IT: A Whole New Approach to Your Body, Brain and Life as a gURL,* from the creators of the enormously successful website gURL.com.

Not all of Pocket Pulse's books are media tie-ins, but Pines says all follow principles that "apply to a book for any-aged human," but are even more critical for teens. First, "capture the voice. I can't tell you how many manuscripts we see wherein the writer thinks kids talk and think this way, and it just sounds lame." Second, "Don't ever try to educate them. They get plenty of that every day. Just tell a good story—any story, it doesn't much matter—that reflects your familiarity with your target reader."

Pines adds, "Don't *say* 'cool.' *Be* cool," and reminds authors that a truly original story will satisfy teens with the feeling that they've discovered something fresh, while the familiar can also offer a comforting appeal. "Teens buy *Buffy* books because they love the show and they want to extend their pleasure in it."

Richter agrees with Pines that successful marketing to teenagers is critical for publishers if they want to keep their audiences. "In general, between ages 12 and 13, there's a 50 percent drop in reading. Reading falls off a cliff. Why should we let that happen?"

Richter expands on Pines's suggestions for writers with some ideas for booksellers. "First of all, no teen wants to be caught dead in the children's section of the bookstore. They want a section that's their own, with teen music, teen apparel, a teen atmosphere." Publishers and retailers must also understand teenagers' lifestyles. "They have more money to spend than we had, but what they don't have is a lot of free time. Any reading they're doing is oriented around their schoolwork. That's the challenge, and it's going to work its way into what kinds of books are made."

In addition to books tied to television shows, movies or the Internet, Richter says teens also respond to books related to music or celebrities. "Teens will buy books on Prince William or the Spice Girls," he says. That interest in light-heartedness suggests, he thinks, that fiction for teens should move beyond the "bleak book," as young adult novels based on social problems like drugs or divorce are sometimes called. "Teens are not only interested in alcoholic Vietnam Vets who commit suicide," he says. "There's no evidence that teenagers want to be miserable!"

New Hand-Selling Opportunities
The ripple effect of Harry Potter (See sidebar, pages 14-15.) has reached the rest of middle-grade children's publishing, too, as kids finish Rowling's books and ask librarians or booksellers what they can read now. "It really has given children's booksellers an opportunity to hand-sell," says Michael Jacobs, Scholastic Senior Vice President, Trade. "What else might they like? Booksellers, librarians, teachers, and parents have a fabulous opportunity to keep kids moving from book to book to book. I think it has expanded the potential universe. That has been the most heartening experience for us as publishers."

Partly driven by Harry Potter, sales of hardcover children's books rose dramatically in 1999—approximately 30 percent—as parents and publishers alike found themselves placing new value on novels for kids. Prepublication interest in new middle-grade novels rose so sharply that one editor reportedly said, only half-kidding, that if one more novel was presented to her as "the next Harry Potter," she'd scream.

Harry Potter isn't the only middle-grade literary character to find surprising success. Louis Sachar's Newbery-winning *Holes* sold well over the figures usually experienced by Newbery-winning novels, and several titles in Scholastic's Dear America series, a group of unjacketed historical fiction hardcovers in diary format, have sold well over 100,000 copies.

Booksellers traditionally reserve space on their shelves only for award-winning hardcover children's novels, but in view of the rising trend in children's hardcover sales, these days many say they're more likely to place orders for promising novels.

Picture Books: A Mixed Forecast
The picture book forecast is currently mixed. "The big news in picture books right now may be that there is no big news," says Donovan. Picture books for kids aged four to seven or eight still

form the heart of most publishers' lists and nobody expects that to change. Still, a slight lull has characterized picture book sales in the last year or two. "It's just a momentary glitch," says Donovan.

Demographics are likely, as with the teen population, to play a large role in the future of picture books. "There've been two baby boomlets, one now going into middle school or junior high, and a new one that has just come, ages one, two, or three," says Donovan. As a result, she says, "There's been more emphasis placed on books for slightly older children, and a lot of emphasis on baby books."

But the younger boomlet is just about to move into prime picture book age, so picture books should be due for another surge in the next few years.

Donovan notes that art is becoming more important in relation to text in modern picture books. "I've always believed that it's a 50-50 partnership, but some argue that there's a resistance to buying books that are text-heavy. That's the myth, anyway; I think it's a self-fulfilling prophecy." If sales representatives and marketers believe that picture books with more text won't sell, Donovan thinks they will carry that message back to the publishers, and fewer text-heavy books will be published. "If they believe it, they make it come true." The emphasis on art is also encouraged by the greater ease of producing full-color art with computers. Donovan suggests, "Compare picture books from today to those from the 1960s. Today's texts are very spare by comparison."

Donovan says today's picture books are published selectively, and companies favor well-known names. "It's a very conservative time right now. It's harder for a new illustrator to break in." A publisher that succeeds with one book by a leading illustrator, Donovan says, is more apt to take off on that success and publish several more by the same artist than to hire new illustrators for those books. "It's expensive to publish a four-color book. It's a gamble. We're betting that we'll make more money than we've paid in the advance. If we win, everybody wins, of course, but it's still a gamble!"

Expanding Stories

Children's books in general are inspiring more new movie or television features than ever before. Literally dozens of movies based on children's novels are planned, in production, or appearing on the nation's screens, from *Stuart Little* and *The BFG* to *Harry Potter and the Sorcerer's Stone*.

Donovan points to a new trend: the development of movies and television shows inspired by picture books. She mentions movies based on *How the Grinch Stole Christmas,* and on *Taxi Dog,* with Robin Williams. "A Disney TV movie was made of *Harvey Potter's Balloon Farm,* not to be confused with Harry," she reports. Disney liked using a picture book instead of a novel "because it leaves them a lot more creative control." Movie makers must expand picture book stories to fill out a script-length story, of course, but that doesn't seem to discourage them. Among many picture books recently mentioned in connection with movies or television series are *Shriek!, George*

Small Press & Special Interest YA

Company	List Size	Queries/Mss yearly	Fiction	Nonfiction
Africa World Press	10	500	Novels set in Africa; African-American, Caribbean subjects.	African history, culture, social issues, education, parenting.
Avalon Books	60	not available	Romance, mysteries, Westerns.	None.
Avisson Press	10	1,000	None.	Biography, multicultural.
Blue Sky Marketing	4	200	None.	Subjects to distribute to specialty markets.
Chaosium	25	100	Fantasy, Arthurian fiction, the occult, horror.	None.
I.E. Clark Publications	6	1,700	Plays: Classics, musicals, holidays, religion, ethnic.	None.
Contemporary Drama	60	1,600	Drama, musicals, social commentary, parodies, skits.	Improvisation, theater arts, speech.
J. G. Ferguson	12	60	None.	Careers, training, college, hi-lo reference.
Highsmith Press	20	4,000	None.	Library-related resources, books on research skills.
Human Kinetics	56	1,000	None.	Sports & related science, medicine, fitness, coaching.
Lion Books	14	100	Younger fiction.	Easy-to-read political histories, biographies.
Masters Press	50	150	None.	Sports, fitness, training, sports figures.
Morgan Reynolds	22	400	None.	Biography series, history, multicultural issues.
Roussan Publishers	8	240	Historical, contemporary, religious, sci-fi, fantasy.	None.
Tor Books	35	1,200	Sci-fi, fantasy.	How-to, crafts, science.
Wordware Publishing	30	100	None.	Texas, the Southwest. Biography, nature, computers, entertainment, humor.

Shrinks, Corduroy, George and Martha, Where the Wild Things Are, and *The Stinky Cheese Man.*

Donovan says that encouraging children, and adults, to become readers should be at the heart of every publisher's marketing strategy. "As a percentage of the population, readers have leveled off over the past 10 years," she warns. "The percentage of people who read for pleasure is embarrassingly low compared to those who, say, rent videos. Publishers are accused sometimes of being elitist, but after a certain age, it becomes a very small clique who read."

Donovan thinks readers are defined at the moment they leave picture books behind and graduate to children's novels. "If kids make the leap from picture books into novels and enjoy reading novels, they habitually become lifelong readers. I think modeling reading is important. Seeing people enjoying books—it makes you want to go and try it out!"

The Spirit Grows

Religious publishing for children has seen special growth, particularly in picture books. Several new children's imprints have launched in recent years, and other religious publishers have added more children's books to their existing lists.

"People have a renewed interest in the spiritual," says Linda Peterson at Zonderkidz, one of the newer children's imprints, from Zondervan Publishing. "They are realizing that they have values that they need to impart to their children." As the news media bombard American homes with news of drugs, violence, and school shootings, parents have turned to children's books for help in raising children with strong morals and religious beliefs.

Religious publishers have responded with increased concentration on quality in children's books. "The quality of products is being raised across the spectrum of religious publishing," says Peterson. "We're using the same technologies that secular publishers are using, that you never used to see in our business, like lift-the-flap books and board books. We're using high-caliber illustrators to make sure the books look the same as those by our general market cousins."

Brian Ondracek, Vice President of Creative Services for Crossway Books, an imprint of Good News Publishing, sees the same stress on quality in his company's general list, which has expanded to include more children's titles. "If we believe, as a Christian publisher, that our message is really important, then we'd better do it every bit as well, if not better, than anyone else," he says. "If the story that we're presenting has a classic feel to it, let's make it look like a book that will last."

What's inside the book matters more than how it looks, of course. Peterson says Zonderkidz books are measured "against whether they deliver the values that we find in the Bible. We do want to make sure that there is an inspirational God-based value." The format of Zonderkidz's books may look new, Peterson says, but the religious message is grounded in traditional Christian faith. "There are timeless truths that have not changed, but today's kids are different from kids

20 years ago. The format must appeal, and then they get good, solid, editorial content."

In Crossway books, Ondracek says, "Our main characteristic is that the story communicates a Biblical truth, not just a moral truth." He sees most of the growth in religious children's books in four-color picture books. In the past, publishers sometimes avoided picture books because of the cost of producing them, but Ondracek says that has changed. It is less expensive to print picture books today because of technological advances, and consumers seem to be more willing to spend money on well-produced books. "There used to be a price-point limit at about seven dollars," he says. "But now books are out there at $14 or $15."

Religious picture books do better than fiction for older children, Ondracek finds. "Christian religious publishers have found it very difficult to compete for the second-to-sixth grade reading audiences. We haven't totally abandoned youth fiction, but if you're going to do youth fiction for us, you have to have a recognizable name, or you have to be able to write a lot of books." A series for young readers can sell well if it's "captivating to kids," Ondracek says, but single titles tend to have a harder time succeeding in the religious market.

There's still more reason for optimism in the children's book world. A recent survey of libraries undertaken jointly by the American Association of Publishers and the Association for Library Collections & Technical Services, found that 60 percent of the surveyed libraries expect their budgets to increase during the next five years, while most of the rest expect their funds to remain stable. After years of budget cuts, this is good news indeed for children's publishing. For librarians, teachers, publishers, editors, booksellers, and last but not least, writers, the new century begins on a wave of hope.

It's a good time for children's writers to ride the surge, turning to our own work with renewed energy and confidence. As HarperCollins's Susan Katz says of children's publishing in the new millennium, "We're thinking that it's a great market to be in."

Market Overview

Magazines & the Millennium

By Vicki Hambleton

"Magazines, the Medium of the Millennium!" So reads the bold headline of a special advertising section found recently in major newspapers across the country. The section goes on to sing the praises of the four-color, glossy world of the printed word with such adjectives as *magnetic* and *memorable*. The praise comes from the Magazine Publishers of America (MPA) and participating magazines sponsor the section. Nevertheless, the self-promotion has a large kernel of truth in it if measured by sheer volume alone.

Statistics show that new consumer launches in the last year for which data is available topped 1,000, the highest ever for new magazines. *The National Directory of Magazines* counted 18,000 consumer titles published in America in its most recent edition, and according to figures from the MPA, on average, 10 titles a week launched.

Veronis, Suhler & Associates, a media industry merchant bank, reports that consumer magazine advertising grew by 7.1 percent. Overall spending on consumer magazines is expected to go from $18.1 billion in 1998 to $23.7 billion by 2003.

For those of us whose heads swim in the face of so many numbers, a trip to the nearest Barnes & Noble or Borders tells the story equally well. The rows of periodicals, four and five deep sometimes, in kiosks that stand five feet high, are an impressive sight, and very welcome to anyone who makes a living freelancing for the magazine market.

While the figures quoted track advertising-based publications (and more and more children's publications fit this category), the numbers in the children's field also indicate strong, continued growth. In the last year, more than 50 new magazines targeting the under-21 set were launched. Add to that the fact that few existing titles have folded and the outlook is very promising.

Play Ball!

For the past few years, industry analysts have always named sports as a possible new niche growth area for children. That prediction proved true beyond expectations. Several specialty titles devoted to single sports have launched, including *Kick!*, a soccer magazine, and *Lax Mag*, for young Lacrosse players. Thanks to women's professional basketball and Mia Hamm et al., women's sports have garnered new attention. *G'Ball*, targeting young women 10 to 18 who play basketball, launched with 150,000 copies. *Amy Love's REAL SPORTS* caters to girls between the ages of 12 and 18 and covers all kinds of sports, from sailing to soccer.

The "grandparent" of them all, *Sports Illustrated For Kids*, turned 10 this year and continues to grow stronger every year. Its circulation now tops one million. "We consider ourselves to be in an evolutionary process," says Group Publisher Cleary Simpson. "If you look at the magazine today, it is very different from what it was two years ago even, much less a decade ago."

There are no immediate plans to launch a *Sports Illustrated For Kids* edition for girls, although there have been rumors of it in the past, but that may be because the group has its hands full with another project, also under the watchful eye of Simpson. Late last fall, Time Inc. announced that its title *Sports Illustrated For Women* will begin publishing monthly in March 2000 with an initial rate base of 300,000. "There's no question that sports is a growth area for Time Inc.," says Chairman and CEO Don Logan. "With the recent explosion of women's sports, *SI For Women* is launching at exactly the right time."

SI For Women was tested with two issues under the name *Sports Illustrated Women/Sport* in 1997 and evolved into four special issues under its current title in 1999. Written for women ages 18 to 34, the publication will cover all women's sports. Editor Sandy Bailey says it "will also offer readers insights on issues of health, nutrition, fitness, and gear."

Scientifically Speaking

Another category of magazines that has been steadily expanding in recent years is science. Two recent major launches are under the aegis of impressive adult organizations. A third is a start-up by two Scholastic veterans.

Scientific American launched *Explorations*, a family publication targeting parents with pre-adolescent children. The motivating force behind the magazine is that a substantial number of parents are concerned about their children's science education. Initially, *Explorations'* goal was to connect the science of the textbook with the science of the real world. Along the way, that goal has been fine-tuned, according to Editor Ari Epstein. "Our focus is on the notion that the world is a really interesting place, your kids are probably already curious about it, and we say, 'Here are ways to help them explore.' We are moving in the direction that science is cool."

Explorations now features a section for parents, another for kids and parents to do together, and a section just for kids. It also features experiments as well as ideas for travel that relates to science. Articles about family trips, with a science angle, appear regularly in *Explorations*. The magazine also attracts the larger audience of readers interested in parenting titles. Epstein says that he considers his competitors to be titles like *Family Fun* and *Crayola Kids*.

Another new magazine, directed at ages 8 to 13, is *archaeology's dig*, pub-

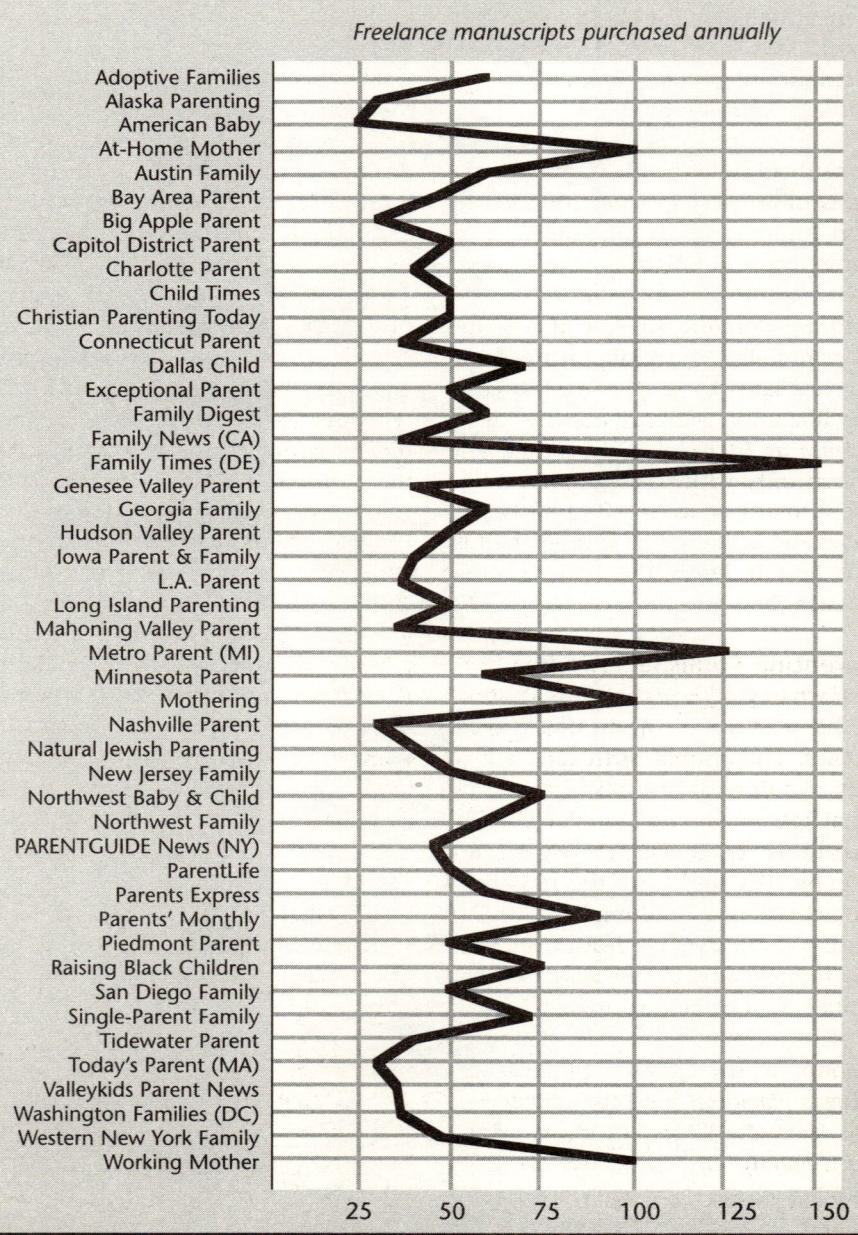

lished by the Archaeology Institute of America. Like *Explorations, dig* is primarily a home subscription publication, although Editor in Chief Stephen Hanks says that they are looking into distribution to the school and library markets for the future.

Connecting parents with the science their children are learning is the basis of *Science at Home,* founded by Lori Andres and Camille Russo, both formerly of Scholastic. They believe that parents generally know how to find the literature, the liberal-arts kind of materials, their children need but are less knowledgeable and less comfortable finding the science they need. *Science at Home* connects home and community with the science children are studying at school. It publishes articles and activities, all strongly hands-on, and it helps the parents learn science themselves.

Parenting Publishers Are Ready

Just when you thought it was all about teens, it may once again be all about babies. The annual birth rate, which has remained fairly steady at an annual rate of 3.9 million for the last decade, is expected to climb to 4.2 million by 2010 and reach the 1957 baby boom high of 4.3 million by 2020. Parenting publishers are ready and looking for new ways to give readers the ultimate in "one-stop shopping."

The Time, Inc., Parenting Group, whose flagship publication is *Parenting*, recently added the Hachette Filipacchi magazine *Family Life* to its list of publications for parents. It also bought First Moments, a sampling-and-distribution company that distributes sample baskets of goodies to new parents—a way to reach parents from the first moment they *are* parents.

Primedia's American Baby Group reaches parents through a whole range of products, from coupons and samples to a television show to prenatal and postnatal print publications including *American Baby; Healthy Kids,* which is distributed through the American Academy of Physicians; and *Childbirth*, a guide to a woman's third trimester.

Gruner + Jahr, publisher of the 73-year-old *Parents,* has increased its presence in the marketplace with the purchase last March of the Baby Publishing Group, a New York publisher that distributes its three titles primarily through gift packs given to new parents. Its publications include titles for parents who are expecting, new parents, and childbirth instructors. *Baby Magazine Infant Care Guide* is distributed to hospitals (nonpaid circulation of 3.7 million); *Baby Magazine* (nonpaid circulation of 750,000) goes to expectant mothers and their doctors; and *Childbirth Instructor Magazine,* a professional health journal (combined paid and nonpaid circulation of 15,000). With a trend towards what is known as

Web-Weaving for Kids: JuniorNet

Virtually every major magazine targeting kids or parents either has or is developing a website. The sites have been the means of extending the magazine's "brand name" and reaching larger audiences. Most publishers and advertisers, however, are still trying to find ways to make the Internet profitable for them without jeopardizing the integrity of their products. This has been especially true in the children's market where fear of Internet stalkers of young children, and inappropriate advertising are at the forefront of parents' minds. A new site may change that.

JuniorNet is the first advertisement-free online interactive learning service for children. Launched in March 1999 by a Boston-based entrepreneur named Alan Rothenberg, JuniorNet is designed for kids ages 3 to 12. The site is unique in bringing together content from some of the best-known names in children's publishing including *Highlights, Ranger Rick, Zillions, Weekly Reader,* and *Sports Illustrated For Kids.*

Ranger Rick has been on the site since its inception. "Alan Rothenberg first pitched the idea of the site to me about three years ago," says *Ranger Rick* Editor Gerald Bishop. "We like them because we have a very strong policy against advertising to children and they had the same policy. So far, we have been pleased with the association and the other publications involved," he says. Still, Bishop had some doubts at first because some of the magazines that would be on the site would be publications that do advertise to children. "We were concerned, but the material on the site is really top-notch," and that concern has faded. Interestingly enough, most of the content from *Ranger Rick* on JuniorNet doesn't come from the print version of the magazine. "We don't package a bunch of stuff up and send it to them. They, being creative folks, use *Ranger Rick* mostly as inspiration and then develop ideas. It's up to us to say, 'Yes, that represents us well,' or 'No, that doesn't.' That was a surprise to us. But it's wonderful. They are doing something we probably would have struggled to do in some form at great expense in the coming years. They are bridging the gap between a print medium and an electronic medium and we are all just waiting to see if they can succeed."

The service costs parents $9.95 a month. Subscribers receive a CD-ROM starter and then go directly to the content on the site. JuniorNet Corporation announced it had secured $70 million in financing, reportedly the largest investment ever in a children's online company. It remains to be seen whether the company can sell enough subscriptions to make it a moneymaker, but at least the demographic numbers are in their favor. According to a report in *USA Today* citing figures from Jupiter Communications, youngsters between 5 and 12 are the fastest-growing segment of all online users. By 2002, 21.9 million children will be online, up from 8.6 million in 1998.

vertical titles—that is, magazines that target narrow niches of the same basic category—coupled with the anticipated population growth in the diaper set, parenting and family titles should flourish for the foreseeable future.

On the News Front

Educational magazines, particularly those with a news bent, are continuing to emerge as well. The venerable *New York Times,* "all the news that's fit to print," is courting the teen market in partnership with Scholastic. Together the two launched *New York Times Upfront.* The magazine replaces *Scholastic Update,* and launched with 200,000 copies distributed through home and school subscriptions. *Upfront* targets teens 14 to 18 and appears twice a month during the school year.

Weekly Reader Corporation joined forces with *Newsweek* to launch its own teen magazine, *Teen Newsweek.* Like *Upfront*, it debuted just in time for the start of the school year. *Teen Newsweek* targets a slightly younger audience, 11- to 15-year-olds, and launched with 130,000 copies. It appears weekly during the school year.

Scholastic had been looking for a way to create a time-sensitive product ever since Time Inc. stepped into the supplementary education arena with *Time For Kids.* That 1995 launch shook both Scholastic and Weekly Reader Corporation, the two leaders in the educational magazine field. *Time For Kids* had the ability to access *Time*'s global resources and get to students in schools much faster than either of the other two.

Time For Kids is in it for the long haul and last year named its first publisher, Keith Garten. He says Time, Inc., will continue to look at new options and ways to expand the company's presence in the education field. "Right now we have two editions," says Garten. "One is for students in second and third grade, the other targets students in grades four through six or seven, and we'll definitely be looking to expand to the very early grades. It is really important to get kindergartners and first graders reading and one way to do that is by giving them a magazine that is just for them."

Garten says the company has no immediate plans to launch a title that targets teens. "The middle school market is very different than the primary grade market, and I think we will look at all the options that might be available to us before we move forward with an edition for older readers. When you talk about middle and high school students, you are talking about marketing to kids at a very important stage of their development. I think we as an industry need to make sure we can deliver the right products."

Asked whether the supplementary education market can support so many different publications, Garten's answer is a definite yes. "When we launched *Time For Kids,* we didn't really take away so much from our competitors. We opened new markets and developed new subscribers that had not used a classroom magazine before."

Scholastic nevertheless did some internal reorganizing in its magazine division in the past year. It announced the formation of the Scholastic Magazine Group, a new unit that combines the 35-title Classroom Magazine Divi-

Teens Take Center Stage

The magazine market for teens continues to be the category to show the most activity. Not surprisingly, one of the biggest players in the market is Time Inc.'s *Teen People.* While established leaders in the teen service field like *Seventeen, YM,* and *Teen* continue to hold their own with circulations that are close to 2 million each, *Teen People,* only a couple of years old, is gaining fast. It has more than doubled its circulation since its debut, going from 500,000 to 1.3 million.

Amy Galleazzi, spokesperson for *Teen People,* says the magazine will continue "to grow our numbers, and expects to report another jump in circulation by the end of 1999." As for content, Galleazzi says, "Last year we did 10 regular issues of *Teen People,* with double-month issues in December/January and June/July. During those months, we did two special-interest issues. One was sponsored by the Milk campaign. In the coming year, we plan to do more special issues. They give us a chance to do something a little different. 'Our Hottest Stars Under 21' issue that came out last year in July was done in conjunction with our first prime-time TV show, and we plan to do more TV-tie-ins."

One factor in *Teen People*'s success is the hunger among teens for anything to do with celebrities. Stars sell magazines in a big way. One company that will try to ride the coattails of all celebrity fever is Primedia. The publishing giant already publishes 10 teen titles, many of them tied to teen idols. The Primedia Group includes *Seventeen, Teen Beat, Teen Beat AllStars, 16, 16 Superstars, Tiger Beat, Superteen, Teen Machine, BOP,* and *BB.* Primedia published a test issue of its latest teen magazine, *Entertainmenteen,* that did so well that the company scrapped future tests and decided to go monthly with the second issue, according to Editor Hedy End.
(continued on next page)

sion (formerly part of the Education Division) with the company's Consumer and Professional Magazine Division. Executive Vice President Hugh Roome will head the new group. Roome says the restructuring will "consolidate the company's marketing resources . . . and give the classroom magazines new attention."

Meanwhile, Weekly Reader made headlines in another arena: It went on the sale block. Parent company Primedia decided to sell off its Supplementary Education Division to help offset a sizable debt. The purchaser is a little-known investment banking concern, Ripplewood Holdings.

According to a report in the publishing newsletter *Subtext,* Ripplewood is a private investment group with diverse interests. Timothy Collins, a former investment banker with Lazard Frères and Company founded it four years ago. In addition to the purchase of the Education Division of Primedia (for a rumored $415 million), Ripplewood also bought

Teens Take Center Stage

(continued from preceding page)

End describes *Entertainmenteen* as "a hybrid of the entertainment magazines and service magazines directed at teens." Distribution for the monthly will be 800,000 copies at 150,000 newsstands, and through subscriptions. End distinguishes the magazine from all the other teen titles: "*Entertainmenteen* is for the girl who is not comfortable with magazines like *Teen* and *Seventeen*, either because of the articles on subjects like sex or because their parents won't let them read them. *Entertainmenteen* is really a light lifestyle magazine. We are very positive and upbeat, and more than anything, we are about fun."

In the category of sizable launches, *Entertainmenteen* is not alone. The teen magazine to garner the most publicity last year was *Cosmo-girl!*, baby sister to the 113-year-old *Cosmopolitan*, published by Hearst. *Cosmo-girl!* launched with 850,000 newsstand-only copies. The first issues of the bimonthly featured—surprise!—celebrities on the cover.

According to a Hearst spokesperson who did not wish to be named, *Cosmo-girl!* will go to 10 issues a year some time in 2000. "The substantial difference between *Cosmo-girl!* and the other teen magazines" in this crowded field, says the spokesperson, "is that the magazine's message goes to the inner girl. It's about their thoughts, their feelings. It speaks to them as an older sister would. We target 12-to-17-year-old girls and we are a younger sister to *Cosmopolitan*. We think of ourselves as being the reader's friend. It's that original Helen Gurley Brown message that you can do anything you want. Part of the mantra of the book is that you can achieve your dream. It also has fashion, celebrity, and beauty coverage."

Jostens Learning, making it a major player in the K-12 supplemental education market. For the time being, the purchase is not expected to have any impact on the day-to-day running of Weekly Reader's publications.

Of Special Interest

Special interest publications, magazines that appear annually or even just once ever, are becoming more frequent in the children's field. Sometimes the titles are special issues of an established publication, which *Teen People* does. Other times, a single issue with no direct tie to an existing magazine is created to test the waters. Two such titles hit newsstands this past year—*Disney's Animal Kingdom,* and *Raising Teens* from the Meredith Corporation, publishers of *Crayola Kids* and *Better Homes & Gardens*. Each did a single issue, and have not scheduled (as of this writing) a second one.

"We have not yet planned a second issue," says *Raising Teens* Editor Richard

Sowienski. "We are waiting to see how well this first issue did before going ahead." One reason behind this special interest strategy is that it's cheaper than a full-fledged launch. Such publications are usually put together with existing staff from other magazines. Sowienski, for example, is also Education and Parenting Editor for *Better Homes & Gardens*.

If they are good, these single-issue publications can make the company money. "To a degree, it's about money," says publishing executive Andrew Friedman of BeachFront Publishing, who has worked for both Primedia and Petersen Publishing. "Single issues can bring in a lot of revenue for a publisher, and as more and more publishers are going public, the bottom line matters more than it ever did."

Whether you are interested in science or soccer, teens or tykes, there is a magazine for your inclinations and experience. If the magazine doesn't exist, it probably will soon. There seems to be no shortage of ideas, or of people interested in building a magazine around them. No niche seems too narrow or too far-fetched. Whether or not all these magazines can make money remains the question. Regardless of who produces what, one group that will continue to reap the rewards of the growth is children's writers.

Technology, Literacy, Government, Kids

■ **GetNetWise.org** has launched. It is "the first comprehensive interactive directory of resources to help guide children in the digital age," according to the the Association of American Publishers (AAP). The AAP, which is a national trade group, and other corporations and public interest groups are participants.

At the website's debut, AAP President and CEO Pat Schroeder spoke of the importance of parent, teacher, and child access to "safe" websites, and of her hope that children could be protected against "online hazards—without heavy-handed government regulation or legislation that violates the First Amendment."

The American Library Association (ALA) makes its criteria for safe websites available through a GetNetWise link (www/ala.org/parentspage/greatsites/criteria.html). It lists "700+ Great Sites" in arts and entertainment, language and literature, people, planet Earth, and science and technology.

■ The AAP, ALA, and the American Booksellers Association (ABA) all opposed the proposal of Congressman Henry Hyde (D-IL) for a **Children's Defense Act** that would have "imposed severe criminal penalties for the sale, loan, or exhibit to anyone under the age of 17 of constitutionally protected material with sexual or violent content." The AAP and ABA addressed a letter to the House of Representatives that condemned "a misguided attempt to address the problem of juvenile violence by destroying basic First Amendment rights."

■ Publishers, the AAP, the American Booksellers Foundation for Free Expression, and other groups filed an amicus (friend-of-the-court) brief in the Third Circuit of the U.S. Court of Appeals in opposition to the **Children's Child Online Protection Act (COPA)**, which has been blocked by the courts although passed by Congress. Under COPA, any commercial communication on the World Wide Web that is accessible by juveniles and that is found harmful to them would be liable for civil and criminal penalties. The amicus brief states that COPA threatens free public discourse and is harmful to constitutionally protected speech.

Timeline

1999 Marched On

By Pat Conway

Anniversaries in Children's Publishing

Books

■ Hardie Gramatky's *Little Toot* celebrated its sixtieth anniversary. Grosset & Dunlap brought out five new titles based on the picture book, as well as *Little Toot: The Classic Abridged Edition.*

■ *Mike Mulligan and His Steam Shovel*, by Virginia Lee Burton, celebrated 60 years in print. Sales for this classic have passed $1.7 million.

■ *Madeline*, the wonderful character created by Ludwig Bemelmans, celebrated a sixtieth anniversary.

■ Margaret Wise Brown's *The Important Book* celebrated its fiftieth anniversary with HarperCollins issuing new hardcover and paperback editions with redesigned cover art.

■ *Paddington*, by Michael Bond, arrived on American shores 40 years ago. Houghton Mifflin marked the occasion with the publication of *The Paddington Treasury,* a collection of stories about the famous bear from Peru.

■ Phyllis Reynolds Naylor celebrated a milestone. Her hundredth book, *Walker's Crossing,* was published by Atheneum.

■ *The Giving Tree* and *A Giraffe and a Half,* by the late Shel Silverstein, celebrated their thirty-fifth birthdays. Silverstein's *Where the Sidewalk Ends* is 25 years old.

■ Paula Danziger's middle-grade classic *The Cat Ate My Gymsuit* (Puffin Books) celebrated a twenty-fifth anniversary.

■ *Bunnicula*, by James Howe, celebrated its twentieth anniversary. To mark the occasion, Atheneum released an anniversary edition of the first book, *Bunnicula: A Rabbit Tale of Mystery,* containing a new afterword by the author.

■ Albert Whitman & Company celebrated 80 years in publishing.

■ Charlesbridge Publishing marked its tenth anniversary.

Magazines

■ *Sports Illustrated For Kids* celebrated its tenth anniversary.

Awards

- The National Book Award for young people's literature was awarded to Louis Sachar for *Holes* (Farrar, Straus & Giroux/Frances Foster Books).

- The American Library Association (ALA) also presented its John Newbery Award to Louis Sachar for *Holes*. The ALA's Randolph Caldecott Medal went to *Snowflake Bentley* (Houghton Mifflin), illustrated by Mary Azarian and written by Jacqueline Briggs Martin.

- The Carl Sandburg Literary Award for excellence in children's literature went to Paul Zelinsky for *Rapunzel* (Dutton).

- The *Boston Globe-Horn Book* Awards named Sachar's *Holes* best fiction. The nonfiction winner was *The Top of the World: Climbing Mount Everest,* by Steve Jenkins (Houghton Mifflin). *Red-Eyed Tree Frog,* by Joy Cowley (Scholastic), won for picture book; and *Tibet: Through the Red Box,* by Peter Sis (Farrar, Straus & Giroux/ Frances Foster Books), received a special citation.

- The Jane Addams Children's Award, for children's books promoting social justice, was awarded to *Habibi,* by Naomi Shihab Nye (Simon & Schuster), and *Seven Brave Women,* by Betsy Hearne and Bethanne Andersen (Greenwillow).

- The Coretta Scott King Award honors African-American authors and illustrators. Winners were *Heaven,* by Angela Johnson (Simon & Schuster), and for illustration, Michele Wood, *I See the Rhythm* (Children's Book Press).

- The Aesop Prize, conferred by the American Folklore Society, was awarded to *Echoes of the Elders: The Stories and Paintings of Chief Lelooska* by Chief Lelooska (Dorling Kindersley).

- The Charlotte Zolotow Award for outstanding picture book writing went to Uri Shulevitz for *Snow* (Farrar, Straus & Giroux).

- The Scott O'Dell Award for historical fiction went to *Forty Acres and Maybe a Mule,* by Harriette Gillem Robinet (Simon & Schuster/Atheneum).

- The NAACP Image Award for Outstanding Literary Work for Children went to Patricia and Fredrick McKissack for *Let My People Go* (Simon & Schuster/Atheneum).

- The Christopher Award went to Donna Hill for *Shipwreck Season* (Clarion).

- The Lee Bennett Hopkins Award went to Angela Johnson, author of *The Other Side: Shorter Poems* (Orchard Books).

- The Spur Award for Best Western Juvenile Nonfiction was awarded to *Cowboy with a Camera: Erwin E. Smith, Cowboy Photographer,* by Don Worcester (Amon Museum).

- On May 10, illustrator Quentin Blake, whose watercolors have graced more than 200 books, was named Britain's first children's laureate. He will promote children's literature during a two-year term.

Reorganizations, Mergers, and Acquisitions

■ HarperCollins added former Hearst properties Avon and William Morrow to its holdings, making it the second largest publisher in the United States after Random House. HarperCollins Children's Books Group, headed by Susan Katz, consists of 8 imprints, down from 17: Greenwillow Books, Joanna Cotler Books, Laura Geringer Books, HarperCollins, HarperFestival, Harper-Trophy, Avon, and Tempest.

The closed children's imprints are Michael di Capua Books; Morrow Junior Books; Lothrop, Lee & Shepard; Beech Tree; and Mulberry.

■ Futech Interactive Products, a privately held children's products manufacturer and distributor, acquired Trudy Corp. Trudy's primary subsidiary, Soundprints, publishes children's books plus packages. Futech also acquired Tiger Press and scheduled 15 new titles to be released under this imprint. For the preschool Little Tiger market, Futech is planning to publish interactive books.

■ Troll, the children's book unit of Torstar Corporation, has been sold to the New York investment firm Willis Stein & Partners L.P. for $70 million.

■ Scholastic, Inc., separated its 35-title Classroom Magazine Division from its larger Education Division and folded it into the Company's Consumer and Professional Magazine Division, creating the Scholastic Magazine Group. Scholastic Executive Vice President Hugh Roome heads this division.

The sole U.S. exhibitor at the Zimbabwe International Book Fair, Scholastic sees an opportunity to establish trade and educational contacts in Africa. The demand is for inexpensive picture books, references, storybooks, teen fiction, and teacher-training material.

Scholastic reported record revenues up 12 percent to $334 million and net income up 61 percent to $22.4 million in the fourth quarter of fiscal 1999. Fourth quarter results were fueled by the strong performance of children's books and distribution, with revenues up 21 percent for the quarter and 17 percent for the year. Growth in book clubs, fairs, and trade properties, particularly Animorphs, Dear America, and I Spy series, helped fuel this growth.

■ Random House bought Listening Library, publisher of award-winning audios for children. Now the children's audio imprint of the Random House Audio Publishing Group, Listening Library releases its first list in spring 2000.

■ Charlesbridge Publishing acquired Whispering Coyote Press, an independent publisher of fairy tales, folktales, picture, and board books. Lou Alpert, founder and publisher of Whispering Coyote, will oversee the editorial direction of Charlesbridge's new imprint.

■ Barnes & Noble scrapped its plans to buy Ingram Book Group shortly after reports circulated that the FTC staff investigating the deal planned to recommend that the Commission reject the merger.

■ The Walt Disney Company restructured its publishing group. The Hyperion adult book group became part of ABC, a division of Disney. A new entity, Disney Publishing, Worldwide, was created with Steven Murphy as Senior Vice President and Managing Director. Murphy continues to be responsible for the children's book group.

■ Bantam Dell Publishing Group President Irwyn Applebaum reorganized several departments in an effort to unify the separate Bantam and Dell operations. As part of the unifying move, four prominent Dell executives left, including the Dell/Delacorte Editor in Chief.

■ Golden Books signed a three-year licensing agreement to publish a range of Pokémon books and products. The agreement was signed with Leisure Concepts, the licensing agent for Nintendo, which developed the Pokémon characters that are featured in the video game and TV show. Products include coloring and activity books and storybooks.

■ For the third quarter, The Millbrook Press reported a net loss of $166,000 on sales of $4.2 million, compared to 1998's third-quarter net income of $311,000 on sales of $4.4 million. The company blamed the sluggish results on a high level of returns from the trade market. Newly appointed Chief Financial Officer Dave Allen is looking for ways to control returns, one of which may be to reduce the number of trade titles or initial printruns.

■ Sales in DK's children's division, DK Inc., jumped 85 percent in the fiscal year ending June 30, 1999. In the United States, revenues in the children's division hit $78.5 million, led by two *Star War* titles that had worldwide sales of $9.3 million and $8 million respectively.

■ The Senate Commerce Committee approved the Children's Online Protection Act requiring libraries to prove they have installed filtering devices on Internet access computer terminals if they are to qualify for e-rate discounts. The American Library Association called this decision "a highly flawed technological approach to protecting children online, forcing libraries to broadly employ that technology in a manner that threatens the rights of all library users to access constitutionally protected material."

■ Simon & Schuster was one of several Viacom divisions that reported double-digit gains in the second quarter of fiscal 1999, with a 19 percent increase in revenues, to $146 million and earnings up 76% to $17 million. This was due principally to sharply higher sales in the trade and children's divisions.

■ Barnes & Noble and barnesandnoble.com will continue to underwrite *Reading Rainbow*, the long-running PBS children's series for an additional two years. Barnes & Noble will promote the show with in-store displays, activities, and story hours. On their website, the book chain will have a special *Reading Rainbow* boutique.

■ Shareholders sued Mattel because its Learning Company software unit is expected to lose between $50 million and

$100 million in the third quarter. The suits claim that Mattel failed to disclose that the Learning Company was having serious financial problems. Mattel acquired the Learning Company in 1999 for $3.6 billion.

Book Launches, Expansions, and News

■ Avon Books for Young Readers launched a fiction line, Tempest, for readers 12 and up. The line consists of mostly reprints but some hardcover originals and reissues of books previously published under Avon's Flare imprint will be included.

■ Hippocrene Books launched a new children's reference line—Hippocrene Children's Illustrated Foreign Language Dictionaries. Each hardcover volume in the 25-title series, geared for readers 5 to 10, contains 96 pages.

■ HarperCollins Children's Books, publisher of the Little House series, brought out a new series called The Charlotte Years, based on the life of Charlotte Tucker, grandmother of Laura Ingalls Wilder.

■ Simon & Schuster's Children's Publishing negotiated new rights to rerelease *Eloise* and its sequels, written by Kay Thompson and illustrated by Hilary Knight. First published in 1955, *Eloise* was an instant best-seller with more than 2,000,000 copies sold.

■ Pleasant Company has added two new lines of books for older readers. American Girl Fiction features contemporary novels for middle-grade readers. The books in the History Mysteries involve preteen heroines solving mysteries set in America's past.

■ The Discovery Channel, in partnership with Dutton Children's Books, released a new line of children's titles—Discovery Kids that will feature science, technology, and natural history.

■ McGraw-Hill and National Geographic Society signed a five-year agreement to joint development and marketing of new science, social studies, and geography textbooks for the elementary and secondary school market. National Geographic will develop original curriculum materials to augment McGraw-Hill's textbook programs in the three subject areas.

■ David Reuther, former Senior Vice President and Publisher of Morrow Junior Books, was named head of a new imprint at North-South Books. The new imprint, unnamed at press time, will publish 25 hardcovers and 30 paperbacks yearly, starting with the fall 2000 list. Titles will include picture books, middle-grade, and YA fiction.

■ Pocket Pulse, a new imprint from Pocket Books, launched in the fall. The teen imprint has six series, including three new lines: two of the lines, TV tie-ins and the third, a teen action series called Fearless.

■ A new imprint for children, Harry N. Abrams Books for Young Readers, made its debut in time to coincide with

Abrams's fiftieth anniversary. Editorial Director Howard Reeves plans to publish between 15 and 20 titles annually.

■ The University of Pittsburgh Press launched a new children's imprint, Golden Triangle Books. The paperbacks are historical fiction for ages 9 to 14.

■ As of March 31, Harcourt Brace became Harcourt Inc.

■ *Harry Potter and the Sorcerer's Stone* and the two other Harry Potter books by J.K. Rowling, have created excitement and a little controversy. Some groups of parents from South Carolina to California have petitioned school boards to pull the books off library shelves and out of classrooms, charging that the stories glorify the occult and popularize witchcraft and sorcery. More than 5 million copies of the first three books from Scholastic are in print, along with over 3.2 million paperback versions.

■ Children's books are big business in Hollywood. Some titles that were made into movies include *Shiloh 2: Shiloh Season, The Iron Giant, Stuart Little,* and *How the Grinch Stole Christmas.* Children's titles to make television debuts are *Olive, the Other Reindeer,* adapted from the Chronicle Book by J. Otto Seibold and Vivian Walsh; *Little Bill* series, based on Bill Cosby's early readers from Cartwheel; and *Roswell,* based on Pocket Books' *Roswell High* series.

■ First Book, the national nonprofit organization that gives disadvantaged children the chance to read and own their first new books, named country singer Reba McEntire as their first national spokesperson. Through Reba's First Book Club, more than 3 million books are being distributed to at-risk children in 300 communities. Publishers such as Houghton Mifflin, Scholastic, Simon & Schuster, and Lee & Low have donated a combined total of 500,000 books for distribution.

■ YALSA (Young Adult Library Services Association of the ALA) has developed National Teen Read Week into an annual event and selected figure-skating champion Nancy Kwan as the national chair. Teen Read Week takes place each October and has received a positive response from teens, librarians, publishers, and booksellers.

YALSA is sponsoring a new award, the Michael L. Printz Award for the best young adult book of the year, to be announced at the midwinter ALA conference along with the Newbery, Caldecott, and other awards.

■ Borders bookstores began teen focus groups to find out what teens are reading and to help the book chain choose titles to feature in their stores.

■ Avon launched Forecasts Club, in which teen readers receive books from Avon in return for their comments.

■ A teen division of the Book-of-the-Month Club is planned.

■ Winning the Newbery Award usually propels sales of a children's novel above 100,000 copies but the 1999 recipient, Louis Sachar's *Holes* (Farrar, Straus & Giroux/Frances Foster), has sold almost double that figure. After the Newbery announcement, there are more than 193,500 copies in print in all editions, including book clubs.

■ Bertelsmann announced an alliance with Xerox Corporation that will allow for on-demand printing of books ordered by consumers through the Internet. Xerox estimates on-demand printing of digitized books reached $54 million in 1998.

Magazine Launches, Expansions, and News

■ In April, Pleasant Company acquired the rights to the newsletter *Daughters*, for girls 10 to 16 and their parents. It contains advice on health, family, friends, and growing up.

■ In April, The New York Times Company and Scholastic, Inc., launched a news magazine for teens called the *New York Times Upfront*, which has replaced *Scholastic Update*. Targeted to students in grades 9 to 12, the biweekly is sold to schools or through home delivery, and features news and politics as well as *Times* stories re-edited for a high school audience.

■ *Teen Newsweek*, a national teen-oriented newsmagazine for grades 6 through 9, was launched in September. Jointly published by *Newsweek* and *Weekly Reader*, this eight-page newsmagazine is published 26 weeks during the school year.

■ A younger version of *Cosmopolitan—Cosmo-girl!*—hit the newsstands with the August/September 1999 issue. Geared toward girls 12 to 17, the magazine will publish 10 issues in 2000 with an emphasis on fashion, beauty, and health.

■ J. C. Penney launched a quarterly in July 1999 entitled *Noise*. Targeted to girls 12 to 18, the magazine, distributed throughout the USA in J. C. Penney stores, covers teen areas from sports and celebrities to fashion and decorating.

■ In July, Primedia launched a magazine for 12-to-15-year-olds called *Entertainmenteen*. The aim of this magazine is to spotlight teen celebrities as real-life models and peers and delve into the behind-the-scenes doings of their private lives.

■ Two sports magazines premiered in 1999: *Sports Illustrated For Women*, in March, and *GBall*, in June. A bimonthly for girls 10 to 17 who play basketball, *GBall* features articles on nutrition, fitness and injury prevention. *Sports Illustrated For Women* targets females 16 and up and features articles on sports, nutrition, and athletes.

■ In April, the bimonthly *archaeology's dig* premiered. Written for readers 8 to 13, each issue offers articles on all aspects of archaeology.

■ *Wild Baby Animal*, a new magazine for ages one to three, premiered its first issue in November. Launched by The National Wildlife Federation, the magazine focuses on baby animals and their needs.

■ *Latingirl* is a new English-language magazine for Hispanic teenage girls.

■ *Young Money,* a new bimonthly for the 13-to-20-year-old market, covers earning, investing, and spending by teens.

■ The Disney Publishing Group previewed a test issue of *Disney's Animal Kingdom Magazine.* Targeted for parents of children between the ages of 3 and 15, the publication features human interest stories about animals, fun facts, and a special section for kids. At press time, no decision had been made about the magazine's future.

■ Retailers are jumping on the teen magazine scene. Footwear retailer Skechers USA introduced a mail order *magalog.* Besides offering a catalogue of shoes, the magalog provides magazine-style articles on travel, as well as reviews of CDs, TV shows and books and has a circulation of 5,000,000. In October 1999, the Target discount store chain and Random House co-produced a promotional magazine, *Teen 'Zine,* which contains write-ups on Random House Books, along with other content.

Multimedia News

■ Warner Brothers and Heyman Films announced plans to produce a film based on the best-selling *Harry Potter and the Sorcerer's Stone* and *Harry Potter and the Chamber of Secrets.*

■ Electronic book publisher SoftBook Press offers readers the option of downloading 100 literary classics, including *Little Women, The Time Machine, 20,000 Leagues Under the Sea,* at no charge when they purchase a Softbook Reader, which retails for $600. The Reader allows users to "turn" pages, simulating the experience of reading a traditional book. Users can also search for key words and phrases and highlight, underline, or write and save handwritten notes.

■ Scholastic launched a comprehensive school-to-home website called scholastic.com for students, parents, and teachers. Free to users, it features content, tools, and online book club ordering for teachers, and editorial content and products for parents.

■ Hasbro has acquired Wizards of the Coast for a reported $325 million. Besides card and role-playing games, Wizards also publishes about 50 science fiction and fantasy books annually.

■ Family Christian Stores launched a new website, www.iBelieve.com, which will feature an online store featuring books, Bibles, and gifts.

■ Random House Children's Books joined forces with Yahoo! Broadcast Services (www.broadcast.com) to bring families a weekly Internet broadcast of children's authors reading from their works. The "Read-Aloud with Random House" program lasts 45 minutes and also includes a brief interview with each author.

■ The Nickelodeon channel is launching a bimonthly interactive magazine called *Nick Jr.* for parents and children. The first issue will be distributed to preschools across the country and will also be available at bookstores, newsstands and through subscription. Each issue will feature a pull-out section, *Nick Jr. Noodle,* for preschoolers. All articles with activities will be specially coded to help parents understand the different learning skills inherent in each activity.

■ Websites for teen readers have sprouted on the Internet. Books for teens are featured on Teenreads.com, Alloy.com, Gurl.com, Gettingit.com. and a new site, Teensatrandom.com, from Random House, which launched late in 1999. A Sweet Valley website, www.sweetvalley.com, from Random House, also features book/music cross promotions.

■ Zany Brainy, the multimedia retailer, went public June 3 issuing a total of 6.1 million shares at $10 per share. Through the offering, Zany Brainy expects to receive approximately $34 million in net proceeds, to be used to open a new distribution center and additional stores, implement new software, and develop an Internet shopping site.

■ Dorling Kindersley began making its entire list available online. Customers can read whole titles on-screen and print out any portion of the contents for free. "It could revolutionize children's nonfiction publishing," DK Chairman Peter Kindersley said. Some DK series that are online include Math Made Easy and the Eyewitness Travel Guides. The idea behind the project is that once consumers see a DK book online, they will want to purchase the print edition. Kindersley acknowledges that if this new venture has a negative effect on sales, they will discontinue it.

■ The entire *Encyclopedia Britannica*, a 32-volume set that retails for $1,250 in book form, has been placed on the Internet (www.britannica.com) free of charge. The site also carries news from newspapers and news wires around the world and from magazines. On its launch, however, the volume of traffic at britannica.com was so great users were turned away and the company quickly purchased new computers to expand service. The Chicago-based company still plans to publish a new 40-volume set and will still sell its compact disc versions of the reference work.

■ Classroom Connect closed a deal with independent school supplier J.L. Hammett Company in which Hammett will distribute the more than 66 web-based curriculum and staff development products of Classroom Connect for the K-12 market. Hammett will also feature Classroom Connect's product line in a general catalogue that goes to schools in all 50 states and 100 foreign countries.

People

Books

■ Children's author and poet Shel Silverstein died at the age of 66 at his home in Florida.

■ William Armstrong, 88, author of the 1970 Newbery Medal winner, *Sounder*, died at his home in Connecticut.

■ Sherley Anne Williams, 54, author of the Caldecott Honor-winning picture book *Working Cotton*, died on July 6.

■ Kate Morgan Jackson heads up the HarperCollins imprint of hardcover picture books, fiction, and nonfiction and Mary Alice Moore heads up HarperFestival, which publishes novelty and audio books, including board books.

■ Barbara Marcus, Executive Vice President of Scholastic, took on the additional title of President, Children's Book Group.

■ Nancy Starr was named Editorial Director of Smithmark Publishers. She oversees the company's children's editorial departments.

■ Cindy Kane, former Editorial Director of Dial Books, was named Supervising Editor at Modern Curriculum Press.

■ Rebecca Davis, former Editor at Simon & Schuster, has been named Senior Editor at Orchard Books.

■ Margery Cuyler was named Editor in Chief of Winslow Press.

■ In September, Karen Lotz, formerly with Dutton Children's Books, was named President and Publisher of Candlewick Press.

■ Stephanie Lurie, formerly with Simon & Schuster Books for Young Readers, was named President and Publisher of Dutton Books.

■ Betsy Gould, former Publisher of Magic Attic Press, has joined Roundtable Press, a New York City-based packager. Gould is in charge of launching their new line of children's fiction and nonfiction.

■ Lisa Holton was named Senior Vice President and Publisher of Global Children's Books, Disney Publishing Worldwide. In this position, Holton oversees Disney's children's books and continuity projects while continuing to oversee Disney's North American imprints—Hyperion Books for Children, Mouseworks, Disney Press, and Disney Editions.

■ David Reuther succeeds Marc Cheshire as President and Publisher of North-South Books. Reuther will also continue to oversee creation of the new children's division being launched by North-South.

Magazines

■ Nancy Axelrad was named Editor of *U*S* Kids*.

■ Rosanne Tolin was appointed Editor of *Guideposts for Kids*.

■ Tommi Lewis was named Editor of *Teen*. The magazine, published by E-Map (formerly Petersen Publishing) is concentrating on a younger audience, ages 12 to 15.

■ Thea Feldman became group Vice President, General Manager of Book Publishing at the Children's Television Workshop. Feldman was formerly Senior Vice President and Publisher at Golden Books.

Closings and Delays

■ Browndeer Press, an imprint of Harcourt Children's Books, was discontinued in August.

■ The magazine *Bluejean* ceased publication after a three-year run.

■ *The Flicker* magazine went out of business in January 1999.

■ *Trails 'N' Treasures*, the bimonthly for ages 6 to 12, has ceased publication.

■ *Young Equestrian* has ceased publication with the March/April issue.

■ *The Mailbox Teacher* suspended publication with its back-to-school 1999 issue.

■ *Topspin*, published by the U.S. Tennis Association, has gone out of business.

Part 2

Market Perspectives

Markets

PreK Nonfiction
Across the Street or Across the Millennium

By Joan Broerman

Knowing what's coming down the street—the products and consumers to come—is a boost for any business. Publishers can take a peek down the road via the census. According to figures gathered by the Population Estimates Program of the Bureau of the Census, the number of people under age five in the United States is close to 20 million. If these potential readers are not yet ready to cross the street by themselves to head for the nearest bookstore, their parents are.

Publishers understand this, and they understand this equation: Population growth plus current nonfiction growth equals more books for a potentially very large, very young audience. The variable in the equation is whether the last wave of baby boomer parents and libraries will spend money on books to give these children a leap into learning.

For generations, parents have enjoyed reading to their toddlers and preschoolers, but in recent years the numbers of magazines and books geared specifically to babies, from birth to four or five, has risen and the content has spread across many subject areas. Board books, novelty books, interactive activity books, and slick, colorful magazines as enticing as any grown-up publication, offer adults a variety of choices as they browse bookstores and libraries and spend hours of quality reading time with their children.

First Steps

Children's librarian June Lacanski remembers reading aloud to her own children when they were babies. Paula Morrow is Editor of *Babybug* and *Ladybug*. Lacanski and Morrow both think that positive feelings transfer in the reading process, whether from parent to child or librarian to child. Instinctively, young children want closeness with special adults. When these adults read to children, Morrow believes, they build readers. What the adult offers with enthusiasm, the children will like. Parents who take their children to libraries are setting them up for a lifetime of learning.

Lacanski runs a summer reading program at her library in Homewood, Alabama, and says when parents and children choose books together, fiction predominates. To introduce her young charges to information sources, she gives program participants extra points for reading nonfiction.

What the Experts Say

Dr. Patricia Edwards, who organized and authored *Parents as Partners in Reading: A Family Literacy Training Program,* recognized by Barbara Bush as one of the top 10 family literacy programs in the nation, notes that as early as 1908 parents were being advised to read to their children. She cites an influential 1984 report, *Becoming a Nation of Readers,* which quoted 10 literacy experts who agreed that "reading aloud to children is the single most important factor in preparing them to read." Project Headstart is a federally funded child development program for ages three to five that takes the approach that the parent is the child's primary educator.

Dr. Edwards received her Ph.D. in reading education from the University of Wisconsin-Madison, and among her many honors is membership on the Board of Directors of the International Reading Association and the National Advisory Board for *Sesame Street*. "I believe that infants and toddlers should be *marinated* or *soaked* in the literature," she says. She thinks publishing nonfiction magazines for infants and toddlers is "a great idea." She doesn't think the literacy problems plaguing our country will go away as a result of the publication of more materials for young children. She expresses concern, however, for the low-income parent who can't afford books and magazines or the nonreading parent who can't participate in the process.

Lacanski and bookseller Marie Peerson, co-owner of Crosshaven Books in Cahaba Heights, Alabama, both note that nature and science predominate in nonfiction books and magazines for the very young. Biographies are being written for younger audiences, says Lacanski, but they haven't reached children ages three to four, and they should. Peerson points to the success of *Who Came Down This Road?,* a history book by George Ella Lyon and illustrated by Peter Catalanotto, for ages four to eight. A *Horn Book* reviewer said it "will start children thinking about history." Peerson says she could sell more books of this kind.

Barefoot Books has identified this opening for topics in prekindergarten nonfiction. The U.K. company opened an office in New York in 1998.

Barefoot's publishers, Tessa Strickland and Nancy Traversy, have seven children under the age of 12 between them and run the company from their homes in London and the Cotswolds. Some of their books introduce children to diverse cultures and they incorporate first learning themes with interactive projects. Barefoot Beginners aims at birth to age six. One of the titles in this line, *The Emperor Who Hated Yellow*, is written and illustrated by toymaker Jim Edmiston. The book teaches the young reader about many things that are yellow—nonfiction—but it does it through a good story. The company also publishes the Barefoot Books line and Barefoot Collections, both with titles beginning with age 4; Barefoot Poetry Collections are written for all ages.

The movement beyond animal and basic science nonfiction topics appears to be spreading. "We consider biographies and all matter of historical topics as well as science and nature themes for all age levels, but with a particular interest in the preK audience," says Melanie Cecka, Editor of Viking Children's Books. "We don't have a plan for publishing a specific number of books for any one age group, but the growing interest in nonfiction, particularly among very young readers, opens up wonderful possibilities for picture books. Because picture books are a major part of our list, I think it's likely that we'll be doing more nonfiction in this format."

Bernette Ford, Vice President and Editorial Director of Cartwheel Books, the Scholastic imprint for preschool and emerging readers, has a different perspective, however.

Ford originally came to publishing for the very young because she found the area excited her personally. The market changed from a library market to an emphasis on trade and mass-market. She could see the preK market growing as baby boomer mothers who worked away from home took up reading to their babies after work. This fueled the trade market. She now sees book production for ages one to three as having reached a critical mass. While Cartwheel has a number of new titles in the works for this group, she doesn't see an increase ahead.

Yolanda LeRoy, Associate Editor at Charlesbridge Publishing, sees government emphasis on early learning as a plus. Her company publishes 80 percent nonfiction and plans to maintain the number of books they are currently publishing for the very young, which is 25 percent of their list. "We do a number of different types of books from board books for toddlers to picture books, alphabet series, concept and counting books, all of which are useful as learning tools for the preK reader."

Williamson Publishing Company plans an increase from its current 10 to 15 yearly children's nonfiction titles to an annual 20 to 25 books. Of those, seven books are scheduled for their Little Hands series for ages two to six. Susan Williamson, Editorial Director, says editorial and marketing factors both play into getting the books to kids and the adults in their lives.

Daycare and preschool markets are more difficult to reach than the K-12 market, says Williamson. Even so, she says the company's Kids Can! line, for ages 6 to 10, and Little Hands "are series we care very deeply about. I can't imagine our not continuing to develop them, as long as we have something new and valuable to contribute to children and their parents and teachers."

In Tandem with Editors

"Successful nonfiction is a combination of the right subject matter and the right voice. It should entertain readers and hold their interest like the very best fiction," says Cecka. Viking "looks for nonfiction topics that are fresh and innovative or offer a unique angle, while staying within a child's realm of understanding and experience. An unusual, untold story is what will grab readers, and us."

Take time to look at the Viking line. The company works directly with authors on most projects, but has worked with packagers and foreign publishers as well. "Viking has a small, highly select list that includes fiction and nonfiction and it's important to recognize the types of books we publish."

At Williamson Publishing, "We encourage our authors to leave ample room for creative expression and open-ended outcomes," says Williamson. "Write directly to the kids even though adults are usually involved. The tone of our books is clear: We think you are great, we are interested in your ideas, we respect your accomplishments."

The kids respond to this, she says.

Williamson is very clear that she is not interested in picture books of any kind. "Go to the library, look at our books, read them, and identify what it is that we do differently. Then, send us a submission that makes sense for us to look at." The company prefers to work directly with authors and illustrators, agented or unagented, and not with packagers; they do read unsolicited material.

At Charlesbridge, LeRoy is looking for unique ideas and extraordinary facts presented in an innovative way. The hook for a Charlesbridge title is whatever it is that makes the book unusual. Note that writers must submit material exclusively to receive consideration at this publisher.

Marketing Director Emily Romero at Barefoot Books suggests prospective writers check their web page (www.barefoot-books.com) and order a catalogue before they send a query or proposal to the Editorial Department, Barefoot Books, P.O. Box 95, Kingswood, Bristol, England BS30 5BH, United Kingdom. This company will work with unagented authors.

Due to a backlog, Cartwheel is not reading unsolicited material, but Ford is open to queries and advises writers to write *query* on the envelope. As for writing for the very young, she advises, "Every word must evoke a picture." For writers, Ford sees more opportunity in early readers noting their strength in the trade and book club markets.

Magazines Stride Ahead

The Cricket Magazine Group has offered more and more to younger readers throughout the last decade, and its

PreK Authors Say . . .

Rebecca Kai Dotlich, author of *Sweet Dreams of the Wild* and *Lemonade Sun and Other Summer Poems,* both published by Boyds Mills Press, also has poetry in many anthologies and has written *What Is Round?* and *What Is Square?* for The Growing Tree, the HarperCollins imprint for infants and toddlers. Dotlich's advice to writers about the preK market: "Researching the market and reading nonfiction books available for the very young is a must." She began reading market guides in college; when she talks about reading books, she is speaking of *stacks* of books.

"I have a fascination for the toddler age," says Dotlich. "I am totally captivated by their innocence and eagerness to learn. They question everything. They notice everything." To reach them, she suggests using playful language. "Remember, consciously and constantly, that what seems simple to you is sometimes complicated, or at the least new, to them. What is old news to you is, to them, a treasure just found. Their excitement over the simplest detail is absolutely joyous." She underscores the importance of being "open to enjoying" children, "listening to them, observing and validating them."

Dotlich considers writing for the very young as both easier and harder than writing for older readers: "Easier because, of course, there is less text and your vocabulary is simple, clean, and somewhat limited. Harder because there is less text and your vocabulary is simple, clean, and somewhat limited." She emphasizes: "Every word counts."

Phyllis Tildes is a writer and illustrator whose personal journey to creating for the very young included marriage, raising a son, running her own graphics design business, and then publishing her first picture book with Charlesbridge. *Animals, Black and White,* an American Booksellers Association (ABA) Pick of the Lists, was named outstanding Science Trade Book for Children. *Baby Animals, Black and White* followed, and was also named an ABA Pick of the Lists. Founding and running her own company gave Tildes an approach to publishing that many writers could take to heart. "This is a business. You are providing a service. It must be something that resonates. Take criticism. Your work is a marketable commodity. Get real. Within these confines, make it the best it can be." Tildes thinks children's writers need a good reason—a burning desire—and a strong focus to build a career. "They must have talent, persistence, and luck in equal quantities."

When Tildes works, her first draft is "overdrawn." Then she rewrites, revises, and simplifies. "The writer needs to leave something to the imagination for both illustrator and reader." Like Dotlich, she says, "Every word must count." She thinks most authors are "visualizers" and don't have to dictate beyond the writing to illustrators. As an illustrator too, however, she doesn't separate the writing from the illustrating but sees them as an organic whole.

overriding philosophy—to produce the highest quality magazines possible—in some sense ignores trends and market studies.

The company has always been research-driven, however, says Bob Harper, President of Cricket Magazine Group. The research stems from the desire to know what children are capable of and what they need to be able to develop good reading and learning skills. Based on such analysis, *Babybug* is tailored to the needs of an audience of six months to two years and their parents and *Ladybug* to ages two to six and their parents.

The two-year-old *Click* has gone about providing prekindergarteners with nonfiction based on similar research into developmental skills and interests and the goal of high-quality. "We feel there is a need to develop science writing that is not a factual parade," says Harper. "Combine nonfiction information with the best elements of storytelling and narrative writing. We're trying to develop a new style of writing."

Following two years of similar research on what children comprehend at each age, the National Wildlife Federation added *Wild Animal Baby* to its other children's magazines in November 1999. The newest publication targets ages 12 months to 3 years. *Your Big Backyard* is also for preK, ages 3 to 6. The third magazine is *Ranger Rick*, for ages 7 to 12. Editor Donna Johnson says *Wild Animal Baby* features baby animals eating, sleeping, bathing, and doing other activities human babies perform too. "Parents want kids to enjoy reading. Animals are a good way to reach kids. We hope we are preaching to the unconverted and will grow our own generation of readers."

The Children's Better Health Institute (CBHI), which publishes the preschool *Turtle*, has no plans for a magazine younger than *Turtle*'s range of two-to-five-year-olds. Editor Terry Harshman says, "While our older readers might participate to a greater degree in the easy recipes and simple science experiments, all readers can participate to some degree."

A False Step: Dividing Fiction and Nonfiction?

The distinction between fiction and nonfiction blurs at the youngest levels of learning because everything is new to a baby, no matter how it is presented. *Ladybug* publishes some nonfiction and

---

PreK Nonfiction Websites

■ **Barefoot Books**
www.barefoot-books.com

■ **Cartwheel Books, Scholastic**
www.scholastic.com

■ **Charlesbridge Publishing**
www.charlesbridge.com

■ **National Wildlife Federation**
(*Wild Animal Baby, Your Big Backyard*)
www.nwf.org

■ **Williamson Publishing**
http://williamsonbooks.com

■ **Rebecca Kai Dotlich**
www.eyeontomorrow.com/
embracingthechild/Bookspecialdotlich

Click may publish some fiction. This can confuse children's writers who wonder what exactly the editors want.

Click Editor Deborah Pool says each issue published in their first year made it clear what the magazine is about—so study those issues thoroughly. Pool's favorite writers do college-level research and are "driven" to be sure of their facts. They write simply, in an interesting way, but understand their subjects at a much deeper level. Themes for the next two years are set and available for a self-addressed, stamped envelope.

Johnson says the spare text in *Wild Animal Baby* will be written in-house, but she is open to finger plays and motion rhymes for lap time, even if they have been published elsewhere. Ilustrations will give those pieces a new look. For *Your Big Backyard,* she would like to see read-to-me stories with a girl or female animal character having adventures. Interested writers should study similar stories from past issues. Johnson also wants poetry with a nature component. She advises that these are very specific needs and she will not read other unsolicited work.

Turtle is receiving more age-appropriate material than in years past, says Harshman. She urges writers to note the underlying message of healthful living in all the CBHI publications and "the shorter, the better" submissions.

For magazines or for books, writers for preschoolers should be both realistic and optimistic. LeRoy says she would never want to discourage writers, but must say, "This is not the most lucrative profession. It is a very rewarding but difficult profession. Keep writing and improving your craft. You have to love what you do, not dollars."

The way a writer connects to the reader, Morrow says, is to "know the kids." Volunteer at church or a place where parents work out and leave their children in supervised care. "Don't read your own work to them because then you are focusing on your writing, not the children. Observe them, play with them, sing with them. Listen."

Twenty million children under the age of five speak in many voices. Editors, publishers, and writers will do well to heed Morrow's advice: "Listen."

Markets

Middle-Grade Fiction
Intense and Funny, Safe and Searching

By Patricia Curtis Pfitsch

Middle-grade fiction has made its share of news recently. Everyone—in publishing and out—is talking about *Harry Potter and the Sorcerer's Stone* and its two sequels, published in the United States by Scholastic. At the height of the rage, the *New York Times* reported 826,000 copies (and counting) in print of this adventure about the schooling of a young wizard, and 915,000 of the second book *Harry Potter and the Chamber of Secrets*. These numbers seem more likely for a successful paperback, but the Harry Potter books are beautifully designed hardcovers. "At bedtime, at the beach, by the pool, in the back of the car, whole families are reading about the boarding school where the food is delicious and the equipment list includes a wand and cauldron," the *New York Times* reported.

The success of Harry Potter seems even more amazing in the face of prior industry belief that fantasy doesn't often sell well, especially to older readers. Perhaps it heralds a trend in publishing for the middle-grade audience? It's too soon to tell, say most editors, but most agree that the books' success is less due to fancy marketing techniques and more to excellent writing and a captivating story. *Harry Potter and the Sorcerer's Stone* is a riveting adventure, but it also explores many of the universal themes of middle-grade fiction—family, school, and friends.

"It's just a great book," says Andrea Cascardi, Associate Publishing Director for Alfred A. Knopf and Crown Books for Young Readers. "At some point a book goes beyond the genre. The message to all of us in publishing is to be ever vigilant to seek books that are exceptional and make sure they get published. We can't say, 'Well, it's fantasy, it's not going to sell,' or 'it's historical fiction, it's not going to sell.'"

Who Am I?

The middle-grade audience spans a large age range, sometimes reaching down to 7-year-olds with chapter books—short novels where each chapter is basically complete unto itself—and sometimes reaching up to teens as old as 14, and exploring deeper and more sophisticated issues. Humor and series fiction are traditional ways of reaching these young readers. But have these children truly changed in interests and reading preferences?

Most editors believe they have not. "They're still exploring their world," says Cascardi. "For the youngest middle-graders, their interests are focused on their families, then friends, and then school. For older readers, friends and school are primary and families are secondary. But they're all dealing with the things that happen to them and asking, 'Who Am I? Who are my friends?'"

Susan Rich, Editor at HarperCollins Children's Books, agrees. "I'd like to hang on to the idea that the great books of the past will always be the greats," she says, but she and other editors acknowledge that the world around children, and their interaction with it, are changing dramatically.

Parents, teachers, and publishers alike know that their world moves at a rapid pace and television, film, and the Internet have made them visually discerning. "They don't have as much freedom as they used to," Mary Cash, Executive Editor of Holiday House, points out. "Both parents work outside the home, and there are more scheduled activities. Middle-graders are more sophisticated in some ways but not in others." Middle-grade novels reflect this. "The kind of families in realistic fiction are changing," says Cash. "There aren't as many stories that show kids riding their bikes to go fishing. More stories show kids going to day camp, or playing with GAME BOYs. Books reflect what kids do."

Trade publishers are not looking for books specifically about these changes in the environment, "but it's important for writers to understand the world in which the child lives today," says Cascardi. "We wouldn't publish a book where the world of the book doesn't reflect the reality of today."

Time Again

Cascardi says some of the differences between recent middle-grade books and those of the past are subtle. "It's not conscious, but it's there if you compare novels of the past to novels of today. Writers are freer in their style than they used to be. They're using more interesting styles; there was more formality in literature of past years. The writing style has to be in tune with the culture. Writers are able to experiment more."

Cynthia Rylant's *Islander,* published by Dorling Kindersley (DK), illustrates. About a boy's encounter with a mermaid, *Islander* is subtly, but effectively, experimental. "It's quiet, personal, a meditative, traditional narrative with a distinctive voice," says Neal Porter, Vice President and Publisher of DK Children's Books. "It's short and it packs a punch in its own quiet way."

The design of this book is a significant part of its appeal. *Islander* is published in an unusual format, short and squarish in shape. "We used decorative elements from seashells in the design; we wanted to suggest the sea," Porter says. The book was meant to have the feel of another time. "The dyed-in-the-wool traditionalist in me regrets the loss of the handmade quality books had in other times," Porter admits, "but on the other hand, the computer gives us a lot of freedom with the way the book looks." To create that sense of another time, DK searched for a typesetter who could set the book in hot type, a technique not much used since the advent of computer printing technology.

On the Edge

Other new middle-grade titles fly in the face of such quiet or subtle experimentation. In these books, the themes of self, family, and friends still appear, but not with the traditional handling of middle-grade fiction.

"There is less fluff coming out," says Jenefer Angell, Assistant Editor at Atheneum Books for Young Readers, an imprint of Simon & Schuster. Atheneum Senior Editor Caitlyn Dlouhy agrees. "Kids are faced with realities they were protected from a while back," says Dlouhy. "Young kids are facing pressures and making choices that were nearly unheard of 50 years ago. It used to be older teens in these situations; now it's the peers of this middle-grade audience. They have more connection with these weighty issues and want to read about them. Middle-grade literature can help kids deal with the ever more difficult issues."

Stephen Roxburgh, Publisher and President of Front Street, believes some adults will not want them to read these books, in a misguided attempt to protect children. "But it is not in our power to protect kids from intense emotion," he says. "I publish to, for, and about those kids at risk. It's important that they have books."

Front Street, a small publisher known for its unusual and sometimes risky books, is bringing out *Bare Hands,* a middle-grade novel by Bart Moeyaert. The story begins as a silly game—running away from an angry neighbor—and escalates into a drama. Either by accident or design, a boy named Ward kills a duck belonging to his neighbor, who then, apparently accidentally, kills Ward's dog.

"It deals with fairly harsh aspects of life," says Roxburgh, "as many of my books do. As an adult reading *Bare Hands,* you might think, 'This is surrealistic,' but remembering back, it's not. One of my recollections of when I was that age is the extraordinary emotional intensity that youngsters have. They haven't developed any elaborate barriers to protect themselves; they're still raw and open to emotion. When I was a child and my dog died, the world ended for me."

Moeyaert captures that intensity. "The story is told from the boy's viewpoint and rises to an extremely tense," says Roxburgh, "and I think true, high-pitched emotional level. The whole book takes place in a few hours: Time is abbreviated so nothing has a chance to cool off. Kids live on this intense level—they won't think it's bizarre—they'll get it."

Emotion and rawness seem to translate to confrontations with violence in more middle-grade books.

Dovey Coe, a first novel by Frances O'Roark Dowell published by Atheneum, is about a young girl on trial for the murder of her older sister's rejected suitor. "It's a match between an astonishing story and an exquisite writer." Dlouhy is seeing more and more middle-grade novels with strong female protagonists, "girls who aren't twirling their hair and longing for boyfriends," and Dovey is one of them. "She's a feisty young girl from the backwoods of North Carolina. The author portrays her with an honesty and integrity that makes you absolutely believe in her. She's the most compelling Southern heroine since Scout in *To Kill a Mockingbird.*"

On the Lookout

Atheneum Books for Young Readers

"I want to publish more middle-grade and YA," says Senior Editor Caitlyn Dlouhy, "and I'm more interested in evocative voices and points of view because of the different perspectives they can give kids." Dlouhy also edits picture books. Send a query first. Titles to study: *Postcards to Father Abraham,* Catherine Lewis; *Spider's Voice,* Gloria Skurzynski; and *Shadow Spinner*, Susan Fletcher.

Dial Books for Young Readers

Dial does not accept unsolicited manuscripts, but does accept query letters. Briefly describe the manuscript's plot, genre, intended audience, and your publishing credits. Send no more than one page of the manuscript of shorter works and a maximum of 10 pages of longer works; any excess will not be read. Never send cassettes, original artwork, marketing plans, or faxes. Manuscript pages will not be returned. In response you will receive a form letter either requesting the manuscript or letting you know it isn't right for Dial.

Dial only keeps track of requested manuscripts. Never call or fax to inquire about the status of an unsolicited submission. Write a letter only if the reply time has exceeded four months. Full manuscripts sent without a prior query will be returned unread. No replies are sent without a self-addressed stamped envelope (send International Reply Coupons (IRCs) if outside the U.S.).

DK Ink

DK books tend not to fall into any particular genre, but reflect the tastes and passions of the individual editors. Send complete manuscripts. Prefers no multiple submissions. DK Ink is reading unsolicited manuscripts but they may be forced to change the policy in the future so check submissions guidelines for current policy.

Front Street

"If you don't accept unsolicited manuscripts, how do you publish new voices?" asks Stephen Roxburgh, Publisher of Front Street. "Half my list are first authors. I'm a truffle hunter—that's what I do." Roxburgh doesn't think of his books in terms of age levels. "I have no interest in age groups," he says. "What is crucial to me is that the book be accessible to youngsters, finding that fine balance point between linguistic skills and life experience. I don't care what the subject matter is. I don't care what the literary sophistication is. What I care about is point of view and life." According to Roxburgh, assigning age levels to books is part of the marketing process, "so publishers can slip books into a slot. *(continued on next page)*

On the Lookout

(continued from preceding page)
For me, that's a problem. These books are unique; they don't go into slots." Front Street's list is made up primarily of picture books or young adult fiction and many deal with harsher aspects of life. Check the website for a catalogue and writers' guidelines (www.frontstreetbooks.com). Titles to study: *On the Stairs,* Julie Larios; *The Copper Elephant,* Adam Rapp.

Greenwillow Books
"We're looking for something new that we haven't read before," says Executive Editor Virginia Duncan. "This is a place for writers who write well, who write individual stories that speak from the heart rather than try to fill a need. We don't publish series for the most part. You can learn a lot by looking at our catalogue and sending for submission guidelines." Greenwillow accepts unsolicited submissions. Titles to study: *Sun & Spoon,* Kevin Henkes; *Beyond the Mango Tree,* Amy Bronwen Zemser; *Unbroken,* Jessie Haas.

HarperCollins
Accepts queries, but no unsolicited manuscripts except from agented authors. Titles to study: *Our Only Mae Amelia,* Jennifer Holm; *Extreme Elvin,* Chris Lynch.

Holiday House
Holiday House is looking for a wide variety of middle-grade fiction, especially humor and literary fiction. To submit, authors must first mail a query. Holiday House will respond by mail, requesting or declining to read the manuscript. Multiple submissions are not accepted. For inquiries about work already submitted, include a stamped self-addressed postcard. Do not call, fax, or e-mail. Titles to study: *Fourth Grade Weirdo,* Martha Freeman; *A Fairy Called Hilary,* Linda Leopold Strauss; and *I Was a Third Grade Science Project,* Mary Jane Auch.

Alfred A. Knopf and Crown Books for Young Readers
Knopf and Crown are looking for books that create a vivid, believable story world, says Associate Publishing Director Andrea Cascardi. "If you strive to make character, setting, plot, and dialogue 100 percent believable, you'll have a much greater chance of being successful." Titles to study: *Sammy Keyes and the Hotel Thief* by Wendelin van Draanen, *The Dreams of Mairhe Mehan,* Jennifer Armstrong, and *Sort of Forever,* Sally Warner.

Walker's Crossing, Phyllis R. Naylor's hundredth book, is another title in the same vein. "It is very timely, very powerful, about a disturbing topic," says Angell. "The main character is a boy who lives in Wyoming and discovers that his brother is involved with a militant white supremacist group. He's trying to figure out how to be part of this family. It's a very edgy topic."

Personally Chosen
Take a step away from these edgy books that push the envelope of the middle-grade experience and you'll find that much recent fiction still deals with other serious topics. Yet middle-graders are an in-between age, still very much children who want security, but who reach toward independence and life's challenges.

"What's special about middle-grade fiction," says Cash, "is that often these are the first books kids have really selected themselves. They are books that the child feels are written especially for him or her, and that makes them memorable."

But, Roxburgh points out, "middle-graders are the most difficult to find books for. That age is such a fleeting moment when children are still innocent."

All Alone in the Universe, by Lynn Rae Perkins, is a new novel from Greenwillow. "It's about that time when you think you have a best friend and then you lose that friend," says Virginia Duncan, Executive Editor. "It's beautifully written, funny, and yet poignant, not like anything I've ever read. The writing is just wonderful."

Middle-grade historical fiction writer Gloria Whelan is known for her fast-paced adventures set in the American past. But HarperCollins is bringing out a different sort of novel by Whelan, *Homeless Bird.* She is still writing for a middle-grade audience, but the book is set in India and the main character is a young Indian girl married and widowed at 13. "It's one of the most affecting, chillingly beautiful stories I've read," says Rich. "Middle-grade girl readers like nothing better than a book that makes them cry—and this is it. It sparkles with the tastes, smells, sights, sounds, the culture of India, but at its heart, it's a gut-wrenching romance."

The Ashwater Experiment, by Amy Goldman Koss, is for older middle-grade readers. "It's funny, but probes more deeply than her first books," says Cindy Kane, former Editorial Director of Dial Books for Young Readers. "The main character, Hillary, is settling into her eighteenth school and creates a whole fantasy world to help her through the experience. Koss handles it magnificently. The book is getting starred reviews. Koss is a very good example of what works and why for middle-grade," says Kane, "because she crosses age groups. She does very young chapter books as well as books for older readers."

A Family Trait, by Terri Martin, and published by Holiday House, is another serious title handled with grace. "It's a lovely story about a girl who discovers a family secret and what it means to be a part of a family," says Cash. "It has humor in it, but at the heart are some more serious issues."

The Lighter Side

Humor is a tool that can help authors carry off many subjects for this age.

"What really works best," Roxburgh says, "is humor, but trying to get it right is difficult. What they find most amusing we adults sort of groan at—finding an adult who can capture that kind of humor is really tough."

Both the Newbery winner *Holes*, by Louis Sachar, and the Newbery honor book, *A Long Way from Chicago*, by Richard Peck, deal with serious issues but are very funny books.

Kane cites *The Trouble with Zinny Weston*, also by Amy Goldman Koss. "She's a California writer and this book has a clear California setting. It has all the ingredients of success for middle-grades. She writes well about family and pets. It has humor—a very funny fresh voice." Koss's second book, *How I Saved Hanukkah*, is a classic chapter book and with a similar mix of ingredients—California, family, humor. "This one outsold the first book two to one," Kane said, "because it was a Hanukkah title. If you have a handle, it's easier to get into bookstores."

Holiday House looks for humorous books. "We love humor," says Cash, "particularly humor for the younger age group." Two of their titles are *I Was a Third Grade Science Project*, written by Mary Jane Auch and illustrated by Herm Auch, and *Third Grade Pet*, by Judy Cox and illustrated by Cynthia Fisher. Cash says that they often try to focus their middle-grade fiction at a very specific age group. "Both these books are illustrated with black and white art. We like to do that for younger middle-grade fiction."

Holiday House is also bringing out some funny middle-grade fantasy. *If that Breathes Fire We're Toast*, by Jennifer J. Stewart, is about a boy and girl who receive a delivery of a dragon. "There's always been a market for younger fantasy," Cash says.

Front Street also publishes humor. Roxburgh points to two books by Douglas Evans, *Classroom at the End of the Hall* and *Apple Island*. "Evans remembers the humor" of that age, Roxburgh says. "He speaks to the concerns and sensibilities of third- and fourth-graders." Both books also use the classroom setting, frequently found in middle-grade fiction.

Dork in Disguise, by Carol Gorman, is a new HarperCollins title about a boy entering a new school. He has always been a dork, but he uses his scientific mind to study up on how to be cool. "He starts school as a cool guy," explains Rich, "but discovers he'd rather be himself. It's fast-paced, funny middle-grade fiction. She hits the middle-grade social scene on the nose."

HarperCollins has launched a mid-

Markets

dle-grade series called A Series of Unfortunate Events, by Lemony Snicket. The author, says Rich, is using a *nom de plume*. "We're all quite excited about it. Its roots are in Victorian children's literature where terrible things always seem to be happening to orphans. It's a bit of a satire, a mind meld between Charles Dickens and John Scieszka."

Without mentioning a definite time and place, the series creates a setting with the distinct feeling of Victorian England. The three main characters are orphans. Violet is 14 and good at inventing things without tools. Klaus, 12, is well-read and often has an interesting bit of information that helps the children save themselves from the evil Count Olaf, who is after their fortune. The youngest, Sunny, is an infant, 'scarcely bigger than a boot.' She can't speak or read, but she has four very sharp teeth and likes to bite. "These books are funny in their own right," Rich says, "and the darkness is balanced by the fact that these kids are resourceful, resilient, and charming. They always foil the plots against them through research, reading, and inventing."

One Is Good, More Is Better?

Familiar mass-market series like Goosebumps and Baby Sitter's Club aim at middle-graders and the off-the-charts sales demonstrate once again that children in this age group will read voraciously.

"Lemony Snicket's books are accessible in the ways a good series is always accessible," HarperCollins's Rich explains. "They all have the same characters and the same world but they're not flat. The author can really write. They have all that I would want a good book to have, but they cater to an audience that is used to serialized stories."

HarperCollins doesn't publish mass-market series but attempts to reach this series-reading audience in other ways. Mindy Warshaw Skolsky wrote several books featuring the same character, Hannah, in the 1980s. Now she has published *Love from Your Friend Hannah*, a hardcover from DK Ink, but HarperCollins is bringing out all the titles in paperback. "They will all look a part of the same package," Rich says. "It's not a series per se, rather it's an opportunity to bring a character to life in several books."

Atheneum, like HarperCollins, does have a few series, though these are not like mass-market either. They have recently published the sixth, and last, title in the popular Bunnicula series by James Howe, *Bunnicula Strikes Again*. "We're also reissuing the original book with a chapter on Howe's experience writing the book," says Angell.

Atheneum also publishes the Alice books by Phyllis Reynolds Naylor. "One interesting thing about the Alice books is that throughout the series, Alice is getting older. We're still calling it middle-grade, but the design of the book reflects a slightly older subject matter."

Other trade publishers address the series phenomenon in different ways. Knopf and Crown are bringing out *Leftover Lily, Sweet and Sour Lily,* and *Accidental Lily*, by Sally Warner. "Lily developed out of some of the books Warner had written for older readers in which she dealt with Lily's older brother," says Cascardi.

A similar set of books developed

from *The Flunking of Joshua T. Bates*, by Susan Shreve, a book for younger middle-grade readers from Knopf and Crown. "Shreve has recently written a book for the junior-high age about Joshua's older sister, Amanda, who's in seventh grade." Cascardi explains that these books are not series in the mass-market sense. "Strong characters sometimes demand their own stories. It just happened organically; we were not necessarily trying for the series effect."

In fact, hardcover publishers would like to dispel the myth that all editors are looking to publish books in series. "It's difficult to launch a hardcover fiction series unless it's by a very well-known writer," says Kane. "Hardcover book sales are review-driven and are mainly directed to institutions—libraries and schools. You can't get the series momentum going. I'd prefer to see a single title. If it does well, let the market set the demand for a second book."

She points to *Titanic Crossing*, by Barbara Williams. "The book had done quite well and was in paperback when the movie *Titanic* came out." Neither the author nor the editor purposely published the book to catch the wave of interest in the *Titanic*, but the paperback sold three-quarter of a million copies, and Williams is working on a sequel.

Titanic Crossing exemplifies another myth editors would like to dispel. Williams wrote the book long before the blockbuster movie and subsequent craze for anything associated with the *Titanic*. Virginia Walter may have sensed 'something in the air' when she was writing *Making Up Megaboy*, a book published a couple of years ago that dealt with a shooting by a 12-year-old boy, but she was not writing in response to events in the news. These happened after her book was in production. Trying to follow trends or events in the news doesn't work, at least not in the hardcover children's publishing industry. "By the time you get the book out the trend has disappeared," Cascardi says.

Similarly, trying to mimic the writing of a successful author doesn't usually produce a sale. "Many aspiring writers look at the market and try to emulate what's already been working," says Rich. "But the best books and ideas come from writers who have their own ideas that are not molded to a market. Something entirely fresh—that excites us most."

"What has made our books most popular," says Cascardi, "is the care and attention the writer pays to details. The best writers really nail everything correctly. They create a solid setting, and strong sense of place and mood. This allows the reader to make a connection with his or her own life. It lets the child both travel to another world and also relate inward. These are the strong underpinnings. Other than this, the details of a middle-grade story can be anything."

When asked what they're looking for, most hardcover trade editors respond as Duncan does. "We're looking for good books. We want strong characters, humor, but I don't think it's a matter of going about finding a spot in the market scientifically. Read. Be aware of what's been published in the past and what people are doing now. But then tell your own story."

Rich agrees. "Aspiring authors should not write the book that's already been done well. They should write the book that nobody has thought of yet."

Poetry

Voices of Verse

By Pegi Dietz Shea

Ferocious Girls, Steamroller Boys and Other Poems in Between . . . No, No, Jo . . . Just Us Two, Poems About Animal Dads. These wildly different book titles reflect the wide use of children's poetry today as entertainment and educational tool. While editors agree that poetry can be considerably more difficult to sell than prose, many are committed to publishing and marketing fresh voices in verse. What's more, they see the need for poetry continuing steadily into the future.

Strengthening Markets

Janet Schulman's 40 years of experience include 13 years as head of Children's Book Marketing for Macmillan. She reigned as Editor in Chief and Publisher for Random House and Alfred A. Knopf for 14 years, before semi-retiring. Schulman edited Jack Prelutsky's poetry anthologies, including two giant Random house collections. She has played a crucial role in keeping poetry in front of young readers.

"An article in *Publishers Weekly* discussed how difficult it is to sell poetry, other than books by Seuss, Silverstein, and Prelutsky," says Schulman. But she reasons, "Someone's buying it—maybe it's the libraries." She also notes that "over the last 10 years, teachers have been learning to use contemporary poetry with children as young as first grade. Before that, the poetry being taught were these chestnuts of didactic, moralistic verse. Poets now go to schools and teach teachers how to present poetry, so I'm hopeful. I'm also encouraged by the success of National Poetry Month, and in April, National Children's Poetry Week." Schulman was also pleased to see the Random House and Knopf catalogue had an entire spread promoting poetry week and the company's poets.

Henry Holt Senior Editor Christy Ottaviano says, "I do feel the market for poetry is improving. Booksellers are now giving more shelf space to poetry collections, and National Poetry Month has carried over into the school curriculum. The challenge remains for publishers to be creative in the ways in which they publish new poets and poetry collections so that the genre will get the kind of attention it deserves."

"At Henry Holt, we are able to choose our poetry projects quite discriminately," says Ottaviano, "since we are not locked into a program that requires us to have a certain number of poetry titles per year." Holt publishes poetry for all ages.

Dinah Johnson's *Belindy Girls* is a picture book poetry collection about the author's vast doll collection, with photographs by Myles Pinkney. Ottaviano also mentions three new works: *Lunchbox Mail*, by Jenny Whitehead, for ages 6 to 8; *Fly Girl and Other Poems,* by Hope Anita Smith, for ages 8 to 12; and *Earth Shattering Poems,* a young adult collection edited by Liz Rosenberg.

Boyds Mills Press believes so strongly in poetry that it has the only imprint in the field devoted to publishing poetry for children. Wordsong, the Japanese term for poem, is headed by Editor in Chief Bernice "Bee" Cullinan. Professor Emeritus at New York University and former President of the International Reading Association (IRA), Cullinan has published 26 books on children's literature and education.

Cullinan emphasizes the high quality and selectivity of Wordsong, which publishes four to six themed anthologies and original poetry books a year. The number depends on economics and quality, she explains. "We like to hand-sell what we publish," at conferences, schools, and bookstores, she says, "and we just can't sell books that quickly."

Orchard Books tends to publish more original collections in picture book form than anthologies, says Editor Ana Cerro. "We do have a few of Paul Janescko's anthologies," which are directed at a young adult audience and which Cerro describes as "sophisticated." She distinguishes between markets for different ages: "Poetry for older readers fares better in the institutional market—schools and libraries—while picture book poetry does well in both institutional and trade markets. Since it's not a genre that flies off the shelf, publishers are concerned about how much poetry they put on their lists." Cerro is proud to note that Orchard has published 47 poetry titles in its 12 years.

While HarperCollins doesn't have a poetry imprint, the majority of its infant and toddler books in the Growing Tree imprint are poetry-based texts. "That's what works best for the youngest audiences," explains Editor Ellen Stein. "For example, newborns may not understand the actual words, but they respond to the musical quality of the language, the rhythm and the rhyme."

At The Millbrook Press, primarily a school and library publisher, Senior Editor Amy Shields says poetry has come back in favor among educators and librarians. Because Millbrook's emphasis is on nonfiction, a fall 2000 poetry title, *Just Us Two, Poems About Animal Dads,* has a special section in the back with photographs and brief paragraphs about the animals in the book. The author, Joyce Sidman, says the poems are "a more playful, more accessible way to learn about the fathers' behavior."

By visiting classrooms, Tracy Gates, Senior Editor at Alfred A. Knopf and Crown Books for Young Readers, sees firsthand the healthy school market for poetry. "Poetry is always a very popular readaloud. The kids always respond to it."

Gates was heartened by the success of Karen Hesse's Newbery winner, *Out of the Dust,* which was written in free verse. "It's tough to get kids 10 and up excited about anything because so many things are tugging at them—TV, computers, horror." She definitely sees a rise in the free verse being written

Poetic Techniques

"I try to get writers away from end rhyme by asking them to write their poetry in prose," explains Bernice Cullinan, Editor in Chief of Boyds Mills Press's Wordsong imprint. "This process forces them to think about meaning, and meaning is uppermost. If the story doesn't hold up, the meaning isn't strong enough." A teacher helped Cullinan understand that thoroughly. "Myra Cohn Livingston pounded that into my head, and many of her students at UCLA—Monica Gunning, Janet Wong, Alice Schertle, Ann Whitford Paul, Kristine O'Connell George—are really coming into their own."

Wordsong has published Gunning's *Not a Copper Penny in Me House.* Margaret McElderry Books has published Wong's *The Rainbow Hand,* and Clarion has published George's *The Great Frog Race.*

Michael Strickland, a poet and anthologist, adds that the same technique can actually help writers come up with fresh rhymes. "Try writing out in prose what you want to say, then go through the words, and see what synonyms you can come up with that sound good together."

If writers do submit rhyming verse, editors and poets agree that the rhythm must be absolutely perfect. "Whenever I get something rhythmic, I immediately read it aloud because that's how most picture books will be read," says Tracy Gates, Senior Editor at Alfred A. Knopf and Crown Books for Young Readers. "If I stumble once, that's all right. But if I keep stumbling, forget it. Sometimes an author says, 'Well, you're supposed to read it like *this*.' I'm sorry, but the author isn't sold with the book."

When asked how he achieves perfect rhythm, author Bill Grossman explains, "Mostly I figure it out by ear: reading it, having others read it out loud. One way to make sure the rhythm is perfect is by using two- or three-syllable anchor words that can be read only one way: *NEIGHbor.* You could never read it neigh BOR. If you have too many one-syllable words, people might read them in more than one way. But if you have a two-syllable word in the middle of a line, it anchors the meter. It makes the meter unambiguous."

Grossman cautions verse writers to shun such cheap words as *very, really,* and *just,* to force the rhythm. "Using them is lazy, unnecessary. Hold yourselves to the highest standards."

and published, especially for teens, rather than publishers trying to bring adult poetry down to teens. "My personal hope," Gates says, "is that more teens will read poetry, see something of themselves in it, and like it." Citing picture books by Hesse and by Carole Lexa Schaefer, Gates says free verse is popular for young children as well but, she says, "People don't always recognize the text as poetry."

Poetry as Book
Gates differentiates Grossman's narrative rhymed verses, *My Little Sister Ate One Hare* and *My Little Sister Hugged an Ape*, from poetry. She sees them as story first. "For picture books, I look for story, voice and character that really capture a kid's attention. Often the language is poetic, because picture books are conducive to that."

Stein says Growing Tree's books for the very young "try to stay away from stories that are overly didactic or message-oriented. We look for stories that are centered in a very young child's world, stories that contain certain situations or elements recognizable to them, and that coincide with the developmental milestones the children are experiencing."

Stein cites *No, No, Jo*, a rhyming book by Kate McMullan: "Two-year-olds can certainly relate to being told 'no' again and again, and the story is designed to invite listeners to chime in with the catchy refrain." Growing Tree's fine-tuned age brackets are newborn and up, 1 and up, 18 months and up, 2 and up, and 3 and up. The editors consult with child development experts on the texts.

While Wordsong's Cullinan allows the book themes to come from the poets' passions, she does advise poets on the overall shaping of their books. "I talk about developing a cohesive theme. The book has to tell a story. It has to have a beginning, middle, and end. There must be a reason that one poem follows another." Cullinan points to Lee Bennett Hopkins's award-winning *Been to Yesterdays*, a book of autobiographical poems chronicling his chaotic thirteenth year.

Shields agrees about the importance of structure. A book of poetry, she says. "is like a picture book in terms of its pacing. The order of the poems depends on the mood the author wishes to create."

Halloween Hoots & Howls, written by Joan Horton and published by Henry Holt, begins with children donning their costumes and ends with them going to bed. Horton stresses that each poem has to have a strong beginning-middle-end structure. "In the beginning of 'Hey Ma, Something's Under My Bed,' I pose a dramatic question that the child solves at the end of the poem."

Ottaviano speaks of *Halloween Hoots & Howls* when she says "I'm attracted to poetry that elicits a response, by making me laugh or by making me consider things in a new light." She says she looks for "a strong, lyrical voice. This can be in the form of rhyme, free verse, or narrative verse. I feel strongly that poetry is often best appreciated when read aloud (especially for children), so it's important for me to hear the rhythm and cadence of the language."

A Real Voice

As one editor states explicitly, editors just do not want singsong, do not want simple, mindless rhymes. The best adult poetry truly speaks on many levels. Even in the most clear-cut verse forms—the sonnet, for instance—poetry must have a real voice, perhaps even more than prose. Prose has the advantage of being (in principle at least!), what we speak. Poetry shouldn't pretend to be anything but what it is, but at the same time the human voice, the insight, emotion, vital humor, must emanate from poetry. That is no less true of children's poetry than of adult's, as different as they may be in other ways. Consider, for instance, T.S. Eliot's *The Wasteland* versus his *Old Possum's Book of Cats*. The first changed the direction of English literature. The second did not, but the quality of the verse is unequivocally high—and light, and fun, and interesting. That's exactly what children's poetry should be.

Horton's signature is a humorous twist at the end of her poems, which have also appeared in *Ladybug* magazine and the Meadowbrook Press anthology, *Miles of Smiles*. One poem shows Dr. Frankenstein at the market buying potatoes with eyes and ears of corn. At the end of the poem, readers find out that he has created a monstrously yummy stew.

Shields refers to Joyce Sidman's *Just Us Two* as an example of a well-structured book of original poetry. The author "arranged the book to reflect the voices of the animal babies from unhatched egg in the first poem to an independent juvenile animal at the end. The structure works because Joyce has been able to make the voices very unique and expressive."

Variety and Freshness

Other essential qualities *Just Us Two* illustrates are range and originality. The author explains how the book evolved: "Each animal 'suggested' the different types of poetic form," explains Sidman, from haiku to rhymed verse to narrative free verse.

Shields says, "Most of the poetry that comes in over the transom is amateurish. The voices, patterns, and rhythms are unchanged from poem to poem." But she has high praise for Sidman. *Just Us Two*'s "Mouse Haiku," for example, is soft and quiet, as Sidman describes how Father warms the nest, "a fragile thimbleful/of fluttering hearts." But the title poem of the book, "Hangin', Just Us Two," about the South American Titi Monkey, has a rollicking, bouncy rhythm. For a third variety, a poem about a crocodile is both ponderous and playful:

> What delight
> to swim along the oozy, snoozy Nile,
> to swing my tail from side to side,
> stretch my pop-up eyeballs wide,
> dunk and splash and dive and glide
> along the oozy, snoozy
>   deep and cruisy Nile.

Orchard's Cerro agrees about the importance of variety in a collection.

"Writers should know that, while I'm not completely averse to verse, they should try singsongy manuscripts on someone else. For most writers, free verse works successfully. People have preconceptions about what verse means. The form does allow for variety. Yes, it has to rhyme and have a scheme. But a whole picture book of singsongy rhyme?"

Timothy Bush's *Ferocious Girls, Steamroller Boys and Other Poems in Between* is populated by "wonderfully oddball characters," says Cerro, who worked at Atheneum, the publisher of the book, before joining Orchard. Other narrative verse she has worked on includes Rhonda Gowler Green's *School Library Journal* Best Book of the Year (1997), *Barnyard Song*, and *The Stable Where Jesus Was Born* (both Atheneum books). Cerro also edited Ralph Fletcher's middle-grade collections, *Relatively Speaking* and *Have You Been to the Beach Lately?*

Gates admits she didn't like rhymed verse at one time. "As an editor, I've seen many examples of bad rhyme. We see an awful lot of Dr. Seuss wannabes. The writers are trying to be something they're not, and it's immediately obvious. I want to see someone's individual voice, and that's why Grossman works. He's his own writer, with his own style, and he tells a great story."

Random House is also looking for voices that stand out. "I would hope we will continue to support poets who have fresh vision," Schulman says. "I was fed up with the thousands of long, boring narrative verses I received when I was Editor in Chief. The cover letters would say, 'This is just like Dr. Seuss.' I would think, 'We publish the *real* Dr. Seuss. We don't need another one!' There are people doing very interesting verse, however, and getting published."

Anthologies: A Toe in the Door

Author and editor Janet Schulman has edited all the poetry anthologies Jack Prelutsky has published with Random House. (Prelutsky published his original poetry with Susan Hirschman, Editor in Chief at Greenwillow Books). In 1981, Schulman started working with Prelutsky on *The Random House Book of Poetry for Children*. Published in 1983, the book of 572 poems sold more than 500,000 copies. Almost 20 years later,

---

Rhyme That Works
By Bill Grossman

Tips

■ Perfect meter every time,
Exactly like a nursery rhyme.

■ Don't count iambs. Don't scan feet.
Just clap your hands and feel the beat.

■ Euphonic writing follows rules
That nobody teaches in poetry schools.

■ Superfluous wording makes poetry worse.
Strive to bring closure to each line and verse.

■ Ears you will hurt,
When words you invert.

■ *Muss* and *fuss* rhyme with *us*,
And so does *bus*, but not *virus*.

the two have worked together on Random House's newly published *20th Century Children's Poetry Treasury,* a collection of more than 200 poems.

In addition to these monumental undertakings, Schulman and Prelutsky collaborate on other projects. When questioned about ideas and themes, Schulman says, "It's hard to know whose idea is whose. We usually discuss what it is we're looking for. He'll raise ideas, and I might say, 'No, there's too much of that.' It's a collaborative effort."

Ottaviano at Holt also says she prefers collections of themed poetry. "Themed collections geared toward particular age groups often indicate that an author has thought about the audience and is writing from a particular point of view."

When asked if Wordsong's themed submissions come in blind or if they are commissioned, Cullinan replies that she works both ways. "I do talk with poets often. Becoming an editor is becoming a good friend to your writers. I might say to a writer, 'We need something in science, or for the social studies curriculum.' I'm very school-oriented."

But if you're not yet on the phone list of an editor, how do you, as a new or midlist author, get your work noticed? Schulman suggests, "Poets should definitely have their publishers send their books to anthologists like Lee Bennett Hopkins and Prelutsky. I know Jack keeps on top of new books being published. When we put these anthologies together, he often has a poem by a new person." Contact them through the publishers of the collections.

Many poets get their toes in the door by submitting an edited anthology that has one or two of their original poems. Cullinan cites Michael Strickland and his book, *Poems That Sing to You.* Strickland is also the biographer of *African-American Poets,* published by Enslow Publishers. Strickland invites poets to visit his website, where he posts his anthology needs. Poets can then submit suitable poems via e-mail. Strickland says he's still looking for realistic poems for separate anthologies on ants, feet, and shoes. "The themes of my anthologies emerge and refine themselves as I edit," he says. He started collecting poems for a collection on shoes and feet, but soon found he had enough high-quality work for two books.

Poet John Micklos also started with collections of other people's poems. His soon-to-be-released books from Wordsong include the tentatively titled *The Daddy Poems, The Mommy Poems,* and *The Grandparent Poems,* which include a few of his own verses. Wordsong is also publisher of Micklos's collection, *Sand, Sea and Surf.*

Cullinan is an anthologist as well. After her son Jonathan was killed while riding his bike, she helped establish the National Council of Teachers of English Award for Poetry for Children in his name. The award is now presented every three years to reward a poet's lifetime work. Cullinan's book, *A Jar of Tiny Stars,* is dedicated to Jonathan and brings together poetry by the award's first 10 winners, including Karla Kuskin, Valerie Worth, Arnold Adoff, Barbara Eshensen, and David McCord. Cullinan hopes eventually to publish a second volume.

Markets

So how can writers learn to write fresh poetry? Editors say they should study the various styles and subjects of today's published poets. A writer's freshness will not come from imitating these poets, however, but from seeing how they use their own voices to evoke the emotion, experience, and humor present in every child.

Part 3

Submissions & Style

Submissions

Win the Day with Queries, Cover Letters, & Other Correspondence

By Susan Tierney

Logic would seem to say that it's easy for writers to draft letters and other correspondence to sell their work. It isn't always. New writers may address editors too cautiously or instead sound overconfident. Even published authors are curious about how other writers compose queries, outlines, cover letters, synopses, and proposals.

Children's Writer Guide to 2000 solicited submission samples to give new writers guidance and established writers alternatives and ideas. All the submissions here were purchased by editors and published, or are soon to be published. The selection covers fiction and nonfiction, magazines and books, various genres and categories. By far the greatest number of materials we received were for nonfiction articles, a reflection of the marketplace. Editors buy more nonfiction than fiction, more articles than books, and fiction usually stands for itself via a complete manuscript and a cover letter that says, in essence, "here it is."

We've reproduced the submissions so that readers can study them one by one. The article gathers the materials together to look at how they work and compare. Review the article first and then turn to the samples, or progress through the article section by section to see how the samples illustrate submission principles. Many examples combine several successful components; noting the possible combinations is a useful exercise.

The selections are blueprints of submission or helpful exceptions full of wonderful detail. They are an array of possibilities derived from the wisdom of experienced authors, who all won the day.

A Face and an Outline

Instincts prevail in these samples. You might guess that you need to use a query style that approximates the publication's, and you do. You know intuitively to tell editors why your ideas will work for them and do it without excess information.

"My philosophy about cover letters is they should be *short*! I believe their purpose is to put a human face on the author," says Marilyn Anderson, "and give any background that might help the editor judge the piece. Otherwise, I try to remember that editors are even busier than I am, and I hate reading long letters that beat around the bush."

Ellen Horowitz has a rule of thumb about query length. "I limit the query to one page when proposing stories under 800 words. My query always starts off with a bang!" The bang of an effective lead is vital and should bear much of the burden of a brief letter.

For longer articles, Horowitz's queries are "an expansion of my one-page query. With this format, I can include more detail and give the editor a better sampling of my style." Short and direct queries work well for 400 to 1,200-word articles, she thinks, because they "demonstrate my ability to write graphically with an economy of words." She looks on the two or three short paragraphs that follow a query lead as "word pictures. Each sentence includes imagery and key words that become part of the story and act as a type of *visual outline*." Finally, Horowitz limits her biographical paragraph to three "carefully chosen sentences."

Brevity works, but cover all bases with enclosures. You shouldn't write so short that an editor doesn't fully understand what you're offering. An accompanying outline, writing sample, or bibliography should also be clear and succinct.

See the following pages for the examples cited in each article section.

Examples

Submission 1, Marshmallow medicine: Submission 1 is simple, direct, brief. Marshmallows are a fun topic for kids, but cover letter author Donna Schmitt mixes into the fun the last thing kids want to do—take medicine. She uses the apparent opposition of fun and medicine in her catchy lead. Schmitt's outline is also short and sweet, specific but not overdrawn. The humorous closing to the article, included in the outline, is as catchy as the lead and leaves a good last impression. Schmitt's bibliography is an interesting mix of sources. Although writers need to be leery of some older works that aren't primary sources, and of relying too much on encyclopedias, Schmitt balances her bibliography with the interview, production information, and recent articles.

Submission 8, Boys' Life *profile*: Using the opening sentence of a proposed article or story as a query lead is a tried-and-true method. Mary Ryan used it when suggesting a profile to *Boys' Life*. Ryan explains, "My lead to this query is actually the lead to my story, which I often suggest to my writing students. After all, you put time and energy into getting it just right to attract a reader. Why not use it to attract an editor too?"

The Genuine Article

As Anderson says, good queries and cover letters put a human face on the author. Successful submissions seem to have this common denominator: The genuine person with an authentic interest behind the letters comes through.

One mark of genuineness, and a strong sales point of some correspondence, is humor. It can surface in the letter alone, but is even stronger when you make clear that the article or story will make kids laugh, too.

Editors value passion for a subject because it helps readers connect strongly, especially kids. Editors want expertise and sincere interest in their writers, whether it comes through education, life experience, or thorough research.

Taking appropriate risks in a query or cover letter, such as being more self-revelatory than usual in business correspondence, can pay off but must be done with caution, courtesy, and restraint. Be sure that a market is likely to be receptive. Exposing the human face behind a query to religious niches, for example, may demonstrate to an editor a conviction important to their publication. You want your genuine enthusiasm and humanity to show through, but do not cross professional lines. While religious publishing is a large market for fiction, editors always ask writers not to preach. That goes for correspondence as well.

Examples

Submission 2, Nature's fast food: Horowitz's query on nature's "fast food" to *Wild Outdoor World* benefits from an assured kid chuckle and from the combination of two topics of ceaseless interest to middle-graders—animals and fast food. The analogies to a menu, restaurant, and gimmicks will speak to young readers, and therefore to the editors. Horowitz sticks to her length requirements, outlined above.

Submission 3, Substance abuse: Christi Reynolds literally slams out with her lead for a "provocative" young adult article. Facing the issue of substance abuse from inside a prison, she conveys sharply and concisely just what her article will do. Her personal reality couldn't be more clear. She went for "dramatic and intense," Reynolds says, qualities likely to be of value to *Listen*, a magazine with the subtitle *Drug-Free Possibilities for Teens*. "My goal was to keep the rest of the query letter intriguing, yet short and to the point."

Submission 4, Cell culture: The opening to Rebecca Bronson's query to *Odyssey* is much more subdued—perhaps more appropriate for a scientist—but the letter as a whole conveys her intense interest in her field and in enlightening children about the importance of science. The letter and bibliography indicate Bronson's expertise, and her outline shows she is able to translate the complex into the language of adolescents. Bronson explains, "When the editor called me to request that I write the article, she surprised me by asking for something completely different from my proposal." Pointing out her education and background, Bronson says, "gave the editor confidence in my ability to write what she wanted. I also targeted a specific issue, letting her know I had read the magazine's guidelines."

Submission 9, Inspirational fiction: A brief, to-the-point lead in Anderson's fiction query to a religious family magazine, *Living*, is something of a gamble in its direct declaration of faith. It paid off. Perhaps the direct lead encouraged the editor about the story's potential to move readers. This approach may be less successful when the piece is nonfiction, and for some religious markets that aim to be general interest publications with a religious slant.

Molding to Form

Query and cover letter variations are sometimes necessary or useful. Established writers with a good number of published projects in a particular area may want to contact an editor to establish a regular relationship, for instance, whether to write a column, contribute to an ongoing series, or do other kinds of assignment writing. Tailoring your background to a particular editorial market is key, just as when you write a résumé for one industry versus another.

Writers may also want to begin to sell an idea with several different markets in mind. The correspondence—letter, outline, synopsis—must also match the diverse markets. An added benefit of shaping a subject to sell to a variety of publishers is that, even if the idea sells to one particular niche, you've already done the basic work to resell your idea in a new format to another market.

Some publishers require prospective authors to complete a form or provide information in a specific way, presumably to encourage, even force, writers to meet their requirements as completely as possible.

A knowledge base and tailoring to market are helped along when an author already has a connection to an editor or publisher, whether because they've met them at a conference, have submitted before and been encouraged, or if they have freelanced for them in other capacities. Do use your connections, but never "push" them. If your brother-in-law is on the Midwestern sales force of a huge publisher, don't share that information with a Boston editor. "Inside" knowledge of a publisher just takes one principle of submissions a step further: Use your close study of markets to make your idea work expressly for that publisher.

Examples

Submission 5, Science assignments: Joan Banks wrote to *SuperScience* to ask the editorial director to consider her as an assignment writer. Although Banks's background is in journalism and library science, she promotes her interest in natural science and backs it up with her solid experience writing on the topic for major publishers. "I didn't realize when I sold my first article to *Ranger Rick* years ago that it would be a building block to later assignments. But it was," says Banks. Her letter is not typical, she says, because it's not a proposal or query. "It focuses on my children's work. I arranged the magazine publication sections of my résumé," not included here, "to focus on the children's magazines as well. I also enclosed several published clips of my children's science articles, which undoubtedly carried the most weight. Editors want to know you can carry through." Banks has since had several assignments from *SuperScience*.

Submission 6, Query form: Cobblestone Publishing's *Appleseeds* uses a query form, which Patricia Cronin Marcello's article on Native American drums exemplifies. At the top of the form an author provides name, address, phone, fax, e-mail address, indicates the issue or interest—*Appleseeds* is theme-based—and title. The form directs the author to describe the idea briefly, include unusual sources, word length, and the unique angle that will speak to the targeted audience of 8 to 10, parents, and teachers.

Authors can replicate the focus of such a form. Mary Ryan's profile submission to *Boys' Life* is an example. (Submission 8, included in the Visual Outline section above.) After the query hook, Ryan concentrates on the angle of primary interest to the scouting magazine: The attractive subject, Trevor Blount, is a scout. Ryan informs the editor she has written for the magazine before and mentions other writing credits. "To seal the deal, I enclosed a few snapshots of Trevor and some hot air balloons in flight. They're so lovely, I thought they'd catch the eye of the editor, too. Guess it worked. The actual photographs of Trevor in his balloon turned out so spectacularly they decided to give the article the cover!"

Submission 7, Runaways: David Schaffer worked at Scholastic, but not in the editorial department, when as a freelancer he wrote two versions of the same query to different Scholastic magazines. Even if most writers don't have an inside connection, Schaffer's submissions illustrate the fine points of writing queries on one subject to magazines with different needs. The proposed article was eventually published by *Choices*, but notice how Schaffer offered a different slice of the pie to *MATH*.

Fiction that Piques Interest

The object of a cover letter for fiction is to pique editors' interest enough to get them to turn to the manuscript. Then deliver the goods in your story. The letter may reveal a story or novel's unique purpose, the singular motivation behind it, or again, the human face that moves the narrative. A fiction cover letter in some brief way conveys inspiration. As artsy or literary as this working of the muses may be, however, don't think that fiction has to fit in less with a market's slants, themes, and editorial objectives. It does.

If you target a publication or company that mixes fiction and nonfiction, including a related nonfiction idea sometimes helps sell fiction. Make an offer an editor can't refuse in this way, then thank them for not refusing, and you're in.

Examples

Submission 10, Multicultural fiction: The hook in Kathryn Slattery's cover letter is an experience in which an idea dawned—that multicultural fiction doesn't have to derive from exotic climes. That was enough to get her piece read, and *Hopscotch* purchased it. Slattery includes in her letter her background as a teacher and scout leader, and her writing credits.

Submission 11, Niche fiction: Catherine Ross also relates the personal experience behind her story concerning disabilities. A picture, a game, a blind teen, and the difficulties of high school friendship are wrapped up in the first paragraph in such a way that an editor of a young adult magazine will keep reading.

Submission 12, Verse play: A verse play for very young children sold for Louise Monohon in part because of the directions for making costumes. Important for a play, she indicates that a class has test-performed the play. Monohon also does a simple, smart thing: She writes a thank you letter to the editor and staff that is warm and informed and that asks for the new submissions schedule she knows the magazine issues. No one ever said a professional letter can't be warm and practical at the same time.

Submission 13, Peer pressure: Rebecca Lugara's cover letter to *Straight* is relatively reserved in comparison to other examples, but it does the job for her young adult story about peer pressure. She effectively describes her story's theme and indicates the humor she uses to convey a serious moral.

Books, The Same but Different

Book project submissions have fundamental differences and similarities from article queries and story cover letters. For obvious reasons, they tend to be longer—they have more to convey. The book submissions materials included here have qualities we've discussed for magazine submissions, and more.

Book proposals tend to be packages. The cover letters remain short enough, perhaps extending to two pages. Remember that book editors have piles of paper to get through that are at least as high as those of their magazine counterparts. Publisher guidelines direct writers to the other materials they should submit, including lengths. But if the guidelines are vague, include samples long enough to give an editor a feel for the scope and style of the book, whether fiction or nonfiction.

The research behind a book is more extensive because of project size and that too must be reflected in submissions packages. Bibliographies tend to be considerably longer for nonfiction, and sometimes for fiction as well. Some companies want to see an extended outline or proposal. Never go too long, and never leave out necessary information.

Examples

Submission 14, Historical novel: Patricia Calvert's proposal for a middle-grade historical novel went straight to an editor with whom she had worked before and delivers the no-nonsense essentials in a synopsis and samples. Her personal style, voice, and mastery of her subject come through soundly.

Submissions 15 and 16, Biography and reference: Two submissions by Ginger Roberts Brackett, one for a biography and the other for a reference book, feature an author with real expertise and great enthusiasm for her subjects.

In her biography proposal, Brackett explains the facts, the angle, how she would treat important issues about a woman writer in the Renaissance, but at the same time the author is very practical and direct about the need to adjust according to editorial direction.

The outline for Brackett's reference book, a romance literature encyclopedia, is a model of completeness and clarity, from subjects to be covered to lengths to front and backmatter.

Submission 17, Educational: Expertise, enough information but not too much, a professional but cordial and enthusiastic style, add up in Cindy Dingwall's proposal for *Storybook Birthday Parties*. She explains why libraries and other markets would purchase her book. She includes her experience in education and libraries. Dingwall's suggested book structure demonstrates that she knows how to target particular ages. A contract with Highsmith Press for *Storybook Birthday Parties* led to two other book contracts.

These book proposals illustrate even better than the magazine submission selections that authors are not tied to format, that neither experienced writers or the editors are overly concerned about small format choices: Write out *enclosure* or not, describe through an outline or paragraph-length synopses. Writers, however, should always remind themselves that the hairs on the back of editors' necks stand up too easily when they see grammatical and spelling errors.

In the end, the correspondence here speaks for itself, just as any writer's query, cover letter, proposal must do. Sincerity, substance, and skill almost always win the day.

Submission 1: Nonfiction Article Cover Letter

Marshmallow Medicine, ages 6-13

Marilyn Edwards, Editor
Boys' Quest
P.O. Box 227
Bluffton, OH 45817-0227

Dear Ms. Edwards:

"It's summer time, time for campfires and toasted marshmallows. Did you know that *marshmallow* was once a medicine?"

This is the beginning of the enclosed 460-word article titled "Marshmallows, a Medicine?" for consideration for the June/July issue of *Boys' Quest* about summertime.

Thank you for considering my manuscript.

Sincerely,

Donna J. Schmitt

encl.:   Outline
           Bibliography
           SASE

Submission 1: Nonfiction Article Outline
Marshmallow Medicine, ages 6-13

Lead sentence: It's summertime, time for campfires and toasted marshmallows. Did you know that *marshmallow* was once a medicine? Thousands of years ago the Egyptians and Greeks used the marshmallow plant to heal.

Body:
1. The marshmallow plant and its medicinal uses.
2. Ancient Egyptians made the marshmallow syrup sweet.
3. The sweet syrup was beaten into a thick foam.
4. An early French recipe for a form of marshmallows.
5. Marshmallow plant brought to the U.S.
6. Machines developed for making marshmallows.
7. Modern marshmallow production.

Closing: Marshmallows have come a long way since the syrup was used as a medicine. It's too bad marshmallow root is no longer an ingredient in modern recipes. If it was, the next time you have a sore throat, maybe your doctor would say, "Take two marshmallows every four hours."

Bibliography

———. "Ask Andy." *Chicago Tribune,* date unknown.
Bianchini, Francesco and Corbetta, Francesco. Health Plants of the World. New York, Newsweek Books, 1977, p. 86.
Interview, Ralph S. Wirebaugh, Chief Research Scientist, Favorite Brands International. telephone, 555-1212.
Edwards, Park. "Around the Mall and Beyond." *Smithsonian*, July 1994.
———. "Marshmallows." Encyclopedia Americana, 1947, vol. 18, p. 369.
———. "Marshmallows." Encyclopedia Britannica, 1993, vol. 7, p. 881.
———. "Marshmallows." Marshmallow Research Foundation, date unknown.
———. "Marshmallow Production: Technology and Techniques." P.M.C.A. Production Conference, 1995.

Submission 2: Nonfiction Article Query
Nature's Fast Food, ages 8-12

Ms. Carolyn Cunningham, Editorial Director
Wild Outdoor World
Boy Scouts of America
P.O. Box 1249
Helena, MT 59624

Dear Ms. Cunningham:

Black bears and beavers dine here. Mice, moose, elk, deer, snowshoe hares, and grouse eat here too. The menu offers many choices, including fast food, specials, and take out. This wildlife restaurant is the quaking aspen, found in more states than any other tree.

Like the most popular restaurants, aspens are easy to recognize by their trademark and advertising gimmicks. The aspen's smooth, cream-colored bark identifies it at any time of year. The music and glimmering lights created by wind in its leaves make it unmistakable.

Aspen shoots that sprout rapidly following forest fires provide fast food for deer, elk, and moose. Bark, leaves, twigs, and catkins add to a menu that makes the aspen a significant source of food and popular restaurant for wildlife.

My 22-year career in environmental education includes 13 years as a ranger-naturalist in Glacier National Park. I am a freelance naturalist who teaches classes on the flora and fauna of the Rocky Mountain region for Elderhostel, Flathead Valley Community College, and the Glacier Institute. My writing appears in *Falcon*.

Please let me know if you are interested in an article on "The Fast Food Restaurant for Wildlife." I look forward to hearing from you.

Sincerely,

Ellen Horowitz

Submission 3: Nonfiction Article Cover Letter

Substance Abuse, Young Adult

Mr. Lincoln Steed, Editor
Listen Magazine
55 West Oak Ridge Drive
Hagerstown, MD 21740

Dear Mr. Steed:

The enclosed nonfiction article, "Paying the Price," begins with the slamming of a steel door in a medium-security prison for men, locking me inside, where my freedom will be severely limited for the next two hours.

Approximately 984 words, this article looks at a class on recovery from alcohol and drug abuse, which I facilitated for nine months at Sheridan Correctional Center in Sheridan, Illinois. The focus is on the particular consequences paid by the young men incarcerated as a result of alcohol and drug abuse. I have been in recovery myself for the past 14 years.

I believe "Paying the Price" promotes prevention in a provocative manner. Please consider this article for *Listen Magazine*. Thank you for your time.

Sincerely,

Christi A. Reynolds

Enclosed: "Paying the Price"
       SASE

Submission 4: Nonfiction Article Query
Science: Cell Culture, ages 10-15

Elizabeth Lindstrom, Editor
Odyssey Magazine
Cobblestone Publishing, Inc.
7 School Street
Peterborough, NH 03458

Dear Ms. Lindstrom:
I am interested in writing an article for *Odyssey* about the use of cell culture as a commonly used technique in biochemistry laboratories. I am a biochemist (I received my doctorate in 1986 from Boston University) and have worked for many years in various laboratory settings. I am currently freelance writing for children, and I am particularly interested in communicating science to children so that they can get a sense of what really goes on in a laboratory.

The article that I intend to write, "A Different Kind of Pet," would describe what cell culture is and why scientists use this technique. It would be approximately 700 words long. A detailed outline is attached, as well as a brief bibliography. Much of this article will stem from my own personal experience with growing cells in laboratories.

I believe that this article would be a valuable addition to your upcoming edition in February, which will focus on cloning. A basic understanding of cell culture would help your readers understand the more complex science of cloning.

I have enclosed an SASE for your response. I look forward to hearing from you.

Sincerely,

Rebecca Bronson

Submission 4: Nonfiction Article Outline
Science: Cell Culture, ages 10-15

I. Introduction
   A. Lead with fact that one square inch of skin has millions of cells
   B. Cells can be grown from living organs
   C. Why study cells?

II. Cell Culture Specifics
   A. Basic definitions
      1. Tissue culture/cell culture
      2. Culture media
      3. Culture flasks (where cells are kept)
   B. Where do scientists get cells from?
   C. Care of cells
      1. What cells eat
      2. How they grow; what is meant by cell growth
      3. Keeping cells clean and sterile
   D. Uses of cultured cells
      1. Drug testing
      2. Manufacturing new skin for burn patients
      3. Cloning

III. Summary/conclusion
   A. Draw analogy between care of cells and care of pets
   B. Restate why cultured cells are important

Bibliography

Freshney, R.I. *Culture of Animal Cells, A Manual of Basic Technique.* Alan R. Liss, Inc., New York, 1987.

Mader, Sylvia S. *Inquiry into Life,* volume 1. Wm.C. Brown, Dubuque, Iowa, 1991, pp. 180-82

Submission 5: Assignment Writing
Letter: Science Contributor

Emily Sachar, Editorial Director
SuperScience
555 Broadway
New York, NY 10012

Dear Ms. Sachar:
I saw an article in *Children's Writer* about Scholastic's science magazines and would like you to consider me for *SuperScience* assignments. My children's nature writing began when I wrote on speculation for *Ranger Rick*. More recently, I've worked on assignment for *National Geographic World*. I also have a book about the rain forest under contract with Soundprints and The Nature Conservancy.

My formal training is in journalism and library science, but I have a strong interest in the life sciences. I have enclosed my résumé and a few samples of my writing. I look forward to hearing from you.

Sincerely,

Joan Banks

Submission 6: Nonfiction Article Query
Query Form, Social Studies, ages 8-10

Author Patricia Cronin Marcello wrote the following to complete a Query Form required by the magazine Appleseeds. *Authors are directed to describe the idea briefly, include unusual sources, and a unique angle that will speak to an audience of children 8 to 10, parents, and teachers. The proposed title: "Caller of the Spirit."*

Nothing is more important to a pow wow than the drum. Native Americans believe that the drum brings the heartbeat of the Earth Mother to the celebration. They also believe that its gentle rhythm brings everyone into balance. At a pow wow, the man who is responsible for the drum is known as the Head Singer. This honorable position is achieved only through wealth of knowledge and experience, and both the drum and the Head Singer are treated with great respect. The Head Singer has the first and last word in all songs and he has total control over the drum, the singers, and the dancing.

I would like to propose a feature article of approximately three printed pages that will explore the significance of the drum, which is central to Native American culture. I will also show how the drum dominates the pow wow, and how it is used by the Head Singer to control his portion of the festivities. Drums of any type fascinate children of all ages. Perhaps including a simple Native American rhythm that they could play themselves or instructions on how to make their own drum would work well with this piece.

I plan to use *Pow-Wow*, by George Ancona (1993), *Eagle Drum: On the Powwow Trail with a Young Grass Dancer,* by Robert Crum (1994), and *Celebrating the Powwow,* by Bobbie Kalman (1997), for my research, along with the Internet and first-person interviews with Native American participants via e-mail. If you are interested in crafts, I am a former craft designer and teacher and I can come up with recyclable materials that kids can use to simulate a Native American instrument, presented in a sidebar with drawings and step-by-step instructions.

I have written for *Calliope* ("Janissaries," January 1996); as well as *Guideposts for Kids, Guide, Church Educator,* and Christian Ed. Publishers. I have written a great deal of material for adults, including articles for *American Cowboy* and *Wild West*. My newest book, entitled *Diana: The Life of a Princess,* will be published shortly.

Native American culture has been one of my interests for several years and I would like very much to be included in this project.

Submission 7: Nonfiction Article Query
1 Query, 2 Magazines: Runaways, Young Adult

This query was sent to two magazines by David Schaffer. Paragraphs one, two, and four are the same, but the third paragraph specifically targets the needs of two different publications.

Lauren Tarshis, Editor
Scholastic Choices
555 Broadway
New York, NY 10012-3999

Dear Ms. Tarshis:

According to the U.S. government, as many as 3 million young people run away from home every year. There are a wide variety of causes, and often running away is simply an overreaction to a family argument, or a part of normal adolescent rebellion. The overwhelming majority of these runaways return home within a short time, usually one or two days.

There are, however, more than 100,000 young people who leave their homes for extended periods—weeks, months, or longer. Most are trying to escape from serious problems. Physical and emotional abuse, substance abuse, economic hardship, and family dissolution are frequently found in the homes of adolescents who have run away. A large and increasing portion of the homeless population consists of "throw-away youth" who have been kicked out of their homes or abandoned.

High-risk youth are not the only ones who face dangers. Crime, homelessness, hunger, and disease can also afflict young people from more fortunate homes if they make bad decisions at troubled moments. Youths who are considering running away can benefit from knowing that there are many services and programs available to help them find other solutions. Hearing about the hardships peers from various backgrounds have faced after leaving their homes can discourage them from making the same mistakes. Knowing how troubled the home lives of some repeat and long-term runaways are can also help them sympathize better with those who live on the streets or in shelters.

I have extensive research on runaway and homeless youth. Would *Choices* consider publishing an article on this topic? I am most eager to discuss this proposal further. An outline/synopsis and list of potential sources is available on request.

To: *Scholastic MATH* Editor

Whatever reason kids may have for running away, the National Runaway Switchboard (NRS) is there to help. "Our hotline operators are able to deal with all the problems that affect teens," says NRS spokesperson Deborah Dabalos. The NRS also compiles a database of the reasons callers give for running away or considering running away These statistics could be the basis for a circle graph article and activity in *MATH*'s graphs and statistics series.

Submission 7: Nonfiction Article Outline
Runaways, Young Adult

For *Choices* magazine.
I. Introduction
   A. Recount recent story concerning Nushawn Williams and the young women he infected with AIDS (1 paragraph)
   B. Present broad view of runaway and homeless youth situation on a national scale, with background statistics and comments from editors. (1-2 paragraphs)
II. Cases of Runaways, Throw-Aways
   A. Personal histories of 3 to 5 youths with runaway experience. (3 paragraphs)
   B. Present personal histories of 1 or 2 youths who were abandoned or fit the category of throwaway. (1-2 paragraphs)
      The personal histories will be selected to represent as much variation in background and family experience as possible. Age, gender, ethnicity, kind of troubled experience, and geographic location will all be considered in attempting to provide a balanced picture.
III. Pros and Cons of Youth Social Services and Alternative Living Arrangements
   A. Cases of bad experiences youths have had in group homes, foster homes, and in trying to live with extended family or friends are described to create an understanding of why some kids don't feel they can count on public services or other people to help them. (1-2 paragraphs)
   B. Examples of programs and services trying to make a positive difference, and showing some signs of success. (3 paragraphs)
      The programs and services described will include outreach and counseling, education and job training, transitional living and life skills, crisis intervention and after-care, and recreational and reward-incentive activities.
IV. Conclusion
      Revisit some of the young people referred to earlier in the article who have overcome their difficulties and describe their accomplishments. Since the kids discussed in the conclusion will all have been involved with one of the programs, the article will conclude that, even if quality help is difficult to find, it is better to seek it out to resolve serious problems than it is to run away. Readers will be referred to sidebars for resources. (2-3 paragraphs)
V. Sidebars
   A. List of sources for help such as national helpline numbers, national agencies and programs, references for further reading, and possibly an Internet source.
   B. In-depth look at one particular program or service agency that is particularly unique or successful.
   C. Family portrait of one runaway.

Submission 8: Profile
Query: Balloonist & Hero, Middle-grade to Young Adult

J.D. Owen, Editor
Boys' Life
P.O. Box 152079
1325 West Walnut Hill Lane
Irving, TX 75015-2079

Dear Mr. Owen:
Trevor Blount is often on top of the world. Well, maybe not on top, exactly, but at least several hundred feet over it.

Trevor, 14 and a First-Class Scout in Troop #123, Palos Park, Illinois, is on track to get his pilot's license in hot air ballooning as soon as he turns 16. He currently has a student license and has already logged several hours of air time. He expects to attend ground school in a year. His father, Alan Blount, was the 1993 World Champion and is a balloon instructor in the Chicago area. He is teaching Trevor himself.

I met Trevor at a recent balloon rally in Chagrin Falls, Ohio, and was impressed with his enthusiasm for the sport and his maturity. A tenth-grader in September, he is an excellent student with tentative plans for going into medicine or research. About four years ago, he rescued a young child who had strayed from her parents and onto a road and he was cited for his actions by the local district. I think he will make an excellent subject for a *Boys' Life* story. I have done preliminary interviews with the entire family.

I am the author of a previous *Boys' Life* article on young magician Dana Berent ("His Hand Is Quicker than Your Eye," December, 1985) as well as the published author of six middle-grade novels. I am proposing a 1,000-1,500-word article on spec.

I look forward to hearing from you.

Sincerely,

Mary C. Ryan

Submission 9: Inspirational Fiction
Cover Letter: Family Magazine

Eugene K. Souder, Managing Editor
Living
R2
P.O. Box 656
Grottoies, VA 24441

Dear Mr. Souder:
I am a piano teacher, a professional writer, and a committed Christian. One day, one of my piano students told his mother he wanted to quit taking lessons. We were both mystified because he was doing very well. On questioning, he admitted he was so afraid of making a mistake that he thought it better not to try at all.

The enclosed story, "Piano Panic," has an important message for those who think they can somehow go through life being perfect.

I hope you enjoy this story and will find it something you would like to publish.

Sincerely,

Marilyn D. Anderson

Submission 10: Multicultural Fiction
Cover Letter: Magazine, ages 6-12

Marilyn Edwards, Editor
Hopscotch
P.O. Box 164
Bluffton, OH 45817-0164

Dear Ms. Edwards:
When we think of multicultural, we seldom think of Great Britain. I enclose a manuscript of 900 words that tells the story of Jenny, a young American visiting relatives in England. Within minutes of stepping off the airplane, Jenny finds herself in culture shock. She discovers there is much to learn about the British language and way of life.

I have recently returned from a trip to England and I know how much fun it can be to discover words that are different from our American English. "Put the Brolly in the Boot and Let's Go" is meant to be both fun and educational. If you are interested in an activity to accompany the story, I have created a simple crossword puzzle, which I also enclose.

I have worked with children for many years as a teacher and a Girl Scout leader. My articles about local Girl Scout activities appear regularly in the *Laguna Coastline News*. I have had a story accepted by the Cricket Magazine Group and it is awaiting publication in *Spider* or *Cricket*.

I look forward to hearing from you.

Sincerely,

Kathryn Slattery

Submission 11: Specialized Fiction
Cover Letter: Magazine, ages 16-24

Richard J. Kaiser, Editor in Chief
Young & Alive
4444 South 52nd Street
Lincoln, NE 68516

Dear Mr. Kaiser:
The enclosed picture was taken at our girls' summer camp during a "blind walk," a game to teach trust and the use of our senses. Recently, a young friend who is blind told me a disturbing story of being abandoned by a group of supposed friends in the middle of her school playing field. I saw the potential for a story by combining the game and the incident.

This 1,400-word story, "Jody's Triumph," addresses many themes relevant to teenage girls: friendship, cliques, anger, and dealing with disabilities.

I am presently a girls' summer camp director and a former junior high school English teacher. I co-authored and published a handbook on canoe trips, *When the Wilderness Beckons*. I am the former editor of two camping newsletters for the Ontario and Canadian Camping Associations. My article "Choosing the Right Camp for Your Child" was published in *City Parent Newsmagazine*.

I appreciate your considering "Jody's Triumph" for publication in *Young & Alive*. I have enclosed an SASE for your convenience.

Sincerely,

Catherine Ross

encl.:   SASE
         manuscript
         photograph

Submission 12: Verse Play & How-to
Cover Letter: Seasonal, Magazine, ages 6-12

Georgiane Detzner, Assistant Editor
Pack-O-Fun
P.O. Box 164
Bluffton, OH 45817-0164

Dear Ms. Detzner:
Please find enclosed my manuscripts entitled "A Bear's Gift" and "Polly and the Three Bears," for your consideration in your Christmas issue of *Pack-O-Fun*. They are companion articles, a short play and a how-to for making the play's costumes.

The how-to is about 275 words and the play is 250 words, or 34 lines. The play is written for the younger grades and has been tested in a kindergarten class. The children memorized the poem, acted it out, and presented it for the school Christmas program. As both a writer and teacher, it was easy to recognize how much this activity was enjoyed.

Thank you for your consideration of my companion manuscripts.

Sincerely,

Louise Monohon

enclosures: two manuscripts/photographs/SASE/résumé

Submission 12: Verse Play & How-to
Follow-up Thank You Letter

Georgiane Detzner, Assistant Editor
Pack-O-Fun
P.O. Box 164
Bluffton, OH 45817-0164

Dear Ms. Detzner:

Thank you for the complimentary copies of the Christmas *Pack-O-Fun*. The Craft-A-Story of "Polly and the Three Bears" tickled my bear instincts. The page layout is great and I loved your costume model, "Polly." The edits to the poem made it much stronger. The Pop-up Tree Card was also well-presented.

Please thank the whole staff for me for a job well done! The entire Christmas publication is beautiful. I look forward to writing for you again. Please send me your new submissions schedule.

Sincerely,

Louise Monohon

Submission 13: Young Adult Fiction
Cover Letter: Magazine, Peer Pressure

Heather Wallace, Editor
Straight
Standard Publishing Company
Cincinnati, OH 45231

Dear Ms. Wallace:

Enclosed is a short story titled "The Pecking Order" for your consideration. It portrays a 13-year-old girl's struggle with peer pressure and self-confidence as she and her two "best friends" get into unexpected trouble for making prank telephone calls to an unpopular classmate.

Mandy, the protagonist, struggles with her conscience as she must choose between taking responsibility for her unkind actions and pleasing her friends, who deny making any phone calls and refuse to apologize to the victim. Through her difficult choice, Mandy learns about the meaning of true friendship. The story uses humor where it is appropriate and delivers the moral in a subtle manner. The story runs about 1,420 words and is written for readers between the ages of 10 and 14.

I hope you will find "The Pecking Order" acceptable for publication in *Straight*. I welcome any suggestions for revision you feel are necessary. Also enclosed is a self-addressed stamped envelope. Thank you for your consideration.

Sincerely,

Rebecca Lugara

Submission 14: Historical Novel
Proposal: Middle-grade

Author Patricia Calvert contacted an editor with whom she had worked more than once, Clare Costello of Charles Scribner's Sons, and submitted the following book proposal, which has been excerpted. The original was seven double-spaced typed pages.

Background
On July 4, 1865, four months after the end of the Civil War, several hundred men gathered along the banks of the Rio Grande near Eagle Pass, Texas. These men, led by General Joseph O. Shelby, commander of the Iron Cavalry Brigade from Missouri, had never surrendered to the Union forces. They vowed they never would.

It had taken the troops 29 days to cross the Texas plains; now they planned to raft across the river and escape into Mexico. There, with the help of Emperor Maximilian, they hoped to rearm themselves, to retrace their steps back across the border, and to restore the Confederacy to the glory they believed it deserved.
. . .

Plot
Tyler Bohannon, a boy of 12, eagerly awaits his father's return from the war. When a stranger stops by the family homestead where Tyler lives with his mother, his younger brother Lucas, and an even younger sister, Rosa Lee, the boy asks for news of the soldiers coming home. He mentions his father's name—Black Jack Bohannon. The stranger allows that he does know that name, that Black Jack, a member of the Iron Brigade, might have followed "Jo" Shelby all the way down to Texas, and likely won't be home for a long while.

The boy is bitterly disappointed, and makes up his mind to pursue his father down through Texas and urge him to return home. His mother is adamantly opposed to any such undertaking, but Tyler is equally determined to go.
. . .

Excerpts from the Novel
The stranger's beard was thin and pale as corn silk, not as thick and dark as a beaver's pelt, as Papa's was. There were blue puddles of weariness beneath his eyes. When he finally spoke, his voice was light and soft as air. Papa's had been as rich and thick as molasses.

"Evening, son."

"Evening," Tyler replied, then added cautiously, "sir."

"You live close by?" the stranger wanted to know. . . .

[This excerpt continues and two others follow.]

Submission 15: Biography
Proposal: Woman Renaissance Playwright, Young Adult

The proposal below is approximately nine single-spaced, typed pages in length and was accepted and published by Morgan Reynolds. The book consists of 10 chapters, 96 pages.

Ginger Roberts Brackett
address, phone

Proposal for biography of Elizabeth Tanfield Cary (1585-1639), English Renaissance writer.

Chapter One Elizabeth "under arrest," seventeenth-century attitudes toward women, and the religion dispute.

The chapter will open outside London, 1627, with an adult Elizabeth writing her history of Edward II while under house arrest by order of the king of England. Her children have been removed from her, her husband will not support her, and her mother wants nothing to do with her, all because she chose to convert from Protestantism to Catholicism. I will include intriguing facts and quotes demonstrating seventeenth-century England's negative attitudes toward women, and I will offer an overview of the religion issue. Here is a possible opening:

> "Who is there?" 42-year-old Elizabeth Cary, the Lady Falkland, cried out. "Will none of my people come near me?" Then suddenly she remembered. Her children had been taken from her. She had no income. Only one servant, her friend Bessie, had remained faithful to her. The other servants had deserted her, on order of her husband Henry. She knelt to pray, remembering Henry's anger when he discovered that she was a Catholic. Perhaps it had been a mistake . . .
> [Excerpt continues, 17 more lines.]

Then I will explain that women seldom pursued any intellectual endeavors, because they were thought to be inherently weak-willed and stupid. They were considered not only incapable of learning, therefore not requiring school, but also evil. This idea came from the story of Eve offering the fruit of sin to Adam in the Bible. Many even believed women lacked souls and were creatures of appetite, craving constant sexual satisfaction. (This particular point I can temper, if editorial direction demands.) . . .
[Explanation continues, approximately two-thirds of a page.]

Submission 15: Biography
Proposal: Woman Renaissance Playwright, Young Adult

We know from his letters, from which I'll supply quotes, that Henry Cary, Lord Falkland, agreed with the negative evaluation of females. He was also a staunch Protestant and anxious to retain his political standing with the Protestant king, James I. Elizabeth made a politically dangerous decision in converting from Protestantism to Catholicism. . . . I will supply a history of the religious conflict dating from the founding of the Church of England by Henry VIII.

This chapter will lead into the next, the biography of Elizabeth, beginning with her childhood.

Chapter Two   Elizabeth's childhood, Renaissance ideas regarding education, an arranged marriage, introduction of *Mariam*.

Chapter Two begins with Elizabeth as a 10-year-old when she accompanies her father, a wealthy barrister to court. There, she applies logic and knowledge of human nature to help establish an accused woman's innocence. This chapter will depict . . . .
   [Explanation of Chapter Two continues, approximately a page and a half.]

Chapter Three   The story of *Mariam*, autobiographical aspects, the drama's plot, and a discussion of its characters.

Elizabeth Tanfield Cary dedicated *Mariam* to her new friend, the "other" Elizabeth Cary, causing confusion for later readers. Because writers never dedicated works to themselves, for years many people thought she couldn't have written the drama. I will relate how this mystery was solved.

   I will explain the term "closet play," one meant only to be read aloud, not acted on a stage, and the significance of women speaking aloud ideas that were forbidden, or at least discouraged. I will briefly discuss the themes of the mistreatment of women that form the foundation for the play *Mariam, the Faire Queene of Jewry*, as a lead into the following chapter.

Submission 16: Reference Book
Proposal: Romance Literature Encyclopedia, Young Adults

ABC-CLIO
OUTLINE FOR MANUSCRIPT PROPOSALS
FOR LITERARY COMPANIONS

Virginia (Ginger) Brackett   Date

TENTATIVE TITLE: Romance Literature

AUDIENCE: Our main audience is users of high school, public, and college libraries. Additional users might include book/reading club members.

SCOPE AND PURPOSE:
Scope: This encyclopedia will offer a review of approximately 675 works, beginning with the "first" romance novel, *Don Quixote,* through twentieth-century favorites. A few Renaissance works will be reviewed to establish the original definition of the term "romance," and to supply the history necessary to understand the development of the genre. Seminal plot lines, such as that of star-crossed lovers, unrequited love, beauty and beast, and the love triangle will be introduced through classic works and cross-referenced to contemporary works to demonstrate continuity as well as change over time in the romance genre.
Purpose: The purpose of an encyclopedia of romance literature should be to provide a thorough investigation of the history of the genre and of its lasting appeal through the consideration of individual works read by high school and college students.

COMPETING WORKS: None known.

RESEARCH METHODOLOGY: The research for possible titles to include in the encyclopedia is based on high school and college reading lists. Background on the genre and early romance works will come from references reflecting contemporary critical theory, translated into lay terminology. Plot and character research will be performed work by work.

ORGANIZATION: The main parts of the book will be: Introduction; A-Z listing of works; Bibliography; Appendixes; Index.

Submission 16: Reference Book
Proposal: Romance Literature Encyclopedia, Young Adults

ADDITIONAL SECTIONS:
Preface: The preface will focus on the encyclopedia as a user-friendly tool, appropriate for students and lay researchers alike.
Introduction: The introduction will define the term Romance, which has various connotations, and will . . . [*Continues for 6 single-spaced lines.*]
Acknowledgements: Assisting researchers will be acknowledged.

BOOK LENGTH: 150,000 words
Introductory Material: Preface, 1,000 words; Acknowledgements, 100 words; Dedication, 20 words.
Entries: A tentative number of entries is 330. The format will be the same as that used in *Utopian Literature*.
  Headword List:
      A. Alphabetical, straight A-Z (list enclosed)
      B. Alphabetical by category (people, concepts, events, etc.; list enclosed)
      C. By length, into 3-5 categories:
           - 60 long entries: 1,500-2,000 words
           - 53 medium entries: 500-750 words
           - 64 short entries: 200-300 words

ILLUSTRATIONS: Illustrations from/of classical works such as *The Faerie Queene* and *Don Quixote,* would provide much visual interest. Copies of some known prints, along with publication information will be forwarded.

PHOTOS: My researcher will suggest locations of photos for many of the contemporary authors and titles, with an estimate of about 10 photos.

SCHEDULE:
  [*Due dates are detailed.*]

COMPUTER/WORD PROCESSING SOFTWARE: WordPerfect 6.1 for Windows.

AUTHOR INFORMATION: Please see curriculum vitae; additional requested information will be supplied.

Submission 17: Educational Book
Proposal: Book Parties, preK to grade 5

Donald J. Sager, Editor
Highsmith Press
P.O. Box 800
Fort Atkinson, WI 53538-0800

Dear Mr. Sager:

STORYBOOK BIRTHDAY PARTIES invites children to celebrate the birthdays of 30 favorite children's book characters. All the characters selected have long-lasting appeal to children and the adults who work with them.

STORYBOOK BIRTHDAY PARTIES is divided into three sections: preschool and kindergarten; kindergarten to second grade; and grades three to five. The overlapping of ages allows for flexibility in planning programs. Each section contains 10 birthday parties for the age group, 5 celebrations for female characters and 5 for male, although both boys and girls will enjoy each of the parties. Parties include storytelling, games, music, activities, projects, birthday treats, and prizes. The games and activities chosen avoid competitiveness and instead engage children in an enjoyable pursuit of the prize.

STORYBOOK BIRTHDAY PARTIES would be a much used addition to schools, libraries, and bookstores. The parties can be used in public and school libraries, in classrooms, and in stores. Some of the parties help children learn to use the library and all encourage children to read. The book will save hours for those who develop and present children's programs. The planning is complete: The presenter only has to gather the materials and prepare for the presentation.

Three years of teaching preschool and kindergarten and more than 17 years as a children's librarian in a large, busy public library have provided me with the experience and inspiration to write *Storybook Birthday Parties*. Highsmith Press publishes outstanding resources for those who work with children and I believe my book will add to your list. I am enclosing three sample chapters, one from each age group, the book and section introductions, a table of contents, and my résumé. The entire manuscript is available for review. This proposal has been submitted to other publishers who specialize in materials for those who work with children. I look forward to hearing from you.

Imaginatively,

Cindy Dingwall

Biography & Characters

Real Lives, Real Stories

By Patricia Curtis Pfitsch

Writers have always blended real life into fiction, especially when it comes to character development. "Many of my characters have a basis in real life," says Zilpha Keatley Snyder, author of 36 books for children and young adults, "even if it's someone I've only met briefly."

The protagonist of her novel *Cat Running,* says Snyder, "was inspired by a schoolmate of mine. I didn't know her very well, and nothing about her family background. But she was small, red-headed, and locally famous for being a fast runner," all characteristics of Cat, the girl in the story.

Joan Goodman's first book, *Songs from Home,* grew from an experience she had in a café while she was living in Rome. "A couple came to the restaurant and sang," she remembers. "They were American, a man and his daughter. That's all I knew about them, that they were street singers. This happened some 30 years ago, and yet it was so vivid for me, so puzzling and intriguing—what these people were doing in Rome begging for tips—that it became the basis for *Songs from Home.*"

But a current trend in historical fiction may be blurring the lines between biography and fiction. While nonfiction writers have often used narrative as a technique to relate real-life events and depict real people, and fiction has always striven for a sense of reality, today some picture books and novels are going a step further in taking a real incident in a real historical person's life to develop a story.

Which Side of the Divide?

A Christmas Tree in the White House, by Gary Hines, is an example. The characters in this picture book are the children of President Theodore Roosevelt. After hearing from their father that they may not have a Christmas tree because of the ecological implications of cutting trees, two of Roosevelt's sons sneak a small tree into their room and hide it in their closet. When the tree is discovered, Roosevelt takes them to Chief Forester Gifford Pinchot, who explains the environmental problems. They're allowed to keep the small tree, but they don't get a large tree. In the back, an author's note explains which parts of the story are known fact: that two of the sons did hide a tree in the closet, and that they did talk to Gifford Pinchot when they were caught. The specific scenes, the dialogue, and the way they got the tree into the White House are all imagined.

Is this fiction or biography? "It's very hard to make the distinction," admits Ginny Moore Kruse, reviewer and Director of the Cooperative Children's Book Center, part of the School of Education at the University of Wisconsin-Madison. She points to the 1999 Caldecott winner, *Snowflake Bentley*, by Jacqueline Briggs Martin, illustrated by Mary Azarian, as another example. "People can't decide. Is it a story? Is it a biography? What is it?"

Kruse sees that new books are falling into a range between fiction and biography. "Some are closer to biography; others are closer to fiction." Kruse herself doesn't feel that these fictionalized stories are really biography. "They don't pretend to give you what a biography needs to offer," she explains.

Peter and Connie Roop, co-authors of both historical fiction and biography for children, agree. "In a biography, you've got to take the whole person's life—like Susan B. Anthony's life—and get all of her adult activities in, as well as the origin of her characteristics," says Connie Roop. "You're limited by space, but have a whole lot of time to cover."

The Roops are working on a biography of Christopher Columbus. "Most biographies deal with the four voyages," Peter Roop explains, "but he had a lengthy life before he ever set sail across the ocean. So, it will be a matter of balancing that out. I would like to split it 50/50 between what we know of his childhood and what we know of his adulthood."

Unlike biographies, the new biographical fiction often looks at one event, period of time, or specific component of a real person's life. In *Grace's Letter to Lincoln*, the Roops look at a short time in the childhood of Grace Bedell who, when she was 11, wrote a letter to Abraham Lincoln suggesting that he grow a beard to improve his appearance and gain votes in the election. In that book, we learn nothing of what happened to Grace when she grew up, only about the events of a few weeks in October of 1860. Yet the characters in the book lived and many of the events actually happened. It's more fact than fiction.

Still other books portray a real person, yet the book is definitively fictional. *Gib Rides Home* is based on the life of Snyder's father, William Keatley. "I wanted to emphasize his wonderful disposition, and his marvelous affinity for horses," she says. "There are bits and pieces of his story in the novel, but the rest is fiction."

Imagined Yet Real

Wherever they fall on the spectrum from biography to fiction, however, the goal of all the books is to portray a real character, to capture reality on paper in terms of the people depicted. The difference comes in how the books achieve this goal.

Even when a book is mostly fiction, as in more traditional historical fiction, the authors start with reality. "Each of my books is sparked by a historical incident," explains Goodman. In *Hope's Crossing*, the incident involves a young woman named Mary Palmer who lived in Connecticut during the Revolutionary War. She was kidnapped by raiders loyal to King George and taken toward New York. Before they reached New York, however, neighbors rescued her. "That's what got me started," Goodman says. But instead of being rescued, Hope, the main character in *Hope's Crossing*, becomes a slave for a loyalist family, escapes with the help of the grandmother, and sets off to find her way home. "Everything in the book either really happened or could have happened," says Goodman. "It's a matter of piecing together different true stories to get to my story."

To understand all her characters' feelings, Goodman uses her own reactions. "On some level, I place myself in this extraordinary situation and see how I'd react." About *Hope's Crossing*, she says, "I did not live through the Revolutionary War, but I have access to that from research that I've done and who I am. I get information and process it to imagine how it would be for me in the same situation." Goodman doesn't figure out all the details about her characters before she begins writing. "In writing the story I get to know my character. I didn't know Hope right from the beginning; I got to know her as I wrote, her strengths and weaknesses."

For Goodman, the history on which she bases her books is an asset. "It helps tremendously to have a few reality hooks: It's like a skeleton and I put on the flesh. It's great that I have these clues from history given to me. It's very exciting to build with that and, hopefully, make my characters real and believable."

A Father's Life

A bit further on in the spectrum, moving from fiction to biography or factual history, is *Gib Rides Home*. Here, instead of working with only a few historical references, Snyder wrote about a character that Snyder knew well. Gib, like Snyder's father, is sent to an orphanage at age six. Instead of being adopted, he was 'farmed out' to work on farms in the area. Also like Snyder's father, Gib has a gentle, patient personality and a great love and understanding for horses, and it's his attitude that helps get him through lonely and often cruel experiences.

"I had thought about using my father's life for a long time," Snyder explains, "because it was interesting, different, and poignant." But she was concerned about the ability to distance herself from the story. "I've seen writers working who base their stories very much on parts of their lives: They drag in things that aren't pertinent to the story line and don't move it forward in any way. If you ask why something is necessary, they say, 'That's what really happened.' I think that's a trap we often fall into. I tried very hard not to."

Snyder's father, for instance, actually had two younger brothers who were also put in the orphanage. "I thought seriously about having three little boys at the beginning, and then I decided that would disperse the emotion of the story too much. I wanted to center the story on Gib and not write a family saga."

In the novel, another character returns from being farmed out. His hands have been frozen; the farmer had punished the boy for losing his mittens by making him stay out in a blizzard. A similar incident actually happened to Snyder's father, but she decided not to complicate the fiction by making that happen to Gib. "A good plot line doesn't exactly follow real life," she says.

Snyder is known for her believable characters. She builds Gib's personality both through his actions and through the comments of other characters. Close to the beginning of the book, Gib and another character are talking about school:

> "Reading and writing," he told Jacob, "is a lot more interesting than scrubbing floors and washing pots and pans. And if we didn't have to go to school in the mornings, chore time would last all day, like as not."

This kind of quiet acceptance and the ability to see some good in everything comes through strongly in Gib's thoughts and words. But we see his strength and calmness through other characters' eyes, too. A bit later on, Jacob tries to explain why Gib is always beaten by the teacher, Mr. Harding.

> "It was because Gib wasn't looking scared enough," Jacob whispered, pulling the other boys away from Gib's cot. "That's what I think, anyway. What I think is, it made old Harding mad when Gib acted so kind of . . . calm and collected like."

Although she didn't have to do it with Gib, Snyder often writes long character sketches for her protagonist and other main characters before she begins the novel. "I write about their personalities, their prejudices, their loves and hates, as well as what they look like. Then I add to that as I get to know them better."

Her editor, Karen Wojtyla, Senior Editor at Bantam Doubleday Dell Books for Young Readers, relates creating believable characters to acting. "The writer has to be an actor inside the head of a character," Wojtyla says. "She needs to know how that character would react. A writer is really a multitalented actor playing all the parts."

Snyder admits to this relationship herself. "As a kid I used to make up characters and then I'd be them, think about what they'd do and say. I was rarely myself. I was always being someone else."

The Way In
Maria's Comet, by Deborah Hopkinson, is a picture book that straddles the line between fiction and biography. It's loosely based on the life of Maria Mitchell, the first woman astronomer

in the United States, but with some important differences.

Maria's Comet is the story of a young girl who lives on Nantucket in the last century, in the same time and place where the real Maria Mitchell lived. The fictional Maria's father is an astronomer and she wants to learn about astronomy as well, all of which corresponds to the life of the real Maria. For her fiction, however, Hopkinson actually turned around some of the facts of the real Maria Mitchell's life.

"The fictional family is not so interested in letting a girl explore her interests," explains Anne Schwartz, Director of Anne Schwartz Books, an imprint of Atheneum Books for Young Readers and Hopkinson's editor. In reality, Maria Mitchell's family was very supportive of her passion for astronomy. "Saying the father was not supportive is historically accurate for the time," explains Schwartz, "although it's not accurate to this particular child."

To create a compelling story, it is vital that the main character's actions have a strong motivation and this usually involves conflict, something that blocks the character from achieving a goal. "By adding the unsupportive family," Schwartz explains, "we created dramatic tension. We had to create the problem, but we created it out of a time and place. It's not as if we created something that could not have happened. We always make sure it could have happened. Fiction gives you the license to heighten reality. And that's what I think we've done—we've heightened reality."

What comes through in Maria's personality is her interest in education, dedication to learning, and love of astronomy and the night sky. Hopkinson shows this through Maria's actions and thoughts on each of the pages of the picture book:

> Whenever I can, I break free from my chores.
> Andrew and I climb to the attic,
> spread the old atlas out upon the floor,
> and imagine we're explorers in faraway lands . . . .
> Our attic hideaway is a treasure trove of books, too.
> Andrew likes tales about sailors best.
> But I love stories of the early astronomers:
> Copernicus, who tried to prove a new idea—that Earth
> and all the planets circle round the Sun.
> And proud Galileo, who first used telescopes to look at the sky.

This love of learning is also an essential characteristic of the personality of the real Maria Mitchell. Hopkinson has changed some of the aspects of Mitchell's life to make it more accessible to children, but she stays true to the spirit of Maria Mitchell.

When does a writer decide to move away from the real person's true life and take a more thoroughly fictional approach? "Some biographical subjects can't be reached through true biography," Schwartz believes. "There are all kinds of amazing lives, but can they be put in an engaging format?" Schwartz and Hopkinson call the process "finding the way to make the story come alive for young readers." Schwartz has noticed that Hopkinson begins with a draft that is very close to biography. "In the revision process, she moves farther away from the research, from the facts, but she doesn't create anything that would contradict real life. We don't want to mislead." She depicts the real and the true in another way, the way all great literature does, and good writing always attempts.

Hopkinson includes an author's note at the end of all her books that explains what parts of the work are factually true and which are imagined. The author's note for *Maria's Comet,* for example, states clearly that Mitchell's family supported her interest in education and points out that this was unusual for the time.

Through the Mirror

Emily Arnold McCully's books feature the interaction of real people and fictional characters. The relationship between them illuminates the history, and heightens good story.

In *The Ballot Box Battle,* she wanted to write about Elizabeth Cady Stanton, the early champion of women's rights. "She was a great wit," McCully says, "ironic, wry, even sarcastic." McCully thought of choosing 1880 as the setting of the story because at that time Stanton and Susan B. Anthony were together writing their *History of Woman Suffrage* at Stanton's house. "I wanted to have them relating all the events of their careers, but that was too unwieldy." She had thought that Stanton's granddaughter was also present, and had planned to use that child as the viewpoint character, but it turned out that she was not born until later. "So I gave Mrs. Stanton a neighbor girl. I was pretty leery of it," McCully admits. "It took nerve, in my view, to make things up."

McCully had read Stanton's writings. She visited her home to see what the house looked like. She met the town historian, who showed her many newspaper clippings and pictures of the town in the 1880s. McCully uses a German phrase which translates *going through the mirror* to talk about understanding history: "Instead of holding up the mirror to history you have to go through it, really try to imagine what it was like then." This process succeeds in creating real characters because, she says, "in many ways the lessons of history happen because there isn't anything that new in the world. Our fascination is with things that seem so strange yet so familiar."

In the story, the neighbor girl, Cordelia, feeds Mrs. Stanton's horse and gets a riding lesson. Although the story takes place in 1880, any child of the 1990s would understand Cordelia's feelings about Mrs. Stanton's stories.

> When she talked about some skirmish in her long battle for the vote, Cordelia always minded her manners and pretended to pay attention, but it seemed to have nothing to do with her. Riding was what she cared about.

At the end of the book, Mrs. Stanton and Cordelia go to the polls and Mrs. Stanton tries unsuccessfully to cast her vote—an event that really took place in Tenafly, New Jersey, in 1880. McCully shows her facing the ridicule of all the men at the polls without flinching.

> Seeing that she could not put her ballot in the box, Mrs. Stanton flung it at the hand covering the slot, saying "I have the same right to vote that any man here has."
> She threw her magnetic glance around the room and extended a hand to Cordelia. "The day will come when this girl may vote!" Two men said, "Hear, hear!"

Here McCully captures Mrs. Stanton's personality. "What she did was completely in character. It really does tell what she was like," McCully explains. "I try to make her brisk—warm-hearted, but a tough cookie." This combination of characteristics comes through in Stanton's own writings; McCully wasn't inventing a personality for Stanton, rather, she was capturing it in a scene.

Emotional Truth

A Band of Angels, by Deborah Hopkinson, is similar to McCully's books in that the story is about a real woman, Ella Sheppard, but the viewpoint character is fictional. Ella was one of the Jubilee Singers, an African-American singing group that raised money for Fisk School, which opened in 1866 as a school for former slaves. A fictional great-great-granddaughter of Ella tells the story of her ancestor. "I tried as much as possible to capture the quality of Ella's character," Hopkinson says. "She was dedicated to learning and determined to get an education. I think she also had high spirits."

Hopkinson shows this in the child narrator's words.

> I imagine Ella, head bent over her work, needle flashing in the lamplight. A book is propped up on the table, so she can study while she sews. And I know my great-great-grandmother had a love of learning inside her that glowed like a warm, bright flame.

Hopkinson presents Ella's feelings in a speculative way by letting the narrator say, "Ella must have felt discouraged . . ." or "I think Ella made herself be brave." In this way, the readers can identify with the character without actually attributing specific feelings to a real person. Hopkinson is able to focus on Ella's motivation without actually making it up. At the same time, we're able to enter into the character's mind as if it were fiction."

But even in a book that's moving closer to fact in its presentation, to present the spirit of the truth successfully, an author sometimes needs to move away from the bare facts of an event or a person's life. "The emotional truth is what you have to get at," says Wojtyla. "The character's responses have to ring true to the reader. There has to be internal consistency."

Hopkinson created scenes to give the story the emotional tension it needed. One scene in particular shows Ella's despair before their last concert. The crowds had become smaller and smaller at the group's performances, and they weren't making enough money for the school. "That part was definitely created," Hopkinson says, but "other dramatic moments were real."

In *A Band of Angels,* Ella becomes the symbol for the Jubilee Singers. It is she who moves the group from singing 'white songs' to singing the songs of her own people, the slaves of the South. Because of this switch, the group becomes successful and saves their school. While historically it is true that the Jubilee Singers became famous when they began singing spirituals, Ella probably was not the sole reason for the change. "That was not the way it really happened," Hopkinson says. "It came out of the demands of telling a story."

Schwartz explains: "The most important thing is to make a story as kid-friendly as possible," she says. "Interest them first. Excite their imaginations. If we had focused on the entire group it would have been much less interesting."

Hopkinson chose to tell the story through the eyes of a child for the same reason. "My first draft was written in the first person from Ella's point of view. There was no child narrator and it didn't have the structure of a told story. It was more like a nonfiction book, and Anne thought it was too dry."

Hopkinson acknowledges the limitations of writing about a real person. "You have more freedom when the character is imaginary," she points out. "There are some things that can't change. I have to make her the age that Ella really was. I have to stick as close to history as possible." But, she adds, "the process is really the same as when you create an imaginary character. When you're working from a historical footnote, you're really making everything up as you go along."

The Telling Details

The Roops, who also write books about children who were 'footnotes in history,' elaborate on how this process works. In *Grace's Letter to Lincoln,* almost all the characters are people who really existed. The authors began with the letter Grace wrote and the information they knew about her family situation. In the book, Grace's family is working to support Lincoln in the election and even her best friend Jennie gets to help. Grace wants more than anything else to do something, too. Early in the book we learn this through her thoughts and actions.

> Grace picked up the apple peeler. She snatched an apple off the counter. She attacked the apple. Jennie helped Jefferson escape from the sheriff. Jennie gets to make banners for the parade. She'll probably even get to march in the parade. All I am doing is peeling apples for a stupid pie. I wish there was something I could do! Grace thought.

It's Grace's feelings that help bring the character alive for the reader. "We don't have historical documentation that she felt that way," Connie Roop says, "but we know she wrote the letter and we have the hooks of history."

"We know that she got the poster of Lincoln," Peter Roop explains. "We know she had a friend named Jennifer, though we had to create the kind of friendship they had. We know her father was an avid Lincoln supporter and that her family had intense discussions. We know that her mother wasn't feeling she could express herself the way she wanted to; we can intuit that from what Grace says in the letter." From this, and from the fact that Grace did indeed write the letter, the authors are able to deduce how she felt.

"When you make up a character out of whole cloth," explains Peter Roop, "you're not tied to the historical person. It's harder in some regards to have a historical person. You have a responsibility to stay true to the real person, to present that person as accurately as you can based on the hooks that history provides."

Connie Roop agrees. "All historical fiction has historical constraints. But there are many more constraints when it's a real person: You're obligated to everything you can possibly find out."

The Roops feel confident about their characters because they know the historical context. "We do a vast amount of research before we start writing the story," Peter Roop says. "There's so much to know—the tools they used, the clothes they wore, the whole historical context, the political discussions of the day. Ninety-five percent never gets into the book, but the five percent are telling details. They move the story forward and give a sense that you, the reader, are there." This is what makes historical fiction so believable.

An Infinite Task

What about true biography? Do authors use similar techniques when doing a nonfiction presentation of a character? "I always worry about biographers," Wojtyla admits. "You have to have a story, a point of view, an angle. I wonder how that distorts what they're writing about. You have to fictionalize to some extent," she continues. "It's an infinite task. How do you know what a letter or a journal entry really means? You can't know what a person really thinks. It takes incredible research to be able to do biography at all."

She points to *Satchmo's Blues*, by Alan Schroeder, a book based on how Louis Armstrong got his first cornet. Even though the story was based on Armstrong's own account, the book was severely criticized by one reviewer because it didn't agree with what had come out in another biography.

"Not much is really known about Armstrong's childhood," Wojtyla says. "Was he making it up? I think it was unfair to the author to give the book such a poor review. I thought the reviewer was taking only one side. But when you're portraying someone real, you get into those issues."

Goodman is now writing a biography of the explorer Henry Hudson. " A lot of it is working backwards into the character. It's like putting together a broken puzzle," she says. Nothing is known about Hudson before his first voyage. It is known that he wasn't a good commander. His crew mutinied three times and ultimately cast him and his son adrift in a small boat and they eventually died. Hudson kept hiring Robert Juet as navigator, even though Juet was very difficult and was able to turn the crew against him. "Why would he keep doing these seemingly stupid things?" Goodman asks. "Hudson wasn't an idiot. He was given a tremendous amount of power and money by investors. They believed in him. He was basing his theories about finding a passage to the Orient on the best scientific information of the day. At the time, it was a credible idea.

"Ultimately, I came up with this man who was obsessed with his vision, with this idea about a northwest passage to the Orient. He felt he was so close to finding the passage and he would do whatever he could to make that goal—which included hiring Juet, who was one of the best navigators around. He put up with Juet because Juet had great skill."

For Goodman, writing biography is similar to writing fiction. "It's letting the facts accrue, to give shape and structure, like the skeleton. Then from there it's making connections, asking how does it all work together to make a man."

Ginny Moore Kruse takes a historical perspective when thinking about the growth of historical fiction and its relationship to true biography. "Various writers have contributed to the standards and what's being published today," she says.

Kruse points to writers like Genevieve Foster, author of books like *Abraham Lincoln's World* and *George Washington's World,* written in the 1940s. "Foster received several Newbery honors for her work. These books look quaint, now, but no one had really taken into account the literal, historical world of the subjects before she did that."

Jean Fritz, well-known for biography and historical fiction, "first started publishing picture book biographies of famous Americans around the time of the nation's bicentennial," says Kruse.

"I don't know if anyone held her illustrators responsible for the level of visual accuracy that an illustrator might be held to today, but the whole idea of having a kind of irreverent, fictionalized story about Paul Revere, for example, was really fresh at the time. Those stories were never wildly popular, but they certainly were welcome."

Fritz went on to write many biographies, some that have been received with more critical acclaim than others. "She always said that she only put something in quotes if it was a real quotation," says Kruse. "Otherwise, she tried to say, 'Perhaps this is how a particular person would have felt,' using qualifying words. She tried very hard to hold herself to that standard."

Writers since have used Fritz as an example of how to write biography. The genre changed. It changed again after Russell Freedman published his photo biography of Abraham Lincoln. "A break-through book stimulates other people's imagination," Kruse says. "Everything any of us does comes from somewhere. We're all building on what we've seen and learned."

Language

At the Service of Story: Dialect, Slang, & Accents

By Catherine Frey Murphy

"One day atter Brer Rabbit fool 'im wid dat calamus root, Brer Fox went ter wuk en got 'im some tar, en mix it wid some turkentime, en fix up a contrapshun w'at he call a Tar-Baby, en he tuck dish yer Tar-Baby en he sot 'er in de big road, en den he lay off in de bushes fer to see what de news wuz gwine ter be."

As he wrote "The Wonderful Tar Baby" about a century ago, Joel Chandler Harris used inventive spellings and contractions to capture the language of the black storytellers who first told it. That language helped make classics out of his Uncle Remus stories. "I begged to hear the Uncle Remus stories, because I could not get enough of Brer Bear's speech," remembers Senior Editor Mary Martin at the Wright Group.

Unfortunately, reading the tales was more difficult than listening to them. In her introduction to Julius Lester's contemporary retelling, *The Tales of Uncle Remus,* librarian Augusta Baker remembers that she, too, loved the Uncle Remus stories that her grandmother used to tell. But when Baker tried to read them on her own, the language made them impenetrable. "They were in a dialect that was like a foreign language and I could not handle it. I was frustrated and, although I loved the stories, I was too impatient to struggle with the words."

Writers who try to reflect the sound and usage of spoken language in written words must overcome a host of difficulties. The misspellings and grammatical variations of dialect can discourage inexperienced readers or perpetuate stereotypes. In historical fiction, incorrectly rendered language can misrepresent the speech patterns of an era. Contemporary slang may date a book, as expressions that were up-to-the-minute when the story was written go out of fashion. But if all writers avoided these hazards by confining themselves to strictly standard English, literature would suffer irreplaceable losses of rhythm, music, and magic.

False Veneers
Dialect poses special problems for young readers. David Gale, Executive Editor at Simon & Schuster, says that a child who is confronted with misspelled words intended to mimic the

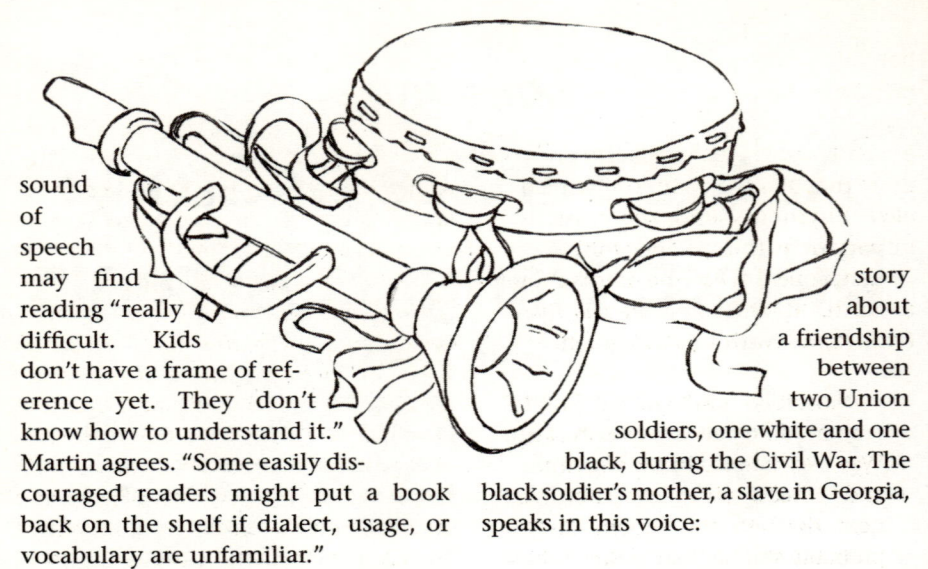

sound of speech may find reading "really difficult. Kids don't have a frame of reference yet. They don't know how to understand it." Martin agrees. "Some easily discouraged readers might put a book back on the shelf if dialect, usage, or vocabulary are unfamiliar."

Julius Lester adds that the difficulty of deciphering dialect isn't the only problem. "The danger of using slang, dialect, etc., in children's books is that it can be overdone in an attempt to provide a story with a veneer of cultural authenticity." Writers who overuse dialect, Lester says, are "forgetting that language is at the service of the story and cannot be an end in itself. I think writers telling stories of cultures of which they are not a part might use more slang or dialect because they want the story to appear more authentic. But for me, authenticity in storytelling means respecting the story, and as I said, putting your language at the service of the story."

Author Patricia Polacco raises the same concern about cultural authenticity. "When you use dialect, it means you are moving into the skin of the people you are writing about. The danger is not being authentic," she says. In *Pink and Say,* Polacco drew on her own family history to write a heartbreaking story about a friendship between two Union soldiers, one white and one black, during the Civil War. The black soldier's mother, a slave in Georgia, speaks in this voice:

"I been gittin' along, though, Pinkus. Warm things got left in the big house when the family left. Dry goods, too. The rest I been gittin' from the woods. They's a freshwater spring. Still have some chickens, even got an ole cow out back that still gives."

For Polacco, the key to authenticity in dialect is to know—and to love—the people and the culture you are writing about. "I gain my authenticity from a loving relationship in a modern life with people of that culture or race. I am relying on the heart, and the heart doesn't lie. To avoid the pitfalls . . . be true to what you know. I would never assume to write from a perspective when I don't have an intimate knowledge and understanding."

"I don't think of what I do as using dialect," says Lester. "What I try to do is to provide enough black English so that the sound of it gets in the reader's ear and this sound pervades the entire

-120-

book. I do this also, and perhaps even primarily, by paying attention to the music of a sentence, to the rhythm of a sentence. Black English involves more than what is commonly called *dialect*. Rhythm, sound, the music is as important as the specific words."

Lester opens "How the Animals Came to Earth," the first story in *The Tales of Uncle Remus*, with this paragraph:

> Most folks don't know it, but the animals didn't always live on earth. Way back before "In the beginning" and "Once upon a time," they lived next door to the Moon. They'd probably still be there if Brer Rabbit and Sister Moon hadn't started squabbling with one another like they were married. The way it come about was like this . . . .

Lester points out that the introductory phrase in the first sentence subtly establishes a conversational tone, reinforced by the choice of the word *squabbling* a couple of lines later. By the last sentence, as Lester explains, "My use of *come* instead of *came* doesn't jar the reader as ungrammatical because I've set a conversational tone using the rhythms and music of black English."

As the story goes on, Lester uses the interjection *well* for its rhythm, along with colloquialisms like "she was looking downright puny" and "you look as po' as Job's turkey." Lester explains, "I use *po'* instead of *poor* because the phrase is a well-known cliché in black speech, at least, and also for the implied rhyme between *po'* and *Job*." Lester uses what he calls "the most ungrammatical of words" when Sister Moon tells Brer Rabbit, "I ain't been feeling like myself of late." Lester explains, "The entire sentence is almost verbatim what I've heard countless older black people say. The reader readily accepts and understands *ain't* because I have established an environment of black English."

The process is a balancing act, combining the Southern black speech Lester remembers from his childhood with normative English to create what he calls "a modified black English." Lester says, "Now, how much of my doing all this is a conscious choice and how much is instinct, well, it's a combination of both and a lot of rewriting. But I am very conscious of using just enough black English to create an environment of sound in which the reader will hear black English even when it is not being used."

The Music of a Place

Martin finds a similar focus on sound in the work of William Armstrong, the author of *Sounder*. "Beyond commonplace conventions such as *ole* for *old* and *in'* for *ing*, he doesn't change the written word much," she says. "Some writers go overboard on inventing new spelling for dialects. But he hears the music in the speech. You can't read the words aloud or silently without hearing the rhythms and knowing they are right for the characters." Martin says the secret of Armstrong's success is his familiarity with the world he describes. "Armstrong starts with a good ear and a dialect he knows. We say, 'He has a good ear,' but we don't know much about what that means. Armstrong wrote about what he knew in *Sounder*, and that must be part of it."

Gale finds the same music in *The Year of the Sawdust Man*, by Alexandra LeFay. "It's not written in dialect, but the phrases she uses give a real sense of place. There are no misspellings or apostrophes, but you know it has to be Southern." To get this sense of place and music across, Gale suggests that writers try using explanatory phrases, like "she said with a lilt," instead of altering spelling or grammar. When changed spellings are necessary, he adds, "Keep it to an absolute minimum—a very light, very minimum level of dialect."

Melissa Roberts, Senior Editor at Eakin Press, often finds herself editing confusing dialect out of manuscripts. "If you have to read it two times, that's too many. It should just roll off the tongue." To make dialect work, Roberts says, make sure it is "clear, easy to read, and avoids stereotypes." She adds that a character who says *gonna* on one page shouldn't switch to *going to* on the next. "Do it one way throughout. Make sure that if you choose a certain word, you use it consistently throughout."

Another Time

In children's historical fiction, capturing the language of another era can pose special problems. Suzanne Coffman of the Colonial Williamsburg Press strives to make the language in the books she publishes about early life in Williamsburg as accurate as possible, while still keeping it accessible. "You don't want to interfere with kids enjoying the story. You want it to challenge them, and let them know there's a difference, but you don't want them to have to work so hard that they lose interest."

"If we make the language truly eighteenth-century, it will be incomprehensible to the reader," says Coffman. Instead of striving for absolute accuracy, she works with scholars at Colonial Williamsburg to find certain turns of phrase, such as *mighty* instead of *very*, as in "she was mighty pleased," that will establish the flavor of eighteenth-century speech. "It's a matter of getting the sense of the language across without making it intrusive."

The historical language used in Colonial Williamsburg's books is grounded in research about the speech patterns of the time. For Kate Waters's *Mary Geddy's Day: A Colonial Girl in Williamsburg,* a joint publication of Colonial Williamsburg and Scholastic, the question of what Mary would have called her parents arose. The family's social class answered the question, says Coffman. "James Geddy was a silversmith, fairly successful—bordering on upper class—so it was *Mamma* and *Poppa*." The precise time period of the story makes a difference, too, Coffman points out. "Just because a slave spoke in dialect in the nineteenth century doesn't mean that a slave in the eighteenth century spoke the same way."

Using dialect obliges a writer to avoid unintentionally demeaning a character by making him appear stupid or uneducated, Coffman adds. "There's a fine line between writing dialect for reality and doing it for what may appear to be a stereotype. When you're writing about the eighteenth century, you have to look closely at class as well as race, and balance it so you don't appear to be making fun of the person."

Writers may also discover that old-fashioned language was less formal and correct than modern speakers sometimes imagine. As Waters worked with the scholars at Williamsburg, Coffman says, "She was a little surprised at how much like twentieth-century language the language in eighteenth-century Virginia was. We were putting the contractions in!"

Waters is a Senior Editor at Scholastic, as well as the author of *Mary Geddy's Day*. She has also written four other photoessays about children in the 1620s, told in the children's vernacular and illustrated with photographs taken at living-history museums. "I have the advantage of the scholars who work with Plimoth Plantation and Colonial Williamsburg," she explains. "The aim is to create language the child might have spoken, that reflects who the child was."

To find the appropriate language, Waters studies the training manuals used to train the costumed interpreters who work in character at the museums. These manuals offer a wealth of information about the life of the time, along with vocabulary lists of words the character would have used. Even more important, she immerses herself in first-person narratives like journals and diary entries, as well as other written materials. "I read prayer books, household manuals, newspapers—everything I can find!"

As she writes, Waters strives first of all for the right rhythm. "I'm trying to use the cadence of the language that I've heard, the rhythm of the sentences," she explains. When the rhythm is right, she adds appropriate vocabulary words like *perchance* or *poppet*. "Eventually, I go back and take many of them out," she admits. "We don't want children to give up after a sentence or two." Each of her books includes a glossary, which Waters says is "essential if you're going to use vocabulary words."

Waters also edits her writing for subjective, motivational words. As Coffman explains the concept, "We say *ought to, have to,* or *need to*. But they said *I must,* or *I am obliged to.*" Waters says, "Today, we equivocate, but in religion-based cultures like the British, Dutch, or the Spanish communities of early America, there was not much leeway for human interpretation of the rules of life! I try not to use motivational words that children of that time would never have used."

Waters adds, "*The Oxford English Dictionary* (OED) is an essential tool." Available at libraries, the OED gives the date by which a word or expression first appeared, with examples of the sentence or phrases in which it was used. "If you're going to say, 'The father had a heart attack,'" in a historical book, says Waters, the OED "will say whether that phrase was used by that time. There's a temptation to say, 'She felt faint.' It sounds quaint and old-fashioned to our ears, but you may find that the word *faint* was not used in that way at that time."

(*Faint* has been used consistently since the fourteenth century to mean feeble, sickly, or wanting in vigor. The word that might have been used for a heart attack in the eighteenth century is *apoplexy,* which was used by Chaucer and on through the centuries before modern medicine.)

Waters also takes into account the psychological climate of the time.

When one of her young characters worried over acceptance by her new stepfather, for instance, Waters suggested most of the child's feelings by implication. "She would never have gone on and on and wondered and worried," she explains. "I hope children can get a chance to appreciate the reticence, the caution of the time."

The result is a passage like this one, from *Sarah Morton's Day: A Day in the Life of a Pilgrim Girl:*

> After milking, I muck the garden to make it rich for planting next spring.
>
> The muck is heavy, and I must often stop to rest.
>
> "Hurry along, Sarah," Mother calls from the doorway.
>
> Oh, marry! I am caught idle again.

"Writers should know that there are experts all over the world who are willing to help them," Waters says, "scholars who are so immersed in the history of the time that they can't help you enough." For information on speech patterns in a particular place and time, Waters recommends contacting the education department in an appropriate living-history museum. But in the final analysis, the important task is listening, to the speech of museum interpreters or "even if it's just a recording of seventeenth-century music. The first thing is just to close your eyes and listen. You'll hear the cadence of the language. It all starts with the rhythm."

Vibrant, Not Disembodied

The rhythms of different times and places is reflected in idiom, but because slang changes swiftly as time passes, writers are sometimes warned to avoid it. "If you write a book set in 1999, and use today's slang, it may date it," warns Roberts, as may references to passing fads. "Kids may think, 'Oh, Power Rangers. That's out.'" David Gale adds, "When you're trying to make your characters do the trendiest, cutting-edge thing, remember that the only reason kids like it is that it wasn't around six months ago, and it won't be around six months from now!"

But Gale adds that the appropriateness of slang depends on the medium in which it's used. "It's appropriate in anything that's not lasting. In a paperback series, for instance, why not? I prefer the use of slang to the use of brand names, or the mention of trendy clothes."

Old-fashioned slang can also help to establish the tone of a time. "If it's congruent with the era you're talking about, then it sets the tone," says Roberts, adding that the passage of time can change usage in startling ways. "My mother used to tell me things that just shocked me. A cigarette was a fag, a pimple was a hickey. She said, 'You have a hickey on your face.' I said, 'What?!'"

In the right hands, as Silver Whistle Editor Paula Wiseman points out, contemporary slang can add an irreplaceable freshness to writing. She says in the Uncle Remus retelling, Lester "used slang and contemporary references, and it made those stories so accessible." The references Lester used in his latest book with Wiseman, *When the Beginning Began,* add what Wiseman calls "vibrant life" to the stories.

When the Beginning Began is a collection of creation tales inspired by Jewish legend and Lester's own translations from the Hebrew of *Genesis*. Lester writes about the creation in a distinctly contemporary tone, as when he describes the time before God created light:

> Once a day or once every million years—what did they know?—Moe, Aviva, Jennifer, or one of the other angels would say, 'Sure is dark.'
> 'Sure is,' God agreed.

"I do not worry that using slang will date my books," says Lester. "I find this question to be an absurd one when we consider the language of Shakespeare's plays which are filled with Elizabethan slang, as well as words nobody has used in conversations since his time. We read Shakespeare today with footnotes explaining the words. But we still read Shakespeare."

"I use slang because stories exist in time. I use slang because I want to communicate with the children of today," says Lester. "I think the belief that one should not use slang gives many retellings a feeling of a disembodied voice, of a voice that is not rooted in time and place. Readers of my retellings feel as if they are listening to a person who loves to tell stories. They feel the presence of a person behind the voice that maybe reminds them of a parent or grandparent. I use slang to help make a connection to the reader."

As Martin points out, a writer who uses slang, dialect, or a regional accent must be immersed in the sound of those voices. "If the writer is not steeped in the dialect or the regionalisms or the slang vocabulary himself or herself, it will ring false." In the end, however, capturing the sound of spoken speech in writing is less a question of following rules than of skill, attention to detail, awareness of rhythm, and the sensitivity of the writer's ear.

Wiseman sums it up, "I hesitate to say there are no problems with slang and dialect, because then everyone will do it and that's not right. But sometimes breaking the rules is the only thing to do."

Focus in Nonfiction

Follow the Thread

By Marilyn D. Anderson

"Needs sharper focus," reads many a rejection note, says Andy Boyles, Science Editor of *Highlights for Children*.

"We receive many articles that are treated too broadly for our readership," says Nancy Axelrad, Editor of *U*S*Kids Weekly Reader Magazine*. In other words, these articles lack focus.

"This is important for writers to understand, but many writers don't know what *sharper focus* means," says Boyles. He offers an example: "Let's say we're talking about the ostrich. The article begins with an attempt at a clever lead, such as a riddle. Then it says that the ostrich is the biggest bird in the world, that it can run really fast, and that it doesn't really hide its head in the sand. The article goes on to say, 'Here's what the female does to prepare to lay her eggs, and after X amount of time they hatch, and the young do thus and so and they leave their parents at age Y.' Then we have another little quip at the end. This article has no focus because it's trying to tell us everything the author knows about ostriches, which isn't very much."

Putting Up Firm Fences

Focus is more than narrowing your subject, however, and it is certainly not researching a subject to death and narrating it all back. "It has to do with audience," says Tanya Dean, Managing Editor of *Guideposts for Teens*. "You must have in mind the person for whom you're writing. What is the reader's age and interest level? What is the information the audience needs or wants?"

Fred Bortz, author of five books and many magazine articles about scientific topics, agrees. Focus, he says, "is the way the reader latches on to a subject and follows the thread right through to the end."

Writers and editors often define focus in terms of other principles or qualities of writing. "It's the slant, what you're aiming toward," says Suzanne Lieurance, co-author of *Kidding Around Kansas City*, and author of many articles about children's computer software. Her co-author, Lisa Harkrader, who has also written many nonfiction articles, agrees that focus is slant, although she uses synonyms—"angle" and "approach." Shannon Zemlicka, who edits nonfiction for Lerner Publishing Group, also defines focus as the writing's angle.

But Kathlyn Gay says, "It's the theme." This author of almost 100 nonfiction books adds to her definition the questions, "What is the point of the book? What am I trying to say?"

Another helpful way of clarifying exactly what focus is comes from Kim Marie Wood, who writes often about horses. She came to grasp the concept through a rejection. "For me, nonfiction has to have a *face*. I once wrote the best article about penguins there ever was and sent it to *Highlights*. I got back a rejection that said, 'Your article lacks face. You need to interview a zookeeper who works with penguins and incorporate your information into what he says about penguins.'"

Nick Cook, author of a wild and crazy book called *Roller Coasters, or I Had So Much Fun I Almost Puked,* relies on familiar, but strong, images to describe focus. "It means putting firm fences around your topic. It's like keeping your eye on the ball."

Turning on a Point

Those firm fences can be erected in different ways, but the best nonfiction writers construct the optimal focus by joining strong structure or organization to a creative perspective.

Focus may begin with your initial idea, but more likely it grows from research. "Often, focus will come from doing the research, but you come up with scads of stuff that doesn't ever get used," Gay says. That broad knowledge must be narrowed down until it is reformed, directed, and if you do it well, absorbing.

More research often means better focus, even before you've hit the keyboard or put pen to paper. "An author should read far more than he writes," says John Allen, Associate Editor at *Cricket*. "Even though you shouldn't say everything you know about a topic, you should know an awful lot."

Interviews are among the most effective ways to come to a slant. "Find someone who has a strong view about the topic," Wood advises. "Don't try to invent the story. Let the story tell itself. In the process of the interview, I even ask the person, 'What is it that you would like to get across to people?' Sometimes that's totally different from what you had wanted to write about."

Bortz, for example, interviewed a renowned scientist to find out about a chemistry concept and found that his subject had a wonderful personal story to tell. "This person wasn't sure he would even go to college until he was out of high school," says Bortz, "but he ended up winning a Nobel prize. This world famous scientist told me, 'Nobody thought I would amount to much, and frankly, neither did I.' That was the story: This guy who's been on the path of self-discovery as well as scientific discovery."

Some portion of the focus may be given to a writer, especially one who has taken on an assignment generated by an editor or one writing for a series. Wendi Old has written five middle-grade biographies for Enslow Publishers, who requires that the first chapter of each book focus on a turning point in the subject's life. Finding that event can be difficult. "When I wrote about James Monroe," Old remembers, "I thought his turning point would be the Monroe Doctrine. I tried that three or four times, but it didn't work. There was just too much background that you had to understand for the Monroe

Narrow Focus, Big Picture

Sometimes the topic you're writing about is almost too big to handle given word count or page limitations. The solution might be to find one example or nugget of truth that will illuminate the big picture.

When Kathlyn Gay wrote a book called *Child Labor, A Global Crisis,* she found herself overwhelmed by all the suffering she learned about. Gay needed to make all the facts and figures hit home. "I found stories of individual young people from all over the world to show the real tragedy."

Suzanne Lieurance ran into a similar problem with a book about Kansas City. She needed very short pieces to introduce each chapter, but she could use no more than 150 words. She walked into the city's Toys and Miniature Museum and wondered what on earth to talk about, out of all the myriad possibilities. Her solution was to focus on something about the museum's history to which the kids could relate. She finally wrote: "Children aren't the only ones who share their toys. Several years ago two Kansas City women decided to share their toy and miniature collection with the entire city."

Doctrine to come up in the first chapter. Finally, I decided to begin with the War of 1812 when Monroe, who was already Secretary of State, had to take over as Secretary of War because an incompetent was in charge. I had to wallow around quite a long time to find that focus." While Old's subjects are usually dead, the focus of her books can still change as she researches. What doesn't change is her aim: "I keep trying to focus on what there was about the person that would interest middle school readers."

A big plus of strengthening your focusing skills is that it can also help you increase your sales. Linda Moore Durston started out to write a book about sponges and called the Oregon Coast Aquarium to learn more about them. That made her turn to Keiko, the whale who starred in the *Free Willy* movies and who was at the aquarium for rehabilitation. "I had seen Keiko there and I suddenly wondered if anyone had done a book about him." No one had. Durston wrote a book, and then wrote an article for *Owl,* each with a different focus. The article concentrated on Keiko's travels. In the book, she says, "I told about Keiko's experiences in the bigger frame of things. I asked what we want to do in the future with animals like Keiko."

Durston observes that this process is not unlike writing fiction when "one character takes over. As you gather information, you might go in a different direction than you had originally planned."

That comparison to the process of writing fiction is one that other nonfiction writers acknowledge. "You must realize that you are telling a compelling

But Will It Sell?

You start with an idea for an article or a book and then you do some research. One of the first things you should research, once you have a solid idea, is the market.

Asked why he wrote his book *Roller Coasters, or I Had So Much Fun I Almost Puked,* Nick Cook laughs and says, "Because I thought it would sell." He had worked at Disneyland and been around roller coasters. He looked for books on the subject, found very few, and decided this was a niche he could fill.

Even one department of a general interest magazine like *Highlights for Children* may look for articles focused in a certain way. Science Editor Andy Boyles says, "We are interested in showing kids that science is a process as opposed to a collection of facts. If we had a writer who had studied tigers (as opposed to someone who just read about them), we would prefer the firsthand approach."

More fundamentally, market focus must begin with the editorial direction of each publication or company. The critical first step in determining focus for your nonfiction is an analysis of your target market's special requirements. Different magazines stress different genres or topics. Associate Editor John Allen says, "We publish more fiction than nonfiction at *Cricket,* but we try to get a little science and/or history into each issue."

Remember, however, just aiming for a theme or desirable genre isn't enough. Focus isn't merely the appropriate selection of a subject, as essential as that is: It is a tight approach to that subject, an article or book structure, and much more.

Guideposts for Teens publishes true stories that inspire readers. "We are an inspirational magazine, not exclusively Christian," Tanya Dean points out. "We have readers who are Jewish, and some who aren't churchgoers at all." Stories for this magazine "need to make some kind of a spiritual point, even if it's as simple as 'God loves you. You're not alone.'"
(continued on next page)

---

true story," says Bortz. "If you care about the subject matter, and if you analyze your own interest, you can find the angle that will give your story focus. Keep the reader in mind and look for that central thread."

Something to Say

Achieving focus continues after the idea sparks, after the research is done, and all through the writing process. For Lieurance, the next step is an outline, and the exercise of constructing one indicates if the work is coming into focus. She says, "David Fryxell explains it perfectly in his book *How to Write Fast (While Writing Well)* when he says, "If you have nothing to say, an outline won't let you say it.'"

Gay puts it this way: "The outline is where you find out what you're really trying to say. It makes you get to the point, or the focus. Otherwise, you're going to go off in so many different di-

But Will It Sell?

(continued from preceding page)

Every issue of *Boys' Quest* and *Hopscotch* is built around a theme. Editor Marilyn Edwards explains, "Editors read each manuscript that comes in to see if it goes with a theme where we have openings. If the writer wants us to pick right up on what they send, it needs photo support." *U*S*Kids* is one of several magazines published by the Children's Better Health Institute. Editor Nancy Axelrad reminds writers, "We have a health and fitness slant. Material that reflects healthy lifestyle habits is encouraged."

When you decide it's time to try a nonfiction book, you need to find out what kind of books various companies publish by looking through their catalogues and reading those that perk your interest. You will find that publisher lists have their own concentrations.

The Lerner Publishing Group, for example, publishes several different series, each with its own particular slant. Editor Shannon Zemlicka explains that the books in Carolrhoda's Creative Minds series, for example, "are for grades three to six and they are narrative in style. Writers who plan to submit to Lerner should also remember to write for guidelines. Due to high volume, submissions are only accepted in March and October."

A book about Kansas City by Lisa Harkrader and Suzanne Lieurance fit into a very specific series put out by John Muir Publishers. Harkrader explains, "They do these books about a few cities each year."

Nick Cook has a new book about downhill in-line skating that is written for a reluctant reader series put out by Capstone Press. "They have very strict guidelines on readability," he says. "I find it a challenge to see if I can stay within their word count, words per sentence, and their format."

rections that no one will know what you're trying to say."

Whether you use an outline, or begin to compose your piece according to another process, Cook advises that the intended audience must be constantly on the author's mind. At this stage, too, the focus is strongly influenced by the age of the reader. Cook is speaking of child development principles and the renowned child psychologist when he says, "Just as Piaget demonstrated, you need to use more concrete examples for little kids, and you want to present something they already know and build on that."

Zemlicka's advice indicates how the form your nonfiction writing takes is an important link to and expression of the focus: "For younger readers, choose a simple, concrete focus. Look for words and phrases that appeal to the senses. Try for very direct images that young children can process. Dialogue is really good for them. It's easier for young children to follow and absorb that than long 'prosey' sentences."

Good Weeding

In the process of the writing, the culling continues: determining what information to include, what to exclude, and how to present it. Bortz, who often writes for older children, knows he has found a subject worth pursuing when he finds himself drawn into the nitty gritty of his subject. "I write for the kid I used to be. I was a kid who liked to go back over and over a text to get more each time. I think many kids will pursue difficult things if the topic moves them. As long as you see a story line, you can hold their focus."

Gay admits she's always tempted to go off on tangents. "I hate to skim the surface of anything," she says. "But you can get onto a topic that young people might not understand if you go too deeply into it. Then you have to pull back. I think, 'Oh, I really don't need to get into this chemistry formula.' Other times you really do want to know this technical data. It depends on the readability of the chapter you're working on."

"The hard part is deciding what to leave out," says Harkrader. "When I did an article called 'Ideas on Demand,' I found there were all kinds of ways to come up with ideas, but I wanted to focus on how you come up with ideas when you need them—like right now. It was hard to weed out all the things that didn't pertain to that particular slant."

Boyles also believes that knowing what to leave out is the biggest problem and adds this comparison to fiction: "Every novel is a book about life, but no single book tells you all about life. The story line and the point of view force the writer to include related events and details and to leave out the rest. If the story doesn't call for a certain bit of information, that information just doesn't come up."

Durston likes to use recurring motifs to help keep her books and articles stay focused. In her book about the whale, she says, "I started with Keiko being moved from Mexico City to Newport, Oregon, with everyone watching and cheering. In one of the last chapters, Keiko is being taken from Oregon to Iceland, and again there are people cheering."

Dean offers this trick for checking your focus as you write: "Our magazine talks about 'the takeaway' rather than the focus. It's what we want the reader to take away from what he has read. Write that takeaway as a headline and keep glancing at the headline as you go along."

Using a similar touchstone, Axelrad uses a question to concentrate her approach. "You write the article with that question in mind," she explains. "When you finish, you ask yourself, 'Have I answered that queston and only that question, or have I answered more than that question?' If you've answered, 'More than that question,' it's time to go back and edit."

Harkrader puts it this way: "If all the little threads go in one direction, you've got focus. If you put the piece away for awhile, something might stick out and make you ask, 'Where is this going?' If I come up with interesting tidbits that don't fit, I'll set those aside and try to put them in a sidebar."

Allen probably speaks for countless editors when he says, "We would certainly like to see more good nonfiction. But the fiction we receive is better than the nonfiction because the nonfiction often lacks focus. Read widely, keep current about what's going on related to your topic, and make the focus as narrow as possible. Hold tight to the focus; don't let anything irrelevant slip in."

Part 4

The Business Side

Business

Networking

How to Connect the Publishing Dots

By Julianne Papp

At a local writers' conference, a children's author suggests to a room full of earnest writers that to be noticed, they should put themselves in front of an editor or agent, shake their hand, and tactfully use them to the best publishing advantage. Great advice, and you have probably heard these as well: "Attend conferences that cater to children's writers." "Meet and mingle with editors and agents." "Socializing with the speakers can be as important as the workshops themselves."

But are you a few hundred dollars and several hundred miles short of rubbing elbows with all those influential people in the children's writing industry? How do you get the same benefits without the flight, hotel, and conference costs? How do you draw yourself into the publishing picture? The answer is right in front of you.

The Start

Networking is like connecting dots: One leads to another to another. Start with strangers, who lead to friends, who lead to authors, who lead to editors. Look locally to writers' groups and organizations, the school media center, the city library, nearby universities, bookstores, and the Internet. Don't discount the grocery store, the auto show, or the dentist's office.

"One day, while in the dentist's chair, I entertained the new hygienist with stories about my unsold books and my quest to be published," says Lee Wardlaw, award-winning author of *101 Ways to Bug Your Parents*. "'Oh, you must talk with my mother,' the hygienist said. 'She's friends with a woman who just started her own children's publishing house!'" Wardlaw met the publisher, was offered a contract, and was invited to be a member of the publisher's partner's writing group.

Another time, while telling friends at a party about her interest in writing a book on bubble gum, Wardlaw was approached by the wife of a 50-year veteran of the gumball vending business who overheard the conversation, apologized for eavesdropping, and cemented a valuable research connection that eventually lead to *Bubblemania: The Chewy History of Bubble Gum*. No flight itinerary, no hotel reservation, no conference or critiquing fee. Just a writer doing what comes naturally—talking about her passion for writing.

The reverse of this situation can also give you a contact strategy that might be called "harvesting conversation." If a conversation floats your way hinting of possible connections, introduce yourself and take it from there. You never know when the perfect research connection, or an editor, may be chatting just an elbow away—or behind you on the grocery line, or at the theater as you're chatting with friends about your latest chapter. More and more freelance editors are working out of their homes in communities like yours, reducing costs for the publishing house and work hours for the editor. Be prepared to take advantage of the contacts that come your way.

Across the Table
You can start networking anywhere, but a good place to begin is at a writers' group—a working membership of writers who meet at regularly scheduled times for productive support, to increase each other's productivity, share information, and help polish each other's work. Notice "productive." If you're not coming away from your meeting with anything more than a caffeine surge and cake crumbs on your chest, then you're not in a writers' group—you're in a coffee klatch.

Writers' groups are a great resource. When one of the writers in our group, Robin, got an encouraging rejection from an editor at G. P. Putnam's Sons with a request to see more of her work, she passed on the editor's name to Barb, who had a manuscript that fit their list. Barb followed up, addressing her manuscript to the same editor, and was rewarded with a similar request to see more work. The connection was right there, just across the table. The bonus is that the editor's suggestions increase Robin's and Barb's manuscripts' marketability, if not for G. P. Putnam's Sons, then for the next house on their list for submitting.

The writers' group connection that Lee Wardlaw made following her dentist visit was 16 years ago and is still going strong. "Their support, critiques, and friendship have been invaluable to my life and my writing career." If you don't already belong to a writers' group, find or start one. Tips can be found in how-to manuals on writing and articles in trade journals.

Volunteer Connections
Another place that provides opportunities to meet authors and learn about their editors is school. Introduce yourself to area principals and media specialists. They have a vested interest and a passion for keeping children interested in books, and many are themselves children's writers. Find out who makes the decisions about bringing authors into the school. Let them know that, as an aspiring local children's writer, you would be grateful for the chance to sit in on selection committee meetings and, of course, attend the author visit. What's an extra body warming up a cold folding chair going to hurt?

Consider volunteering to help prepare for that wonderful visit. Could you make your family's favorite cookies for the author's tea? Type up flyers to send home with students announcing the big day? Treat an author to dinner? Be a chauffeur from and to the airport or hotel?

In *Networking at Writers' Conferences, From Contacts to Contracts,* Steven and Lee Spratt give sensible suggestions for "the art of careful volunteering," and extend the same idea to editors attending conferences: "Give the editor a ride, and you have her attention on you, as an individual, for the duration of that ride. By using this tactic, we have both sold an agent on representing us and in another case, sold a book." Whether squiring a writer or an editor, be friendly, but do not try to be a tour guide. Be inquiring, not annoying. Even though your hands may be perspiring, and your heart racing faster than the speedometer, try to relax and be friendly; the rest will come naturally.

Besides the obvious education you can get from learning another writers' experiences and points of view when volunteering to assist in their visit in some way, you have the benefit of establishing a relationship with an author who may remember your name should their editor ask for a recommendation.

The media specialist in one of our town's schools makes it a point to invite local writers to hear visiting authors in hopes of fostering publishing connections. Through a school visit, my writers' group colleague, Robin, became acquainted with John Reynolds Gardiner, who discussed her manuscript. He didn't have time to read the entire story, but he made suggestions and advised her to send it off to an editor he knew. The result was the editor's personal response with a request for a rewrite.

Connections to county school personnel can also help get you curriculum guidelines (great information for the educational market). These people may also be, or know, representatives for various county, state, national, and international reading and writing programs. It might not be a bad idea to create your own holiday: "Take a Media Specialist to Lunch Day."

Public Libraries

The other professionals to connect with, and celebrate, are the children's librarians at the main library and its branches. This dedicated group, many of whom are published authors themselves, may prove to be a valuable networking link. University and college library, and teaching, connections may also prove invaluable.

If your public library hosts local authors, learn who arranges author visits and writing programs. The more you know about the library system, the better your chances are of becoming acquainted with the person who can connect you. A personal introduction by the person in charge may carry weight when a visiting author has some spare chat time.

If you can involve yourself in the invitation process, you may be able to suggest one of your favorite authors, or

Meeting and Greeting Tips

Use your writing talents to flesh out a go-getter character—you! Make writing friends; it's easier to talk with a friend than it is a stranger. Ask names and don't forget to use them. Use titles (Professor, Dr.) until you are invited to drop them. Think of meetings as interviews, taking notes afterwards. The next time you plan to meet, review your notes and make a point of connecting your last conversation to this one, making your name and face a stronger memory. After the first few meetings, you will move from stranger to acquaintance, to business friend, and if you're fortunate, to friend.

Be Prepared
Do have:
- business cards readily available
- two working pens
- small hard candies or breath mints
- a networking notebook or tabbed section of a journal. Start each entry with a full address, phone, e-mail and referral name. Leave room for dated notes; if you expect more contact, leave a full page. Slip business cards into an attached pocket or envelope.

Be Presentable
Think of what your mother would say before you rushed out the door as a child. Be groomed, and keep on hand waterless hand wash, a comb, hair clip, and for women, perhaps a cover stick or lipstick. Even a tucked shirt and a swipe at dusty shoes can make a big difference.
(continued on next page)

---

better yet, an author/editor. Be ready to offer your services in the same manner as with school visits. If an author you suggested is to be invited, be willing to assist with the connections.

A shortcut to tapping into English departments and the people on campus most associated with children's literature is to meet the head librarian. He can often direct you to just the right people. Keep your eye on the area newspaper for university-sponsored events where writers and editors are featured speakers or are available for book signings and conversation.

Most universities offer one or two noncredit courses or workshops for children's writers, generally led by published authors. Instructors with a passion for children's literature are happy to encourage promising writers, sometimes to the point of becoming mentors, sharing friendship as well as expertise and information.

Large universities often have satellite campuses and bookstores. These may be more accessible to you, so be sure to get names and numbers of personnel and

Meeting and Greeting Tips

(continued from preceding page)

Find the balance between the just-stepped-out-of-the-catalogue look and frump, and try to maintain that. Steven and Lee Spratt, authors of *Networking at Writers' Conferences, from Contacts to Contracts,* suggest finding "something that helps you express not only your personality, but your sense of business self—something that is uniquely yours and communicates your own individuality." First impressions do count.

Paybacks
Write thank you notes when appropriate. Volunteer, support fund-raisers, or feature an organization in an article for a local paper. Paybacks generally become reciprocal and can take as much or as little of your time as you like. Be careful not to overcommit yourself, however.

Be Professional
- Be conscious of business hours, especially peak hours.
- Check school policies regarding visitors.
- Shake hands and smile.
- Be personable, not personal.
- Describe your manuscripts in one or two brief sentences.
- Don't monopolize speakers.
- If you're out with the kids or friends, make introductions as necessary, keep it short, exchange names, business cards, and follow-up as soon as possible. Your new contact will be more impressed if he has your undivided attention later.

---

request to be put on a mailing list for upcoming writing-related events.

Some universities sponsor community festivals that focus on reading and storytelling. Young Authors, a workshop for young writers, is supported by the University of South Florida in conjunction with the county school system, and hosts authors who offer recognition, support, and encouragement to young writers. You'll hear about these events through both the university and district grade schools. Get behind the scenes early to maximize your opportunity to discuss possible writing connections.

A Special Event
Individuals who work in the public sector are essential resources, but trade contacts are vital as well. No matter what bookstore you frequent, the megastores or the independents, make it your business to become more than a passing acquaintance with the manager of the children's department as well as the store manager.

Depending on the size of the store,

Author Visit Preparations

✔ Become familiar with the author's work. Does the author credit an editor in a dedication? Who is it?
✔ Check bookseller's and publisher's websites, or catalogues for book reviews and the author's bio.
✔ Check a current writers' market for publisher information. Do you have a manuscript that fits the publisher's list?
✔ Plan a few short, but useful, questions.

Internet Sites

Keep linking manageable with an Internet notebook, highlighting interesting addresses and adding a brief description of the site. Bookmark favorites and surf selectively. Many companies use their name, acronym, or an abbreviation plus .com for an address. Academic institutions end in .edu and organizations end in .org. Here are some general areas to search:
- publisher sites
- writer sites (Inkspot.com is a great place to start.)
- university and district school Web pages
- writing and reading organization Web pages (Society of Children's Book Writers and Illustrators, American Library Association, Children's Book Council)
- online writers' chat groups.

In a Nutshell

✔ *Who they are.* People in the industry, or those who have already made the connection with others in the industry—published writers in book, magazine, trade journals, textbooks, newsprint, radio, television, film, online magazines, and information sites.

✔ *Where they are.* Author visits at bookstores, libraries, schools, in residence at universities, newspaper offices, TV and radio stations, the Internet.

✔ *How to contact them.* By phone, in person, via introductory note (mail or e-mail), acquaintance introduction.

✔ *Make the best of the contact.* Be prepared with questions, be presentable, be polite, assertive not aggressive, be brief, obtain permission to follow up on contacts.

✔ *Follow through and pay back.* Write a thank you note, follow leads, keep in touch. Volunteer, reciprocate the connection.

one person may fill both positions, and may also serve as the Community Relations Manager (CRM). Large booksellers employ a CRM or Special Events Coordinator (SEC) who arranges book signings and other in-store or community events. Take a minute to stop in and chat with this person and be sure to get the latest on writing-related events. The local Barnes & Noble CRM saves publishing catalogues for me and lets me know in advance when authors are scheduled to give in-store presentations. The CRM or SEC know marketing representatives from major distributors who may be willing to speak to large gatherings of writers. Could you be the liaison between schools, libraries, or writing organizations and endear yourself to a member of the industry?

When visiting bookstores to shop-talk with personnel, be considerate. Don't drop by during peak hours and expect the staff to eke out 30 minutes to accommodate your budding career. Keep in mind how favorably the bookstore staff will look on you when it's time for you to find the perfect hometown venue to do your first book signing. Independent booksellers are happy to play host to local writers who make it big.

Aside from all this, people who sell children's books are lovely people. Take some time to socialize occasionally over a good book and coffee.

Over Long Distances

The face-to-face encounters are fun and rewarding, but the Internet is also a wonderful resource, providing writers with long-distance connections. Some libraries have Internet access computers for public use. Time limits are generally imposed, so keep an address book of favorite sites, adding links as you find them.

Online writing groups cover just about every genre. Writers and editors discuss, applaud, and commiserate about the writing life in a casual and supportive way. These groups are wonderful ways to network.

Sasha Tomey, a romance writer, e-mailed an author telling him how much she admired his work and asked a specific writing question. She received a long reply and over the next weeks, the author advised her on her work and suggested websites that would help. Would this author, having advised Tomey, suggest her to his editor? Maybe. And it's the *maybe* you've got to work for in networking.

Writing to publish is a business with many departments that all need your attention. The writing, market research, and the submission process can be made more hopeful if you increase your publishing opportunities with networking. Talk up your current story or article idea to friends and strangers, keep your eyes open for events showcasing children's authors, associate yourself with staff and committee members who make scheduling decisions for authors, be professional, follow-up leads, make friends.

One of the characters in the John Guare play, *Six Degrees of Separation,* says, "Every person is a new door, opening up into other worlds. Six degrees of separation between me and everyone else on this planet . . . But to find the right six people." Networking helps you find those people, and along the way you're going to meet many who are intelligent, caring, and helpful as you connect the dots of your publishing picture.

The Making of a Magazine
Set the Tempo
By Vicki Hambleton

Imagine a difficult jigsaw puzzle, perhaps one of those that are round and all one color. Now imagine three, four, eight people coming to the table with pieces of the puzzle and putting it together. Some go for the edges first, while others like to work piece by piece, studying shapes and developing a pattern.

That process is not unlike putting together a magazine. Just like the puzzle solvers, each editor brings pieces of the final work to the table. The difference is that the way the editorial players put together the pieces of the magazine is as unique as each finished product, the magazine that arrives in the mailbox or on the bookstore rack.

The staffs of three magazines, *Highlights for Children*, *Campus Life*, and *Footsteps*, opened their doors and let us peer behind their glossy covers to see just how the creative process flows from idea to manuscript to final product. The business of making a magazine is fluid. Editors constantly look at, re-evaluate, their editorial process, tweaking it and searching for ways to make it better.

As Managing Editor of *Highlights*, Christine Clark describes herself as the conductor of an orchestra. "I set the tempo," she says, "and the other editors make the music. I think the music we are playing was composed by the founders of *Highlights* 52 years ago. My job is to allow the editors to interpret the music without ever straying from the original score."

Hitting the High Notes:
Highlights for Children

The process of building an issue of *Highlights* begins with the purchase of manuscripts. Nonstaff writers are responsible for 95 percent of the magazine's articles and stories. Each of the editors reads material that comes in unsolicited over the transom. They make recommendations and Clark makes the final decision to purchase based on their comments.

Marileta Robinson and Rich Wallace, *Highlights* Senior Editors, share duties for the magazine's fiction. Robinson oversees stories for younger readers, while Wallace is responsible for older readers.

"When I get a story I feel we should consider for *Highlights*, the first thing I do is to pass the piece around to a few editors for their comments," says Robinson. All the editors at *Highlights* routinely look at different types of articles and stories submitted, but at the same time, "I might ask for a specific editor's comments," she explains. "If I get a story that has to do with science and I want to make sure the science sounds right, then I'll ask the Science Editor, Andy Boyles, to read the piece."

Once purchased, a piece becomes part of the *Highlights* inventory. Unlike many publications, the three million circulation monthly works with a very large inventory. It may take several years from the time a piece is bought before it sees print.

Each issue begins to take shape at what *Highlights* calls a *nominations meeting*. All the editors attend with one or two pieces they think should run in a given issue. The goal is to create a good mix of materials in terms of variety, age range, and subject matter. Sometimes a piece is held because it is too similar to another one selected. "If we have a science article on horses, and I have a story with a horse in it, we'll decide to hold one for another issue," says Robinson.

The *plan and balance* committee, a group of three or four editors chaired by Clark, next reviews editors' nominations. Wallace describes what they look for when it comes to balance: "Our magazine has to cover many different areas and meet the needs of an audience with a vast age range, 2 to 12. For each issue, we want as many pieces as possible to have as broad a range as possible. If one piece is good for 2-to-4-year-olds, then we want another that reaches 5-to-8-year-olds, and another for 7-to-12-year-olds. We also want to make sure there are some surprises that kids aren't expecting and, overall, that there is a lot of fun and humor."

Clark says that the editors must also consider how each issue fits in with the plan for the entire year. "We consider how long it has been since we ran, say, an art piece or a profile of a sports figure when we plan an issue."

Out of the plan and balance committee meeting comes the final plan for an issue that will be published 10 months later. At any given time, four or five issues are in some stage of production. Clark estimates that there may be as many as 100 different pieces of the puzzle circulating the office: layouts for one issue, sketches for another, word processing copy, and dummy proofs.

Once the decisions are made about which pieces will make up a given issue, editors edit each article or story for content and for length—to fit the space allotted in the issue. The piece is then trafficked to the copy editor, to a secondary editor, and to Wallace who, in addition to being a fiction editor, acts as Coordinating Editor. He and the copy editor see everything that goes into an issue at every stage of its creation.

Each editor has a secondary editor who acts as backup—a kind of editing partner. "The more eyes you have on a piece, the better," she says. "My partner makes comments on things that maybe they didn't understand, or notes that something could be made clearer. The copy comes back to me with comments and then I do a final edit before the copy is sent to our Art Director, Janet McCaffrey."

McCaffrey makes the copy come alive with illustrations and, in some cases, photographs. Editors may recommend a particular artist or offer suggestions about a character's age or ethnic background. "When a story comes to me," McCaffrey explains, "I read it first to get a feel for who I might want to illustrate it. Certain artists are better with one kind of story than another. I also start to think about how I might lay the piece out, what parts are best illustrated."

McCaffrey has about 50 artists with whom she works on a regular basis, and twice that number of artists whom she uses less often. Each issue of *Highlights* represents the work of as many as 20 or 30 artists. Once McCaffrey has assigned stories, the artists have six weeks to come up with preliminary sketches, which are circulated to the editors for comment. When a sketch is approved, the artist begins work on the final art.

"When the final art comes in, we have what we call a *page-through*," says McCaffrey. "We hang up all the pages in the conference room and see how the flow of the magazine is going. Do we have too much, say, for younger readers at the front of the book? We decide on a final order and then the art is coded. The code tells us what will go on which page." Five months elapse between the coding and the printing process of color separation. Clark looks at the final pages, and when she approves it all, the issue is sent digitally to the film house, the final stage before the issue is printed and ready to go.

Current and Connected:
Campus Life

Campus Life, a Christian monthly with a circulation of about 100,000, is put together by a staff of 15 editors. While many of its features are written by freelancers, *Campus Life* is produced almost completely in-house and editors do double duty as editors and writers. The magazine staff includes a managing editor, part-time senior associate editor, two assistant editors, part-time designer, assistant design editor, and editorial coordinator.

Each issue of *Campus Life* is born at

one of two staff retreats held to plan the six regular teen issues. The three annual college issues are planned separately. Managing Editor Christopher Lutes explains the purpose of the retreat: "Each editor is expected to bring to the retreat five ideas that will get us through three or four issues." These ideas fall under what Lutes describes as specific *grid* points. Each issue includes very specific kinds of articles, such as first-person stories, student profiles, celebrity pieces, and issue-oriented articles. Other ideas fall under a more general heading that encompasses photo features, humor, and general interest.

The retreat is also the time for brainstorming, to come up with ideas for new features or columns, a time to evaluate the content of *Campus Life*. "Our audience, teens, is constantly shifting," says Lutes. "Some topics, such as dating, remain constant, but sometimes we decide that a particular column is going stale, or isn't connecting to the current crop of young people, and we need to pay serious attention to these things."

As editors present their suggestions, they are asked to come up with a rationale for each piece. "Don't just tell me you like an idea," Lutes instructs the editors. "Tell me why the reader should like the piece. Every idea we come up with needs to go back to what we feel is going to connect with and help our audience."

Part of each editor's job at *Campus Life* is to stay current in some way with the magazine's audience. Many of the editors are involved with youth at church or in other groups and Lutes stresses the need to be in touch with leaders such as youth pastors. "We go to people like youth pastors to feed us ideas," he explains, "and to keep us informed about what is important in young peoples' lives."

At the end of a retreat, Lutes, as the managing editor, puts the ideas together into various issues, usually three at a time. His outline for an issue includes all the ideas discussed and he budgets pages. "I need to come up with the number of pages each article will cover, the number of words it should be, any sidebars needed, and how many columns will run. I keep juggling until I make it work, but sometimes there will be holes. Maybe we didn't come up with a really strong idea for one piece of an issue, so I'll leave space to fill that in later at an editorial meeting."

Each editor gets a copy of Lutes's issue plan. Over a period of a few weeks, it is discussed until the staff feels it is right. Feature articles are assigned to editors, each of whom is also responsible for writing columns.

Approximately 20 percent of the magazine is now freelance-written and that number may continue to grow, according to Lutes. Assistant Editor Alicia Hodge is one of the editors who works regularly with queries. Lutes says she "excels at screening queries and focusing writers so that we get material that works well for us."

For every five queries she receives, Hodge asks one writer to submit a manuscript. Surprisingly, she never hears from many of them again. Hodge says she makes her selections by gauging from writing samples whether she thinks the writer, with guidance, can come up with work that will fit *Campus*

Life's style and needs. At her suggestion, a line was recently added to the writers' guidelines that specifies that the magazine prefers writers who "are willing to be edited and work with editors." Hodge explains, "We have a very specific audience in mind and we have advertising needs to meet. We also know the mentality of the churches our readers attend and have to be mindful of their expectations as well."

When she receives a manuscript she had requested on speculation, Hodge routes it to the other editors with comment slips. Each editor makes comments and then recommends whether the piece should be purchased, rewritten, or sent back. All material, freelance and staff-written, is reviewed in first draft form by all the editors of *Campus Life*. Once a piece is reviewed, the responsible editor prepares a final draft that includes suggestions from the rest of the staff. The final draft goes around to editors one more time before being sent to the design team.

The art in *Campus Life* is all photographs, and with the exception of photos used in celebrity profiles, the pictures are all staged specifically for the publication. The art director arranges for the photographs and assembles these and text into the page proofs.

Finally, all the editors look at everything in the issue one last time. Working with a small staff means constant interaction and "give and take at every step," says Lutes. "Everything that we publish is the result of teamwork."

Create Anew: *Footsteps*

Publisher Malcolm Jensen describes *Footsteps* as "one of my children." A year old, the magazine is one of three new publications added to the Cobblestone Publishing family of educational magazines that also includes *Cobblestone, Calliope, Faces, Odyssey, Appleseeds,* and *California Chronicles.*

Jensen says his role as publisher is to "pace the sidelines and coach." He does, however, participate in the yearly planning sessions that take place each February. Also present at this meeting for *Footsteps* are Managing Editor Lou Waryncia, Editor Charles Baker, Art Director Ann Dillon, and Marketing Manager Manuela Meier.

Footsteps addresses topics related to African-American and African history and culture. While the issues do not tie directly to the curriculum, as *Cobblestone* issues do, Jensen hopes that the magazine will be used by teachers as supplementary material. Issues are planned a year in advance in part to allow teachers to see what is coming and determine how it can be used in the classroom to enrich lesson plans.

While Editor Charles Baker comes up with the list of possible themes, everybody in the planning sessions makes suggestions. When a final theme list is set, deadlines are mapped out to the last detail: when articles will be assigned, when they are due back, when they go to the consulting editors and copy editors, when they go to design.

Baker then creates an issue outline that is based on research. He takes almost weekly trips to a large university library and stays current through magazines and newspapers. Many of the topics *Footsteps* covers relate to current news. An issue on Thomas Jefferson's slave Sally Hemmings, with whom Jefferson may have fathered children, was being written just as Jefferson descendants were meeting with Hemmings descendants for the first time at Monticello.

When the outline is set, it goes to Waryncia, who is located at the Cobblestone home office in New Hampshire. Baker lives in Massachusetts, so most of the work is done via fax, telephone, and e-mail. Everyone who attended the initial editorial planning session also reviews the outline. Waryncia describes the process as "a constant talking back and forth." He says it is his goal "to make sure that each issue is consistent, accurate, and basically fun to read." Baker, in turn, appreciates the input from other members of the staff. "Sometimes when you are researching a topic, you get so into it that you forget what people don't know." Thanks to Jensen, for example, an issue on black cowboys included a piece on cowboy gear.

Next, articles are assigned to writers, who receive a go-ahead letter and a copy of the issue outline. Sharing the outline in this way helps cut down on overlap among pieces. The writer has five weeks to complete an assignment. During that time, Baker is at work finding the art that will accompany the editorial. At *Footsteps* it is the editor's job to compile all the art for each issue.

Each issue of *Footsteps* and other Cobblestone magazines is budgeted for everything from writers to art to proofreading to design. The editor may juggle these budgets as he sees fit: One issue may need more money for writers, another for art.

When copy is back from the writers it is put on disk and sent to the consulting editor and managing editor for review. Because *Footsteps* is an educational magazine, each issue has an expert who acts as consulting editor to make sure that every word in the magazine is historically accurate.

Waryncia reviews the content for readability. "I go through the manuscript looking for ideas. Sometimes I go through and circle words because if it is a word I don't understand how will a fifth grader understand it? In our issue on black cowboys, I told Charlie [Baker] I wanted to be able to feel the dirt beneath the cowboys' fingernails, smell the horses and the cattle. We have a chance in this magazine to make people come alive for our readers." Waryncia not only looks at the first edit, but also reviews a writer's original manuscript and sometimes may request that something be put back in that had been left out of the edited version.

Baker then incorporates the changes into a final draft that has been copy-edited and that goes back to the writers for a final read through and fact-check. With this version back in-house, Baker begins to lay out the issue. "I have a good idea of what I want the entire issue to look like," he explains. All the while, he talks with the art director, Ann Dillon, about different aspects of the final magazine's look. Each story has its own folder containing the final edited copy, artwork, and any notes Baker may have for Dillon.

No detail is too small to consider. Each issue of *Footsteps* has a different border that runs across the top and bottom of each page that is the brainchild of the editor/art director collaboration. The border in the issue on the Massachusetts 54th Infantry was made up of stars and the American flag; for the black cowboys issue it was a collage of symbols that evoke the American West, everything from cowboy boots to cacti and armadillos.

"With *Footsteps*," explains Waryncia, "we made a conscious effort to make it look different from the other Cobblestone magazines. It is still a work in progress. *Footsteps* definitely has more white space than our other magazines, and we want it to be more stylized—same borders, same introductions, but with very different departments. So far, we are very pleased with the way things are going."

When final proofs are delivered, they are reviewed again by Waryncia, Baker, and a proofreader. The issue is at this point virtually done. Final minor changes are made if needed and it then goes back to the art director who gets it ready for pre-press. The editors have 24 more hours to review final page proofs before they are sent out for printing. Time elapsed from initial planning to final form is ideally six months.

Like the puzzle that is finally complete, or the piece of music ready for an orchestra, the newly printed magazine stands out as a thing of beauty. For those who collaborated in the process, there is pride and satisfaction in the creative product, but pride as well in the contribution to words and pictures that pass on knowledge and pleasure in a unique form.

Business

Distribution
Getting Books to Readers

By Patricia Curtis Pfitsch

Distribution. It's crucial for a book's success. Publishers talk about it. Writers complain about it. But what is it and what can writers do about it?

In the simplest terms, distribution is the process by which a book gets from the publisher to the individual who buys and/or reads the book. "Every publisher wants to find cost-effective ways to get a book to the end user," explains Walter Mayes, co-author of *Valerie and Walter's Best Books for Children: A Lively, Opinionated Guide.*

Publishers have a variety of ways to access that consumer. Many large and medium-sized publishers have sales representatives who visit the buyers. Some visit bookstores, schools, and libraries. Others contact drugstores and supermarkets, and still others visit specialty stores. "That's the start of the distribution cycle," explains Alan Smagler, Vice President of Sales and Marketing at Simon & Schuster, whose Children's Division has its own dedicated sales reps who visit bookstores and other retailers and talk about books on their list.

Although much smaller than Simon & Schuster, Boyds Mills Press follows a similar process. "Our sales reps call on stores two to four times a year," says President Clay Winters. "We make an attractive offer to the retailer; we offer an extra discount or free freight. We want them to sample the new line and also buy from the backlist right at that moment. That gets the books in stores so when reviews or advertising occurs, the books are available."

That first order is usually given directly to the publisher through the rep, and the books are shipped directly from the publisher's warehouse to the retailer. But booksellers can't afford the time or the money to make separate orders from every publisher every time they need more books. So for re-orders, they often go through wholesalers or distributors.

Both wholesalers and distributors buy books from many different publishers at a discount and sell them to buyers. This allows a bookstore to do one-stop shopping, rather than contact all the publishers separately. Sometimes wholesalers are referred to as distributors, but technically the difference between them is significant.

A Matter of Momentum

"A distributor has an exclusive rela-

The Writer's Role in Distribution

Is there anything writers can do to help distribution of their books? "You can't have control over distribution," says Walter Mayes, co-author of *Valerie and Walter's Best Books for Children; An Opinionated Guide*. "You might as well not even think about control. But you can certainly influence it and make sure you are knowledgeable about what's happening."

Of course, there are many reasons why a particular book isn't available at a particular bookstore or conference but, says Alan Smagler, Vice President of Sales and Marketing at Simon & Schuster, "often an author sets up an appearance and doesn't understand exactly when the books will be available. Sometimes authors are not informed of when the book is shipping."

Smagler suggests that authors need to know the release date and the publication date of their book before beginning to publicize it. (The release date is when the book can first be shipped to stores. The publication date is when the publicity and marketing efforts begin.) Sometimes a book's release and publication dates change due to hold-ups in the publication process.

Here's another hint from Mayes: When writers or conference organizers check with bookstores about availability, "they should make sure the person they're speaking to at the bookstore has experience doing special orders or conference orders. It's not unusual for one person to be assigned as the special orders person. Any good independent bookstore will have someone who does that."

To give your books the best chance of being available, Mayes suggests writers first contact the publisher to be sure of the publication date and that the books are in stock. It can also help to know which wholesalers carry the book, but it's not a good idea to call the wholesaler for that information. The wholesalers are not set up to deal with individual writers. "It's not that we're not interested," explains Susie Russenberger, Assistant Vice President of Book Products at Ingram, "it's just not the most efficient way." Instead, your publisher might be able to give you statistics about which wholesalers are carrying your book, and how many copies they have on hand. Or, if you have a close relationship with your local bookstore, they might be able to find out for you.

Armed with that information, talk to booksellers in the region where you want your book to be available. "If you as an author know where your book is and which wholesalers are carrying it," Mayes says, "you have a better shot at helping that bookseller know how to order your book."

When writers show up at an appearance and find their books unavailable, says Mayes, "what it frequently boils down to is that there are not enough copies in the distributor pipeline to make up for a publisher's shortfall when a book has ceased to sell. Your book is old: They've shipped out all the copies, they're not

(continued on next page)

The Writer's Role in Distribution

(continued from preceding page)

reprinting it, and the copies they've shipped out haven't come back, but haven't sold, either. That bind is what messes up author appearances a lot of the time. It's not that the publisher or distributor doesn't have the book. They just don't have enough copies."

But even in this case, given enough time, booksellers may be able to fill the order by going to a number of different sources. "It depends on how important the event is and how well they think your book will sell. If they don't know you from Adam," Mayes says frankly, "I'm not sure they are able to go to extreme lengths to have your book at a conference. Each time they order books and they can't consolidate that order into a larger order, their discount goes down, and the profit on sales goes down. And their profit on sales is very slim to begin with."

Valerie Lewis, co-owner of San Francisco's Hicklebee's Bookstore, agrees. She points out that it can cost more to pay the extra staff hours for doing special orders than the bookseller makes on the books, especially when booksellers are handling books for author appearances and conferences. Lewis takes her role as a community bookseller seriously, and she, like many, believe it's part of her job to make as many books available in the store and at conferences as possible. "But booksellers are also responsible for staying in business. When we carry books that we know won't sell, we're being foolish. It's a very fine line."

She notes that it helps when an author who's speaking at an event communicates with the bookseller. "If the author calls, saying, 'this is the book I'll be mentioning in my talk,' then we know that's the one most likely to sell."

Sometimes it works better to have the publisher call the bookstore. "It's often easier for a publicist to ask about book availability than for an author to do it," says Lewis. "Then the publicist can tell the author that the books will be there."

The bottom line is that both publishers and booksellers want to sell books. Writers who want to influence the distribution process should market their books by doing author appearances. "Work tightly with the publisher," says Lewis. "Have an idea of what kinds of distribution the publisher plans to do, how well the book will be promoted."

"Keep in contact with booksellers you've met and let them know when you have a new book coming out," Mayes suggests. And he goes even further. "It would be a tremendously good idea for authors to join American Booksellers for Children (ABC). Know the names of booksellers around the country who sell children's books. Include them in your promotion efforts. If you're speaking in Madison, Wisconsin, for example, know the names of the booksellers there." To influence book distribution and sales, it's what you know and who you know that will make a difference.

Small Press Distribution

"Small publishers have a very hard time creating a distribution process," says Walter Mayes, co-author of *Valerie and Walter's Best Books for Children; An Opinionated Guide.* For this reason, many small presses and self-publishers use the services of distributors. "These are companies that consolidate the sales, marketing, shipping, billing, invoicing, and returns for a number of small publishers."

This system works well for small publishers for several reasons. First, by hiring a distributor, they get expertise in marketing, accounting, etc. that they may not have on their own. Second, when a number of small publishers join under the umbrella of a distributor, they enter the market with what Mayes calls "critical mass." Chain stores, which usually can't order from individual small presses or self-publishers, can order from distributors. A distributor can then place books with a larger wholesaler. They may have representatives that visit retailers.

"The downside is," says Mayes, "that you are one of maybe 200 publishers the distributor is selling in a list. It's easy to get lost, but it's easy to get lost if you're a small press and you're trying to do it all yourself, too."

Industry Requirements
Partners, based in Michigan, is both a regional wholesaler and a national distributor. They don't carry too many single title children's storybooks in their national distribution program, but they do carry educational material. "We have a full line of teacher-created materials and instructional materials," says Public Relations Manager Barbara Cooper.

Cooper points out that distributors don't work with every publisher who contacts them for representation. "Their books have to go through a review process," she says, "and I probably reject more than I take." She stresses that it would be to the author and publisher's advantage to go into a bookstore and take a look at what's out there. "They need to do their homework before they spend their money to get the book printed. I see so many books that don't meet industry requirements," she says. "They don't have an ISBN number, a price, and a bar code on the cover. The title isn't always on the spine." She would like to see as much energy put into the cover of a self-published book as into the text itself. "The cover is what sells the book," she says. "You have 20 seconds for the customer to pull the book off the shelf. What do you have to convince them to do so? The spine—that's all you have."

Brett Waldmen, Vice President of The Bookmen, a wholesaler based in Minnesota, also works with self-publishers and very small publishers who want their books to be carried by wholesalers. "We wish they would talk to us in the

(continued on next page)

Small Press Distribution

(continued from preceding page)
very beginning stages. They're naturally so excited to get the book out there that they don't know some of the necessities, like creating a bar code or putting an ISBN number on the book. We can help so they're knowledgeable going into it."

Time and a Good Product
Jerri Garretson left her six-year career as Head Children's Librarian for the Manhattan, Kansas, public library in the last year to concentrate on her role as owner-publisher of Ravenstone Press. As a librarian and writer, she was very familiar with industry standards for books. She began her publishing venture in September 1997 with *Johnny Kaw—The Pioneer Spirit of Kansas,* her retelling of a tall tale. Her second book, *Izzie—Growing Up on the Plains in the 1880s,* was originally written by her mother, Marion S. Kundiger. Garretson revised it, redrew the illustrations and added photos.

"It's very hard to get any sort of distribution if you don't have an ISBN number. You need to register as a company with Bowker," the publisher of *Books In Print,* Garretson says. "You need a bar code, the specific type required for books. The book has to follow the proper format, the copyright page should be set up properly. A self-publisher can do all this, but I felt it wasn't worth it for just one book. One ISBN number costs $175; you can get 10 numbers for the same price."

So Garretson founded Ravenstone Press, which will "publish books on Kansas and the Great Plains That's the direction I'm looking at, a niche I believe will work for my company. I'm willing to publish books by other people eventually, but so far I've only done books I've personally worked on." She has several books in various stages of production and is not encouraging submissions at this time. Garretson's books are well designed and meet industry standards and requirements, but she didn't immediately approach distributors. "I have to decide if it will be of help," she says. "If your market is local, there's not much point in being national. As a new small press, you can't attract a distributor; you have no track record."

Garretson believes that in her situation, it's best to start out by hand-selling. She visits bookstores and gift shops and offers the standard 40 percent discount. She also presents programs, sends out advertising flyers, and takes direct mail orders. Her books are currently carried in about 20 retail stores, are listed in the *Book Kansas!* catalogue and with wholesaler Baker & Taylor, and appear on the major book sales websites and the Kansas Originals Market website. Recently, she and her mother promoted *Izzie* in Fergus Falls, Minnesota, where the true story took place. They sold 300 books. "If you have a good product, it works," Garretson says, "but it takes a lot of time."

tionship with its publishers," explains Brett Waldman, Vice President of The Bookmen, a book wholesaler based in Minneapolis. "All books sold go through that distributor and the publisher gives the distributor a significant discount, perhaps 75 percent. The distributor reaches out in a marketing way; they may have reps that go to bookstores. They try to create momentum for the books they represent."

In effect, the distributor performs the role of publisher for the actual publisher. "Sometimes, the negotiation with a company that does distribution includes warehousing, billing, collecting on the bills, handling returns," says Mayes. "It's usually smaller houses that choose to go that way, but I also know some larger publishers that go to a distributor. Sometimes it's more efficient to have a company that is doing distribution handling your product."

Partners is a Michigan-based distribution company. "We represent small publishers who then use Partners to distribute their books," explains Barbara Cooper, Publisher Relations Manager. Like a publisher, they put out catalogues twice a year to be used as sales tools by their reps. These include the entire current list (frontlist) and backlists (books still in print, but not on the current list) of the publishers they represent. They also deal with larger wholesalers as if they were a publisher. "All the titles that we pick up for national distribution are placed with Ingram and with Baker & Taylor," Cooper reports, mentioning two of the largest wholesalers.

A wholesaler, on the other hand, reacts to demand. "We're not creating the momentum for the book," explains Waldman. "We do have some marketing programs, telemarketing, telefax, ads in catalogues, billboards on trucks, but in no way do we think that this takes the place of publisher marketing."

Although wholesalers do create catalogues to let buyers know about the books they stock in their warehouses, they don't focus on selling specific books. "Our main purpose is serving our customers," says Susie Russenberger, Assistant Vice President of Book Products for Ingram Book Company, one of the largest wholesalers in the country. "If we're getting a lot of requests for a book we don't carry, we will research and contact the publisher, but generally we rely on publishers to contact us with information about the books."

The Challenge of Numbers
From the wholesaler's viewpoint, the process begins when the publisher sends them information about books months ahead of the publication date. "We get it into our database," Russenberger explains. "Then the publisher makes a presentation of the titles," and the wholesaler decides what books to carry, and how many copies.

"Ingram is trying to carry everything," says Russenberger. "We wouldn't carry textbooks or nonreturnable items, but we're expanding our inventory, so the question for us is not really which books to carry, but how many copies of a particular book to have on hand." Ingram tries to keep a two-month supply of a title; the tricky question for them is how many copies of a book might sell in a month. "We look at what the author's other books have done," explains Russenberger. "The sales reps help us understand why a particular title might sell more. But generally we have to trust our gut feeling."

For a smaller wholesaler like The Bookmen, decisions about which and how many books to carry is the biggest challenge. They can't carry every book published, but they need to have the ones buyers will want. "Publishing is very risky these days," Waldman admits. "Around 60,000 books are published each year. Think about going into a bookstore: Most of those books might just be spine-out on the shelf," while it's much better for a book's chances if the cover is displayed. "We rely on our experience, history, our sense of the category or genre, and sometimes we look at trends. It's not a perfect science, but fortunately we're right more than we're wrong."

Partners also acts as a regional wholesaler for some publishers. "When we're doing wholesaling, we carry Random House, Penguin, Simon & Schuster, HarperCollins, etc.," explains Cooper. But Partners also carries very small publishers at wholesale. "Their titles are probably regional. They have something to do with one of the states—whether it's a novel with a murder taking place in Ohio or the lighthouses of the Great Lakes, it's region-specific."

Although booksellers and libraries often get a bigger discount on orders they place directly with the publisher, they order from wholesalers because one-stop ordering saves time and money. They also order from wholesalers because they can get the books faster. "If books are available in the warehouse," says Smagler of Simon & Schuster, "we can have the books to them within ten days to two weeks, depending on where they are. We recommend to our stores and libraries to place orders 30 days in advance."

Wholesalers can often get books to the retailer in one or two days. A smaller wholesaler like The Bookmen tends to have a regional clientele, and many of The Bookmen's accounts are in the Midwest. "Bookmen ships the same day," says Waldman. "Orders that are in by one o'clock are guaranteed to ship the same day—all orders are shipped within 24 hours."

Ingram has warehouses in various parts of the country, so they have a national presence, but they tend to ship regionally. "Most publishers have only one warehouse on the east coast," says Rossenberger. "Ingram has two superwarehouses, one in Nashville, and one in Roseburg, Oregon. We also have smaller warehouses in Virginia and Connecticut, as well as in Denver, Ft. Wayne, Indiana, and in southern California. Our turn-around time is very quick."

Just in Time

This fast turn-around has encouraged booksellers to use what's known as just-in-time ordering. Instead of keeping a large inventory of books on hand at the bookstore, they can keep a small inventory on hand and still satisfy their customers' needs because the wholesalers can get books to the bookstore within one or two days.

There are hazards in ordering from wholesalers, however, especially for independent bookstores. "When we started back in 1979-80," says Valerie Lewis, co-owner of Hicklebee's Bookstore in San Francisco, "we weren't aware of the distribution channels. We were going directly to the publisher, and I think that was the best thing we could have done. It gave us a sense of partnership with the publishing houses, rather than feeling once removed from the source."

She also sees a more subtle and insidious problem with dealing only with wholesalers. "The power behind being an independent bookstore is that each one is unique. The more distribution channels I use, the more I'm narrowing down my choices: I'm depending on other people's choices, and I'm becoming a little more 'chain-like.' I worry about independent bookstores that order primarily from distributors and wholesalers; they might miss that little gem that the distributors don't carry. They're yet another step away from being totally different from the other stores around them."

The distribution process is one of those invisible elements of the publishing industry. When it's working properly, neither the writer nor the reader really notices it. When an individual goes to the bookstore or library, the book is there, available for purchase or borrowing. When a writer shows up to speak at a conference, a stack of her books is on the sale table, waiting for participants to buy. But when the process breaks down and the books aren't available, then everyone notices.

Special Sales & Niche Marketing

Reach an Expanding Marketplace

By Kim Childress

Think of bookselling and you may think talk shows, book signings, those cardboard stands called "dumps." Odds are you don't picture cereal, cat food, or potato chips, but, believe it or not, these consumer products all represent special sales and niche marketing opportunities to sell children's books. With a little creative thinking and the right combination of book and placement, special sales can sell hundreds, thousands, even hundreds of thousands of copies in one transaction.

Special sales involve book purchases made outside normal trade and retail stores. They involve a group or business buying a set quantity of books at a discount for resale. The discount may range anywhere from 40 to 75 percent, depending on the number of books and the situation.

"Publishers are willing to give all kinds of breaks," says Susan Salzman Raab, President of Raab Associates, a public relations firm specializing in children's book promotion. "Say a food company was contacted about a children's cookbook, and the company wants their name listed on the book, and asks the publisher to go back to press for X number of copies. That can be done, though it would have to be a very sizeable number; the publisher would consider this when negotiating the price for purchase."

All kinds of deals are cut when it comes to special sales. When successful, they can reach untapped consumers and reap substantial profits. "One of the nice things about special sales is that they reach an audience that may not go into bookstores," says John Kremer, Publisher of Open Horizons and Editor of *Book Marketing Update*. "We probably sell more in the specialty markets than we do through the bookstores," says Lorrie Allen, Vice President of Special Sales for Element Books.

With all the changes in publishing and consolidation in bookselling, authors should think about niche markets where their books may fit. Some common outlets include catalogues, special interest groups, and premiums, but the potential for special sales is limited only by the imagination.

Special Sales Markets
It is important to understand that special sales occur distinctly from the work of regular publicity and marketing de-

partments. A publicity department develops promotional materials, sends out review copies, and sets up signings, tours, and interviews. "Special markets, on the other hand—or at least the special markets group in Penguin Putnam—deal with catalogue, premium and promotional sales, direct marketing, corporate and custom sales, and more," says Melanie Cecka, Editor at Viking Children's Books.

Catalogues

Catalogues are perhaps the most common and successful special sales outlet for children's books. Museum, toy, and gift catalogues are ideal for selling picture books. "We often work with Heartsong, Chinaberry Book Service, Signals, and Seasons," says Christina Figel, Mail Order and Direct Marketing Manager for Random House. "Even adult catalogues occasionally pick up children's books, including American Family Publisher, Reader's Digest and Publishers Clearinghouse."

Many special interest groups, like the National Wildlife Federation put out catalogues that offer children's books among their merchandise. Companies also do expanded gift catalogues for holidays. "If an author goes into a store and sees a catalogue that he thinks his book would fit into, if it would complement the other item, then we'll make the contact," says Allen. "The ideal is to look at catalogues ahead of time and see how your book fits," says Kremer.

Premiums

Another fruitful avenue is premium sales. "Premiums are any ways that corporations or associations might use a book in the normal course of their business," explains Kremer. Books might be given away with membership or for a purchase. Many professionals, like attorneys and therapists, like to give books away to clients. Other companies, like those that sell cereal or food products, offer books for sale for a small payment plus proof of purchase. "Publishers have had success in getting exposure for their books on the backs of cereal boxes," says Robert Lombardi, Director of Special Sales for Harcourt Brace and Company. "But premium sales are challenging because the cost of producing a book is high when compared to the cost of producing other types of children's premiums—small toys or Frisbees for example."

Yet, books have a number of advantages over other types of premiums. They educate, entertain, and are available to suit almost any audience. People tend to keep and cherish books for a long time, and they have a high perceived value while being relatively cheap to purchase. "We always try," says Lombardi. "We're in touch with the big companies, like Nabisco and Proctor & Gamble, and whenever applicable, we mail to all of them."

Special Interest Groups

Special interest groups and associations also use premiums. Working with these groups can provide access to appropriate audiences that would otherwise be unaware of your book, and group members may be especially receptive to offers that are associated with the organization.

Churches, clubs, and other organi-

An Inventory of Sales

Grosset & Dunlap sold more than a million Nancy Drew and Hardy Boys books when they were offered on 20 million boxes of Post Raisin Bran cereal. Meow Mix offered *The Meow Mix Guide to Cat Talk* to people who bought the cat food. The book was customized for Meow Mix by changing the title of Jean Craighead George's *How to Talk to Your Cat*. Random House made its largest single sale in company history to Kellogg cereals. Besides giving away 500,000 copies of Dr. Seuss books to 2,000 schools, Kellogg offered another 1.6 million copies free to kids who returned box tops from four different cereals. General Mills had to come back for three additional orders when it offered books from the First Time series featuring the Berenstain Bears in exchange for two UPC symbols from Kix cereals. Frito-Lay inserted three 20-page mini-books written by R.L. Stein, collectively called the Goosebumps Thrillogy, into 32 million bags of Doritos, Ruffles, and other Frito-Lay chips. Goosebumps also formed partnerships with Taco Bell, Pepsi, Hershey and Pizza Hut. Dorsey Laboratories, in cooperation with Random House, developed a children's book, *The Care Bears Help Chase Colds,* to promote the sale of their Triaminic cold-care products. More than 3,000 Dairy Queen restaurants featured *The Busy World of Richard Scarry* in a summer-long promotion in 1996. Finger puppets featuring book characters were also given away inside of children's meals. James Malinchak, self-publisher of *From College to the Real World,* found that corporations will pay him $3 to $5 per book and then give away copies to students if he speaks on behalf of the corporations at colleges.

Business

zations sell books for fund-raisers. Books might be given away when someone joins the organization, or they may be sold to members as part of a regular catalogue. "We did a book called *Talking to Angels,* by Esther Watson, about a little girl who had an autistic sibling, which we sold to the National Autistic Society," says Lombardi. "They bought the book in bulk from us and distributed it themselves, but we created a special flyer that they included in their mailings. It was a simple black-and-white announcement, above and beyond what we normally do, but we felt the book was so special that it was worth every penny. Two hundred copies of the book sold, and we continue to sell it as a result of making the initial contact."

Many museum stores have also been expanding their children's book sections because patrons are often impulse buyers of picture and gift books. "We did a book called *The Blue Butterfly: A Story About Claude Monet,* by Bijou Le Tord," says Tammy Cabot, Director of Gift Markets for Random House. "I went on the Internet to look up all the museums that the traveling Monet ex-

Expert Advice

"If you or your book have connections with any companies, clubs, or associations, be sure to let your publisher know." *John Kremer, Open Horizons Publishing and* **Book Marketing Update**

"Give anecdotal stories about creation of the book, how you did something, how the illustrations were done, the inspiration behind the writing of the book. I personally enjoy anecdotes because they are part of my sales pitch." *Robert Lombardi, Harcourt Brace*

"Think creatively. Look at your book and think about who could be out there who might be interested, even if it's a stretch. Then go back and develop your ideas. Provide your publisher with the information." *Susan Salzman Raab, Raab Associates*

"Before a book actually goes to press, listen to the recommendations that the sales force makes, such as tips on the cover. The author has influence over that. Everything gets run by the author." *Tammy Cabot, Random House*

"Work closely with the publicity department." *Lorrie Allen, Element Books*

"Think about new ways to reach consumers." *Stephanie Owens Lurie, Simon & Schuster Books for Young Readers*

"Authors should run special sales ideas by editors before approaching the sales department, primarily because publishers are often already exploring the markets authors are suggesting." *Christy Ottaviano, Henry Holt*

---

hibit was going to hit, and that's how I got the sales lead to present the book to those museums. Now we sell about 15,000 copies a year."

Author as Distributor
Your publisher may also be willing to set you up as a distributor. You would then buy your books at an agreed upon discount (50 to 75 percent) and resell them in bulk at a profit. You can take a case of your books with you whenever you speak or visit a new city where you may discover a specialty store that would do well with your book. The publisher benefits from having an expert on the subject selling quantities of books, and you get more money than you would have received through royalties alone. "This tends to be fairly event-driven, but it is a common thing, and we welcome it," says Allen. Lom-

bardi also encourages authors to act as a distributor, and he has worked with some who sell their books very successfully through their own website.

The Internet
The Internet is the tool of the future, and its impact on publishing is still being determined. With billions of companies online and more signing on every day, the Internet offers unforeseen possibilities in special sales, through an author's own website, a specialty store, or an online newsletter. Book buyers are increasingly going to alternative media to find products. Cabot says Random House's online special sales have become so substantial that a new department was created to handle them.

"Authors can use the Internet to do research and identify catalogues and specialty groups that might be interested in carrying their books," says Kremer. For broader titles, many consumers will probably continue to rely on bookstores, but the Internet should be a great help in marketing very niche titles. Plus, the Internet has the potential to reach customers who normally don't go into bookstores. "The sales channels for books are constantly changing," says Stephanie Owens Lurie, Vice President and Editorial Director for Simon & Schuster Books for Young Readers. "All of us need to think about new ways to reach consumers."

From the Internet to the grocery store, special sales are a win-win situation. The more you know about them, the more you help your publisher sell your books. As you sell more books, you receive more exposure, which in turn helps sell even more books. And a higher sales history will help sell future manuscripts (not to mention increase royalties).

Use What You Know to Sell Your Manuscript
When you submit your initial query, manuscript or proposal, mentioning market possibilities shows your professionalism and may prompt editors to take a closer look. Quality of writing and overall story still matter most, however, even if an author has a "guaranteed" advance special sale.

"I'd be fairly skeptical about an author's prepublication assurance of guaranteed sales to a niche market," says Jeannette Larson, Editor at Harcourt Brace. "A trade book often takes several years to produce, and by that time the market and book buyers may have changed. But we love to hear about such contacts once the book is closer to publication."

Kremer believes that authors should propose possible markets in the initial proposal, and Lurie agrees that special sales suggestions could be a hook for the publisher in acquiring the project. But overall, special sales won't make or break a submission.

"First and foremost, the manuscript must be well-written and well-conceived, especially within the context of the marketplace," says Christy Ottaviano, Senior Editor at Henry Holt. "I would only recommend that an author offer special sales markets in a proposal if he has a solid, researched angle that specifically pertains to the project."

Cecka believes, "These days the prospect of an outside sale can be a real

Business

factor in deciding to publish manuscript, but only if the editor is confident that the book shows strong sales potential in more mainstream markets first."

Author and Publisher Together

Because policies vary from house to house, it is important to ask questions and learn how things work so that you are in a position to do as much as you can without stepping on any toes. Find out how special sales are handled by your publisher and what role you will play.

Sales efforts often depend on the size of the house. Larger houses usually have a greater sales force, with departments and individuals who focus on various aspects of special sales. Smaller and medium-sized houses may have fewer people doing more work, which doesn't mean they are less effective, but they may not do as much for all of their titles simply due to lack of manpower. Some publishers brainstorm niche ideas for all their titles, while others work on books with more general interest.

"We select books that we feel most appropriate for our marketplace and put our energy into those," says Figel. Lombardi and Raab consider niche marketing ideas for all the books they handle. "We look at the most straightforward things, like sports organizations for sports books and horse magazines for horse books," says Raab. "We also contact a few other organizations and media to feel around and see if there is any potential for this book beyond the straight publicity. For example, many children's books we've worked with have potential to reach into the New Age market, and that's an area often overlooked."

Regardless of your publisher's policy on the books that receive attention, at most houses authors work through their editors. Authors fill out questionnaires that cover all their marketing ideas, and this is passed through the editor to the appropriate marketing department. Viking, Random House, and Simon & Schuster all prefer that authors work through their editors first although Larson explains that once an author gets approval and a contact with marketing has been made, "then it's common for authors to go directly back to that department with any follow-up ideas."

Figel is not averse to authors contacting her directly, but she says it makes more sense for them to work through their editor or marketing liaison. "That way, editorial, marketing, and publicity all know what's going on."

"Take into consideration the size of the publisher and how it would be if every author contacted us," Cabot agrees. Plus, as Ottaviano and Raab point out, usually the publisher is already exploring the markets authors suggest. "But this shouldn't discourage authors from making contact," Cabot says. "They definitely have the best feel for where their books should be."

Lombardi sees authors as "invaluable tools," and he usually works with them directly. "I'll often call the authors myself and pick their brains, rather than wait for them to make the contact." Raab also encourages authors to make suggestions to the publisher and believes that it is not bad to approach sales personnel in a nonthreatening way with an attitude of cooperation. "It lets a publisher know you're willing to help without going where you shouldn't, and by asking you get a feel for which areas you can cover."

"Publishers may be doing a hundred titles a year," Kremer says. "Realistically, they're not going to be paying that much attention to each book. Authors need to take a proactive role."

A Marketing Guerrilla

Regardless of your primary contact, at some point you will have the chance to pitch your promotional ideas. The idea is to think creatively, before, during, and after the writing of your book.

Let special sales potentials brew in your mind along with your stories. Think about who would be interested in your book besides children, parents, and grandparents. Write down any contacts as you go along, including people and companies who helped with research.

Any time you see or hear of an organization or catalogue that relates to your book, write it down and put it into a file for future reference. If you are a member of any organizations, or if you have specific contacts who might be interested in your book, map this out for your publisher. "If your dad wants copies, give us his name and address," says Lombardi. "Anyone who is interested, we want to know."

In some cases it's more sensible for the author to make a contact. Perhaps in a small place where you have an "in," it would be better for you to send a personal note rather than an informal query from your publisher. But when dealing with organizations like the American Library Association, which gets calls from authors all the time, the publisher should make the contact since they know people there.

Above all else, write from your heart, not for the market. "We just published a book last season called *Tell Me Something Happy Before I Go to Sleep*," says Lombardi. "In addition to having huge success in trade stores, we easily sold 150,000 copies through special sales, and it's still selling. For a children's book, $16 hardcover, that's unusually successful. Buyers just love it. The minute they pick it up and start to read it, they're sold. The story is so strong and wonderful. This is one of the things I look for, that universal story that everyone relates to, something that tugs on your heart strings. Whether it has practical applications in history or language arts doesn't really matter. That would just be an additional selling point."

"Ultimately, I think a manuscript will catch an editor's eye because it will make a really great children's book—not because it could be sold to store Y or catalogue Z," says Cecka. "The fact is that many of the books being published for children today will never sell outside the normal channels, but they still manage to delight plenty of young readers—and that's what it's supposed to be about."

Marketing Resources

1001 Ways to Market Your Books, by John Kremer, Open Horizons, $27.95. An absolutely indispensable resource book that covers all aspects of the publishing industry.

Catalog Sales Directory. Open Horizons, P.O. Box 205, Fairfield, IA 52556. (800) 796-6130, (515) 472-6130. Features more than 500 catalogues known to carry books, $40.00.

American Association of Museums. 1575 I Street, NW, Suite 400, Washington, DC 20005. (202) 289-1818. Mailing lists of museums categorized by type of museum. Call for price information.

An Author's Guide to Children's Book Promotion, by Susan Salzman Raab. Pennsylvania: Raab Associates, 1998. $12.95. An excellent overall guide to the children's book industry.

Book Marketing Update. www.bookmarket.com

Directory of Premium, Incentive & Travel Buyers. R.R. Bowker, P.O. Box 31, New Providence, NJ 07974. (908) 464-6800. www.reedref.com. Lists corporations and premium buyers by name, title, address, phone, and fax.

Encyclopedia of Associations. Gale Research Company, 835 Penobscot Building, Detroit, Michigan 48226. (313) 961-2242. Lists nearly 20,000 associations.

Promo Magazine. 11 River Bend Drive South, P.O. Box 4225, Stamford, CT 06907-0225. (203) 358-9900. www.promomagazine.com. Covers all promotions.

Resources Directory of Mail Order Catalogs. Gray House Publishing, Pocket Knife Square, Lakeville, CT 06039. 860-435-0868. Updated annually, call for current price.

Book Fairs & Clubs
The Right Book in the Right Place
By Joan Broerman

Book fairs and clubs have been part of the school scene for generations. Parents, children, and teachers delight in them: At the fairs, children look at all the selections, make their choices, pay with their own money, and bring home books that day. Brochures of monthly book club offerings give students the wonderful anticipation of the day their chosen books will arrive. Parents are informed about the fairs in advance, and can read through the club brochures with their children. Teachers are pleased with any tools to encourage reading, and the schools also profit from the fairs and clubs. It's win-win-win. What do fairs and clubs do for writers?

Know the Players
Susan Salzman Raab is author of *An Author's Guide to Children's Book Promotion* and the To Market column in the *Bulletin* of the Society of Children's Book Writers and Illustrators (SCBWI), and is President of Raab Associates, a public relations firm specializing in children's book promotion. Raab advises writers to train themselves to ask publishers when a book contract is first drawn up, "How do you see selling a book like this? Could you take it to Scholastic or Troll or other companies that run book clubs or fairs?"

That inquiry, says Raab, "is part of understanding the overall picture" of marketing children's books. The value to writers, she says, is in knowing the possibilities for their books. Fairs and clubs are among the opportunities worth pursuing by an author. While a publisher sees the whole picture for marketing a book, an author knows a work's ins and outs, its nuances, and can provide insight to the publisher. An educated writer who can explain how a book fits a niche or meets an unusual need will be comfortable saying, "I know of this special book club where I think my book could be submitted. May I approach them, or do you prefer to do it?"

Raab advises writers to enter into discussions with a publisher with the intention of learning the promotion plan for their books and determining how to help optimize the books' exposure. Authors should not meddle in areas that are inappropriate, says Raab, but it is perfectly reasonable to bring the publisher informed ideas. It's a matter of figuring out what is useful, and considering the players involved.

If a publisher gives the author a

green light, the next step is to submit the book for possible inclusion in a book fair or club. Some fairs and clubs are open to a writer's direct approach, but one large door is closed to authors and admits only publishers and packagers. That door is marked *Scholastic*.

The Book Fair Elephant

Scholastic has been in the book fair business nearly a quarter of a century and committed to children's education for more than three-quarters of a century. As far as children's book fairs go, Scholastic is the elephant that sits where it wants to. Every year, Scholastic purchases about 2,000 titles from 150 to 160 publishers and packagers, to appear at 80,000 book fairs that reach 40 million students in kindergarten to grade eight. Scholastic's own titles make up only 30 percent of their book fair offerings.

Alan Boyko, Vice President of Product Management for Scholastic Book Fairs, says, "We reach kids in every corner of the country, kids who have never been in a bookstore. We want to help kids find the right books." Scholastic Book Fairs has its own acquisition team within Scholastic, Inc., consisting of 12 to 15 publishing professionals—editors, former librarians, booksellers, bookstore owners, and others—who meet to discuss every book proffered at each book fair. Scholastic sells these new, frontlist books at a fair for about six months and then moves on to other books.

While 80 percent of the books available in bookstores are backlist, 80 percent of the books Scholastic sells at book fairs are frontlist. "We want the newest books in front of children," Boyko says. He enjoys the thought of young readers marching into the school cafeteria, looking over a selection of quality books, and making important purchases with their own money.

A Scholastic fair may also feature a smaller number of titles, such as classics, from the backlist. These are older books still in print that Boyko says Scholastic hopes all children will read when the timing is right for them. The books are a mix of hardcovers and paperbacks and cost the same for the fair customer as for a bookstore patron.

In preparation for a book fair, Scholastic sends a school a promotional kit that includes a video for students and a letter for parents. By the day of the fair, books and authors should be well-known to parents and children. In one video presentation, Dav Pilkey, author of *Captain Underpants* and many other titles, told third graders he had trouble sitting still when he was their age. The young readers understood. The video was Pilkey's opportunity to connect with the kids headed to the book fair, and connect he did. His book became a best-seller, with more than a million copies sold.

A plus for schools is that a book fair run successfully as a fund-raiser can make good money. Scholastic book fair profits for the schools—not Scholastic's profits—have been reported as high as $75 million annually. But Boyko balks somewhat at this aspect of the fairs. "We don't consider ourselves a fund-raiser," he says. "The school must have a reason to have a fair. Do they want each child reading? Teachers can teach skills, but children must read. They must read good books. We find the books we think children will want to read."

Before school ends, Scholastic offers buy-one, get-one-free fairs, which are not fund-raisers. This is one more opportunity to put books in the hands of young readers, who have summer reading time stretching before them.

Cynthia Maloney, Scholastic Book Club Marketing Director, details how a book goes into a Scholastic book club program so that it ultimately makes its way into a child's hands. "Although we see the same books as the book fairs, we operate independently. Additionally, our book club editors are not the same Scholastic editors who buy for our publishing house. Our book club editors, aided by an advisory panel that we consult if we want a reaction to a book before we offer it, make selections and come up with a balance for our customers (teachers, parents, young readers). The editors consider awards lists and reviews and learn every aspect of a publisher's list. The key is child and classroom appeal." Once the selections are made, the deals begin.

Scholastic is not open for solicitations from writers. All deals are between the book club company and publishers, packagers, and agents. "Once deals are struck, the contracts mean that a book will be showcased for 2 months and 20 days." This short-term exposure takes into account that not all the children who are exposed to a book will have been the one to buy it: Friends will trade; a teacher buys a book and keeps it in the classroom. Once a child has held a book, or heard a chapter read by a librarian or teacher, he may want it. The author's audience continues to grow but the newly interested readers will have to go to a library or bookstore to search for a book, when it is no longer a book club selection.

Boyko notes that a book exposed at a fair in a school of average size, about 500 students, and an indeterminable number of parents and grandparents, makes thousands of impressions. Five copies of a given book may be sold at the fair, but the book might be sought out at stores the next day. The author pens another book and readers are waiting. Repeat this scenario in every school hosting a book fair. Boyko sees fairs as a huge opportunity for writers and sellers.

Open To Writers
Another name that figures prominently in school book fairs and clubs is Troll. Julie Scarpa, Director of Market-

ing for Troll Book Fairs, says the company first started conducting fairs in elementary and middle schools in 1958. Over the years, Troll expanded to a full-service children's publishing company that also runs book clubs and fairs.

During the school year, Scarpa says, "Tens of thousands of public and private schools in the United States hold Troll Book Fairs, reaching tens of millions of students, teachers, and parents." Although primary schools, kindergarten to grade six, are the major audience, Troll also holds book fairs in preschools and middle schools.

An acquisitions team consisting of editors and educators meets often to discuss and select new publications for both the fairs and clubs at Troll. Scarpa says new authors, illustrators, and developers who would like to be included in a Troll book fair or book club are encouraged to send materials to Elise Daily, Troll Communications, 100 Corporate Drive, Mahwah, NJ 07430. "If they are considered appropriate for our children's market, the books will be reviewed and discussed at editorial meetings and perhaps selected for inclusions in fairs and/or clubs."

Troll's services to schools that host fairs begin long before the book tables are set up for business. From the first phone call to the pick up of any remaining books, the school librarian or PTA/PTO volunteers running the fair are assured of help. Fair representatives help them pick the best dates, work to customize the selection of titles appropriate for the school, and make a point of being available to answer any questions before, during, and after the fair.

Troll does not send representatives to each fair, however. The librarian or volunteer is completely responsible for organizing and conducting the fair in each school. Troll invites book fair organizers and school librarians to "Preview Parties" with displays of an actual book fair, to give firsthand looks at a fair in action. Troll also uses telemarketing and sends independent representatives to visit schools. Four weeks before the fair, a complete planning kit is mailed to the fair organizer. The kit includes promotional materials, ideas for increasing sales, and how-tos for involving the whole community and ensuring that the fair runs smoothly. The books are delivered three-to-five days before the fair dates and the drivers even help set up the displays.

Although some schools are in session year-round, most still take a summer break. Book clubs do not. Web pages for both Scholastic and Troll keep teachers and students aware of the books and interactive materials available for summertime as well as school time. Just as clubs are categorized by age group and special interests, summer activities offer packages geared to the same groups.

Not Just for Schools Anymore

Books Are Fun (BAF), the largest direct marketer of books in North America, took the idea of school book fairs into the workplace in 1988. BAF holds more than 20,000 fairs each year in companies of at least 100 employees. In 1998, the company grossed $70 million for school book fairs, $70 million for corporate book fairs, and $20 million in their newest market, day care centers.

At corporations, the purchasers are

Librarians as the Link

If book fairs and book clubs have strong support from school librarians, the likelihood is that these programs will continue to put books in the hands of children and funds in the school coffers. Kate Vogel is the librarian at Inverness Elementary School in Shelby County, Alabama. Her children call her "The Library Goddess" and their essays won a prize for the school when *Child Times*, a local parenting publication asked kids to tell them, "What's Cool at the Library?"

Every year, Vogel runs a successful book fair. The most recent one netted $6,000 for four days' work, including one thousand dollars in free books for the teachers and $500 in bonus points. The classes in her school also participate in many book clubs.

Scholastic and Troll have clubs for each age group as well as for special interests. While book fairs take place once or twice a year, clubs are a monthly or quarterly opportunity for young readers to make book selections. Vogel says the teachers like the bonus points and prizes they can earn from the clubs because this helps them build a classroom library or place books in the hands of children who cannot afford them.

While some schools may use their book fair profits for computer games and software, Vogel spends her book fair profits on books. "I don't think a computer program will ever change a child's life the way a book will." To librarians like Vogel, book fairs and book clubs are an important way to introduce children to books and authors.

---

primarily women—70 to 80 percent—and BAF market studies confirm that women are far and away the major buyers of children's books. Consequently, BAF prefers to approach companies with large numbers of women employees. To set up the fairs, BAF representatives contact human resource departments and present the idea as an employee benefit. United Way has also worked with BAF in conjunction with fund-raising. Many fairs result from referrals and networking.

At a recent BAF fair, Arkansas BAF representative Bill Meers set up 350 titles in a company cafeteria, 50 percent of them children's items, including educational materials. BAF makes it possible for workers to pop into a fair during a break, hold children's books in their hands, and buy them. "We're selling lots of books," Meers says. BAF has recently expanded into day care centers. Now, every six weeks, more than 85,000 schools and day care centers in North America put on a Books Are Fun book fair.

BAF had tested a signature program that would bring authors to the fairs to sign their books. Author Darcy Pattison participated in the test, signing copies of her book, *The River Dragon*. She liked the exposure, but reveals that writers

Customized Clubs

Book clubs are targeted to fit particular interests and age groups. The lists below indicate how Scholastic and Troll target their marketing in this way.

Scholastic Clubs
   Age-based clubs
      Firefly (Preschool)
      SeeSaw (Grades K & 1)
      Lucky (Grades 2 & 3)
      Arrow (Grades 4, 5, and 6)
      TAB (Grades 7 and Up)
      Spanish/English Club (PreK-5)

Accessing the web page also gives readers the option of browsing books by category such as award winners, favorite authors, illustrators, and characters, holiday/seasonal, nonfiction/reference, and science/math/nature.
    Scholastic web page: www.scholastic.com/bookclubs

Troll Clubs
   Troll has book clubs designed for age groups:
   Preschool to kindergarten
   Kindergarten to grade one
   Grades two and three
   Grades four to six
   Grades six to nine

   Troll web page: www.troll.com/bookclub

---

made less money from sales because BAF buys books in bulk and gives deep discounts to its fair customers. An author signing in a bookstore reaps the rewards of full-price sales.

Logistics caused BAF to discontinue the signature program, but Tim Hildebrandt, Vice President of Corporate Book Fairs at BAF, responds to Pattison's view: "It is difficult for a new author to get exposure. No, they won't make much money at a BAF fair, but word of mouth is very important. Fairs give authors tremendous exposure. Books get out there. People read them, get interested, and go to bookstores to buy them."

A writer who wishes to have books test-marketed by BAF should send a copy of the book and a short biographical sketch to Buying Department, BAF, 123 N. Main, Fairfield, IA 52556. BAF will look at the book and may buy 200 copies, which it will test at a fair. If the book sells well, BAF may buy another 250 and could place an order in six to nine months. The order could be as high as 30,000 to 100,000 books. While an author might salivate over that prospect, Pattison points out that authors need to consider the difference in potential profits of high volume sales at deep discounts versus fewer sales at regular royalties.

For authors who make frequent personal appearances, the high volume sales may leave the author with no books to sell when speaking at schools or conferences, especially if no additional printruns are planned, thus sending the book out-of-print.

A Club with a Twist

Traditional book clubs feature new books, whether from a front or a backlist. Harriet Logan, owner of Loganberry Books in Cleveland, Ohio, has combined old books with new technology and created a unique book club. Loganberry Book Clubs feature used books that may be hard to find titles or books out-of-print. Logan's work can extend the life of a title that has already been around the traditional book fairs and book clubs.

Logan says she buys her inventory mainly at auctions and library and book sales. Eighty percent of the selections that go to her club members are from the pool she has created, customized for the individual. Her web page gives new life to old titles and simplifies choosing books for young readers (www.logan.com/ loganberry).

Logan's interesting approach highlights the ultimate purpose of book clubs and fairs: Even if a young reader does not buy a book at a fair or through a book club, a friend may. Later, the two might trade books or ask their parents to take them to the library or bookstore to search for an author they discovered at a fair or through a club. Every time a young reader holds a book and looks at the cover, an author's name becomes more familiar, and that is the author's goal on every level, from pure literature to the child's learning to the writer's career. Book fairs and book clubs are important tools in getting the right book to the right reader for all the right reasons.

Summary Thoughts

For a reader, the difference between buying a book at a fair or through a club and buying it at the bookstore comes down simply to a trip to the store. The writer has other differences to consider. If a book is sold through a club or at a fair, the income per book is probably lower. But these sales might not have taken place at all otherwise. The more books sold, obviously, the greater the total income even if some of the sales return less to the author. Book fairs and clubs also provide authors with wide and very immediate—straight to the child—exposure.

Career Concerns

Insurance for Freelancers

By Veda Boyd Jones

On December 12, 1989, the Berlin Wall had come down, the Soviet Union was dying, and greeting card illustrator Cheryl Harness quit her day job. It was not an easy decision, but resenting her "employer buying the right to waste the creamy middle of my waking-working hours," and discontent with promotions of people other than herself, gave her the incentive to strike out on her own. Having already illustrated seven books and written and illustrated one of her own, Harness set out to make it as an author/illustrator. Now some 15 books later, including the well-received *Ghosts of the 20th Century* from Simon & Schuster, Harness has no regrets, even though "when you're self-employed, the hours are longer and your boss is tougher."

Did she consider the high cost of health insurance before she quit her day job? No, but it quickly became an issue. Harness knew a serious illness or injury could financially devastate her, so she had to find an insurance carrier. She discovered she could extend her group insurance coverage for a limited time. Employers with 20 or more employees are required by the Consolidated Omnibus Budget Reconciliation Act (COBRA) to make coverage available for 18 months. The former employee is responsible for the entire cost of the policy. Coverage is available longer if there are other factors (disability, death of a spouse, divorce). This window of opportunity allows a former employee to find another job with insurance benefits or make arrangements for an individual policy.

Through a recommendation from a friend, Harness contacted a Mutual of Omaha agent and obtained a major medical policy. It offered no disability or dental plan, but "it came in very handy when I required major surgery."

Jim Nolan, First Vice President of Public Affairs at Mutual of Omaha, says that a variety of factors, such as age, gender, tobacco use, general health status, location, and type of coverage, determine the rate for an individual policy. Because there are so many variables, it is impossible to give a rate that would apply to all writers across the nation, but he calculated a typical rate. For a female, age 45, nonsmoker, in good health, and located in Joplin, Missouri, the monthly rate would be $128. That individual policy has a

A Special Vocabulary

- **Coinsurance or copayments:** the amount you pay on a claim after you've paid the annual deductible. Fairly standard is 80/20, with the insurance company paying 80 percent and the insured paying 20 percent.
- **Deductible:** a fixed annual amount that you must pay on medical bills before the insurance company will pay a benefit.
- **Drug Card:** a special benefit that pays a certain amount for prescription drugs.
- **Health Maintenance Organization (HMO):** an organization that provides health care services for subscribing members in a particular geographic area. A primary care physician decides whether a patient needs to see a specialist.
- **Preferred Provider Organization (PPO):** a group of hospitals and physicians that makes a contract with insurers to provide comprehensive health care services at discounted fees.

$2,500 deductible, a prescription drug card that sets the price for generic medicine at $10 and for name brands at $20, 100 percent coinsurance, and a pre-existing condition clause that would exclude for one year any condition treated in the six months prior to the insurance policy taking effect.

Case Studies

Freelance writer Gary Blackwood, whose award-winning middle-grade novel *The Shakespeare Stealer* (Dutton) is among his many books, went for years without insurance and was lucky that he had no major illness. But then one day, "after a very minor health problem that resulted in a small procedure to the tune of $2,000, my eyes were opened to the high cost of health care." He and his wife started looking for health coverage and found it at a most unlikely place.

Posted on a bulletin board at a local discount store was an advertisement for Americans for Financial Security, an association of self-employed people who wanted group status for an insurance rating. Although a membership fee is required to join, it is included in Mega Life and Health's monthly premium of $212 for Blackwood and his wife, who live in Missouri. They fall into the lower-50 age group and have a deductible of $2,500 a person each year. If they use doctors on the insurance plan's in-network list, the Blackwoods pay 20 percent coinsurance on any charges after their deductible is met. If they use doctors not on the list, they pay 50 percent coinsurance on each claim. This plan does not have a drug card.

Diana West, a freelance writer for adult and children's magazines, serves as a reservist with the Federal Emergency Management Agency (FEMA). When called for an emergency, she packs her bag, but when not working a disaster, she's a writer.

Since she works intermittently for the government, West doesn't receive federal benefits. Another FEMA employee told her about the *Christian Brotherhood Newsletter,* whose members share each other's burdens. Although not an insurance company, the newsletter operates like one. For $100 annually, West is a member. Once a month for 11 months, she is sent a card about another member who has a need, and she sends $100 to that person. If she has an *incident* (an illness or hospitalization), she pays the first $200 then sends her itemized bills to the newsletter. The total bill is published, meaning it's divided up and sent to other members, who send their dollars directly to Diana, who is responsible for paying her own medical bills. Each incident is limited to $125,000. The Brother's Keeper program ups that amount by $100,000 for an additional donation.

Levels of monthly voluntary giving ($100, $50, and $25) dictate medical coverage. Factors such as age, gender, and location—important since Midwestern and New York hospitals usually don't charge the same amounts—don't affect the monthly donations, although there is a standard pre-existing conditions clause. "I know it sounds unusual," West says, "but it works." She has had no complaints about the payments, which are called *gifts*, she has received when she has sent in her incident bills.

As a single parent, romance writer Lois Kleinsasser (aka Cait Logan and Cait London) was meticulous about arranging her freelance career before she quit her good-paying day job with the government. She didn't decide to stop everything and take the leap; she planned for it. "I did not want to lie on my deathbed wishing that I had tried for a career that I loved." She also didn't want to be in a financial bind.

When she made the leap, Kleinsasser was debt-free and had multibook contracts from two different publishers, but insurance was still a huge consideration. "I started hunting and comparing policies, and nothing could beat my government policy or price. I knew I would be paying lots more for much less."

Although hesitant to endorse a certain insurance company, Kleinsasser found a major medical policy that worked for her. She supplemented this coverage with a separate cancer policy, since cancer runs in her family. She also chose a bank that offered an accidental death and dismemberment policy at a minimum charge. She advises writers to "ask if good health will get you a discount on the premium. Also see if there's a small life insurance policy that comes with the health insurance."

Research Your Options
We're writers, and writers research before they begin a project, whether fiction or nonfiction. We must research this insurance area of our lives just as carefully. With so many health insurance policies on the market—

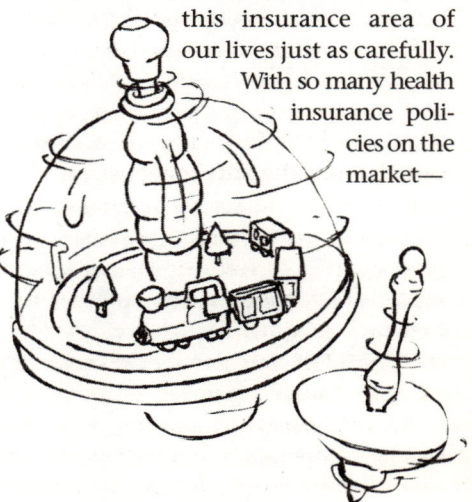

those that dictate which doctors can be used, those that pay only a set dollar amount, those that require high coinsurance payments—you must learn which one best fits your needs. Even after you find the one for you, check around at renewal time. State and federal regulations change periodically, and new laws could mean a better policy is available at a lower cost.

Independent insurance agent Bill Hinman, who represents several insurance companies, says health coverage isn't a cut-and-dried issue.

"Ask a question about insurance coverage and rates, then give me any set of circumstances, and my answer will be different," says Hinman. He warns writers to ask companies for a definition of pre-existing conditions and to list every condition on application forms. He advises writers to learn the difference in a major medical policy that pays a "usual, customary, and reasonable" fee for procedures and a hospital/surgical policy that lists how much the company pays for each medical procedure. Many times, the premium is small for the latter policy, but the coverage is also small. "A benefit of $1,600 just isn't going to cover brain surgery."

There are two ways for a freelance writer, who isn't covered under an employer's or spouse's insurance, to obtain health insurance—an individual policy or a group policy through an association or organization.

An Individual Policy

The insurance commissioner of each state maintains a list of insurance companies and managed care plans (see sidebar on page 178 for definitions of HMOs and PPOs) that are licensed in that state to offer medical coverage for individuals. Obtain that list, and then visit the public library. Several rating services (such as Standard & Poor's and Weiss Research) rank insurance companies for consumers, but the volume most libraries own is *Best's Key Rating Guide* by A.M. Best Company.

Although rankings are not the final word on an insurance company, a writer should pay heed to the financial health of insurance companies. Check Internet websites for insurance companies that interest you, and become familiar with the types of coverage they offer. The site www.insweb.com answers frequently asked questions about health insurance and gives rates from several companies. It includes a comprehensive glossary of insurance terms.

Make your own list of top insurance companies, and then call agents and request a quote. Ask questions. Compare rates and coverage. Take notes, make a chart—whatever works best for you—but be thorough.

Many companies that offer policies to individuals won't touch writers with severe pre-existing conditions such as diabetes, kidney disease, previous cancer, and heart conditions. Most states operate a high-risk pool, however, that allows people with these conditions to obtain coverage, but at a very high cost.

Group Coverage

If you belong to an association or organization that offers a group plan, send off for information about the company that insures the group. Many times, a group can obtain rates lower than those for individual policies, but that's not always so, and certain plans for groups may not be available in all states. When investigating these insurance companies and plans, be sure to find out what happens to the insured if the group disbands.

Several writers' groups make group insurance available to members:

■ *Society of Children's Book Writers and Illustrators* offers group major medical insurance to writers in most states through Manufacturers Life Insurance Company. All writers may join the Society of Children's Book Writers and Illustrators (SCBWI), whether published or not, for a $50 annual membership and one-time $10 initiation fee.

■ *National Writers Union* members may be covered by Aetna/US Healthcare Quality Point-of-Service Health Plan. Payment of benefits differs if a patient uses a doctor in the plan's network or one outside the network. Published writers and those who have not sold their work, but are actively seeking to, are eligible for membership in the National Writers Union. Annual dues are based on writing income, starting at $90 for income under $5,000 a year.

■ The *Authors Guild* is an association of published authors with dues of $90 for the first year, and based on writing income in subsequent years. The Guild offers a major medical plan from Manufacturers Life Insurance Company.

Don't forget to look at organizations you belong to that are not writing related. These might include:

■ The *American Association of Retired Persons* (AARP) offers basic and special health insurance such as cancer policies and supplemental Medicare policies.

■ *The American Association of University Women* (AAUW) also makes group rates available to members.

■ Many college alumni associations offer group insurance.

The federal government realizes health insurance is expensive and wants to make it more affordable to the 10 million self-employed people who currently have no coverage. In the tax year 1999, the self-employed may exempt 60 percent of health insurance premiums from income tax. By the year 2003, all of the premiums can be deducted from gross income and not be taxed.

A thorough search for health insurance is worth your effort. You'll find the coverage that suits your needs and at the best price available. Mutual of Omaha's Jim Nolan offers this advice to freelancers: "Explore your options. Look at two or three association group plans, not just one. Talk to agents about individual policies. They have a vast wealth of expertise and can guide you through the process and tell you what has worked for others in your situation. Do the research, just as you would if you were reporting a story, and make an informed decision."

Agents

Forecast: Sunny, a Few Clouds on the Horizon

By Elaine Marie Alphin

"Children's book sales are up and should increase over the next five years," reports literary agent Andrea Brown. "Baby boomers are buying books for their kids, and schools and librarians have gotten some of the funding issues straightened out and are buying. The mood in publishing is more optimistic than it's been for the last three or four years."

It is essential for agents like Brown to keep up with changes in the children's publishing industry, to serve their clients. Agents meet with editors, review the books in the field, and scout for new works. As a result, they can offer special insight into what's being published in the early years of the millennium and into just how welcoming the publishing climate is for writers.

Writers will be happy to hear what many have to say: That climate is "extremely healthy," pronounces Ruth Cohen, who heads her own agency. Amy Berkower, of Writers House in New York, broadens the perspective even more: "The culture seems very vested in children reading."

"I'm optimistic," says Ginger Knowlton of Curtis Brown, "I've been in the business for 13 years, and every year it just keeps getting better, even though I'm told this has been the worst 10-year period in a long time."

Yet another agent, whose firm wished not to be identified, says, "We're reading so much in trade magazines predicting positive sales, and seeing children's titles on the *New York Times* best-seller list. It was a down market in 1993 when I started in the industry, so it's great to see it on an upswing now."

Not every agent sees completely sunny days ahead for children's publishing. "I think it's somewhat cloudy on the horizon," says Barbara Kouts. "I do believe quality will come through. I stand for that, and that's why I'm in the business, but it gets more difficult every day." Explanations for both outlooks come from the growing megacorporations that publish children's books.

Big Brother Is Publishing

"Children's publishing is much more of a gentleman's business than adult publishing," says Steve Malk, of Writers House in California, "but there's no doubt that publishing has changed over the years. Some editors today have become very market-driven, and these

Not Your Same Old Age Groups

"In the past, the market was defined by age group," says agent Amy Berkower. "Main characters had to be about the same age as readers, and adults didn't have major roles. Now that's opening up: The canvas has enlarged and authors have an opportunity to explore relationships between kids and adults in a new way. The Junie B. Jones books are good examples of a series that broke all the rules. The main character is in kindergarten, yet the books are written for second grade. When the publisher learned that [author] Barbara Park had broken the sacred rule, she was tempted to cancel the series, but didn't because of the editor's enthusiasm and the author's stature. It turned out that kids love 'reading down' about this particular character. The series includes more than a dozen books so far, and the latest one made the best-seller list."

"One thing I hear often from my clients is that they want to do board books," says one agent, whose agency wishes her to remain unnamed, "but most board books are reissues of classics, so there's no market for new books there at all."

Other age groups are changing also. "Editors are really looking for fun middle-grade books, and by that I mean both single titles and series for third and fourth graders," says agent Ginger Knowlton. "There's a great demand for chapter books," says agent Barbara Kouts, "because the children who read picture books are growing up. But chapter books are hard to write. Too many of them tend to be dull and flat." The unnamed agent says, "It's tough to find good middle-grade writers, because these books are so short. Everything has to happen in 64 pages, but you have to have a whole story—character, action, humor and you may also have spot illustrations."

Sound young for middle graders? The middle-grade category has broadened to include chapter books, and even adolescent books that used to be categorized
(continued on next page)

---

huge corporations have to be profitable. You have to wonder if some day in the future, books are going to become homogenized because there are so few publishing corporations, all doing the same thing, all courting the same market." He hastens to add, "I don't think so, but it's a scary thought."

As small publishers are purchased by larger publishers, and then large publishers merge to form megacorporations, the process of acquiring and promoting books has evolved from the days when editors published books they liked without challenge. "Instead of just saying they'll take it, especially the story for a picture book," says Kouts, "editors have to find an illustrator first, and then present the complete package." Brown has seen similar changes. "If a book wasn't perfect," she says, "if the ending needed rewriting

Not Your Same Old Age Groups

(continued from preceding page)
with young adult titles. "I think there are more award opportunities for middle-grade books," says the unnamed agent, "so for manuscripts I might think are YA, I'll do a contract but call it middle-grade."

But true young adult novels haven't completely disappeared. "It's always been that awards focus on middle grade, but YA focus is increasing," says Kouts. The Young Adult Library Association (YALSA) "is going to have a YA award, the Printz Award, and the National Book Award has focused attention on YA books. YA was just dead a few years ago, but it's coming alive again. Now editors are actively asking for it: 'Send me a great YA!' Libraries are making more effort. They're setting up special rooms to draw teens in."

"To write for this group it's important to keep in touch with the culture," says the unnamed agent. "Writers could watch MTV, or go to the library and watch teens. If they have teen relatives, really listen to them—not slang that will become dated, but the teen voice that will keep the dialogue ringing true. Some of them can talk really fast, for instance. Listen to the way they're expressing their feelings—is it in a subtle way, or is it right out there?"

Berkower says, "YA needs to be reinvented from the ground up—beginning with what the genre is called. The phrase 'young adult' simply doesn't work anymore. New lines are being created by a number of YA publishers with a fresh look designed to appeal to a visually sophisticated generation. They're also working with retailers to find new ways to display these books—as far away from board books as possible—as well as figuring out ways to cross-promote books on the Internet and with other popular teen products such as clothes. Though YA as a market has been in trouble for a long time, it's promising to see publishers begin to find new and creative ways to reach this growing audience."

---

or something, it used to be they'd work with the writer to polish it, but not anymore. They just won't buy it."

Knowlton recalls, "One Harper-Collins editor loved a picture book, but other people didn't share her vision. Because they'd just acquired Morrow, with its strong picture book list, they chose not to make an offer on the picture book from an author who was new to Harper, even with 20 books to her credit. They wanted only stellar manuscripts from best-selling authors."

"We're hoping the shrinking market won't translate into shrinking possibilities," says the anonymous agent source. "In the end, though, we're still selling to an individual editor." The catch is that individual editors don't have as much power as they used to. "Tried and true editors can get behind a book and say, 'Yes, you must publish this,'"

Recreating Nonfiction

One of the genres agents are selling is creative nonfiction. "Now editors want to involve the kids in a story," says Andrea Brown, "then the kids learn the facts through the story." Barbara Kouts says, "You can't do the same old thing. It has to be something very different, or else the books don't sell. Editors are looking for more diary series, but it will glut soon because everybody is jumping on the Scholastic Dear America bandwagon. But kids love the books, and teachers can use them in the classroom."

According to Amy Berkower, "There used to be a rule that you couldn't mix fact and fiction. Then *The Magic School Bus* was published. Its success paved the way for a new breed of book that does both. In the adult market we've seen the tremendous success of *Midnight in the Garden of Good and Evil* and *The Perfect Storm,* a kind of narrative nonfiction, which I think could also work well in the children's book market."

Berkower recalls, "Doris Orgel had been writing novels based on mythological figures that were well-reviewed but just weren't selling well, so we put our heads together and came up with *We Goddesses*—beautifully illustrated creative nonfiction written as three autobiographies of those mythological figures." Brown has had a similar experience. "I sold a creative nonfiction book by Ginger Howard that was a good story, but also taught kids about a specific historical time, and taught them how to build a house out of clay and water, so it worked on three levels. It sold right away, and the editor wanted Howard's next two books."

Knowlton says. "But there are also young editors who have to go through committee. And on top of the whole structure is the big publisher asking: What's the bottom line? What's going to make us money?"

Marketing Reality

According to Kouts, "An editor likes a book and takes it before the board, but marketing people can say 'No, that won't sell' or 'We've tried something like that before, and it didn't sell' and the book is rejected. That really bothers me, because the editors' judgment should be the bottom line. Editors know what's a good novel, and it's important that good novels be published even if they don't sell well."

Cohen sees the acquisitions process a little differently. "Editors have to produce successful books that have to sell in certain quantities because their salaries, their reputation, their longevity depends on it. But very rarely will they tell me that marketing doesn't like it—in adult publishing, yes, but not in children's publishing. I tell an editor: It's a good book and I think you should read it and it should have a place on your list. Most every editor will read it very quickly. I've sold a book in three days because I knew it was a good book and the editor knew it was a good book. Neither of us knows if it will sell a million copies, but that's not important."

To some publishers, the numbers are particularly important, both in the form of sales history and predictions. "With writers who have been published before," Kouts explains, "the editor wants to know the sales figures on previous books, and that gets pumped into the meeting. If previous sales were good—great. But this hurts midlist writers."

Some agents don't see the changes brought about by megacorporations as all bad. "You may see that these conglomerates will create more efficient companies and more profitable businesses," points out Berkower. "Perhaps if publishers are fiscally stronger, they'll take more risks. With fewer publishers, it's more important than it was before to find an editor who has a vision and a plan for promoting the author and the book." Brown sees this happening already. "Publishers have cut their lists. Those that used to publish 40 books now only publish 25. But they're paying higher advances and putting more money and effort into promoting each book so they can see a better return on their investment."

Malk believes that ensuring that publishers properly promote titles is a major part of an agent's job. "You have to do everything in your power to get the book out there so people can see it and buy it," he says. Big corporations understand promotion in a big way. Malk wonders, "If Scholastic hadn't been so behind [J.K. Rowling's] *Harry Potter* and there hadn't been all this buzz, who knows if it would have done as well? It's a fabulous book, but who knows?"

Hot Sales Prospects

The question of which books will sell well and which will fail plagues writers who try to market their own books. Agents are in a better position to know what editors think is hot, and what's frozen over.

"I hear the same line from everybody about picture books," says the agent who didn't wish to be identified. "Not text-heavy, lots of humor and action, and definitely not quiet. Too many quiet books got published, and the market was saturated. Editors are very into picture books for toddlers. This is based on recent scientific studies that the younger you read to children, the faster they learn. I'm getting manuscripts of five to six pages, and that's way too much! Three or four pages, or even two or three pages will sell much better." But can writers always trust what editors say?

According to Knowlton, "Editors have told me they want sweet, short texts, like *Guess How Much I Love You* from Candlewick. But then I send them a book like that, and they say 'No, it's too simple; there's not enough text!' I used to sell more picture books, but now I'm selling more middle-grade books, and many of the picture books I do sell tend to be long and literary or poetry." Brown finds that the picture books she's selling are "quirky—books that are sort of out there, a little weird, but not too weird! Rhyme is back, but editors are looking for interesting wordplay that rhymes. If someone comes along with a great folktale, forget it! There's just a glut because so many of them were published."

Malk agrees. "It's a copycat industry," he explains. "You're certainly going to see a lot of fantasy in the wake of *Harry Potter*. But too many will get published. After the success of *The True Story of the Three Little Pigs,* which is a wonderful book, everyone wanted to publish retold fairy tales, but too many of them got published and some weren't any good. Now, there's a backlash. If I have a retold fairy tale that is very good, it's hard to sell. I try not to be influenced by trends. I represent books that I love. It doesn't matter if it's coming out this fall or 10 years ago or 20 years in the future. Good work will always sell." *The True Story of the Three Little Pigs* was written by Jon Scieczka and illustrated by Lane Smith.

Cohen works the same way. "I don't think it matters what the year is," she says. "Editors look for strong characterization. They want books that are people-driven. Kids want to read about characters and like them or dislike them. I think the whole *Harry Potter* thing is a good example of that: Readers care about Harry." She adds, "When the parent reads to the child or the child reads to himself, they should feel they just have to talk about it. Good fiction must be integrated with your mind and your heart."

"Editors don't want just a sweet little novel," says Brown. "Books must deal with characterization and issues. Editors want more literary fiction. They want to see characters grow in the book, and learn something fresh and interesting."

Willing to Grow and Change

Fresh seems to be the key to what publishers want. "Editors are looking for a distinctive voice," says Berkower. "They want books with strong emotional impact, books that are edgy and fresh."

"I know authors who have gotten contracts in the past, and now they're writing the same good books and they're getting kind letters, but not contracts," says Knowlton.

Brown points out, "You have to give editors what they want. Writers have to be versatile and willing to try new things. There are some writers who, after they've published 25 or 30 books, are resistant to change. They're good writers, but they're totally clueless, isolated at their computer desk, still writing the same old things. Not everyone can write a certain type of book, of course, but you can try."

Berkower agrees. "If I see no growth from one book to the next, or if sales go down, I say let's look at the picture here. Let's see if you can correct this. I approach it as a matter of managing their career. Some writers are not receptive, of course. It's totally their choice. But I see it as my job to advise them."

Malk sees his job as more a matter of matching the quality books he believes in with the right editor. "I come from a different place than others do, because my background is different," he explains. "My mother owns an independent children's bookstore and I worked there for seven years, interacting with customers. It was all hand-

Alternatives in an Electronic World

Ginger Knowlton proposes an unusual reaction to changes brought about by demanding megacorporations and new technology. "I think more authors will self-publish," she says. "Many publishers want all rights, especially if you don't have an agent and, generally, publisher contracts are becoming increasingly unfair to authors. Because of technology, authors can print their own books. They can publish, and promote and sell them through their website—anyone can have one. Based on orders, the author could print just four or five copies, as needed. I can even see a bunch of authors banding together and hiring a distributor and selling that way."

Self-publishing has increased in the adult market, with good success. "Look at some of the best-sellers that started out as self-published books or as small press titles," Knowlton points out. "The authors got exposure, and their books were promoted by Oprah or whatever, and then the book just took off and was picked up by a big publisher. There's no reason this can't happen in children's publishing as well."

selling, and I got a really good sense of what people want, what they would like. Now I think I have a really good sense of what editors will like." He laughs. "I guess I'm noted for being really, really enthusiastic about stuff I represent! It probably annoys some editors, but you have to be really passionate. If it doesn't sell right away, you don't want to lose your enthusiasm. If a book speaks to me, if it has a really good voice, I'm going to find a place for it."

Brave, New, and Electronic

With the introduction of electronic books, or e-books, the face of publishing may be changing as dramatically as it did when the printing press made monastic scriptoriums obsolete. Agents are scrambling to deal with the implications of this new technology.

"I think it's affecting the entire business and the entire publishing world," says Cohen. "We have to be sure we try to put into the contract words or phrases that keep most of the e-rights available to the writer, but that's not always possible. Some publishers won't change e-rights percentages at all." Knowlton agrees. "It's been a bear as far as contracts are concerned. How can we determine a fair royalty when we don't know how much money we're talking about?" Kouts complains, "So far, publishers have been really hardnosed about what they'll give you on electronic rights. They say: 'We don't know what's going to happen, so we insist on a 50/50 split.'"

Berkower comments, "I'd prefer to make deals based on term of license rather than copyright, as is sometimes done in Europe. I've seen a few British contracts that take the uncertainty of these new markets into account and offer the author a chance to renegotiate if market conditions become more favorable. Most American publishers haven't offered authors this opportunity, and are therefore making it very difficult for authors and agents to feel good about signing contracts these days."

Writers are also concerned that their books may never go out of print (and their rights never revert to them) if publishers can download even a single electronic copy in a year, and claim the book is still in print. Malk says, "In out-of-print clauses, I try to limit it to when a standard U.S. print edition is not available anywhere, so that doesn't include single online titles. We're trying to protect our clients, but we're just not sure how the whole thing is going to shake down."

"I tend to be optimistic," says Berkower. "You can market film products through television, movies, DVD, and video and it hasn't hurt the film industry any. I don't think e-books will necessarily hurt print books." Berkower points out that it all may be a fuss over nothing. "When CD-ROMs came out, we spent a lot of time fighting over these rights. It ended up being a huge waste of time since the market never matured." She pauses, then admits, "But I think electronic rights are going to be more consequential."

Will e-books replace print books, however? "There will always be children's print books," says Knowlton confidently. "Children will always want cuddle time, and you can't cuddle up to a piece of machinery." Kouts isn't so sure. "Electronic publishing goes against my sensibilities," she admits, "but people always want something fast and quick, so I can see it succeeding."

Brown has a more immediate answer. "I just met with the people who do Rocket Books," the big electronic book publisher who launched a year or so ago. "They'd love to do children's books, but they can't—they can't do color yet!" she announces triumphantly. "So it won't affect any of us for a few years. First will be novels for teens, probably science fiction, the sort of stuff kids on computers like to read. As it spreads to the rest of children's publishing, in some ways it will help authors. It will be a new market for them, especially for books that have gone out of print. This won't happen for 10 or 15 years, but when you can get 20 books on a disk for the price of a hardcover, well, it's inevitable." Brown pauses, then adds, "This generation's kids probably won't see paper books."

Knowlton isn't certain. "Lewis Carroll's *Alice in Wonderland* is one of the premier e-books, since it doesn't need color, just those black-and-white illustrations. Frankly," she comments, "it doesn't look very nice."

Crystal Ball, Anyone?

Agents admit they're not sure what will happen with electronic rights, or with other developments on the horizon. "I don't know," says Cohen. "If I knew where publishing was going, I'd be a whole lot richer! We talk about e-rights, but you never know. Someone may suddenly find a new way of publishing that makes these problems less important. We can't control many of the things that are going on right now, like Amazon.com or e-rights, so we shouldn't obsess about them. What we must focus on is what we can control: the quality of the writing."

"These are all generalizations. Every manuscript has its own personality. Every editor does. Every author does. So it's a matter of matching those up," says the unnamed agent. Brown reminds authors, "There are so many things that are hot right now—historical books, humor, New Age books. It was big in the adult market, and now New Age and spirituality has hit the kids' market. With people worrying about the millennium and kids shooting each other, there's a need for books that emphasize values. Editors want to see books about angels. I think kids' memoirs will be big."

"I wish I had a crystal ball!" the anonymous agent says, laughing. "I'm interested in seeing if books about girls' sports will grow, especially with the women's soccer World Cup win! I see a resurgence in young adult books."

Knowlton also says, "I wish I had that crystal ball so I could see what's going to sell! Good writing, certainly, but with that certain edge and fresh voice."

In the end, however, what sells is a good book. "Quality is what it's always been about," says Kouts, "ever since the great children's books of the thirties and forties." Malk agrees. "The market is fickle, and trends come and go, but at the end of the day it's the time-tested classics, and new books that have that timeless feel, that sell. I think people have a yearning for them."

"In the Ursula Nordstrom days, the constant for a writer used to be the editor," says Malk. "Now, with the mergers and with editors moving all over the place, the constant is the agent."

Business

Part 5

Reference & Research

Research

Resources

The Wondrous & Complex World of Five Research Libraries

By Carolyn Yoder & Susan Tierney

Your local library has become more complex and easier to use. It connects to a much wider world than it did even a few years ago. The computerizing of local libraries allows readers and researchers to gain access to books, periodicals, and documents at libraries, archives, and museums statewide and beyond.

Imagine, then, the complexity and the possibilities of major research libraries today. They offer matchless resources, especially for writers, and at an increasingly rapid pace they are connecting to each other, giving researchers admission to an international array of primary and secondary sources. Research libraries offer millions of books, manuscripts, letters, photographs, documents, artwork, recordings, and more. All libraries today are in the process of great change as they work to create a harmony between digital and print information.

This evolution has been made possible through electronic technology such as databases, CD-ROMs, and other formats that make reference materials more readily available to researchers.

Undoubtedly, the most important resource links are being forged through the medium of the Internet, whether the researcher is wired at home or at the local library. Investigate online library holdings and certain acronyms begin to appear: OPAC (Online Public Access Catalogue), IRIS (Integrated Research Information System), and others. These are the networks that open access to catalogues and collections and bridge research sources around the world.

The researcher who needs direct access to special collections still needs to make a trip and be fully prepared to take advantage of the physical access to materials. Most research libraries welcome you only after you have exhausted local, regional, and academic resources. Research is serious business. It pays to know where you are going, what you will be allowed to use in what way, and what is expected of you once you are there.

The following five major research facilities—the libraries of the University of Chicago, the British Library, the Pierpont Morgan Library, the Getty Research Institute for the History of Art and the Humanities, and the Library of Congress—represent a diversity of collections and capabilities. Some are small, some huge; one concentrates on manuscripts and rare books, another deals with art and architecture; one takes an academic focus, and two are general research libraries. One is the largest library in its country, another is the largest in the world.

THE UNIVERSITY OF CHICAGO

The University of Chicago's several libraries serve faculty, staff, and students primarily, although the general public may use the school's library system and, given special privileges, take out books. Like every major research university, UChicago can brag about quantity as well as quality: Its collections number more than 6 million volumes, 7 million manuscripts and archival holdings, and 390,000 maps and aerial photographs. Many of its resources are in electronic format as well as print.

The William Rainey Harper Memorial Library is the general "college" library, used primarily by undergraduates. It covers the humanities, social sciences, and what the library calls *nontechnical* sciences.

The primary research library and the repository of the university's largest collections, is the Joseph Regenstein Library. It is the site of a general reference collection, business and economics periodicals and services, and reference materials and current journals in anthropology, geography, political science, sociology, library science, history, Western languages and literature, linguistics, film and theater, music, the military and naval science, psychology, philosophy, religion, the classics, Africa, the Ancient Near East, the Islamic Middle East, East Asia, and Southern Asia.

Of special interest to many children's writers, the Regenstein maintains a collection of standardized tests, educational documents, and elementary and secondary school textbooks,

---

The University of Chicago Libraries

All the libraries operate under their own set of guidelines and hours.

- **The William Rainey Harper Memorial Library:** the college library of the University of Chicago.
- **The Joseph Regenstein Library:** the humanities; social sciences; and several area-studies collections relating to East Asia, Middle Eastern Studies, Slavic and East European Studies, and South and Southeast Asia.
- **The John Crerar Library:** Science, medicine, technology.
- **The D'Angelo Law Library**
- **The Chemistry Library:** organic, physical, theoretical, inorganic, and analytical chemistry.
- **The Eckhart Library:** mathematics, statistics, and computer science.
- **The Social Service Administration Library:** child welfare, public welfare, mental health, and social urban policy.
- **The Yerkes Observatory Library:** astronomy and astrophysics; located in Williams Bay, Wisconsin.

in addition to its reference works in education. Researchers can find gold, too, in the University of Chicago's Rare Book Holdings, which includes the Encyclopedia Britannica Collection of Children's Literature. Other rare holdings cover history, literature, and drama of the U.S. and Europe, and special collections of Judaica, the history of science and medicine, economics, and German literature.

In the Manuscript Collections are the editorial files of *Poetry Magazine,* the William E. Barton Collection of Lincolniana, and the papers of Stephen A. Douglas, Saul Bellow, and Ida Wells, to name a few. Manuscripts date from the second century to contemporary times.

Another special collection is the University of Chicago Archives. They contain the works of past and present university faculty, including Enrico Fermi, Edith and Grace Abbott, George Herbert Mead, Charles E. Merriam, and Marion Talbot. The Chicago Jazz Archive and the Map Collection are also part of the special collections.

The Regenstein has just undergone a building renovation and continues to grow from card catalogues and print to more electronic sources and uses, including greater online access.

Library Privileges
Visitors from outside the University of Chicago community are welcome at the libraries and can obtain short-term library privileges through the Privileges Office.

A *day pass*, one each quarter, allows visitors to "consult resources in all units of the library during scheduled hours of service for that day only." *Infopasses*

The University of Chicago Online

Online access sources at libraries around the world are changing almost daily.
- **LibInfo Subject Guides:** Web server, a starting place for print and electronic resources.
- **Sources A to Z:** comprehensive list of electronic resources.
- **Online catalogue:** access to the university catalogue, and links to other libraries.
- **WorldCat:** bibliographic database of about 30 million items at 21,000 libraries.
- **RLIN:** Research Libraries Information Network. Another bibliographic database of about 23 million items from major research libraries.
- **ESTC:** English Short Title Catalogue. Access to early printed materials in U.S. and Europe.
- **Hand Press Book:** Access to early printed materials in U.S. and Europe.
- **ArchivesUSA:** Archives and manuscript collections in 4,700 libraries and repositories.
- **Online Computer Library Center:** a nonprofit membership library computer service and research organization.

In addition, the University of Chicago libraries have:
- Electronic indexing and abstracting services, organized by subject.
- Electronic Journal Collections.
- Other reference sources, such as *Britannica Online, the Oxford English Dictionary, Books in Print.*

are available to the Chicago public and operate the same way. A *reference privilege card* is good for one quarter, with no other time restriction, but does not grant borrowing privileges. The *borrowing privilege card* is issued for one quarter, provides access to all "units" of the Library, and allows holders to borrow circulating materials.

Extended privileges for scholarly research are available to full-time faculty from other accredited institutions. Reference privileges are granted without a fee and borrowing privileges for a fee.

THE BRITISH LIBRARY

The glory that was England is undoubtedly reflected in The British Library. Its new Manuscript Reading Room—barely a year old although the library dates from the founding of the British Museum in 1753—is situated next to the St. Pancras Station in North London. Billed as a research facility and not a public reference collection, the British Library is the national library of the United Kingdom. In 1973, the British Library was "re-founded" formally as a distinct entity from the British Museum although the two remain closely tied.

Currently in a period of growth, the St. Pancras Building will eventually house a large portion of the collections: more than 150 million items, including books, journals, patents, manuscripts, maps, music, stamps, and sound and video recordings—along with the majority of the reading rooms, designated to certain areas of research.

The Open Access Reference Collection, considerably larger than its forerunner at the British Museum, is open to visitors to the Reading Room. It uses the Dewey Decimal System. Certain manuscript facsimiles and a pamphlet collection are also open access.

Most of the Library's holdings, however, are in closed-access storage and are ordered through catalogues and bibliographies. Many of the books and other materials, such as illuminated manuscripts, are so valuable, they may not be seen without the advance written recommendation of a "manuscripts curator," such as a colleague or teacher with strong academic credentials. Facsimiles or microfilm are available for some.

Among the many irreplaceable holdings are manuscripts of *Beowulf, Sir Gawain and the Green Knight, Le Morte D'Arthur,*

The British Library Online

- **Website:** large website with information for visitors and researchers, and links to other research sources.
- **The British Library's Automated Information Server (BLAISE):** access to 21 databases, more than 18.5 bibliographic records.
- **Current Serials File:** search more than 62,000 periodicals.
- **Gabriel:** the World Wide Web server for Europe's National Libraries.
- **inside:** access for educators, businesses, and governments around the world to the Library's journal and conference collection. Available on CD-ROM, with Web access under way.
- **OPAC 97:** access through the Web to British Library collection catalogues.

British Library Holdings

Highlights of the British Library's many unique collections include:

- **The King's Library:** the 65,000 volume library of King George III.
- **The Manuscript Collections:** letters and documents "from almost all of the British sovereigns and statesmen, prime ministers, diplomats, and military officers"; the papers of scientists, medical researchers, explorers; the works of major figures in English literature.
- **Early Printed Books:** books in English, Dutch, French, German, Spanish, Italian, and Scandinavian languages, printed before 1851.
- **The Oriental and India Office Collections:** materials on all cultures of Asia, North Africa, and on the European interaction with them. Records on the East India Company and Britain's India Office.
- **Music:** manuscripts and printed British music dating from the Middle Ages through modern composers; European music.
- **National Sound Archive:** thousands of hours of recordings of poets reading their work, beginning with Tennyson and Browning; musical recordings.
- **Modern British and Irish Collections:** British publications covering the humanities and social sciences since 1915. British and Irish twentieth-century history. Modern British and Irish poetry collections. Publications of literary, historical, and cultural societies, including The Beatrix Potter Society, archaeological societies.
- **Overseas English Collections:** publications from countries outside Britain where the research language is English.
- **Philatelic Collections:** the National Philatelic Collection of the U.K.
- **Maps:** Maps, atlases, and globes from all parts of the world dating to the fifteenth century.
- **The John Ritblat Gallery:** a permanent exhibit that displays the eighth-century work of Bede, the *Anglo-Saxon Chronicle, Lindisfarne Gospels, Magna Carta,* Shakespeare's First Folio, a Gutenberg Bible, among many other rare and historic works.
- **Science, Technology and Business:** five reading rooms contain reference materials in the physical and life sciences, technical literature that is generally at a postgraduate level, and a "collection of patents from almost every issuing authority in the world."
- **Newspaper Library:** extensive journalism collections of periodicals in the U.K., but also around the world. One of the online resources is a list of newspaper libraries and collections around the world, including many in the U.S.

classical texts, and modern texts and letters from Virginia Woolf, Evelyn Waugh, and others, antiquarian collections of local history, the writings of scientists, medical researchers, and explorers.

With its many historical resources, the British Library is nonetheless embracing modern technology. It is in the process of developing a Digital Library System (DLS). Accessible to researchers throughout the world, this electronic resource "will be made up of words, still images, moving images, sound and any combination of these." One manuscript already in this digital library is the *Electronic Beowulf*, "an image-based edition of *Beowulf*" and other historical materials concerned with the manuscript, such as eighteenth-century transcriptions. The Magna Carta is also available, and online at the British Library researchers can find a site called, "The Nineteenth Century 'Live' on the World Wide Web."

Library Privileges
People who are interested in "seeing" the British Library can do so through programs and exhibits, and by reading its publications. Access for researchers, however, is only granted to individuals who have reached a stage in their research where the British Library is their only recourse. Some, limited, books are available through interlibrary loan.

Applicants must apply in person at the Reader Admission Office, be interviewed, complete a registration form, and supply two-color passport photos and a proof of identification bearing a signature. Reader passes are then issued free of charge to researchers, usually over the age of 18. The passes are time-sensitive, the length determined by the extent of research to be done. Most passes are for one month, one year, or five years.

The British Library offers special considerations for "postgraduates and academic staff carrying out research to support academic studies (five-year pass), students at the undergraduate level (one-year pass), people carrying out research on behalf of a company or place of work, and people carrying out personal research."

THE J. PAUL GETTY CENTER

The J. Paul Getty Center in Los Angeles, California, is made up of the J. Paul Getty Museum, the Getty Research Institute for the History of Art and the Humanities, the Getty Conservation Institute, the Getty Education Institute for the Arts, and the Getty Grant Pro-

---
The Getty Online

- **Website:** overviews and links to the different segments of the center, with descriptions of collections, and information on access, publications, grants, educational programs. Links to research access sites.
- **IRIS (Integrated Research Information System):** online catalogue available on the Web; bibliographic record of books, serials, auction catalogues, archives, photos.
- **Online Research Services:** database searches.
- **CIC (Collections Integrated Catalogue):** makes Web and Telnet resources, databases, and other resources available to researchers at the Library.
---

gram. Until last year, the Getty Information Institute was an "operating program" working toward technologically improving art history and humanities research. That Institute has now been integrated with other Getty programs.

The Center has two museums. One is located in Malibu and is devoted to classical antiquities. Presently closed, it will reopen in 2001 as a "center for archaeology and cultures." The other museum in Los Angeles is devoted to European paintings and decorative arts, illuminated manuscripts, sculpture, drawings and photographs.

The Research Library of the Institute for the History of Art and the Humanities "supports advanced research in the visual arts and the humanities" with general and special collections, "visual resources," and a Photo Study Collection. Holdings at the Library extend from the Bronze Age through antiquity and all of European history. Western art and culture are the Institute's primary focus, but in recent years the collections have embraced materials from cultures connected to Europe, such as the Americas, ancient Near East, and Islam.

The general collections contain books, serials, and auction catalogues on art, archaeology, architecture, culture, historic preservation, and even in applied science and technology. Special Collections and Visual Resources contain rare books, rare photos, manuscripts, archives, prints, drawings, artist journals and sketchbooks, architectural drawings, and more. The Special Collections are particularly notable in nineteenth- and twentieth-century materials and in the avant-garde art and cultural movements—Dadaism, Surrealism, Bauhaus, Russian Constructionism, and others. The Photo Study Collection contains two million photos of art, architecture, and decorative arts.

In all, the Research Institute has 700,000 books, serials, and auction catalogues; 43,000 rare books; 6,000 linear feet of archives, manuscripts, and architectural drawings; 14,000 prints; 460 collections of rare photographs; and two million study photographs.

The J. Paul Getty Center

- **J. Paul Getty Museum:** collections are Antiquities, Decorative Arts, Drawings, Paintings, Sculpture and Works of Art, and Manuscripts, which includes the Ludwig Collection. The Photograph Collection contains more than 25,000 prints, thousands of daguerrotypes, 30,000 stereographs and *cartes-de-visite*; it is strong in the early 1840s and for the last decade and a half has concentrated on the major photographers of the first half of the twentieth century.
- **Getty Research Institute for the History of Art and the Humanities:** library and research facilities at the Center.
- **Getty Conservation Institute:** works to protect "cultural heritage through research, training, field work, and information exchange."
- **Getty Education Institute for the Arts:** furthers education in the arts, through information and curriculum resources. (www.artsednet.getty.edu)

Library Privileges

The Plaza Reading Room at the Institute is open to the public on a "space available" basis. Visitors can request materials to be used in the reading room or can use the general reference collections directly.

Access to the general collection's open areas, which make up 40 percent of the Library, is immediately granted to *stack readers*—graduate students, arts professionals, and other members of the "scholarly community." These areas contain reference, book, periodical, and auction catalogue stacks; a multimedia area; public terminals; a periodicals reading room; and the browsable stacks of the Photo Study Collection.

The Getty Library policy is to allow access to its special collections based on "research need" rather than "reader level," but all researchers must make appointments in advance.

Materials in the closed areas of the Library must be requested through the online catalogue, IRIS (Integrated Research Information System), which is accessible on the Web. Visitors to the Library have other database and electronic resource options.

Stack readers must show proof of institutional affiliation or "other suitable identification" and photo identification. The Library also honors *extended readers*, with extended hours of access to the open areas, reserve shelves, and assigned study carrels.

A researcher must complete an application form that describes the research project, materials needed, and includes two references. Appointments are needed for a trip to the Special Collections and the Photo Study Collection. Specific guidelines are in place for the loan of monographs, periodicals, auction catalogues, certain scholarly books, Art in Fiction, Los Angeles Collection, and audio-visual materials. Special permission is needed for the loan of microforms.

THE PIERPONT MORGAN LIBRARY

The Pierpont Morgan Library in New York City began as the private library of the wealthy financier Pierpont Morgan, who, in 1890, began collecting "illuminated, literary, and historical manuscripts, printed books, drawings and prints." In the 1920s, the library opened to the public and since that time has expanded to include music manuscripts, children's books, Americana, and twentieth-century materials. It is an important center of research internationally because of its many unique holdings.

The Morgan's major collections are Literary and Historical Manuscripts, Medieval and Renaissance Manuscripts, Printed Books and Bindings, Music Manuscripts and Books, Ancient Near East Seals and Tablets, and Drawings and Prints.

While many of the materials owned

The Morgan Online

- **Website:** provides basic information about the collections and about availability of resources and access for visitors and researchers. Currently limited search capabilities.
- **OPAC (Online Public Access Catalogue):** now being installed and expected to be fully accessible through the website in two years.

by the Morgan will appeal to writers—Thoreau's journals, letters of Jefferson and Lincoln, manuscripts and letters of Voltaire, Austen, Dickens, Charlotte Brontë, Steinbeck, Einstein—the collection of classic early children's books is of greatest interest to children's writers. The remarkable artwork includes 10 centuries' worth of illuminated manuscripts; printed books from the fifteenth century to the present, including Lewis Carroll's *The Nursery Alice* with hand-colored proofs by illustrator Sir John Teeniel; musical autographs "unequaled in this country," according to the Morgan, and the largest collection of Gilbert and Sullivan materials in the world; and 10,000 sketches, drawings, and prints from the fifteenth to the twentieth centuries, including works of Dürer, Blake, Degas, Rembrandt, and others.

Of particular interest on deposit at the Library is the Gilder Lehrman Collection, a large compilation of historical documents dating from the time of the discovery of the New World to today. Its highlights include Columbus's letter describing his discoveries, Gerald Ford's pardon of Nixon, and a copy of the Thirteenth Amendment, signed by Abraham Lincoln and others.

Library Privileges
The Reading Room is open to students and scholars who need to consult the rare materials. There are no open stacks and no borrowed items. Researchers who are interested in prints and drawings must make appointments ito use the Drawings Department's study room. Special considerations are also needed for the Ancient Near East tablets and seals

The Pierpont Morgan Library

Collections:
- **Literary and Historical Manuscripts:** books, manuscripts, correspondence in the fields of art, literature, history, politics, science. The privately owned, extensive Gilder Lehrman collection of American historical documents is on deposit at the Morgan.
- **Medieval and Renaissance Manuscripts:** 1,300 illuminated manuscripts from 10 centuries, and papyri.
- **Printed Books & Bindings:** comprehensive and diverse collection, from all times, but very strong in the fifteenth century. Classic Early Children's Books Collection; three Gutenberg Bibles.
- **Music Manuscripts & Books:** includes very large, high-quality collection of manuscripts in the composers' hands.
- **Ancient Near East Seals & Tablets:** engraved seals and artifacts from Mesopotamia through the fifth-century BCE Persian empire.
- **Drawings & Prints:** more than 10,000 drawings and prints from fourteenth to twentieth centuries.

and the Gilbert and Sullivan collection.

The guidelines for handling the Library's holdings are strict because most of their materials are precious. A request to do so must be made in writing and accompanied by a letter of reference from a scholar or an educational institution. Approved researchers receive a reader's ticket good for a year, but must call a week before their visit.

The Pierpont Morgan is currently installing an online public access catalogue (OPAC). It should now be available on-site to scholars and staff and in about two years, available through the Morgan's website. That site currently indicates that "[f]uture plans include enhancing the descriptions with images, full-text transcriptions, and links to electronic resources."

Photographs of the many beautiful works in the Morgan's holdings may be purchased as 35 mm color slides or 8-by-10-inch black-and-white photos or color transparencies, and in black-and-white microfilm. If the photo is to be published, whether it is artwork or text, the purchaser must request and obtain permission from the Morgan and the copyright owner.

THE LIBRARY OF CONGRESS

With 115 million items, the Library of Congress (LOC) in Washington, DC, is the largest library in the world, specializing in "all formats, languages, and subjects." The LOC's "mission is to make its resources available and useful to Congress and the American people and to sustain and preserve a universal collection of knowledge and creativity for future generations." Housed mostly in three buildings on Capitol Hill—the Thomas Jefferson, James Madison, and John Adams Buildings—the collections are extremely wide-ranging and comprehensive in scope.

The Library of Congress bills itself as a research, not a lending, library. It is made up of 22 reading rooms, with the Main Reading Room (MRR) the "primary entrance into the Library's research collections and the principal reading room for work in the social sciences and humanities." Its main card catalogue and online catalogue let the researcher know if material can be found there or at another reading room.

The MRR materials cover art, education, history, language, literature, philosophy, political science, psychology, religion, and sociology. Books on science, business, economics, music, law, and other subjects are housed in specialized reading rooms. The Children's Literature Center, which not only offers reference services and produces its own publications, but also develops programs and exhibits, is located in the MRR.

The other reading rooms, detailed in the sidebar on pages 206-207, are: African and Middle Eastern; American Folklife Center; Asian; Business Reference Services; European; Geography and Map; Hispanic; Japan Documentation Center; Law Library; Local History and Genealogy; Manuscript; Microform; Motion Picture and Television; Newspaper and Current Periodical; Performing Arts; Prints and Photographs; Rare Book and Special Collections; Recorded Sound Reference Center; and Science.

Of particular interest to many writers, the Manuscript Collection includes the papers of Clara Barton, Ben Franklin, Booker T. Washington, and Walt Whitman, as well as presidential papers, Thomas Jefferson's rough draft of the Declaration of Independence, and Washington's First Inaugural Address. The Rare Book and Special Collections houses, among much else, the libraries of Susan B. Anthony, Thomas

Jefferson, and Woodrow Wilson.

The LOC's research services include on-site and online aids. Online resources include three main catalogues: for the collections, for prints and photographs, and for braille and audio materials. (See the sidebar on pages 208-209.)

The researcher may also take advantage of highly specialized bibliographies and indexes. Most important for many researchers is the LOC Finding Aids, which helps users search archives, manuscripts, and other primary sources. The Library website also links to the catalogues and databases of more than 300 other libraries nationally and internationally, and has specialized tools directed to publishers, K-12 educators, and the blind and handicapped.

A small percentage of the LOC's total holdings are available in full text online. The doorways to these are the American Memory: Historical Collections; Country Studies/Area Handbook Program; and the Science Tracer Bullets (SCTB) Online. These illustrate how much the LOC tailors its research aids to the distinct needs of users.

The American Memory collection, for example, was developed with the assistance of educators and historians who contributed "ideas for these collections according to their relevance to U.S. history, social studies, and language arts." A Learn More About It site online provides research resources and educational approaches for teachers and others who want to take advantage of American Memory, and the LOC's Center for the Book offers companion reading lists.

Other highly targeted resources include databases on cold regions science and technology, Latin American studies, and Korea. Another very focused LOC database is a microform reference source for government documents concerning Americans killed, missing, or taken prisoner in the war in Vietnam. Of course, the LOC is the prime resource for researchers looking for information on government. Other government resources are to be found through the Federal Libraries and Information Centers; Global Legal Information Network (GLIN); THOMAS, the source of legislative information; and the records of the U.S. Copyright Office.

Note the difference between the Library of Congress and the National Archives, however. The Archives, also housed in Washington and at the University of Maryland, are the *"repository for the official records* of the U.S. government."

Library Privileges

All Library of Congress reading rooms operate under separate hours, guidelines, and access policies and each has its own web page. As at other research libraries, researchers are asked to exhaust the references at their local, academic, or special libraries before coming to the Library of Congress.

To obtain a library issued user card, one needs a photo identification showing current address. Users must be over 18, although high school students may use the LOC under special considerations. There is no fee for a card. Because of the vastness and density of the Library, it is strongly suggested that people new to the collections start their research at information desks either at

The Library of Congress

The materials and services available at the Library of Congress are so vast that it would take many pages to do them justice. The LOC is a resource arguably unequalled in the world. The following descriptions of organization and services only begin to highlight what it has to offer.

Reading Rooms:
- **Main Reading Room (MRR):** the general reference collection of 200,000 titles in 70,000 volumes, but with coverage only of the humanities and social sciences, and containing bibliographies. Access to materials in the other, specialized, reading rooms is available through the MRR. The MRR also houses the Congressional Hearings Collection, a Biography Alcove with 1,300 biographies and related references, telephone and city directories for the entire U.S., the Microform Guide Collection; 150-plus volumes of the Quotation Book Collection.
- **African & Middle Eastern:** materials on countries and regions from South Africa to the republics of Central Asia.
- **American Folklife:** part of the American Folklife Center, although coverage is international. More than one million manuscripts, recordings, photographs, and moving images.
- **Asian:** materials on and in Asian languages, on Asians in America and around the world, and on the Pacific islands. Includes the Japan Documentation Center.
- **Business References Services:** covers banking, commerce, economics, finance, industries, insurance, investment, marketing.
- **Children's Literature Center:** founded in 1963, an "advocate for the study of children's books." Book collection, lectures, symposia, exhibitions.
- **European:** a very large collection, but many materials relevant to Western Europe are available in the MRR, especially concerning the U.K. and Ireland. Resources on Spain and Portugal are found in the Hispanic Reading Room.
- **Geography & Map:** the largest collection of maps, atlases, and "cartographic materials in other formats" in the world.
- **Hispanic:** covers Latin America, the Caribbean, Spain, and Portugal, Hispanics living throughout the world and their cultures.
- **Law Library:** at the service of Congress, federal courts, and executive agencies, but also available to researchers and the public generally. World's largest library of law materials for all nations.
- **Local History & Genealogy:** local, national, and international publications.
- **Manuscript:** 11,000 separate collections, 50 million items.
- **Motion Picture & Television:** film and television in the U.S. and internationally.
- **Newspaper & Current Periodical:** the public means of obtaining access to the

(continued on next page)

The Library of Congress

(continued from preceding page)
LOC's Serial & Government Publications Division's materials. Includes U.S. and foreign newspapers, past and present, in Western European languages; other current periodicals; government documents from the U.S. Federal Depository, the United Nations, and the European Union.
- **Performing Arts:** part of the Music Division. Eight million items, including music, books, manuscripts, microforms, copyright deposits.
- **Prints & Photographs:** more than 13.6 million photographs, prints, drawings, posters, architectural and engineering drawings.
- **Rare Books & Special Collections:** a broad collection that takes many forms, including books, manuscripts, pamphlets, broadsides, playbills, title pages, prints, posters, photographs.
- **Recorded Sound Reference Center:** audio collections that "reflect the entire history of sound technology, from wax cylinders, through LPs and tape, to compact audio discs."
- **Science & Technology:** all areas of science and technology except clinical medicine and technical agriculture, which are found in the National Library of Medicine (part of the National Institutes for Health, Department of Health and Human Services) and National Agricultural Library (part of the U.S. Department of Agriculture).

Other:
- **Center for the Book:** an LOC division created by Act of Congress to promote reading, libraries, study, and America's literary heritage. Works with Congress, government, and with private organizations. Runs events, arranges projects, and publishes.
- **Federal Libraries & Information Centers:** FLICC, the committee directing these, works "to foster excellence in federal libraries and information services through interagency cooperation and to provide guidance and direction for" FEDLINK, the Federal Library and Information Network.
- **Digital Collections & Programs:** See sidebar on the Electronic Library of Congress on pages 208-209.

The Electronic Library of Congress

Catalogues, Databases, Indexes, Guides
- **LOC Online Catalogue:** searches of bibliograpies and information on the LOC collections.
- **Prints & Photographs Online Catalogue:** 250,000 records in this database, referring to more than 5 million items in the collection. About 90 percent have some digitalized form. Crosses over with various collections, like American Memory. Copies of many are available through the LOC Photoduplication Service, but users must ensure they obtain rights to use from the LOC and copyright holders.
- **Braille/Audio Materials Online Catalogue:** bibliographic listings of publications in braille or that have been recorded.
- **LOC Finding Aids:** specialized, detailed information specifically on manuscripts and primary sources.
- **Other Libraries' Catalogues:** provides links and information from more than 300 library online catalogues nationally and internationally.
- **Science Tracer Bullets (SCTB) Online:** full-text resource. Bibliographic guides meant for users with general knowledge.
- **Vietnam Era POW/MIA Database:** specialized index to microform materials on U.S. and the Vietnam War.
- **OCLC :** Online Computer Library Center, part of the Federal Libraries and Information Services Network, **FEDLINK.** Open to member libraries.
- **Microform Guide Collection:** The microform collection is organized into more than 400 guides, located near the Main Reading Room. Microforms cover books, periodicals, manuscripts, photographs, documents, transcripts. Microform collections are also available in some of the specialized reading rooms, such as Law and Manuscript.
- **CD-ROMs:** disc indexes to journals, documents, dissertations, other materials.

(continued on next page)

the Jefferson Building or the James Madison Building, attend orientation classes, or ask reference librarians for assistance. The Library publishes helpful materials, including the booklet, "Information for Researchers: Using the Library of Congress," and a leaflet, "Public Services in the Library of Congress."

The LOC is a closed-stack library, and no books may be removed from the reading rooms. Books are requested by using call slips online or manually and are delivered to a desk or a designated book service hold area. Researchers may request books one day in advance and use a reserved area set aside for those spending more than one day at the Library. Up to five books may be held for three days. Researchers should use the reading room "located

The Electronic Library of Congress

(continued from preceding page)
- **EUREKA**: a variety of databases in the arts, history, humanities, science, technology, and social sciences offered by the Research Libraries Group. The LOC subscribes to them and offers them through the reading rooms.
- **Research Guides:** miscellaneous relatively brief guides to various subjects and to the collections. Also available in print.
- **Indexes, Abstracts, and Bibliographies:** an index to indexes, bibliographies, etc. Indexes of titles, subjects. Also available in print.

Text Resources Online
- **Digital Collections & Programs:** A relatively small proportion of LOC holdings are digitalized, but among them are the American Memory Historical Collections and the Country Studies. Also under the umbrella of Digital Collections is Thomas, GLIN, and some portion of the Prints & Photographs collection. These programs are described below.
    - **American Memory Collection:** more than 60 collections accessible online in full-text, digitialized photos or prints, maps, recordings. Primary sources, archives. All on American culture and history. Links to Learning Center, ideas for teachers and students.
    - **Country Studies:** studies of the culture, politics, economics, national security of more than 100 countries.
    - **Global Legal Information Network (GLIN):** database, full texts, abstracts of national and international legal documents.
    - **THOMAS Legislative Information:** a primary source of information about Congress and government. Full texts of bills and other documents. Roll call votes, bill status, committee information, the Congressional Record. Site also includes the Thomas Jefferson Papers from the LOC's Manuscript collection.

in the building where the materials they are requesting are housed."

If you can't make it to the LOC, and you have exhausted local or regional resources, write for research help to the National Reference Service at the Library. Your letter should list the resources you have already consulted. The Service does not provide a "compilation of bibliographies, response to requests for information connected to school assignments, debates, and contests, and genealogy and heraldry research."

Yet there is hardly anything you couldn't research at the LOC, or the other fine research libraries. For writing ideas, to develop projects, for background, for accompanying photos or art, the treasures of libraries are closer at hand than ever before in history.

Library Access Numbers

- **The University of Chicago Library:** www.lib.uchicago.edu
  - William Rainey Harper Memorial Library, 1116 East 59th Street, 773-702-7959
  - The Joseph Regenstein Library, 1100 East 57th Street, 773-702-7874
  - Special Collections, 773-702-8705
  - Privileges Office, 773-702-8782
  - D'Angelo Law Library, Laird Bell Quadrangle, 1111 East 60th Street, 773-702-9631
  - The John Crear Library, 5730 South Ellis Avenue, 773-702-7715
  - Chemistry Library, 5747 South Ellis Avenue, 773-702-8775
  - Eckhart Library, 1118 East 58th Street, Room 217, 773-702-8778
  - Yerkes Observatory Library, Williams Bay, WI 53191, 414-245-5555
  - Social Service Administration Library, 969 East 60th Street, 773-702-1199
- **The British Library:** www.bl.uk
  96 Euston Road, London NW1 2DB, United Kingdom
  0171-412-7676
- **The Pierpont Morgan Library:** www.morganlibrary.org
  29 East 36th Street, New York, NY 10016
  212-685-0008, ext. 376
- **The Getty Center:** www.getty.edu
  1200 Getty Center Drive, Los Angeles, CA 90049-1681
  - Getty Research Institute for the History of Art and the Humanities, Research Library Services, 1200 Getty Center Drive, Suite 1100, Los Angeles, CA 90049-1688, 310-440-7390
- **Library of Congress:** www.loc.gov
  101 Independence Avenue, SE Washington, DC 20540
  General: 202-707-5000
  Reading room hours: 202-707-6400
  Reference: 202-707-5522
  Researchers: 202-707-6500
  Visitors: 202-707-8000
  Directions: 202-707-4700

Sports Research & Writing

All About Stats?

By Kim Childress

Sports books today stretch kids' minds along with their muscles. They reflect the growing health and fitness movement, with new sports series for children popping up all over the field. Bookstores host a wide range of sports-related fiction, nonfiction, and even poetry. Not only does sports writing inspire readers to get up and go, it has long been a pull for reluctant readers, appealing to those who might not otherwise pick up a book. What kids learn on the playing field and in the pages of a good sports book translates to the rest of their lives.

"Sports is life, and life is a sport," says Maureen Holohan, former Northwestern basketball star and author of The Broadway Ballplayer series. "It's a place where people learn about teamwork, sacrifice, commitment, and loyalty."

Margaret Blackstone, former editor and now the author of sports books for the very young, says her mission is to get kids to read a book and then get out of their seats and do something. "One of the biggest thrills I get out of these books is that I can give a learning experience about words and a learning experience about using your body. If kids don't pick up a sport early, they may not know about it, but if they read about it, they may want to try it."

Research and writing about sports are like fine-tuned teammates in a championship game. When all the components come together, they result in a win.

Sports Vehicle

Just as athletes are motivated to play for different reasons, inspiration for sports writers comes from a variety of sources. It may come from memories of childhood games, an unfulfilled desire to play, or an interest in role models.

Personal experience is often the first step in research for sports writers. Chris Crutcher combines past experience with a desire simply to write good fiction for young adults in such books as *Running Loose, Staying Fat for Sarah Barnes*, and most recently, *Ironman*. "Looking back through teenage eyes, so many times they're your own eyes," he says. "I just use my own experiences and my own take on things. My adolescence had so many sports in it, they became a vehicle to tell the story. But I consider the sports a backdrop, more than the theme, of the story. Many times the sport is part of the structure of the character's life; the rules are clear; and sometimes you can draw analogies between sports and other events in real life. *Staying Fat for Sarah Barnes*, for example, was a balance between being a sports story, a friendship story, and a testing of the narrative's character."

Sports were a way for Dean Hughes to connect with young people. Hughes has written more than 76 books, half about sports, including his new Scrappers series. "I had wanted to be a writer from the time I was in school. I played as a kid, but I was the one who became the coach because I wasn't a great player. When I got interested in writing for young people, I knew that sports are a big part of kids' lives and I knew a lot about sports, so I decided to try it."

Author Dan Gutman was also a poor player but a huge sports lover, so he used writing as a way to keep sports in his life while influencing children. "When I was a kid, I didn't like to read, but I loved sports. I wanted to find out about sports, so I started reading about them, and that's what made me into a reader. I visit many schools and see the same thing happen with kids and my books. Many kids, particularly boys, are reluctant readers. They are also fanatical sports fans. It's very gratifying to hear some parent say their kid wouldn't pick up a book, but when they read my book, they couldn't put it down. I always tell kids that even though I wasn't good at sports, I was able to find a way to make sports my career, and if they love something, even if they're not good at it, they can make it their career too." Gutman's most recent titles include *Jackie & Me,* *Honus & Me,* and *Virtually Perfect.*

Author of nine nonfiction sports books for children, including *Rock Climbing, Mountain Biking,* and *Surfing,* Larry Dane Brimner "had absolutely no interest in sports writing until I saw some kids performing stunts on their bikes in my neighborhood. It intrigued me, and I realized that this was a book idea. I asked them if what they were doing had a name, and they called it BMX freestyle. I did my homework and learned there were no other books out there on the subject. It became my first sports book."

Concentrate on the Ball

Having the motivation to write sports stories is well and good, but concentrating on the ball—subject and genre —takes writers to the big leagues.

Brimner and Gutman started out writing nonfiction and now focus on fiction. From their own experiences as teen readers, Sue Macy and Holohan decided to write for girls because they could never find enough books on strong female role models, especially athletes.

Once writers find that focus, research carries them over the next hurdle. "Researching transports you into a different dimension. It is the best part of what I do," says Macy, author of several nonfiction books for girls, including *Winning Ways: A Photohistory of American Women in Sports* and *Play Like a Girl.* "I'm always clipping things from the newspaper, and *Winning Ways* came about simply from organizing my notes. I didn't know what I wanted to write about, but I started to organize information into a timeline to see how women's sports developed, and I realized I needed to write a history."

"Usually, I read about an incident, something in the newspaper, that will get me thinking in that direction," says Crutcher. "I think about what would happen if one of my characters were involved in that incident. Sometimes I create a character who will respond the way I want for my story. I usually start right in the middle of the book, with an event that moves me. I want to hit the ground running. Since I'm not an outliner, I never know in the beginning where a book is going to go, and I don't worry about it when I start. The story has a better chance of carrying me than me carrying the story."

Similarly, Virginia Euwer Wolff may read of an event and then create a scene in her head. Her novel *Bat 6* combines sports and history and involves two softball teams battling it out in post-World War II Minnesota. She envisioned a panicked rush towards first base. "I saw a bright sunshiny day and all these people standing around the base because something had happened. It was something terribly serious, and I had to ask myself what was going on. I had to decide in my conscious mind what had happened."

From Idea to Reality

Once an idea begins floating around, what's the best way to catch it and turn it into a home run? Where does the "hard stuff" come from? For Wolff, it took years of research before her vision became a reality, and she had additional research to do since her book was historical fiction.

"There was a book in the library, a 1943 softball book for girls, which I kept for six months. I ended up photo-copying the whole thing, including the index. I watched Ken Burns's baseball documentary, *The 5000 Hours of Baseball*, and from that I got some really important information. I watched the old *Angels in the Outfield,* and many other forties and fifties movies. I watched the 1995 World Series and took pages and pages of notes. I brought home coaching and hitting videos from the library. I did a thousand times more research than I could ever use, but it made me ask questions that I wouldn't have known to ask, like was the character Shazam a home hitter or a base hitter? Did she bat right or left? Some authors use the additional research to write something else, a related picture book or poetry story."

The old movies helped Wolff capture the feel of the times, but she also considered the changes in equipment and uniforms. To compare the then and now, she ordered old Sears catalogues and contacted sports equipment manufacturers for old catalogues. The extra effort paid off in accuracy and helped her story "ring true."

When Brimner began the preliminary research on his first biking book,

Personal Inspiration & Perspiration

Virginia Euwer Wolff—On writing *Bat 6*
"Don Gallo had asked me to write a story for one of his anthologies. I had not done any short stories for kids yet, so his postcard said 'I know you haven't written about sports before but maybe you'd accept the challenge.' That's when I checked the movie upstairs, that one that's going on in my head all the time, and I saw all these people panicked running towards first base. All these people were standing around because something had happened. I knew that it was more than a short story. From there I procrastinated for about five months because it looked like such a huge job, and I wrote a scuba diving story for Don Gallo's anthology instead. But I kept gathering information, I was so enthusiastic about it. I kept thinking of Edith Horten's quote, 'I dreamt of an eagle but gave birth to a hummingbird.' Getting it onto the page takes a tremendous amount of guts because it always turns out so differently from what you envisioned."

Chris Crutcher
"I didn't intentionally start out as a sports writer. I started writing stories with adolescent protagonists. My own adolescence had so many sports in it that they just became part of the stories. I grew up in a small town where everyone played sports, and there were just enough people to field a team. I played football, basketball and track in high school, and I was a swimmer in college. I'm probably less likely to consider myself a sports fiction writer, yet when I wrote a book of short stories I called it *Athletic Shorts* partly because I recognize how others view me."

Margaret Blackstone
"I grew up in Oyster Bay on Long Island and played lots of sports. I loved baseball. It ran in the family because my grandpa was a big player. I grew up in
(continued on next page)

---

he went to the library and literally pulled out every sports book in the children's section. "I organized them by publisher, looked at them and decided what I wanted to do. Franklin Watts published closest to what I wanted. I queried them and they sent me a contract."

As a fiction writer, Crutcher writes mainly from experience, but when he needs to look something up, he finds the fastest place to go is the Internet. "I'll give a character a disease, or I may need to know a sequence of events that

Personal Inspiration & Perspiration

(continued from preceding page)
the country, learned to swim when I was three, and I was a good runner. I ran the six-hundred faster than any girl ever in my school. I also started ice skating at the age of four, and then became a competitive figure skater. I was a jock, but I also studied very hard. I became very intellectual and went to Yale. Writing my stories gave me time to think about the good times of my youth. I've always been a poet, and all the books that I write begin as a poem, in a kind of stanza form. This form helps me keep the writing authentic and fresh."

Larry Dane Brimner
"I was barred from playing sports in school because I am blind in one eye, but I at least try the sports I write about. Making the attempt will give your book a sense of realism, until you get past that and think 'What am I doing here?' That happened to me when I was rock climbing. I went rock climbing over a three- week period with an instructor. At one time I looked down and panicked. My instructor was 90 pounds and I'm about 160. I thought, if I fell, could she really hold me?"

Sue Macy
"Sit down and think about some general questions that you'd like to answer involving your topic. Then figure out at what research facility you might find the answers. It might be the public library, or a university library, or a museum, an archive, whatever. Then go there—set aside at least a whole day and try not to go on weekends, when things may be crowded or some services, such as photocopying centers, might be on reduced hours. You might even call ahead to confirm that they've got the stuff you're looking for. Some facilities keep certain materials off-sight, so they may need a few days to bring them to the building for you."

happened a long time ago," he says. "I'm not an Internet expert, so I usually punch up some key word on AOL [America Online] and let them do the work for me. I'm amazed that you can type in a word, follow the possibilities and usually come up with the answer."

Macy agrees that the Internet is a good source, but she feels it is much more productive to go to a good library, preferably at a university, and search their archives. "If you're just looking for details on current events, the Web is great," she says. "When I was writing

Winning Ways, I needed to find some facts about women's sports at the upcoming 1996 Olympics. I was able to visit some Olympic sites at two in the morning and find answers to my questions. So in that instance, it made my work much easier. However, whenever you see historic material on the Web, you've got to realize that someone decided what to put on and what to keep off. In effect, they've censored what you find. I prefer to go to a good library or an archive and discover things that might not have been looked at for decades. The exploration process is an important part of my research, and it's just not the same on the Web."

When Macy starts a new book project, her first step is to go to Princeton University's library and search their archives and open stacks. She has the benefit of being a Princeton alumna, but she says that most university libraries make some arrangement and allow writers access.

Once there, Macy immerses herself in her subject by being physically surrounded by old books, magazines and microfilm, which often lead to other books on related subjects and new areas to explore. "I don't spend a lot of time taking notes," she says. "Instead, I search, gather material, and then photocopy so I can carefully read things and take notes at home. A good day at a research facility for me is one when I come home with at least 100 photocopied pages. Often, that forms the bulk of my research material for a book."

All the News

For Macy, and all the writers interviewed, newspapers are essential in sparking story ideas and gathering information.

"You can find things from the newspapers that never get repeated—great details and quotes that completely get lost after the fact," says Macy. "The best newspapers for sports research are the ones in the home cities of the teams you're focusing on. The *Grand Rapids Press* had excellent coverage of the All-American Girls Professional Baseball League because one of the teams was based in Grand Rapids." Macy also says you can save weeks of research if you find someone who kept scrapbooks of articles, such as a player on a team you're writing about. She found Pitcher Fran Janssen of the All-American Girls league, "who kept a scrapbook of all the coverage of the league's two traveling teams in 1949, saving me lots of legwork in tracking them down."

For *Winning Ways,* which "goes back 150 years," says Macy, "it was really hard to find information on African-American athletes because they weren't reported on in the mainstream press, so I went to African-American newspapers from the thirties and forties and found photos and stories of women you would never find otherwise."

Macy found the first African-American newspaper, the *California Eagle,* through a reference to a specific article in Arthur Ashe's book, *A Hard Road to Glory.* Most of the African-American papers didn't have indexes until the last few decades, so Macy ended up scrolling through issue after issue on microfilm. "There's a library in New York City that specializes in African-American material: the Schomburg Library on Malcolm X Boulevard. I looked at my first newspapers there, and then I also looked at some at Princeton. Other major papers that I used, besides the *Eagle*, were the *Chicago Defender*, the *Philadelphia Tribune*, and the *Pittsburgh Courier*."

To find old copies of local newspapers, Macy recommends trying state or local historical societies, or the newspapers themselves if they're still around. But archivists live to help writers and researchers, and talking to them is another important part of any research project.

In the Arena
Part of the fun in writing the sports story is the research takes you beyond the library and into the playing field. Whether you are a player or a spectator, all the writers interviewed attest to the importance of watching the games, live or televised. "If you are writing about a 13- or 17-year-old," Crutcher says, "get to know some of the kids who are playing, like in Little League. Go and listen to the kids talk about it."

Macy agrees that it is important to attend sporting events because "not only do you show support to the teams, but you get story ideas. When you go to an NBA game, you learn more about the league by seeing who is in the audience. You can see the effect the games have on girls and boys."

"I went to a Knicks game for my basketball book," says Blackstone, "and what I got out of it was the *squeak squeak squeak* of the sneakers. With baseball, I watch too much already. I use research as an excuse to watch a few more games."

Playing the game has its pluses. It is especially helpful if you're writing fiction, says Macy, because you're more in the moment, versus writing a series of researched details. Brimner agrees that you don't have to be proficient, but you should attempt a sport to help with a sense of realism in story and voice.

Hughes doesn't believe it is necessary to play. "One of the great things about writing is that we don't really have to have done everything we write about," he says. "We can transfer our feelings. Say, if a woman has been in a dance recital, she can remember that kind of nervousness. It's easy to put yourself in another's situation."

"Anything that's competitive in your life, you can draw a parallel to sports," says Crutcher. "Music can be competitive, for example. If you don't have experience in competitive sports, rely on your experience in anything else where the pressure's on, you're feeling stressed, and you could choke. Those feelings are exactly the same."

Some writers develop unusual ways to find out what they need to know. During the four years it took Wolff to write *Bat 6*, she kept a softball in her office and tossed it from hand to hand. For *Surfing*, Brimner hired teens in his neighborhood to take surfing lessons, paid for their boards, then watched and asked questions. Listening to announcers analyze games on the radio is another source for Hughes and Wolff, as well as watching television shows and movies. Still, much sports research comes from simply observing.

"The research I do is just paying attention," says Crutcher. Organization is another key component in researching and gathering information. "When I do

Recommended References from Sporting Writers

Chris Crutcher: "One of my biggest influences when I started was watching Terry Davis write *Vision Quest*, being able to use Terry as a resource and use the book as an example of how sports have changed."

Dan Gutman: The *New York Times, The Reader's Guide to Periodical Literature,* and *The Baseball Encyclopedia.*

Maureen Holohan: *How to be a Successful Self-Publisher,* by Dorothy Kavka.

Dean Hughes: "Most sports have some kind of an encyclopedia, like *The Official Major League Baseball Fact Book,* that gives the history of all the different teams and stats. I used that in Scrappers a lot—I have the kids talking about past players and their stats."

Sue Macy: The Women's Sports Foundation (www.womenssportsfoundation.org or (800) 227-3988); Women in Sports and Events (WISE) (www.womeninsportsandevents.com or (212) 726-8262).

Virginia Euwer Wolff: "There was a book in the library, a 1943 *Softball for Girls,* by Viola Mitchell. I had the third edition in 1952, and I kept it for six months. I kept renewing it over and over until finally I photocopied the whole book, all the pages, including the index."

---

interviews and type the transcripts, I store the pages in one of those portfolios with plastic page holders," says Macy. "This essentially makes the interviews into a book, and it's easy to highlight and flag sections or quotes. Once I have a chapter outline for a book, I'll go through all my notes, flag pertinent pages or quotes, and write the chapter number on the flag to show where that bit of information fits."

Macy approaches each chapter as an article and makes a folder for each. "I place relevant articles and other notes in the folder, and I keep those articles in their folders even when the book is done in case I have to go back and check any facts."

Whatever methods you use, establishing a system of organization is crucial in bringing together those winning components.

Sporting a New Look

Current sports books are as fast-paced and nonstop as a track-and-field event. They pack their pages with accessible information and exciting pictures. The sports writer needs to consider sidebars, information tidbits, and captions, and how they will all fit together with the main text. "The overall look of sports books today is much more lively, using more color and a breezy, magazine style, which is more natural, if not always grammatically correct," says Brimner. "There are also more lively sidebars. Kids may skip the text and

Favorite Writers

Chris Crutcher: "Terry Davis, Will Weaver, Dan Jenkins, and Frank Deford are some good sports writers. Some books that were the most influential for me are not really sports books, like *The Things They Carry,* by Kim O'Brien, *The Color Purple,* by Alice Walker, and anything by Kurt Vonnegut."

Dan Gutman: "Ring Lardner and Jayson Stark in *The Philadelphia Inquirer.*"

Maureen Holohan: "Rick Telander, Jack McCallum, and a bunch of the writers from *Sports Illustrated* are the best around."

Dean Hughes: "*Memories of the Mick,* by David Halberstam, and nonfiction books that try to give you the flavor of the sport."

Sue Macy: "I particularly enjoyed *A Kind of Grace: A Treasury of Sportswriting by Women,* edited by Ken Rapoport; and *Babe: The Life and Legend of Babe Didrikson Zaharias,* by Susan E. Cayleff. *Babe* was an academic study, but a terrific example of social history centering around an athletic figure."

Virginia Euwer Wolff: "I'm a thrift shop buyer. If I like it, I buy it, and I found *Baseball's Hall of Fame,* by Ken Smith. In another thrift shop book, *The World Series Encyclopedia,* I found Hank Greenburg, and he went straight to my heart and into my story."

---

read the captions and sidebars, and if there's good information, it may draw kids back into the text. I use sidebars all over the place. They expand on the information without actually being a part of the text itself."

Photographs are another factor that many writers should think about. Many an author has not considered what the photos would add until after their book has been released, and if they don't appear as the writer envisioned, by then it is obviously too late.

"I select the photos in my books," says Brimner. "As I'm doing research, if I notice any photographs that I really like, I make a note of the magazine and contact the photographer. When I was researching *Rolling . . . In-line!,* I came across some outstanding photos in a skating magazine. I contacted the art director and asked how I might contact the photographer. The art director, in turn, gave me the name of a stock photo agency that represented the photographer. It turned out that the agency, Outside Images, specialized in sports photography and was owned by the photographer in question. I've worked with Outside Images on three or four books now, and they've been very flexible by notifying their stable of photographers of exactly what I'm looking for and even setting up particular shots that I felt were important to the book when those images were not found on file." (Outside Images, 24 Preble Street, Suite, 200, Portland, ME 04101. www.outsideimages.com)

Brimner has obtained photographs through networking too. In some cases, he says, "a magazine's art director has given me the phone number of the photographer, and I've dealt directly with the photographer. Publishers also have photo researchers, which I have used in some instances, but for my sports books the photos and visuals are an extremely important part, and I want to maintain control."

Hitting the Mark

Nonfiction, especially how-to children's books, need to be up-to-date and technically accurate, as Brimner emphasizes. After doing his preliminary research, going to the library, interviewing players, and trying out the sport, Brimner researches equipment. "I'll go to a sporting goods store and ask for the most recent information on a sport. If possible, I'll visit a manufacturing company to see the equipment being used, or I'll write and ask for a press kit. This gives me an idea of how a sport is changing, and it's especially important, so I'm not writing about equipment from 10 years ago. I realized this after doing a revised edition of one of my books. I sent it to one of my readers to check it out and found that the equipment was no longer being used. You need to be very, very current. Just because it was written about last year doesn't mean it's current."

Sports fiction needs to be absolutely accurate also, although for different reasons. "If I see a movie about sports, and the contest doesn't look right or the character is not good enough to play competitively, it blows the story," says Crutcher. "It's also true for books. Once I was reading to a group of students from my book, *The Crazy Horse Electric Game,* about baseball. I played less baseball than other sports, and a player in the audience raised his hand and said a pitcher wouldn't do something in this particular circumstance. I asked what he would do, the student told me, and I wrote it all down."

From sports reporters, to coaches and players, all the writers interviewed have someone they consult once their books are finished—some expert in the field—who knows everything from rules to jargon. Macy suggests using the Internet to find an expert. "If there's an organization that touches on the material you're writing about, go to their website and post a message asking for someone to consult with," she says. "If you're writing about the history of fly fishing and there's a Fly Fishing Veteran's group, you should be able to find someone there."

Brimner offers three methods for new writers to find an expert fact-checker. One is sports museums. *Surfing* was fact-checked by someone at the Surfing Museum.

A second is, "as you're doing your research, keep track of important names in the sport. I've found contacting these individuals directly and simply asking them to check my manuscript for accuracy usually pays off with a positive answer, especially if I have interviewed that person for content. People seem willing to help if asked."

The third avenue Brimner has used, as he did for an in-line skating book, "was to contact the leading manufacturer in the sport—Rollerblades, Inc.—and ask if they could have somebody check it. Almost all of these companies have 'professional teams' to demonstrate their products and they're usually happy to assign a manuscript to an expert."

Brimner recommends caution here, however, because along with their comments, Rollerblades, Inc., sent a form requesting final approval of the manuscript. Authors should not give up creative control to corporate entities, he says. Brimner returned the Rollerblades form to them unsigned and explained that nonstaff writers do not relinquish creative control. This seemed to cause no problem.

Beyond technicalities is a certain attitude that athletes possess. To capture that on paper, writers must immerse themselves in the sport, which Hughes does by interviewing players, coaches, watching movies, videos, and reading countless books on his subjects. "More important than just knowing the rules of the game is trying to get the essence of what makes that particular sport what it is," says Hughes.

"What I found when writing about karate is that there's almost a religious quality brought to it, this whole mentality, a mood, to this sport that is difficult to understand," Hughes continues. "The same with soccer. It's an international sport that has never really been big in America, and the players have an understanding of the sport that goes beyond scoring. People who love the game love to watch the moves, the passes, the ball-handling. It was surprising to see how much experts talked about things beyond the practical. There's this mystic quality that kept coming up about how you have to feel the way the ball was part of your body. I read about players who sleep with the ball. To write about soccer, I had to get a real feel for that."

The Wave of the Future

Sports and sports books are sure to continue growing in popularity, opening up room for new and expanded subject matter. Brimner, Macy, and Holohan all see increased need for more girl-related sports books, fiction and nonfiction.

"I think things are going in the right direction," says Macy. "When I started writing there were hardly any books out there that had girls in sports, even in secondary characters. But I still think there is room for more. You often have the same biographies, the same women featured again and again. I also think there are many African-American athletes who haven't gotten fair coverage."

Hughes sees a need for books and stories about more individual sports. "There are many sports that kids love but for some reason there aren't many books about them, like swimming, track, and wrestling. I've always wanted to do one about skiing. If kids like sports, then they like to read about them, but publishers tend to stick with bigger sports, like baseball, football, soccer and hockey."

As writers tap into the excitement of sports—the constant playing, cheering, and emotion—they are essentially transported into a child's world, tapping into an inner voice of their own. It is that place that writers need to reach to deliver inspiring stories. Perhaps no other genre can deliver as much fun on so many levels throughout the process as writing about sports.

Online Research
Lost & Found on the Internet

By Mark Haverstock

During the last decade, writers have embraced the computer as an indispensable tool. Without it, many would feel lost when it comes to drafting a magazine assignment or composing a book.

With the expansion of the Internet, the computer has also become a jack-of-all-trades—mailbox, delivery service, and even telephone substitute. Instead of dropping a manuscript in the mail, many writers pack it into an electronic message and fire it off to that editor who wanted it yesterday. Rather than wading through a maze of voice prompts on an office telephone system, they opt for e-mail messages. But most valuable of all is the Internet's ability to be a first-rate research assistant, helping you sort though a vast repository of information.

Start Here

Many writers and editors use Internet websites as their first stop for research. "They are important to my homework, the preparation I do before I call to make an appointment for an interview," says author Joan Broerman. "If I plan to interview an editor, I read what the publishing house says about itself and its current books and authors on its web page." She notes that websites are helpful in finding phone numbers, reports, data, population figures, new books and research papers on a topic. "Websites also list e-mail addresses that I can use to request more information."

One particular website saves Broerman considerable time. "The one I check most often is my Southern Breeze SCBWI web page," she says of the site for one of the Southern regions of the Society of Children's Book Writers and Illustrators. "As Regional Advisor, I've found that our own web page frees me from answering the same questions over and over again. I just refer people to the web page and ask them to call me if they have more questions." Besides providing information and links to writing sites, it has also benefitted authors regionally. "The list of school and library visits on our web page has meant more calls from librarians and teachers who are looking for speakers," says Broerman.

Writer Susan Molthop, a writer's host for the Writer's Exchange Guide at About.com, starts most of her research projects at About.com, Alta Vista, or one of the other search engines. "What I'm looking for is a big site for the topic I'm researching," she says. "From there, I go to that site's links page. That's where I find the best stuff, because the web masters of really outstanding sites spend hundreds of hours researching the best links." In contrast, search engines list almost anything.

When not working on an assignment, Molthop spends time on bulletin boards and forums—gathering places for people with common interests. "America Online has a huge network of boards on just about anything you could imagine," she says. On the Web, she prefers Delphi and its variety of forums. "When you join a forum, they notify you by e-mail when new posts are added. They also have a great search feature, so you can browse all their public forums by topic."

Writing queries based on current news can be easy if you know where to look. Author Aline Newman searches news archives and downloads the articles she needs. "I read somewhere that a dog had pulled a poisonous snake off a little boy before it had a chance to unload its venom," says Newman. "I looked up the location from where the AP (Associated Press) report had been filed, went to the Web, and found the local newspaper in which the story had been written." Newman then wrote her query based on the article information.

The Internet also helped Newman track down information about an albino buffalo. "I surfed several sites until I found a phone number for the National Bison Association," she says. "They referred me to Bob Pickering, an anthropologist at the Denver Museum of Natural History, who had written a whole book on the subject."

Allison Payne, Assistant Editor at *Guideposts for Kids* and *Guideposts for Teens*, finds the Internet an invaluable resource. "It's great for checking facts quickly and finding contact information for people and organizations," she says. "Using search engines, I often find information and trivia that would have taken significantly longer to find using traditional resources." When Payne fact-checks an issue, she can usually confirm the bulk of information using the Web, saving a huge amount of time.

She also uses the Web for filler. "I often do short articles and sidebars, and I get a lot of that information from the Internet," says Payne. "Often, the information I need for articles like this is not readily available except on the Web. A couple of my recent sidebars involved movie special effects and stunts. For a movie that has only recently been released, the only place I'm going to find detailed information is on a website."

Other websites not specifically aimed at writers can be valuable and time-saving resources. Bookstore sites such as Amazon.com and BarnesandNoble.com are a quick, easily accessible alternative to *Books in Print*. Scope Systems, an industrial electronic repair facility, incorporates one of the best historic event and birth date reference sites on the Web. If you're researching a specific topic, the Web can deliver the goods directly to you. CNN offers free news clipping services that seek news wire articles on topics you select. Enter your home page and you're greeted with the latest news from those categories.

These are only the beginning. Start finding your own most useful and favorite websites with the many and varied sites listed. Go get lost—and found—on the Internet.

The Year's Best Sites for Writers

Ready to do some digging for details? Here is a sampling of best sites recommended by writers, arranged by category:

Reference

- Lists of books in print: www.amazon.com; www.barnesandnoble.com; www.borders.com
- List of books out of print: www.bowker.com/bop/home/BOPformsrch.html
- Free custom news service: Gathers news stories on topics of your choice. www.cnn.com
- Learn to do almost anything, from driving a stick shift to preparing for an earthquake: www.learn2.com
- Birthdays and historical events by date: www.scopesys.com
- The Phrase Finder: Contains 5,000 common phrases with meanings and origins. www.shu.ac.uk/webadmin/phrases
- The Polling Report: Recent public opinion poll results from leading polling firms. www.pollingreport.com
- Babel Fish translates French, German, Italian, Portugese, and Spanish text or websites to English and vice versa: www.babelfish.com
- Download content from a variety of books, newspapers, magazines, transcripts, photos, and maps from the Electric Library. Free 30-day trial/$59.95 a year subscription: www.elibrary.com
- *Information Please* online almanac. www.infopls.com
- Mail call: Check ZIP codes, rates, fees, and track express mail packages: www.usps.gov/ncsc
- Who said that? It's the 1901 edition of *Bartlett's Familiar Quotations*, but it's free. www.columbia.edu/acis/bartleby/bartlett
- Alphabet soup: Got an acronym, but don't know the meaning? www.ucc.ie/acronyms/acro.html
- Need directions? Door-to-door and city-to-city driving directions available in map or text form: www.mapquest.com
- Space, the final frontier: NASA delivers a wealth of information on space projects and current science: www.nasa.gov
- Visit the New York Public Library without leaving home: www.nypl.org

Directories and Search Engines

- Detailed index of online phone books, with links to *Yellow Pages, White Pages*, business directories, e-mail addresses, and fax listings from around the world: www.teldir.com

(continued on next page)

The Year's Best Sites for Writers

(continued from preceding page)
- The best search engines on the Internet, all in one location: www.locate.com
- Dogpile checks dozens of search engines, news wires, and newsgroups with one click: www.dogpile.com
- Want something? Ask Jeeves. Type in a question, and you'll get an answer and/or a set of links that can lead you to an answer: www.askjeeves.com
- Improve your Internet search techniques with SearchIQ: www.searchiq.com

Dictionaries and Encyclopedias
- A huge list of dictionaries available for every language imaginable: www.facstaff.bucknell.edu/rbeard/diction.html
- Stuck for a rhyme? Try the *Semantic Rhyming Dictionary:* www.link.cs.cmu.edu/dough/rhyme-doc.html
- *Encarta Online Encyclopedia*: encarta.msn.com/EncartaHome.asp
- Reference tool kit: *Funk and Wagnall's Encyclopedia,* research center, and Reuters News. www.fwkc.com
- My Facts page, links to 54 encyclopedias: www.refdesk.com/factency.html
- Dictionaries, encyclopedias, and other ready references for writers: www.sharpwriter.com
- Mythology: Find out about gods, goddesses, and other mythical figures in the *Encyclopedia Mythica:* www.pantheon.org/mythica
- Need to find someone? Navyspies Investigations Organization has free tips for tracking down hard-to-find people: users.aol.com/navyspies/tips.htm
- Need a translation of up-to-date slang? Try the online slang dictionary: www.umr.edu/~wrader/slang.html

Expert Sources
- Before you pay your attorney, check this site for free legal advice: www.nolo.com
- Reputable sources of scientific information: www.mediaresource.org
- Interactive guide to thousands of the country's leading experts and sources. www.yearbooknews.com
- Free advice from Astronauts to Zoo Keepers: Select from 12 categories with hundreds of websites and e-mail addresses where you can find experts to answer your questions. www.askanexpert.com
- Get in touch with experts from universities, corporations, national labs, medical centers and more: www.profnet.com

(continued on next page)

The Year's Best Sites for Writers

(continued from preceding page)

Health Issues
- Stretch! Exercise breaks for computer users: www.computerfit.com/ch2pt2.html
- Tips for preventing Repetitive Strain Injury: www.engr.unl.edu/ee/eeshop/rsi.html
- Tired eyes? Check these Computer Vision Syndrome resources: www.visionguard.com/resources.htm

Writer's Resources and Organizations
- The Children's Literature Web Guide: links to children's writers' and illustrators' websites. www.acs.ucalgary.ca/~dkbrown/index.html
- The Institute of Children's Literature: Rx for Writers chatroom and weekly discussion group with authors and editors hosted by Kristi Holl; many articles posted on writing techniques, morale and inspiration, and more. www.InstituteChildrensLit.com
- Online writers' magazines: Contains market info, writing tips, networking opportunities. www.inkspot.com
- Society of Children's Book Writers and Illustrators: www.scbwi.org; (National) hometown.aol.com/southbrez (Southern Breeze: Alabama, Georgia, Mississippi); www.star-telegram.com/homes/scbwi (North Central/Northeast Texas); members.aol.com/nescbwi (New England)
- The Purple Crayon: an archive of information and advice for children's writers and illustrators. www.users.interport.net/~hdu/index.html
- For publishers, agents, and authors: news, information, and marketing services: www.authorlink.com
- Writers' Exchange, hosted by Susan Molthop: hints for beginners, info on markets and marketing, research tools, books, newsletters, celebrity chats, and more. www.writerexchange.About.com
- Stories, one-act plays, and thoughtful critiques from writers all over the world: workshop.fcoppola.com

Supplies and Software
- Tip World: Get handy how-to tips for your favorite programs delivered to your e-mail address. www.tipworld.com
- Online store jam-packed with products and services for freelancers: www.masterfreelancer.com
- Software, books, and writers' supplies with an emphasis on script writing: writerscomputer.com

(continued on next page)

The Year's Best Sites for Writers

(continued from preceding page)
- Computer and software solutions for Mac or PC: www.zones.com; www.egghead.com; www.cybout.com

Free and Inexpensive
- Clip art, invoice and press release templates for Microsoft Word 97: officeupdate.microsoft.com/DownloadCatalog/dldWord.htm
- Almost a free lunch: Check out the oldest free stuff site on the Internet:.www.volition.com/free.html
- Software downloads: Some are free, others are try-before-you-buy. www.softseek.com; www.filepile.com
- One less thing to carry around: Keep your planner and address book online. www.planetfall.com; www.calendar.yahoo.com

Fun Stuff
- The Center for the Easily Amused: Full of games, animations, quizzes, trivia, jokes and more. www.amused.com
- Rejection slip revenge: Try rejecting editors' rejection slips first. www.prairienet.org/youthtopia/or002.html
- Dumb lists: If you think Letterman's top 10 are funny, try these. www.dumb-lists.com
- Wonder what the rest of the world is searching for? Catch a glimpse of some of the searches being performed on MetaCrawler, at any moment: www.metaspy.com
- Fall asleep during Art Bell's program? Want to hear live sports broadcasts from across the country? For recorded archives and live events: www.broadcast.com (Note: You'll need to download the free RealPlayer G2 from www.realplayer.com first.)
- Bring out your voyeuristic side: See what everyone else is doing on this webcam site (all G-rated): www.szym.com/cameras/us.html
- Need a crash course in photography for an assignment? Learn some tricks of the trade from professionals: www.photo-seminars.com
- Trivia, Quotes, Quizzes, Useless Facts and More: www.uselessknowledge.com

Online Research

In Search of Photos on the Web

By Mark Haverstock

Picture it. The right photograph can lure readers into a magazine article or make your book stand out among others on the shelf. It can illustrate how a laser works, help a reader visualize life during the Civil War, or reinforce the spine-chilling mood of a gothic novel. But finding that perfect photo can be as difficult as tracking the elusive Yeti, or catching Leonard Nimoy smiling.

The Right Image

"Photo research is a bear," admits Ken Sheldon, interim Editor of *Cobblestone*, indicating the great lengths the American history magazine takes to find the right photos and illustrations. All the magazines in the Cobblestone Publishing Group use dozens of photos for each issue, and they tap four major resources to find them.

"Every issue of *Cobblestone* has a consulting editor who is an expert in the field," says Sheldon. "These people are often associated with museums and institutions. They often have resources and contacts that can point us to good photos." *Cobblestone* recently did an issue on Benedict Arnold, for example, and the Fort Ticonderoga Museum was very helpful in providing images.

A second resource is authors who submit picture ideas and sources with their manuscripts. The Cobblestone magazines also look to photo houses as well to fill in gaps when necessary. "But in the last few years, the Internet has become a gold mine for finding pictures," says Sheldon. "As far as starting off and getting leads, we've used the Web quite a bit." The primary advantage to using the Web, he says, is the ability to cast a broad net and search all over.

At *Guideposts for Kids* and *Guideposts for Teens*, Photo Editor Julie Brown gets a "shopping list" from her editors and art staff for each issue. "If it's something specific where stock photography will work, I'll go to stock houses like Tony Stone or FPG," says Brown. "I can call them and they'll do the research for me and send me photos, or I can go to their Internet sites, put in a keyword, and preview photos online."

If it's a news item, Brown goes to the Associated Press (AP) website. "AP lets you do a keyword search and the photo will come up," she explains. "Sometimes you have to use several different search combinations to come up with the right photo. If you put in 'Jordan,' you'll get everything from the River Jordan to Michael Jordan."

Whether it's from a stock photo house or a wire service, Brown prefers to get the pictures directly from their websites. "That's a huge advantage to us; it saves a lot of time," she says. "We've already seen the photo, we know we want it, so we can get it immediately. It's amazing how quickly it can be downloaded. Usually, I get a call within the hour to tell me it's been downloaded to our site or e-mailed to me as an attachment." If she needs higher quality images, she requests that the photos be sent on CD-ROM or Zip disk, or she may request the original photo.

Although *National Geographic* has an unmatched reputation for outstanding photo work, the kids' version, *National Geographic World,* rarely uses the in-house library. "We feel that very few photos shot for adults work equally well for children. Most of those photos don't have the kind of information or storytelling flair that appeals to kids," says Alison Eskildsen, Senior Illustrations Editor. "I look to photo stock agencies and a number of photographers, such as natural history photographers whom we've worked with over the years. We have a good idea of what kind of pictures they have and the subjects they shoot."

If Eskildsen isn't using established photographers or stock agencies, she's surfing the Web. "We use the Web for tracking down unique sources, usually in the areas of science, history, and archaeology," says Eskildsen, "those areas where there might be experts in the field shooting pictures who would probably never market them." She cites a story on mummies: "I did a Web search. I found museums that had mummies in their collections, university professors doing historical work on mummies, dig sites, and news articles on mummies. They not only provided leads for information sources, but leads for photos as well."

The Web has really been most helpful to *National Geographic World* for science stories, hunting down high-tech information and photos. "Tech-savvy people are more likely to post the information on the Web," says Eskildsen, and "many universities are posting research on their sites."

By the Book

Editors at children's magazines usually welcome leads and suggestions for illustrations and photos, but many seek their own images and budget them in-house, relieving the writer of most responsibility. Book authors work under a different set of parameters.

Author James Cross Giblin routinely does photo research for his popular nonfiction titles. "On books like my biography of Charles Lindbergh, I've been responsible for gathering the photographs and prints to be used as illustrations, as well as obtaining the permissions for their use. The publisher is responsible for reimbursing me for photographic costs, up to whatever amount is negotiated." (See sidebar on opposite page, Staying on Budget.)

Whether you do your photo research on the Web or by using traditional research methods, you should begin to identify the images that will help you illustrate your book or article early in the research process.

Staying on Budget

Writer and editor James Cross Giblin advises that photograph expenses should be covered by a standard part of the book contract. Writers negotiate the cost of prints and permissions as part of the package. Don't count on a blank check: Photo and permissions budgets, when you can get them, are modest at best, although the amounts are increasing. "In the 1980s when I wrote some of my first books, my budget was only $500," Giblin says. "A contract I signed last year included a $5,000 budget."

Start by seeking photos from free or inexpensive sources as much as possible. "A great many of the photos we get are ones we don't pay for," says Julie Brown, Photo Editor at *Guideposts for Kids* and *Guideposts for Teens*. "We just contacted the U.S. mint for photos because we featured a piece on the new quarters. You contact them, and they'll send you slides or whatever you need free of charge." That reduces the bottom line when it comes to producing a magazine issue.

Alison Eskildsen, Senior Illustrations Editor for *National Geographic World,* says the same. "We use NASA as a source for space and astronomy photos. They go out of their way to provide us with images," she says. "I also use other government sources for photo research, such as the Center for Disease Control (CDC) and National Park Service, but they're less likely to have the photos we need."

To hunt down free and inexpensive photo sources on the Web, author Hope Marston goes directly to the search engines. "I usually try Ask Jeeves first; then I check Dogpile as well as others," she says. "I don't go to stock photo sites because they are too expensive for my budget." Marston has also gone to sites related to her topic and asked for help. "I checked out fire investigators when I needed pictures of accelerant detection dogs. These queries don't always get a response, but it is worth the effort."

"Stock photo agencies have wonderful pictures, but I only go to them as a court of last resort because they are so expensive," says Giblin. "I have always tried to find sources that fit within my budget, since the publisher's contribution is fairly limited." After he had finished the Lindbergh biography, he did fill-in photo research at the stock agency Corbis. "Three years ago, these cost a minimum of $125 for a half-page picture. In contrast, print and permission fees at the Library of Congress run about $35 to $40."

Royalty-Free Images

Free pictures? Not exactly. But royalty-free images deserve a second look, especially with the growing number appearing at established stock photography houses. It's an attempt to streamline the image licensing process and keep costs down.

"With the advent of digital images, a new clip art model is emerging in which the CD-ROM publisher pays the photographer a one-time sum, rather than a royalty each time someone licenses the picture," says Paula Berinstein, author of *Finding Images Online: Online User's Guide to Image Searching in Cyberspace.* This resembles a typical work-for-hire arrangement, unless the photographer has the foresight to negotiate an arrangement where he can sell the same photos himself, leveraging his investment.

There's a second definition. "*Royalty-free* may mean that no royalty is paid to the photographer if the buyer uses it in certain predefined ways," explains Berinstein. An example of this might be the hundreds, if not thousands, of photo library CD-ROMs that can be purchased for personal use, like on a website or to make personal greeting cards. If the buyer wants to use a picture for some other purpose, perhaps in a book or promotional materials, a special higher license fee applies, and the photographer receives a royalty.

According to Rohn Engh, publisher of *Photo Stock Notes,* there is a third definition for royalty-free that generally applies to the buyer, not the photographer. The buyer doesn't have to pay extra reuse royalties like traditional or rights-managed arrangements. The buyer pays once and can use an image in any way.

If you choose to use royalty-free, be sure to read the fine print and ask questions to be sure the photos you choose are cleared for publication needs. Licensing photo rights can be a complicated process, so be informed.

Check out these sources on the Web for more detailed information:

- Paula Berinstein's Online site: www.online.com/onlinemag/OL1998/berinstein9.html
- Comstock Stock Photography: www.comstock.com/web/PhotoStore/StoreMAINFRAME.asp
- Rohn Engh's Photosource Web Page: www.sellphotos.com/psn/February_98.txt

"What I do is make a list of likely sources as I go along," says Giblin. "When I do research in other books, I might not want to use their exact photos, but I would look at their photo sources." Sometimes he finds pictures that lead him to incorporate some information in the text. Text and pictures "feed on one another," Giblin explains. He routinely makes photocopies of interesting pictures he finds, noting sources and catalogue numbers.

In the case of the Lindbergh biography, Giblin found a wealth of photos at the Minnesota Historical Society in St. Paul, not far from Lindbergh's boyhood home in Little Falls. He also found a not so obvious source in the Missouri Historical Society. Lindbergh was backed by St. Louis businessmen, hence the plane's name, *The Spirit of St. Louis.*

"This is where the Internet can become a big help," Giblin says. "Many historical societies, including the Minnesota and Missouri Historical Societies, have websites with indexes of their holdings, which could save you a lot of letter writing and phone calls."

Digital Images
Whether you choose photos from museums, corporations, libraries, or stock photo houses, you'll be faced with another choice: traditional prints or digital format.

Stock houses like Corbis, which acquired the extensive Bettmann Archive in 1994, are going digital to make their collection available to professionals as well as consumers on the Web. "The archive has about 70 million images—historical, news, and celebrity," says Michele Glisson, Corporate Relations Coordinator. Not all 70 million will appear on their Web catalogue. Instead, Corbis has hired photo editors to go through the images, compiling a sampling of the best to be digitized. "We're scanning the best and most demanded images," says Glisson.

Digital images bring up the issue of resolution. Resolution refers to the clarity and amount of detail present in the image, usually referred to in dots per inch (DPI). The more DPI, the better. A photo scanned at 72 DPI might be adequate for a small print or website picture, but totally unsuitable for books or magazines, which usually require 300 DPI or greater. "The higher resolution images should be sufficient for most books, newspapers, and magazines," says Glisson. "The exception would be when people are looking for a detailed portion of an image. We'll go back and rescan the part they want, to give them the resolution they need for that detailed work."

There's also another choice to make

Research

for digital images from Corbis: permissions and licensing. "There are two models we work under," says Glisson. "The first is the traditionally licensed or rights-managed model where, for example, a magazine negotiates a price with us for an image, based on use, circulation, and their standing as a customer. The second, royalty-free model works differently. As a user, you can go online, choose an image for a set price, $39.95 for example, and you can use that image as much as you want for commercial purposes."

The advantage to the royalty-free choice is price, and under the same arrangement you can order thematic CD-ROMs, giving you a hundred or more images for $100 to $300. The traditionally licensed model, according to Glisson, offers some exclusivity: You are guaranteed you won't see the picture on the cover of a competitor's magazine next month.

But are digital photos the answer to the future of photo research—from websites or stock photo houses? Not in all cases. "Sometimes I've had to go back to the original photo because they didn't have a high-quality digital scan for good reproduction," says Eskildsen. But savvy Web masters are beginning to respond. "They're not only posting low-resolution files, but higher quality files as well, and some will post high-resolution files if you ask."

Despite some trade-offs in selection and quality, the Web is an invaluable source for tracking down those elusive photos, and as technology improves, it may become a one-stop shopping center for image research. "The Web has dramatically changed how we do things," says Eskildsen, "by making pictures immediately available."

Sources for Photo Research

Archives and Links
- Archives of American Art (associated with the Smithsonian Institution). 7th & F St. N.W., NMAA-NPG Bldg., Balcony 331 MRC 216, Washington, D.C. 20560. 202-357-2781 www.siris.si.edu
- Archival Resources for History at Bobst Library, NYU. www.nyu.edu/library/bobst/research/hum/history/archives.htm
- Canadian Archival Resources on the Internet, University of Saskatchewan. www.usask.ca/archives/menu.html
- Center for the Humanities. The Miriam & Ira D. Wallach Division of Art, Prints and Photographs, Photography Collection, Room 308, The New York Public Library, Fifth Avenue and 42nd Street, New York, NY 10018-2788. 212-930-0837. www.nypl.org/research/chss/spe/art/photo/photo.html
- The Getty Museum. www.getty.edu/museum/main/Photographs.htm
- Library of Congress National Union Catalog of Manuscript Collections. Web interface to approximately 500,000 records for archival collections in libraries, museums, state archives, and historical societies throughout North America are searchable in this database. lcweb.loc.gov/coll/nucmc/nucmc.html
- Minnesota Historical Society. www.mnhs.org/library
- Missouri Historical Society. www.mohistory.org
- Museum of Modern Art, Collections. 11 West 53rd Street, New York, NY 10019. 212-708-9400. www.moma.org/docs/collection/index.htm
- National Archives and Records Administration search page. www.nara.gov/nara/searchnail.html
- Ready, 'Net, Go: an archival "meta index," or index of archival indexes that refers users to the major indexes, lists, and databases of archival resources. www.tulane.edu/~lmiller/ArchivesResources.html
- Repository of Primary Sources, University of Idaho. www.uidaho.com
- Links to collections and archives. www.uidaho.edu/special-collections/other.html

Books/CD-ROMs
- *Finding Images Online: Online User's Guide to Image Searching in Cyberspace.* Paula Berinstein, Information Today Inc. Updates to book/additional information located at: www.berinsteinresearch.com/updates.html
  Also check the picture resource page and directory of Web image sites: www.berinsteinresearch.com/pics.htm; www.berinsteinresearch.com/fiolinks.htm
- *Stock Photo Smart: How to Choose and Use Digital Stock Photographs* (Book and CD-ROM) Joe Farace, Rockport Publishing.

(continued on next page)

Sources for Photo Research

(continued from preceding page)
- *Stock Photo Deskbook.* The Exeter Company, Inc., 767 Winthrop Road, Teaneck NJ 07666. 201-692-1743. www.stockphotodeskbook.com
  This website has a search feature to match photo categories with stock agencies.

Directories, Databases, Web Links:
- 1-Stop Stock: quick search of 11 major stock photo suppliers. www.1stopstock.com
- A.G. Editions Photo Network contains online image catalogue and the Guilfoyle Report, which contains industry news, annotated directories, and a current photo want list. www.ag-editions.com

Part 6

Profiles

Mary Azarian

Picture the Moment

By Patricia Curtis Pfitsch

"I've always done art, back to my earliest memories," says Mary Azarian, winner of the 1999 Caldecott Medal for her artwork in *Snowflake Bentley*. In a sense, she has always been an illustrator as well.

"I started out as more or less an abstract artist," she explains, "but I've always recognized that my work is very much based on illustration. I tend to illustrate a scene or a quote." Azarian has a printmaking business in her home in rural Vermont; she says her prints, which are not true illustration, "feel very illustrative. I always feel that I'm illustrating something."

Azarian majored in art at Smith College, and at first both painted and made prints. Her later focus on printmaking was mainly a business decision. "After I moved to Vermont, taught school for a while, and had children, I wanted a home-based business. I decided prints are easier to sell than paintings," she explains. "I was equally interested in both, but I didn't want to have to go to the city" to work. Eventually, Azarian concentrated even further, on woodcut prints.

Although Azarian has done many kinds of illustration for cookbooks, poetry, novels, and short stories, most of her illustration work is for children's publishing, where, she says, "There are many more opportunities."

Her first book, *A Farmer's Alphabet*, appeared in 1981. Later books include *Sea Gifts, Symphony for the Sheep,* and *Faraway Summer.* Coincidentally, the real-life Snowflake Bentley shows up as a minor character in *Faraway Summer*. "The illustrations for both books were done at the same time," Azarian says. "It was rather curious that Snowflake Bentley was a character in both books."

Simple Yet Elegant

Azarian was first attracted to the *Snowflake Bentley* manuscript because of the writing. "I liked it immediately. It is very simple, yet elegant. There aren't too many words." She says author Jacqueline Briggs Martin "makes the important points in a pleasing way." The book is the story of Wilson Bentley, a Vermont boy who was fascinated with photography from an early age. He grew to become famous for his pictures of snowflakes and admired for the principles and development of his technique.

Azarian was a bit worried about the subject matter because it parallels her printmaking scenes so closely. "I was uneasy about doing yet another series of illustrations based on Vermont scenes. I was worried that I couldn't make the illustrations fresh enough." After she got to work on *Snowflake Bentley*, however, she stopped thinking about that. "I just began enjoying the process."

She didn't need to do much research for the book. "The text was accompanied by explanations of the science, so that information was supplied." She did visit the Jericho Historical Museum in Vermont to see Bentley's camera. "I wanted to get it as accurately as possible." Azarian also looked at the museum's collection of Bentley family photographs, although she did not attempt to reproduce accurate portraits of family members in the book, with the exception of Bentley himself. This decision came partly from the dictates of the woodcut medium.

In large part, that is a factor in her chosen medium, woodcut art. "The characteristics of the medium are so strong," she explains. "The drawing can be an accurate rendition but the characteristics of the woodcut take over, so the final result is not like the drawing."

Hands On and Off

When she begins illustrating a manuscript, Azarian first does a dummy to decide where the figures should go. "That's as detailed as I ever get in the dummy," which is then approved by the publisher. "I usually meet with the art director to discuss what works and what doesn't."

Azarian has taken quite distinct approaches for the books listed by different publishers. "I did *Barn Cat* for Little Brown; they're very hands-on. We talked about every detail. Houghton Mifflin is very hands-off. They're certainly willing to help out when I need it, but basically they just let me go." Azarian is comfortable with both approaches. "Both are fine. Sometimes it's nice to have everything set and clear so I'm a little more secure in the format, but I can't say I prefer one or the other."

After she does the dummy and confers with the book's art director, she does the illustrations. "I print the block in black and white and add the colors by hand. I sometimes do two, three or even four versions of the coloring before I decide how I want it to go."

"I don't do many preliminary sketches," she explains. "I do a detailed pencil drawing right onto the block, working until I get it the way I want it." She works right on the wood because of the problems involved in translating a drawing on paper to the block. "If the drawing is very detailed, there's the problem of reversal. It's very hard to reverse the drawing without it looking too mechanical, too sharp-edged."

When Azarian sends the finished illustrations to the publisher, they are usually accepted without revision. "Sometimes they don't like something

Mary Azarian Titles

- *Barn Cat: A Counting Book.* Carol P. Saul, illustrated by Mary Azarian (Little Brown, 1998)
- *Faraway Summer,* Johanna Hurwitz, illustrated by Mary Azarian (Morrow, 1998)
- *A Farmer's Alphabet,* illustrated by Mary Azarian (to be re-released)
- *The Man Who Lived Alone,* Donald Hall, illustrated by Mary Azarian (Godine, 1998)
- *Sea Gifts,* George Shannon, illustrated by Mary Azarian (Godine, 1999)
- *Snowflake Bentley,* Jacqueline Briggs Martin, illustrated by Mary Azarian (Houghton Mifflin, 1998)
- *A Symphony for the Sheep,* C.M. Millen, illustrated by Mary Azarian (Houghton Mifflin, 1996)
- *The Tale of John Barleycorn: Or from Barley to Beer,* Mary Azarian (to be re-released)

and ask me to redo it," she says, and in those cases, "I must say, they're almost always right; the second version is usually better."

For Azarian, the easy part is the actual woodcut. "I never worry about that," she says. "The hardest part is breaking the text down, deciding what goes where in the required number of pages." The decision of how to illustrate the text is entirely up to her. "Sometimes it's obvious when there is a strong and specific theme. Sometimes I'm not sure how it will go, but as I complete some drawings, I get a better idea."

Azarian has been in the business of printmaking and illustration for almost 30 years and has an art studio in her home. "Unfortunately," she says, with a laugh. "I save the commute but then I'm never finished working." She does try to work regular hours, usually in the morning, and then stop to do other things. "I have an absolutely enormous garden," she says. She has cut back on its size in recent years, but still spends time planting, weeding, and putting up food for the winter.

In recent years, Azarian has slowed the pace of her art work. Since winning the Caldecott, however, that process has reversed itself. Now she's working more. "It's fun," she admits. "I work better at a hectic pace." She has been doing one or two books a year and doesn't expect that to change much. "I do hope I'll get offered interesting work."

Azarian illustrates books for others, and she also comes up with her own ideas for books. *The Tale of John Barleycorn: Or from Barley to Beer* is her illustrated version of a folk ballad. Her new book, *A Gardener's Alphabet,* "focuses on garden activities rather than individual plants," Azarian explains, "and I'm trying to get a little bit of humor into it. It's for very young children, but I see it as a book to be read with a parent; the parent might enjoy it as well as the child."

As the titles reveal, Azarian tends to illustrate books concerned with the outdoors and rural life. "I live in a rural area and I appreciate it," she says, "and I grew up on a small farm. I tend to choose as subjects things that I see around me." Azarian's inspiration comes from her experience in the moment. "I don't spend time intellectual-

Profiles

izing about what I choose to do. I look out and see a lily that looks particularly wonderful. It becomes an image in my mind, and then I may or may not turn it into a print."

Marilyn Edwards
Values-Added Publishing

By Mark Haverstock

Marilyn Edwards grew up in the small town of Deshler, Ohio. It was the kind of place where people knew their neighbors and traditional values were revered. Kids could be kids and revel in the joys of childhood without being pushed headlong into adulthood. It's these down-to-earth qualities that are emphasized by her two children's publications, *Hopscotch* and *Boys' Quest*.

Although Edwards was not formally trained as an editor, she had considerable exposure to journalism: Her father-in-law was Editor of the *Bluffton News*, in Ohio, and her husband has been a writer and publisher for the newspaper for 30 years. Motherhood expanded the exposure into juvenile publishing. "When our kids were growing up, I subscribed to every mainstream children's magazine that was out there," says Edwards. "That's how I became familiar with children's magazines." Much of what she puts into *Hopscotch* and *Boys' Quest* comes from experience with her own kids, and from several years' experience as a teacher.

Edwards also worked with the International Brotherhood of Magicians publication, *The Linking Ring*. "Our family printing business had published their magazine for 60 years. We didn't do much with editing, just production," she explains. In 1988, she was asked to computerize their operation and handle fulfillment. "Since we'd learned all that, my husband and I figured that if we could do it for the magicians, we could do it for our own publication. So we looked into purchasing a magazine," says Edwards.

Demonstrate and Reinforce

Originally, *Hopscotch* was published by journalist Don Evans and his wife Jane, an elementary school librarian. They started the magazine for girls in 1989 because Jane Evans was frustrated that her school library's magazine collection contained next to nothing for girls. She thought it was geared more toward boys. The Evanses created, financed, and edited *Hopscotch* for several years, but serious illness compelled them to find a buyer for it. The sellers found highly compatible buyers. "Sometimes there are things that are meant to be; this was one of them," says Edwards. "Things seemed to click in conversations with the Evanses. We had some of the same goals and philosophies. This is the kind of magazine we would have published for our own kids if they were still young. We signed the papers at their kitchen table and then went out to dinner. In a sense, the magazine was their child, a labor of love, and we were adopting it." The first issue of *Hopscotch* that the Edwardses published was dated February 1992, but the Evanses are still listed in the masthead as the founders of the magazine.

Several years later, Edwards gave birth to a sibling, *Boys' Quest*. This second publication was created after parents and librarians asked for a wholesome magazine similar to *Hopscotch* that would help boys to develop an interest in reading. "After carefully considering various marketing studies, we decided to launch *Boys' Quest*," says Edwards. "There are fewer freelance opportunities here, but it is the freelance articles that often help in the selection of a new theme."

The shared goals and philosophies that sold the magazine still drive *Hopscotch* and *Boys' Quest*. "We believe that some of the problems in society today result from the breakdown of traditional family values," Edwards says. "Children should learn appropriate behavior at an early age. If this behavior isn't reinforced throughout childhood, it can be lost or forgotten by the time children reach adolescence. This behavior includes respect for adults, respect for others, honesty, integrity, purposeful living, and adopting a caring attitude toward other living things." *Hopscotch* and *Boys' Quest* continually stress these principles and virtues in stories that "demonstrate and reinforce."

Edwards cites a *Hopscotch* story about a girl news carrier acquainted with a lonely, ill, elderly woman. The girl makes a point of checking in on the woman every day. "That isn't the main plot of the story," says Edwards, "but it's a part that sets an example children can identify with. We like stories that have some kind of moral, and a subtle moral works best. This allows us to appeal to a wider audience. "

To Give Children Their Time

The formal editorial philosophy for *Hopscotch* and *Boys' Quest* states explicitly that the world is pushing kids to grow up too quickly. The two magazines aspire to ease the transition from childhood to young adulthood.

"Pushing kids into adulthood is a matter of what we present to them," Edwards says. "Do we present boyfriends, makeup, fashion and fads, or do we present childhood themes? All our themes relate to childhood. Childhood doesn't change. It's what society tries to do to childhood that may change. Many families, teachers, and librarians want a magazine that reflects traditional values instead of fads or trends."

Edwards sees the specifically distinct orientations of the two publications to boys and to girls as a means of helping the young maintain their childhoods. "Though all kids have common interests, like pets, we have two magazines to meet the differing interests of boys and girls. We frequently choose themes that may be more often of interest to boys for *Boys' Quest*—trains, cowboys, cars, planes—and for *Hopscotch,* themes of interest to girls, such as dolls, tea parties, cooking, and babysitting. We are careful not to stereotype by gender, however. *Hopscotch* carries science and math pieces in every issue. *Boys' Quest* regularly includes cooking projects, because I think boys need to know how to cook, too."

The format and content of the magazines also differ to meet the needs of each audience. *Boys' Quest* takes a more hands-on approach by offering puzzles, games, building projects, and experiments, many of which are written by contributing editors. *Hopscotch* typically runs more fiction and poetry. Where *Hopscotch* may approach something in a *cute* fashion, *Boys' Quest* would treat the same with humor.

Material length also differs. Stories in *Hopscotch* are typically 1,000 words, as compared to 500 words in *Boys' Quest*. Neither accepts advertising. "We will never publish these magazines with advertising," Edwards states definitively, "because we feel that's one of many things that can hurt children. Too many societal factors," she says, "are trying to turn them into mini-consumers. If children's magazines aren't carrying outside advertising, they're promoting their own products. Our policy not to carry advertising isn't going to change society, but I also know that we're not promoting those objectives."

Stealth Learning

Another defining quality of *Boys' Quest* and *Hopscotch* is their thematic approach. Edwards explains why they have chosen to adhere to themes: "Teachers, librarians, parents, and home-schoolers have told me they use our magazines as research tools, so theme-based issues make it easier for them. Themes also give kids a chance to read about topics they might not otherwise explore."

One *Boys' Quest* issue included a variety of poems, projects, articles, and puzzles revolving around the theme of time. "I think it's easier to make the issue both educational and fun if you have a focal point," says Edwards. "We want kids to enjoy reading, but also to learn something. Sometimes, we have to trick them into learning, so we take a subtle backdoor approach—a kind of stealth learning. In our horse issue, we did an article on the center of gravity, which could have been very dry. But the idea was designed around how to make a rocking horse: Changing the weights on a rocking horse changes the center of gravity."

Hard-Edged Advice

Themes also offer advantages to writers. "From a writer's standpoint, themes narrow the scope," Edwards thinks. "We have our themes planned through 2003, and we're always adding to the list. There's really no time constraint because we read and select articles as they come in. When an issue is filled, we're done. It could take a year, six months, or even less." Edwards is convinced that this strategy "helps authors better target their articles, and gives us the specific topics we need."

Not surprisingly, Edwards also has very clear-cut opinions on writers and what is required of them. "First, all writers should read the editorial guidelines and several issues of the magazine to which they plan to submit material, to understand clearly what the magazine is about. If there is a philosophy or a statement of purpose, writers should also read that. Based on that information, a writer should send only material that has a chance of publication because it matches the magazine's philosophy or typical content."

For *Hopscotch* and *Boys' Quest*, the serious writer's process must include a close review of the theme list and sample copies. "Writers must know the kinds of stories we look for, the kind of photographic support we need, and the lengths we publish."

Author John Hillman, Edwards recounts, "sent us a short sports story. It was something unusual; you wouldn't find it in *Sports Illustrated For Kids*. It was within our word count guidelines, had excellent photo support, and matched our theme. We snatched it right up, and let the author know that it was just the kind of piece we were looking for. Just about everything else he sent we also bought. A book publisher read several of his articles in our magazine and contacted him to write a book. Since then, he has written several more books."

Equally encouraging to authors is Richard Reegan's experience. The author, Edwards says, "sent us an article that was right on target and he became one of our regulars. Sometimes, I've even created a theme around his stories." The lesson, Edwards says, is "Try to find your niche, whether it's with one magazine or a dozen."

Every Writer a Somebody

In comparison to some other magazines, *Boys' Quest* and *Hopscotch* are relatively small, with circulations of 10,000 and 15,000 respectively—in contrast to the 3 million circulation of *Highlights for Children*, 80,000 readers of *Cricket*, and 700,000 girls who read *American Girl*—but Edwards and her husband "are constantly looking at ways to expand the current magazines and perhaps introduce others."

Don't mistake Edwards's passion about values and quality for a laissez-faire approach to the business of publishing. "One thing that's boosted our circulation is being involved in school magazine sales programs. It has increased our exposure, and we receive many subsequent renewals. Being in Barnes & Noble has helped us out considerably. We also maintain two websites where potential subscribers can order."

But values remain the dominant motivation behind *Boys' Quest* and *Hopscotch*. "No matter how large we become, we will still run the magazine as if it were small," Edwards promises. "We will not treat individuals like numbers. We have a state-of-the-art telephone system, but there's always a human voice to greet subscribers. Everyone who sends a manuscript, whether we accept it or not, is a somebody. Each manuscript gets a handwritten response. There's such stiff competition for writers that I think it's important to treat them with some dignity and respect. We've even received letters from authors thanking us for personal responses. One said, 'I could not let your kind comments come without commenting myself. Such a rare rejection is as uplifting as acceptance itself. I, too, regret that you could not use any of my poems, for it would have felt very home-like in such a gracious place.'"

Edwards has her rewards. "I have to say I love my job here; I look at it as fun. I'm 49, but when I go into the office, I put on my 9-year-old hat and think like a kid."

"We will continue to see new children's magazines on the market," she thinks, "but the Internet will never replace the printed page. Receiving a magazine in the mail is special. There's no joy that compares to sitting under a tree or curling up in a favorite chair with a favorite book or magazine." She also never forgets the educational dimension: "As teachers, we're always concerned about children and reading—not only being able to read, but encouraging them to read. Many children are intimidated by books, but a magazine can serve as a good substitute. Magazines have more illustrations and often have larger type, making them more kid-friendly. The pure joy of reading will never be instilled other than through the printed page."

Frances Foster

Open to Story

By Elaine Marie Alphin

"I started out with children's books in 1955," Frances Foster recalls. "I looked at people who had been in publishing for a long time then, like Ursula Nordstrom and May Massey, and they seemed so great, so unreachable in what they were doing. It feels funny to have lasted that long myself, at least in terms of years." She laughs warmly, not at all unreachable, despite having edited some of the great children's authors of the last half of the century.

Foster was fortunate in her apprenticeship. "I started out as an assistant to Alice Dalgliesh, who had begun the children's book department at Scribner's," she says. "It was a great place to start because she was a born teacher. That's where I got my foundation and my roots." In 1961, Foster left Scribner's to do freelance editing while her children were small. She first worked for William R. Scott at Young Scott Books, and then worked under Margaret McElderry at Harcourt Brace, and at Alfred A. Knopf and Pantheon.

"It's a little bit different freelancing than being on the staff of publishing houses," Foster explains. "You're not out of touch completely, but you're not as actively involved in the whole publishing process. That changed with the recession of 1973 when divisions of publishing houses were cut back. At Knopf, rather than laying off people on staff, they cut back on freelancers. So, when a position opened up on staff, I applied and that worked out well for everyone."

A Distinguished List of Authors

Unlike some editors, who start out working with adult manuscripts, Foster always wanted to edit children's books. "A lot of it was the look of them," she explains. "I was interested in art, and it seemed to me that children's books combined art and story in this very appealing way. I was also interested in developmental issues. I thought of majoring in developmental psychology, but then I became more interested in literature and decided from the very beginning that I was interested in doing the children's book end of publishing."

Foster found out quickly that working with talented authors could be rewarding—and challenging. "My very first editorial project, when I was freelancing, was the revision of Roald Dahl's *Charlie and the Chocolate Factory*," she recalls, "when the editor

An Editor's Perspective

"Some of the special books I worked on were books I sort of inherited," Foster explains. Rather than individual books, however, Foster thinks "in terms of authors, because most of the people I've worked with have become ongoing contributors to the list. I think when you get just one or two books from somebody, you might tend to think more of 'the book.' Certainly, when I'm working on a book, I'm very much focused on that title. But when you take a historical view, it's definitely the author I think of."

- Roald Dahl. *Danny, Champion of the World* (Knopf, 1975); *The Enormous Crocodile* (Knopf, 1978); *The Twits* (Knopf, 1981).
- Leo Lionni. *Cornelius* (Knopf, 1983); *It's Mine* (Knopf, 1986); *Matthew's Dream* (Knopf, 1991); *An Extraordinary Egg* (Knopf, 1994).
- Lore Segal. *The Story of Mrs. Lovewright and Purrless Her Cat* (Knopf, 1985).
- Mavis Jukes. *Blackberries in the Dark* (Knopf, 1985); *Like Jake and Me* (Knopf, 1987), a Newbery Honor Book.
- Ann Cameron. *The Stories Julian Tells* (Pantheon, 1981); *The Most Beautiful Place in the World* (Knopf, 1988); *The Secret Life of Amanda K. Woods* (Farrar, Straus & Giroux, 1998).
- Suzanne Fisher Staples. *Haveli* (Knopf, 1993); *Shabanu: Daughter of the Wind* (Knopf, 1989), a Newbery Honor Book; *Dangerous Skies* (Farrar, Straus & Giroux, 1996).
- Kate Banks and Georg Hallensleben. *Baboon* (Farrar, Straus & Giroux, 1997); *And If the Moon Could Talk* (Farrar, Straus & Giroux, 1998).
- Margaret Anderson. *Children of Summer* (Farrar, Straus & Giroux, 1997).
- Tomek Bogacki. *I Hate You! I Like You!* (Farrar, Straus & Giroux, 1997).
- Claire Nivola. *Elisabeth* (Farrar, Straus & Giroux, 1997).
- Mordicai Gerstein. *The Wild Boy* (Farrar, Straus & Giroux, 1998); *Victor* (Farrar, Straus & Giroux, 1998).
- Louis Sachar. *There's a Boy in the Girls' Bathroom* (Random House, 1988); *Holes* (Farrar, Straus & Giroux, 1998).
- Peter Sis. *A Small Tall Tale from the Far Far North* (Knopf, 1993); *Starry Messenger* (Farrar, Straus & Giroux, 1996), a Caldecott Honor Book; *Tibet: Through the Red Box* (Farrar, Straus & Giroux, 1998), a Caldecott Honor Book.
- Elizabeth Spires. *The Mouse of Amherst* (Farrar, Straus & Giroux, 1999).

wanted Dahl to change the description of the Oompa–Loompas to avoid racist criticisms and characteristics, I had no idea what I was getting into! I didn't know that Dahl had a legendary temper and could be very difficult, but I had enough sense to realize that this might be a pretty ticklish subject, and so I wrote a very careful letter, and got a very, very nice, reasoned response from him, where he was totally cooperative! The editor in chief was amazed by this response, because everybody else in the department had burned bridges with Dahl over past books. The assignment had been given to me because I was the only fresh one there. By virtue of my not having alienated Dahl further or anew, I came to work with him on subsequent books."

Foster inherited a few writers she feels particularly honored to have worked with. "I became Leo Lionni's editor when his original editor retired in the early seventies. Other authors I worked with were Mavis Jukes, who was a Newbery Honor winner, and Suzanne Fisher Staples, who also won a Newbery Honor. I did the first book that Peter Sis both wrote and illustrated, *Rainbow Rhino*, and his next book, *Follow the Dream*."

Discovering Sachar

When Foster saw the first manuscript from Louis Sachar, the National Book Award and Newbery winner in 1998 for *Holes*, she was torn. "I was very interested in *There's a Boy in the Girls' Bathroom*," she says thoughtfully, "but it was deeply flawed. Louis has this way of exaggerating characters. I think it's a genius that he has, but in the first draft the parents and the teacher and the guidance counselor, and even Bradley, seemed so exaggerated that they were sort of caricatures. But I felt he had an amazing story to tell, and that they were all amazing characters. He had just taken them too far for me."

So, she rejected it, but sent Sachar a lengthy letter explaining her concerns. "I didn't make any suggestions for revising it, partly because I didn't think he could revise it. I knew nothing about him at the time, but I just thought, 'It's a shame, this could be really good.'" But Sachar, who is a lawyer who gave up practice, didn't give up on his book. He had his agent contact Foster to say he was coming to New York and wanted to see her. "I remember grudgingly agreeing to see him—grudgingly, because I didn't think anything could come of this." She laughs. "And that was something I'll never regret! A lesson in that is always be open."

Foster and Sachar discussed everything in the book. "I remember him disagreeing with some of the things I'd said. When I'd tell him, 'I don't really believe the teacher,' he'd say, 'This teacher a friend of mine had said that very thing, and it's absolutely true.' So, then, what was I to say? Except, 'Well, sometimes the truth doesn't work in fiction, so your challenge is to do whatever you have to do to make it believable.' It was clear to me that he knew what he was doing, that he had a reason for doing and saying everything. Sometimes seeing his reason made me realize why something hadn't worked, or that he just had to go back and rethink it. In a month or two, the manuscript came back. He had done such a total and successful revision that it was very, very exciting!"

The lessons learned on *There's a Boy in the Girls' Bathroom* paid off in Sachar's subsequent books for Foster. "He's certainly a quick study. He's such a good self-editor that he doesn't leave much structural work that needs to be done. That's the only book of his that I had much input into the shaping. The other books have all involved more line editing. I don't have to salvage something or redirect it, because he's already done that. If something feels a little loose, you question it and he tightens the connection, but the connections are all there. I think that's what makes *Holes* so intriguing, because it's like a giant puzzle. I think this reflects the way his head works. I think his legal discipline has a lot to do with what a trap his mind is."

When to Break the Rules

While Foster worked to shape the structure on *There's a Boy in the Girls' Bathroom*, she was careful not to limit Sachar's style. "He does all sorts of things you're not supposed to do," she comments. "He'll step outside the story and address the reader directly, and he knows he's doing it. Sometimes, I start to question something with him, and then pull back and edit my own question before I ask him, when I realize that what he's doing really does work. I think he's guided not by rules, but more by instinct, and his instincts are right on the mark."

Foster didn't know what Sachar was writing until she had *Holes* on her desk, but she trusted his instincts. "I never know what he's got in the works until it's done. He'll say, 'I'm working on a novel,' or something like that, so it's not as if he says nothing, but he doesn't tell me anything more than the bare category. When he started *Holes*, he didn't know what to call it, because he didn't know what he was going to write about, but he was going to try to write something. So he named his file *Try*. Each day when he opened up his file, he would have to type in 't-r-y.' He said at one point he thought 'Maybe I should rename this.' But then he decided that this was really a good reminder to him, just to try."

When she got *Holes*, Foster knew that Sachar's try had paid off. "*Holes* didn't surprise me at all, because I saw the seeds of it in his earlier books. I think the reviewers who said they didn't think he had it in him were really reflecting the way they were suddenly looking at him in a different way. But I didn't see *Newbery* written on it! Partly, of course, because you don't want to jinx a book by holding out any hope for it. You can't help but have high hopes, but I can't tell you how successful I have become over the years (as I think most editors do), in not letting ourselves entertain too much hope for awards. Louis has, for much of his career, been ignored by the establishment. It was the kids who discovered him and who really loved his books, not the reviewers."

Foster laughs, a little sadly. "You get so accustomed to really wonderful books not getting the attention you think they deserve. I work almost with blinders on. I know what's going on in the industry, but I don't read everything the way some of my colleagues do. I

Life After Downsizing

Writers in 2000 dread the news that one more publisher has been amalgamated into a huge industry that will cut back on editors, leading to cutbacks on unsolicited submissions, and making it that much harder for a new writer to break in. But there's hope after downsizing—even for the editors who find themselves let go! After 20 years on staff with Knopf, Frances Foster found herself given early retirement in a downsizing move. "It was a rather large downsizing operation," Foster says, "where 20 or 25 of us in the juvenile division of Random House Knopf were let go. The offer from Margaret Ferguson to start my own imprint at Farrar, Straus & Giroux came instantly when the news came out. I might have taken early retirement, actually, if this hadn't been offered. It was a great opportunity; it could be that I needed to be booted to take advantage of it."

Foster tends to stick with her writers, and they stick with her, even to the point of moving from Knopf to Farrar when she began her imprint. "I think one of the miscalculations that was made at Random House —and these decisions were made by a part of the company that wasn't at all close to the editorial book publishing end of it—was the assumption that authors would stay with the house. It wasn't a case of my campaigning to get people to follow me. An author, I think, feels very loyal to the house, but that loyalty is felt through the editor. That's the connection you make. So a number of authors, including Louis Sachar, Peter Sis, Suzanne Fisher Staples, and Ann Cameron, have come with me. Those are just a few of the people that I had worked with for many years at Knopf. We had a long and pretty solid relationship."

don't have quite the feelers going out in all directions. I pay close attention to the books I'm doing, so I'm maybe not looking at things in as comparative a way as anyone else might. Even before the Newbery, the National Book Award was such a thrill—and it was completely unexpected! We submitted the book, but we'd submitted other books. And anything that has a jury—well, you learn to realize that you can't predict what the outcome will be."

Acquiring New Authors
With the many writers that Foster has acquired over the years, "It's the work that draws me. With a first novel or a first story, it's a leap of faith that you have to take. There's no track record to tell you whether or not it's going to be successful, or whether or not this person is going to write anything else. But it's the substance of the story that draws me."

In this day of emphasis on voice, Foster finds herself attracted to different components in a manuscript. "I guess I'm less inclined to be drawn to what we used to call *atmospheric* stories, something that's beautiful and poetic, but doesn't have a story. I look for a certain amount of substance, something to sink my teeth into. It's a mixture of plot, character, theme, but I find I don't think so much in terms of plot. I want the book to *say* something. I want it to *mean* something. Leo Lionni always talks about picture books as being like theater, and it's true. The presentation, the setting—the whole book is important."

Nancy Gruver & Joe Kelly

Girl Power & Media

By Patricia Curtis Pfitsch

When Nancy Gruver and Joe Kelly, founders of *New Moon*, were first thinking about starting a magazine, they talked to their eleven-year-old daughters and a few of their friends. "They thought it was one of Mom's crazy ideas," Gruver recalls.

By traditional standards, it was. Gruver's background was in regional development, and Kelly had been a reporter and host for a local public radio show. They had no prior experience in publishing. "We were too naive to know not to do it," Kelly says.

"We started by taking a book out of the library on how to start a magazine," Gruver adds, "and we found out that we didn't meet any of the criteria. We didn't live in New York City. We didn't have millions of dollars." They live in Duluth, Minnesota, and began with $10,000 in personal savings.

What they did have was the passionate belief that girls entering adolescence need support to stay true to who they are in the face of strong cultural messages telling them to change themselves. "I was looking for resources that would provide this kind of support, and I couldn't find anything," Gruver explains. That is what they provide in *New Moon,* a magazine for girls.

The Right Message

She and Kelly were and are concerned with the messages communicated in traditional magazines for girls, especially those that contain advertising. "By definition, advertising creates a need that will motivate readers to buy the product. If what you're selling are products that change the way you look," Gruver says, "then the way to create that need is to make you feel you don't look good the way you are. There's nothing wrong with enjoying make-up and clothes," she continues. "What's wrong is when girls are persuaded to do this because they don't feel good about who they are."

Inspired by *Meeting at the Crossroads,* by Carol Gilligan and Lynn Michael Brown, which documents the psychological development of girls eight to sixteen and discusses the hurdles girls face during adolescence, Gruver and Kelly, their daughters, and other girls in the Duluth area, determined that the girls themselves could act as editors for the magazine. "Gilligan and Brown say that girls need to express who they are in the world," explains Gruver, "and they need the help of adults to do that."

Not only is the editorial board of *New Moon* composed of girls the ages of the readers, 80 percent or more of the writing in the magazine is done by girls between the ages of eight and fourteen. "That's the other way we're very different," Gruver says. "*New Moon* allows girls a voice, and brings the voice out into a larger arena in a way that it's accorded great respect. The magazine is professionally produced." That was one of the decisions made by the girls themselves. They wanted to make a real magazine, not something that looked like they'd run it off on the copy machine during lunch hour. They wanted work that girls were doing to be accorded as much respect as an adult magazine.

Gruver and Kelly talked about the new project in a holiday letter, and mentioned they were looking for writing by girls. "We have a network of family and friends from all over the country, and in some cases outside the U.S.," Gruver explains. "There was a huge need for something like this. It was the right idea at the right time. People were so excited that they told other people. We had five hundred subscriptions before the first issue was even printed."

Skeptics often believe that the involvement of girls in the decision-making process is only window dressing or a focus group, but one visit to a meeting soon shows them their mistake. "Almost universally they say, 'Wow, this is a real editorial meeting!'" Kelly reports.

A Collaboration

"It's not that the girls do everything," Gruver says. "We do have a staff of adults as well. Adults have experience in how to get things done in the world." Sometimes the adults help with revision; when the girls like the idea in a submission but not how it's expressed, the adults can help with rephrasing. "Our experience as adults helps their voices to become clearer," adds Kelly.

The magazine is really a collaboration between the adults and the girls. How do the adults know when they've gone too far in pushing their own ideas? "The girls tell us," Kelly says. "They develop the confidence to challenge us as peers. They have as much authority as we do."

Kelly and Gruver believe that collaboration is at the heart of what they do. "We're working in the gray area," Gruver says. "We're listening and respecting each other. We're not cutting off other people's passions. We're modeling tolerance."

The internal process of collaboration and respecting the passions of others that's integral to assembling each issue of *New Moon* shapes the spirit of the magazine, and letters to the editors show that the readers value this as well. Many readers say things like, "I really love the fact that there's a place where we can disagree."

Gruver and Kelly are delighted with this response. "Girls need to learn how to disagree," Gruver points out. "They don't get a lot of experience in how to do it."

Over the New Moon
Since the advent of *New Moon*, Gruver and Kelly have expanded their message to other forums. *New Moon Network* is a newsletter for parents, teachers, youth workers and other adults who are concerned about girls' development.

"We've also been publishing a magazine called *Hues* for college students," Gruver says, "but we've recently made the difficult decision to suspend publishing. It doesn't have the kind of circulation we need to keep it going." They found that college-aged readers prefer to buy single issues from the newsstand rather than subscribe. Without the stable income from subscriptions, Kelly and Gruver found it impossible to keep the magazine going without selling advertising. Rather than compromise their mission, they decided it would be best to stop publishing.

"We've got a few other exciting things going on," says Gruver. "One is a series of New Moon Books, published by Crown." The topics for the first four books are friendship; money, power, and independence; sports; and writing. "These books have been edited by girls as well," explains Gruver. "We've pulled together a group of girls from around the country to do the books."

They've also been developing a pilot for a television show. "That's quite exciting. Our goal is to have the show on public television. We just recently got a distribution agreement with a major distributor to PBS stations around the country. Now we're looking for underwriters to fund the production of 13 shows."

The idea is to create a newsmagazine show for girls. "We'll be taking the same types of stories that are in *New Moon*, profiles of girls and features about things girls are doing, and putting them on television," says Kelly, "and there's a section where girls will be able to create their own videos and send them in." As with the magazine and the books, their TV show will have a production board made up of girls 8 to 13.

"All these girls are not unusual," Kelly says. "Things like this can happen anywhere—if an environment is created in which girls get to exercise their power." Gruver adds, "They've already got the power. There are just shamefully few places to exercise it."

To that end, Gruver and Kelly are presenting more and more workshops and conferences where adults can learn to share power with girls. Kelly has recently developed a national nonprofit organization called Dads and Daughters. "Its purpose is two-pronged," explains Kelly. "First, it will help fathers deepen our relationships with our daughters, and second, we'll be working to change the cultural messages that value girls for how they look rather than who they are and what they do. Fathers have a unique impact on their daughters. We need to be aware of what that is and how to make it a positive impact."

Information about all the *New Moon*

publishing projects is available on their website: www.newmoon.org.

Now, seven years after the beginning of *New Moon*, Gruver and Kelly have great hope. "We've become a focal point," says Gruver, "a clearinghouse. People tell us what they're doing; we hear about wonderful things that are happening. People are taking girls seriously. I was recently at a conference in Los Angeles, a summit on girls and television. Throughout the day, they repeatedly used our buzz words—why we should listen to girls, and how we can change the way the media relates to girls.

"We believe in the power of media created by girls. We think that has so much power to change the world. We still have a long way to go," Gruver adds. "I don't want to minimize that. But there's been a lot of positive change."

Mary Heaton

When Words Call

By Vicki Hambleton

Mary Heaton had all the hallmarks of someone destined for a career as an editor: a passion for words, including grammar, a love of books, an early interest in journalism. Today, whether it is her task to write, edit, or flow text together with art, as Managing Editor of *Crayola Kids,* her joy comes from crafting words into work that educates, entertains, and illuminates.

From an early age, writing has been her well-loved avocation. "I won some essay contests as a kid, and when I was in the Camp Fire Girls, I started a newspaper for the group I was in. As I grew older, my summer jobs were always at a newspaper. Then in college, I edited the school paper."

College for Heaton was the College of St. Catherine in her home state of Minnesota, where she majored in French and chemistry. When asked why she, a budding writer, chose these majors over English, she is quick to answer. "I decided that the English majors were doing what well-educated people should do anyway, so I pursued other subjects." She laughs as she recalls being a French major editing the school newspaper "on a campus full of English majors." But she is a strong advocate of a liberal arts background for anyone interested in pursuing a career as a writer or an editor.

Heaton continued her education with a master's degree in French language and literature from the University of Iowa. She began her career as a teacher at the University of Montana and taught for two years before taking a hiatus to start a family. She has two children, both now grown and working in education.

When her children were in grade school, Heaton went back to work. "When I resumed my career, I went back to journalism," although her first job combined an educational setting with communications, as a public information officer at St. Francis College in Pennsylvania. She also freelanced as a copy editor. She went on to earn her teaching certificate at St. Francis, but never got the chance to make use of it. She answered an advertisement for a job at *Highlights for Children* and has been in children's magazine publishing ever since. Her magazine career began in copyediting. She credits her background in French with helping her get that first job: "Because I had taught French language classes, I was considered something of a grammarian."

Critical Thinking

Heaton was with *Highlights* for nine years, in many different positions, culminating with the job of Contributing Editor. She describes the experience as "invaluable" because "I learned so much about editing and selecting and critiquing. Because *Highlights* accepts so much material over the transom, editors there really learn to develop critical thinking and how to cultivate freelance writers. The editors do a little tweaking, some work on how a piece should be presented or what it needs in the way of art or illustration. They really get a thorough grounding in all aspects of magazine editing."

When Heaton left *Highlights*, she returned to freelancing and writing for a local newspaper. "I wrote a weekly column for a local paper for which I got paid $15 a week. But I wanted to see if I could do it—come up with a new idea on deadline each week. I did it for two years and built up quite a collection of essays. It was something that was fun and free-wheeling, and that also gave me great fulfillment."

Heaton also went back to work as a freelance copy editor. "I did a lot of textbook editing and I loved it. What is fascinating about copyediting is that you learn so much about subjects that you might otherwise never have explored. I did a book on the history of art from the Pre-Christian to the contemporary, and I thought, 'Let me be a contestant on *Jeopardy* now!'" Heaton loves copyediting and considers it an important skill for an editor.

Next Stop, Iowa

While she enjoyed her freelance work, Heaton continued to look for a full-time position that would present new challenges. The answer came in the form of a telephone call from a good friend, Don Stoll, former Executive Director of EdPress. He called and asked how she felt about Iowa. Her answer was, "Well, Des Moines is all right." Next stop, Iowa, to edit a magazine being launched in 1991 by the Meredith Corporation: *Crayola Kids*.

Heaton arrived in time for the second issue. She describes the early days of the magazine as exciting and challenging. "It was a very different experience for me, to be working on a new venture, especially coming out of *Highlights,* where the philosophy had been set in tradition. We began *Crayola Kids* with a minimum of staff—an editor, an art director, and myself, and for a time, I was the only full-time employee."

Crayola Kids has evolved to become a magazine for the whole family, although it began as a publication for kids that had a parents' section. Originally, it was primarily subscription-based. Today, it is very much advertising-driven for revenue, rather than dependent on subscriptions.

Ads, for Better or Worse

The subject of advertising in children's magazines is a constant topic of debate in the industry, and it was one at *Crayola Kids* as well. "We have a parents' panel," explains Heaton. "We send them questionnaires that help us develop our pages and learn what kids like best. We finally bit the bullet and asked them what they thought about the ads in the magazine. Out of 35 people, 34 said the ads were just fine."

"Ads," she says, "have become, for better or worse, an integral part of all our lives, and they don't take away from the benefits of the magazine. I think magazines are tremendously important in kids' lives. The niche publishing that is going on right now is just wonderful. When you think of what Carus or Cobblestone Publishing have done—hitting different age ranges and interests—it's really great for kids. The kids can scratch the surface of a subject, and if they want to go further they can or they can move on to something else."

Heaton is very proud of the work she and her colleagues have done in creating *Crayola Kids*. "Success, for me," she explains, "translates to helping kids learn without them feeling as if they are being taught. Information should be useful, but also fun. We take a topic and make it fun and at the same time leave our readers, I hope, with a desire to go away and learn more and we try to show them how to unleash their own creativity."

In her mind, one of the best parts of *Crayola Kids* is the trade book printed in each issue. "We print every word and every illustration, so it's not just an excerpt. We have a very small staff and so we use books that have already been published, but sometimes we have chosen one, as with *Miss Spider's Tea Party*, that has just come out and then it really takes off."

While a small staff often translates to long hours, Heaton loves the diversity and demands of her job. A typical day might include planning for a photo shoot, working with the art director on a final page proof, talking with a freelancer, and answering reader mail. She calls copyediting a "flow experience" and admits that it relaxes her.

Asked where she might be 10 years from now, she laughs and answers, "Probably retired and birdwatching and copyediting. I have some book ideas that I have been collecting, but haven't had time to get to. You know, I think I'd love to do another newspaper column." The avocation of writing continues to flow into Mary Heaton's lifetime vocation.

Profiles

Jacqueline Briggs Martin
To Bear the Weight of Story

By Patricia Curtis Pfitsch

When Jacqueline Briggs Martin's children were small, they lived in the country. "We had few close neighbors to visit," she remembers, "and fewer neighbor children to play with Sarah and Justin. We amused ourselves, often by reading children's books." It was that enjoyment that led Martin, writer of the 1999 Caldecott Medal winner *Snowflake Bentley*, to write for children. "I wanted to write books that children and parents, grandparents, aunts, and uncles could share. I bought a pen and tablet and started."

Although she has now published 11 books, success didn't come easily. "It was over two years before anyone wanted to take a second look at any of my submissions," she explains. Until five years ago, she taught preschool part-time, in addition to writing. Now she is able to write full-time. "I try to do my writing in the morning and do other jobs—letters, house jobs, and such—in the afternoon."

Martin's love for writing, specifically in the picture book genre, comes through in her words. "I love that each word is important and must bear its share of the weight of the story," she says. "I only write about subjects that interest me so much that I cannot not share them with others."

She wrote *The Green Truck Garden Giveaway, A Neighborhood Story and Almanac* after reading about a man in Oregon who gives away gardens. "I love gardening, so I knew I had to make a story out of it." In addition to the story, the book includes instructions for growing plants in containers, starting a butterfly garden, and various recipes for food and for bug repellent. Martin also loves trees and acorns, the core ideas behind *Button, Bucket Sky*. She grew up on a farm in Maine that was in her family for seven generations, and was personally interested in researching eighteenth-century life in Maine. Much of that research found its way into her historical fiction picture book, *Grandmother Bryant's Pocket*.

Bentley's World

Martin first learned about Wilson Bentley, the man who photographed snowflakes, in 1979, when she read an article about him in *Cricket*. More recently, at the urging of her children, she decided to turn that interest into a book.

"Picture books are what I write," she says, "so I had a picture book format in mind from the start." *Snowflake Bentley* features the basic story of Bentley's life in large print. More complicated details of his life and career appear in sidebars next to each picture. "I like the sidebar approach," Martin explains. "I used it with the gardening book, and thought of using it with *Washing the Willow Tree Loon*. We decided to use it with *Snowflake Bentley* because it allowed us to add more details of his life while still keeping the story short enough to be of interest to younger children."

At first glance you might think a book like *Snowflake Bentley* is easy to write. The text is deceptively simple, spare and full of specific concrete sensory details that drop readers right down into Bentley's world. They can taste the snow on their tongues, see the lanterns flickering through the darkness, hear the swoosh of sleds pulled by oxen. Here is the book's first sentence:

> In the days
>   when farmers worked with ox
>   and sled
>   and cut the dark with lantern
>   light,
>   there lived a boy who loved snow
>   more than anything else in the
>   world.

But Martin researched for six months before even beginning to write, and continued researching even after she began writing. "I visited Bentley's home and the museum set up by his children and now operated by the Jericho Historical Society. I read books: books about farming in New England in the late nineteenth century, a Bentley biography for elementary students (*Snowflake Bentley, Man of Science, Man of God,* by Gloria May Stoddard), and many of the articles Wilson Bentley published in magazines." She also read many articles about Bentley and talked several times with the archivist at the historical society, Ray Miglionico.

The book went through a number of drafts before she was satisfied with it. "In telling any story the writer has to decide the 'best' way to tell it. Sometimes the only way to decide is to write it one way and see whether or not it works. I had to decide if I wanted to tell his story in one day, in one snowstorm, or more chronologically." Eventually, she, and others, decided that a chronological approach would work best.

"We worked very hard on the book," Martin says. "I say 'we' because many are involved in making a picture book: writer, artist, editor, book designer." She was proud of the book when it was done and felt that the love and care of all the people involved showed. "I didn't know if it would be a book that would have a small band of followers or find a larger audience, but I did feel that those who read the book would see it in our admiration for Wilson Bentley and our efforts to tell his story."

The Vision Remains

Martin is now working on another nonfiction book, *The Lamp, the Ice and the Boat Called Fish,* about the *Karluk,* a

Jacqueline Briggs Martin Titles

- *Bizzy Bones and the Lost Quilt,* illustrated by Stella Ormai (Lothrop, Lee & Shepard, 1989)
- *Button, Bucket Sky,* illustrated by Vicki Jo Redenbaugh (Carolrhoda Books, 1998)
- *Good Times on Grandfather Mountain,* illustrated by Susan Gaber (Orchard Books, 1992)
- *Grandmother Bryant's Pocket,* illustrated by Petra Mathers (Houghton Mifflin, 1996)
- *The Green Truck Garden Giveaway: A Neighborhood Story,* illustrated by Alec Gillman (Simon & Schuster, 1997)
- *Higgins Bend Song and Dance,* illustrated by Brad Sneed, (Houghton Mifflin, 1997)
- *Snowflake Bentley,* illustrated by Mary Azarian (Houghton Mifflin, 1998)
- *Washing the Willow Tree Loon,* illustrated by Nancy Carpenter (Simon & Schuster, 1995)

ship of the Canadian Arctic Expedition of 1913. "It got trapped in the ice in August, 1913, and eventually sank," Martin explains. "The party on board included crew, scientists, and an Inupiaq family, including a father, mother, and two girls aged eight and two. My book is an account of how the people on the *Karluk* coped and tried to survive cold and ice and little food." Houghton Mifflin is publishing the book this year.

Martin has published with several different companies. "Different publishers are comfortable with different formats and subject matters," Martin explains, "and editors move a lot, and that often changes what a publishing house wants. When Norma Jean Sawicki went to Tichnor & Fields Children's Books, at that time an imprint of Houghton Mifflin, she took Martin's *Higgins Bend Song and Dance* with her. So when I had finished *Grandmother Bryant's Pocket,* I sent that to her also, and when I was looking for a home for *Snowflake Bentley,* I sent that to Houghton Mifflin as well. I have had the good fortune to work with several very fine editors at various houses: Dinah Stevenson, Virginia Duncan, Judy Levin, and Ann Rider."

Since *Snowflake Bentley* won the Caldecott Medal, Martin's life has changed a bit. "I'm busier now. I am adjusting to that, and trying to find a new schedule that still allows time for writing, which is what I love to do."

But her vision of her writing is the same. "I've always wanted to write books that would be shared and enjoyed the way my children and I enjoyed books in the farmhouse in Lisbon, Iowa. I have always wanted to write books that would introduce children to characters, either in fiction or nonfiction, that they would remember and carry with them for all of their days. My goals have not changed.

"I feel very fortunate to be able to do what I do. I can't imagine another career for myself and I'm grateful to family and friends for their support and encouragement."

J.K. Rowling
A Magical First
By Vicki Hambleton

Picture this: Scholastic buys your first published novel's American rights. The book is published in the United States, and immediately jumps to the best-seller list and stays there. The book is so popular that American readers go to Amazon.com's British site to order the second book, already published in the United Kingdom. Much to the dismay of Scholastic, some American booksellers are stocking the British edition of the second book. This, in turn, prompts Scholastic to announce that it will publish books two and three of the series months ahead of schedule in response to public demand.

Rather than the plot of a best-seller, this scenario is the true story of first-time author J.K. Rowling, who is indeed living a life as fantastic as that of Harry Potter, the character responsible for her rags-to-riches story. For anyone who has been living on Mars for the past year or so, Harry Potter is the star of Rowling's delightful novels, which have struck the hearts of readers of all ages. Originally published in the U.K., where Rowling lives, *Harry Potter and the Philosopher's Stone* (renamed *Harry Potter and the Sorcerer's Stone* for the American audience) won Rowling international attention almost immediately. The second and third books, *Harry Potter and the Chamber of Secrets* and *Harry Potter and the Prisoner of Azkaban*, immediately appeared on best-seller lists.

Harry Potter and the Sorcerer's Stone won Britain's National Book Award, as well as the Smarties Prize, a kind of Booker Prize for children's literature. *Harry Potter* rose to the top slot on the British best-seller list—something no children's book has ever done before. The author thinks one reason that the books have "crossed over" between adult and juvenile readerships is because she didn't write with a specific audience in mind. "What excited me was how much I would enjoy writing about Harry. I never thought about writing for children. Children's books chose me. I think if it is a good book, anyone will read it."

Fantastically Funny

Scholastic bought the American rights

to the book for more than $100,000, the most ever paid for a first-time author's children's book. Rowling has signed a seven-book contract, and a seven-figure movie deal with Warner Brothers. As amazing as all this seems, anyone who has read one of the Harry Potter books understands at least in part the reaction the first book garnered from critics and fans alike.

Harry Potter is a delightful character who has fans from 8 to 80. The story of his trials as a wizard-in-training is fantastic enough to transport the reader deep into another world, filled with dragons and ghosts, games of Quidditch (a kind of airborne soccer), and sorcery classes. Yet, Harry and his friends retain a humanity that lets each reader relate to the emotions they all experience. Who can't identify with Harry's fears as he sets off for the first day of school and wonders if he will make friends?

The humorous elements of the story keep it all from getting either too frightening or too sad. In one wizard class, the task is to change a mouse into a snuffbox. "Points were given for how pretty the snuffbox was, but taken away if it had whiskers." The author says that she really wrote the book for herself. "It is my sense of humor in the book, not what I think children will find funny, and I suppose that would explain some of the appeal to adults. On the other hand, I think I have very vivid memories of how it felt to be Harry's age."

Mapped Out
Rowling's work has been compared to the books of Roald Dahl and C.S. Lewis. The Harry Potter books may or may not join the ranks of *Chronicles of Narnia* as eternal classics, but they at the very least have become a phenomenon of children's publishing.

Harry Potter was "born" on a train trip between Manchester and London, England. Rowling says the idea for the story "just fell into my head." It would be five years before that idea would become a finished novel. From the beginning, the author envisioned the story as unfolding in seven books, one for each year Harry spends in wizard school. She mapped out all seven books at once and even wrote the final chapter of the last book to remind herself of where she was going.

Rowling keeps notes on everything from the laws of wizardry to interesting names she can make use of in the books. She even collects names. "*Hedwig* was a saint, *Dumbledore* is an old English word for bumble bee, and *Snape* is the name of a place in England."

A History
While she was writing the first Harry book, Rowling's personal life was falling apart. Her mother died at the age of 45 from multiple sclerosis. Rowling was robbed and then lost her job. Determined to start over, she packed her bags and moved to Portugal to take a job teaching English. While there, she met a journalist, married, and gave birth to a daughter. The marriage didn't last and four months after giving birth, Rowling and her infant daughter were heading back to the U.K. to settle in Edinburgh.

Rowling found herself in an all too familiar trap, faced by so many single mothers. She could not work because she couldn't find affordable child care and so lived on welfare until she was able to get situated. Her days were spent wheeling baby Jessica around the streets of Edinburgh until the infant was asleep. Rowling would then "run, literally, to the nearest café" and sit and write Harry's story. She quickly learned which cafés would let her sit for an hour and a half and nurse a single cup of coffee, which was all she could afford.

Harry Potter and the Sorcerer's Stone was written in longhand and when the book was completed, Rowling typed it on a manual typewriter. She sent copies to two agents whose names she pulled from the British version of *Literary Marketplace*. The first agent returned the manuscript almost immediately. The second agent, Christopher Little, saw something in the work and began to shop it to publishers. Three publishers turned down the manuscript on the grounds that it was too long for children. The fourth, Bloomsbury, snapped up the book. Bloomsbury was responsible for showing the manuscript to Scholastic's Arthur Levine, and the rest is publishing history.

Casualties to Come
Rowling is regularly asked what will happen in the succeeding books in the series. "The theme running through all seven books is the fight between good and evil," she explains, "and I'm afraid there will be casualties!"

Still, her fans breathe a sigh of relief knowing that there are more books to come. A good book is hard to find, a potentially great series of children's books even harder. Harry Potter may prove to be that something special, an experience that readers carry with them as they grow up and then look forward to sharing with children and grandchildren.

Rowling wrote her first book at age six and has been writing ever since. She has no plans to rest on her laurels. "I have always written and I know that I always will; I would be writing even if I hadn't been published. Even if writing is now my full-time profession, it is also my greatest pleasure."

Louis Sachar

Writing for the Fun of It

By Elaine Marie Alphin

"I was an economics major," Louis Sachar recounts. "There weren't a whole lot of required courses for that, so I had to fill the rest of my schedule. One day, a cute little third-grade girl was handing out pieces of paper that said 'Help! We need teachers' aides at our school.' This was for college credits. It sounded easy—no homework, no tests. I really had no interest in kids at that time. I never would have imagined I'd have a career writing children's books. But I loved being an aide."

From that experience came Louis Sachar's first children's book, *Sideways Stories from Wayside School,* and his wacky stories found their way into more than three million children's hearts and funnybones.

Despite his reputation for humor, Sachar is laid-back and thoughtful as he chats, rarely making jokes or laughing out loud, the way readers laugh as they enjoy his books. He has discovered that writing children's books is full of opportunity. "I think the state of children's writing is probably at an all-time high," he says. "There's a lot of good literature out there for kids, and schools are using children's literature to teach reading and writing, instead of primers."

Making Time

Sideways Stories from Wayside School was published in 1978, while Sachar was in law school. "I came from a family of doctors, lawyers—professional people, so I felt channeled in that direction," explains Sachar. "But writing was always my passion. In high school I dreamed of being a writer, but I didn't know I'd ever really get published. I went to law school because I knew it was difficult to earn a living by writing." Writing books while going to law school sounds daunting to most writers who have trouble balancing their writing with jobs or families, but not to Sachar. "I just made time for it," he says. "I only wrote about an hour or two a day, in the mornings, and went to class in the afternoons."

Practicing law could be even more time-consuming than going to class, but Sachar felt his writing continuing to call him. "When I graduated law school, I kept thinking I need to get a job," he recalls. "I remember I really agonized over it. Meanwhile, I would write primarily in the morning, and do part-time legal work in the afternoon to pay the bills. But I kept thinking, I really ought to get a job. Finally, after four years, it occurred to me that I'd obviously made a decision not to look for a job, so I forced myself to quit worrying about it. Then, maybe four years after that, the books started selling well enough for me to drop the law work."

Critical, and Parental, Reactions

While Sachar's books have been popular with children and teachers from the beginning, the critics weren't so enthusiastic. "I don't really think about critical acclaim," Sachar says, "I guess because I never really get that much.

"Several years ago, the *Horn Book* came out with a list of all these books that have been published over the last however many years. They gave them a rating of one to five, for what they recommended for libraries. I was just shocked that they gave *Sideways Stories from Wayside School* the lowest recommendation. You think, 'Well, they don't like it. But the book has become sort of a classic, and it's just odd that they wouldn't recommend it.' You wonder if someone has a grudge against you."

Sachar must be more than a little pleased that in the end, those reviewers were won over. His novel *Holes*, published by Farrar, Straus & Giroux, won the triple crown of awards: the National Book Award, the Newbery Medal, and the *Boston Globe-Horn Book* Award for Excellence in Children's Literature. This is only the second time any book has won all three. The other was *M.C. Higgins, The Great,* a 1975 book by Virginia Hamilton.

Remembering one reviewer who complained that his writing was pedestrian and his plots predictable, Sachar gives one of his rare laughs. "Well, I know my plots aren't predictable! I guess the ones that get to me are the reviews that I can see truth in, the reviews where they point out things and I go 'Yeah, that's right, I did tend to do that.' But when they say something like the plot is predictable: Well, what I constantly hear from readers is that the plots are very unpredictable! So when I get that, I ignore it."

It's harder to ignore parents who try to ban his books. *The Boy Who Lost His Face*, about the pressures of adolescence, has been the target of censorship groups because some characters in the book use obscenities. "People who complain haven't even read the book," Sachar points out. "One boy checked the book out of his school library, and then his mother complained about the language in the book. They had a school meeting and a committee was formed, and then the principal and the parents met, and they all voted to keep the book. This took about three months. So the book's back on the library shelf, and that same boy checks it out again. The librarian says, 'Are you sure? You know the way your mom feels about this book.' And the boy says, 'Well, I never got to finish it.'"

Sachar lets the story make his point, just as he does in his writing. "You don't have to set out to write a preachy book," he contends. "You just make a fun book with characters kids care about, and they will become better people as a result."

Bubbling Inside

Sachar has learned to trust his own idea of how to make his points. After his early success with *Sideways Stories from Wayside School*, his novel *There's a Boy in the Girls' Bathroom* was initially rejected by Frances Foster at Alfred A. Knopf. While she thought the book had promise, she concluded that the manuscript was too deeply flawed to be revised. But Sachar believed in the book, and got his agent to make him an appointment with Foster. Sachar asked for clarification of Foster's comments, then went home and revised. A few months later, he sent her the book again, in nearly the form it was ultimately published.

Writers often form critique groups to support each other through rejections, encourage each other through the challenges of writing, and discuss manuscripts. Not Sachar. "I never let anyone read a book until it's finished," he declares. "Nobody. Not anyone. I never talk about it. Once it's read, it's gotten out: It's no longer this thing bubbling inside me. If I've been working on a book for a year, the only way I can tell anyone about it is to finish it. It makes me want to write it that much more." An exacting editor of his own work, Sachar doesn't ask anyone to critique his books. "If somebody says they like it, that makes it hard to find the effort to improve upon it. If they say they don't like it, it might discourage me."

Not showing anyone his works-in-

Louis Sachar Titles

- *Sideways Stories from Wayside School* (Follett, 1978)
- *Johnny's in the Basement* (Avon, 1981)
- *Someday Angeline* (Avon, 1983)
- *Sixth Grade Secrets* (Scholastic, 1987)
- *There's a Boy in the Girls' Bathroom* (Knopf, 1987)
- *Wayside School Is Falling Down* (Lothrop, 1989)
- *The Boy Who Lost His Face* (Knopf, 1989)
- *Dogs Don't Tell Jokes* (Knopf, 1991)
- *Sideways Arithmetic from Wayside School* (Scholastic, 1992)
- *Monkey Soup* (Knopf, 1992)
- *Marvin Redpost: Kidnapped at Birth?* (Random House, 1992)
- *Marvin Redpost: Is He a Girl?* (Random House, 1993)
- *Marvin Redpost: Why Pick on Me?* (Random House, 1993)
- *Marvin Redpost: Alone in His Teacher's House* (Random House, 1994)
- *More Sideways Arithmetic from Wayside School* (Scholastic, 1994)
- *Wayside School Gets a Little Stranger* (Morrow, 1995)
- *Holes* (Farrar, Straus & Giroux, 1998)
- *Marvin Redpost: Class President* (Random House, 1999)
- *Marvin Redpost: A Flying Birthday Cake?* (Random House, 1999)
- *Marvin Redpost: Super Fast, Out of Control!* (Random House, 2000)
- *Marvin Redpost: A Magic Crystal* (Random House, 2000)

progress allows Sachar to leap right into writing without any outline or advance planning. He starts with an idea, plays with it, and lets it take him where it will. Sometimes, this leads to a dead end. For two years he worked on a novel for adults that "just never came together," he admits. "Maybe I was trying too hard to be adult instead of just writing a fun story like I do when I write for kids. But the characters never quite came alive for me, and the plot never got me excited. Finally, I just didn't want to finish it, and so I started to write something for kids again."

That something was *Holes*. The young adult novel grew out of a hot Texas summer, and the idea of a curse. Sachar returned to Texas heat after a vacation in Maine, "and that's how I got the idea for a detention camp in the desert. I was just tired of writing about school, so I was trying to come up with a different setting. The story grew out of the setting. Then I tried to write a fun story. I know it sounds weird to say that, because the setting sounds grim, but to me it was always my intention to write a fun adventure story. I thought kids would be intrigued by what it's like to be sent to prison."

The other idea that got Sachar going was the curse. "I had used a curse in an earlier book, *The Boy Who Lost His Face*," he explains. "I wouldn't have used the same idea, except that I was told the book was going out of print, so I thought I can use the idea again. But then it turned out they'd made a mistake, and it wasn't going out of print. If I'd known that I wouldn't have used the curse, because I don't want to repeat myself. But by then I'd already incorporated the curse into the story."

Piece by Piece

Holes is an intricately plotted story of destiny, of friendship and loyalty, responsibility and redemption, all filtered through an understated humor. At least, that's how the book reads in its published version. But Sachar had no idea how the pieces of the puzzle would fit together when he began writing.

"Some of the connections I made right away, but how to get there and what was going to happen between then and now, I didn't know. I just tried to come up with really colorful characters, like Kate Barlow, the kissing outlaw, and the Warden. When I first made them up, I really didn't know how I was going to use them."

Sachar solved plot problems as they arose. Once he had a solution, he found other ways to work the idea throughout the book. "At one point, I was trying to figure out how Stanley and Zero were going to survive out in the desert. I found out about native plants, and came up with sweet onions. It hadn't occurred to me to connect Sam with the onions yet; he was just fixing the school. Then I got the idea that he was selling onions, and the boys would survive by eating onions. I rewrite about five or six times, and by the time I got to the third draft, I had the book pretty well plotted out."

Once *Holes* was finished, Sachar read it aloud to his daughter's fellow fifth-graders. "It was helpful to me to be able to read it out loud, to get the feel of it, with an audience. Somehow, when I read aloud to a group, I'm able to get caught up in the story and see it through their eyes."

Sachar sent his revised *Holes* to Foster, having no idea that he had written a book that would receive critical attention and prestigious awards, "but many people said it was a contender. I always thought awards involved a very secretive process, so I certainly didn't want to base my hopes on what people were saying. That's not why I write books, to win awards, so I didn't want to have a feeling of failure if it didn't win.

"When Farrar first came out with the cover, I wasn't really happy with it," Sachar says. "I talked to Beverly Horowitz at Bantam Doubleday Dell about whether we had to use the same cover for the paperback. She made a comment: 'Well, wait and see what happens in January,' so she was obviously thinking about the Newbery. She just didn't want to jinx it by putting it into words, but she was suggesting that by January the book might be so identified with the present cover that we wouldn't want to change it."

Telling the Story

One of the most surprising aspects of *Holes* wasn't its cover, but its voice. Sachar shifts back and forth from a conventional third-person voice that focuses on Stanley, the main character, to an omniscient voice that relates stories from the past about Stanley's "no-good-dirty-rotten-pig-stealing-great-great-grandfather," and about the history of Green Lake.

In a time when so many writers strive for a compelling first-person voice, or at least a voice that stays with one viewpoint character, Sachar refuses to be limited. "I do what's necessary to tell the story," he states. "I would tell it all from one character's point of view if I felt that told the whole story, because I know it's kind of bothersome to the reader to have to switch. But there are times when I just can't tell the story from one point of view, so I'm required to draw back and show other things. That's tricky. That was the hardest part about writing *Holes*—all the different stories, the different time scenes."

Despite the hard work, Sachar would have been pleased with *Holes* even without the critical recognition. "We're all very excited about the awards, but to me, the greatest reward for the book is still the actual writing. I tend not to think about the fact that so many kids like my books. Writing, to me, is such a personal experience. It's maybe a year-and-a-half with the book, not talking about it with anyone. By the time the book comes out two years later, I feel a detachment from the actual writing of it."

By that time, Sachar is already working on something new, but, of course, he won't talk about that yet. All he'll say is, "I'm just trying to write a fun story."

Stella Sands

Honest Work

By Vicki Hambleton

"With *Kids Discover*, I feel I am doing something meaningful with my life," explains Editor Stella Sands. "Opening kids' minds to new ideas and experiences is the most fascinating thing one can do. I call it honest work. I don't think I'd be happy making a living say as a broker on Wall Street."

Sands has spent her entire career working for and with children. She was born in Florida and spent her childhood in New Jersey. After college at New York University, where she decided she wanted to be a writer, and graduate school at Fordham in American literature, she went to work as a teacher. She taught English and writing in New York in junior and senior high school and at the college level.

But with writing still very much a consuming interest, she moved from teaching to writing the textbooks used in the classroom. Sands spent time at Henry Holt and Scholastic, writing language arts texts primarily, and along the way continued her own writing. She wrote a children's novel, *Odyessea*; she wrote plays, one of which was produced at Ensemble Studio Theatre; and she wrote film scripts. "I've always been someone who enjoys working on more than one thing at a time," she says.

In 1990, Sands's work was brought to the attention of Mark Levine, who was developing an idea for a new children's magazine. "When we conceived of the idea for *Kids Discover*," recounts Levine, "a friend recommended Stella to me. I met her and felt that she was exactly what was needed to make the idea work. She understood from the outset the concept of *Kids Discover*. The magazine is a bit unique in that it is not a traditional kids' magazine. We see it as being more like a book, really, and Stella had tremendous experience in educational book publishing. She has been our founding editor and I think she is a great selection for us, and we for her."

The Workings

Sands describes her job at *Kids Discover* as "a match made in heaven," and as editor she has remained true to the original concept, with only a few changes. Sands attributes this unusual phenomenon to the fact that her vision for the magazine, and the publisher's, were on the same wavelength from the outset. "Over the years, we have debated changing our style," she says, "but we haven't because it has been so successful."

Kids Discover explores a theme each month to educate 6-to-12-year-olds colorfully. Topics covered over the eight years the nonfiction magazine has been published are as wide-ranging as pyramids, the brain, robots, Pacific Rim, Columbus, garbage, television, soccer, elephants, the Vikings, the equator, and glass. Sands says she tries to vary the themes so that each year covers a wide range of topics. "We try to sprinkle some geographical concepts with some historical themes, with some science themes so if you look back over a year, there is variety."

Sands thinks *Kids Discover* is a hit with kids because of the approach it takes to learning. "A kid's magazine," she explains, "should give its readers the impression that knowledge is cool, give them the sense that they can absorb knowledge and enjoy it at the same time. Learning and having fun don't have to be opposites."

One way the magazine achieves this is through design. "We as readers take in information in paragraphs," she explains, "but we, and kids especially, can only process so much at a time, so to enhance that kind of learning the magazine uses a lot of pictures. It is sort of a double whammy—the pictures reinforce the text. And although we use a lot of art, the pictures are never gratuitous. Some of our pages are meant to be read in order, others stand alone, but each one is connected to the next and together they flow as a book would."

Part of the success of this approach comes from the way the writers put together their information. "We break each issue down into spreads," explains Sands. "Then the author comes up with six parts of the story or six discrete parts of the topic that we want to cover, and then we decide how to flow those parts together."

The Impact

The letters she receives from young readers, says Sands, are proof that *Kids Discover* must be doing something right. "I can't tell you how many great letters we get from kids saying they just love an issue. They often quote facts from the magazine that they never knew. I get letters from kids saying they can't wait to get their next issue in the mail. It's so rewarding for me to know that we are making an impact."

Kids Discover originated as a subscription-based publication mailed primarily to homes, but in recent years, it has found a new audience in the school and library markets. While Sands is very pleased with this, she says the magazine will continue to operate independent of the school curriculum. "We do consider the school curriculum when we plan our issues," she explains, "but that doesn't mean we won't do a topic that is not defined by a school need."

"For example, we just did an issue on the subject of blood. Now, I don't know any curriculum that studies blood, but we liked the idea of taking apart the body in an interesting way and doing a whole issue on blood. A textbook would never approach the subject in that way."

While *Kids Discover* keeps her busy, as one might imagine Sands is also working on other projects. One is creating computer simulations used in high school classrooms. The simulations are designed to help kids learn how to become decision-makers. Sands compares the writing to writing dialogue for a play.

Whether it is editing *Kids Discover* or writing a film script, Sands says her career will always involve kids. To her, the explanation is simple. "I love writing and I love knowledge and I love reading and I love kids—what more could I do than work for children?"

Judith Woodburn

A Bookshelf to Be Filled

By Vicki Hambleton

"I didn't come to children's publishing until much later in life," admits Judith Woodburn. That may be, but as Vice President and Editorial Director of Pleasant Company, she has landed in the thick of it.

Launched by Pleasant T. Rowland in 1985, Pleasant Company has sold more than 56 million American Girl books, as well as the company's extraordinarily successful dolls, their accessories, clothes, and other lines of books. As Editorial Director of the company Woodburn is charged with growing the company in new directions and overseeing its print and CD-ROM products.

How Woodburn ended up at the head of such an empire is serendipitous. "My path is unusual," she admits, "but then I think everyone's is." But few have such an unusual story.

Secret Admirer

Pleasant Company first hired Woodburn in 1994 as Editor of *American Girl* magazine. At the time, she was teaching magazine writing and editing at Marquette University and freelancing as a writer and editor. Her areas of expertise included urban design, architecture, and psychology. Prior to that she was Editor of *Milwaukee Magazine*, an award-winning regional.

So how does an editor get from urban design to a girls' magazine? For Woodburn, the answer is through a secret admirer. "I received a call from a recruiter who had gotten my name from someone in New York—who I may never know. This individual knew my work at *Milwaukee Magazine* and suggested I might be a candidate for editor of *American Girl*."

Woodburn wasn't sure she wanted to go into children's publishing, but went on the interview nonetheless. One visit to Pleasant Company headquarters in Middleton, Wisconsin, was all she needed to convince her. "I was just astounded by the caliber of people that I encountered and the passion and energy of the women—and I do say *women* because at the time there were very few men—who were running this company."

Woodburn says she was "smitten" and made the decision to give up freelancing in exchange for the world of girls. While the leap from complex adult subjects to the concerns of preadolescent girls seems daunting, she says, to the contrary, her training in the adult world was perfect for her job as Editor at *American Girl*.

"First of all, I think in my core there had always been a passion for this kind of work that had gone untapped. I also think I was better at editing a children's magazine because I had edited one for adults for so long." Woodburn's previous writing often involved complex, highly specialized subjects. Her task was to "take complex concepts and make them intelligible to readers who were intellectual but not necessarily informed about the subject matter." She could do the same for the young readers of *American Girl,* and besides, she says the magazine helped her "tap into my inner 10-year-old."

Like many who write nonfiction for children, Woodburn understands that explaining a concept to a child takes a writer who has a deeply grounded understanding of the subject matter and an editor who acts as a complement.

A good editor, she says, is "one who can read deeply enough to understand what the author is trying to do, even if the author doesn't always understand herself, as opposed to deciding what you the editor want and trying to convince the author that that is what she should want too."

Re-Evaluating Image

After two years as editor, Woodburn and other top management at Pleasant Company sat down to re-evaluate where the company was going and take a hard look at its publishing program. Pleasant Company started as a company about dolls and books. That image of the company, says Woodburn, has brought it under criticism by some who didn't take the books seriously because of the dolls.

"Pleasant T. Rowland," states Woodburn, "*never* wanted to be known as the doll lady! In fact she insisted that a book come with every doll. You couldn't buy a doll without a book." The books have sold into the hundreds of thousands, even purchased without the doll.

Given the success of the books, Pleasant Company began to explore other publishing opportunities. In 1996, the company was already publishing The American Girls Collection books, as well as *American Girl* magazine, and the American Girl Library line of advice and activity books.

"We really saw that we had a base to build on," says Woodburn. The company decided to broaden its base to appeal to a wider audience of young girls. Woodburn was promoted to Vice President and Editorial Director and was charged with identifying the needs of the American Girl audience and determining how to best serve those needs.

"The American Girl Collection is of interest, obviously, to many girls," she explains, "but there are so many other kinds of girls for whom we could be publishing great books."

In answer to those needs, Pleasant Company launched two new fiction lines for 1999-2000. The books are for slightly older girls, age 10 and up;

Woodburn estimates that readers top out around 14.

History Mysteries are targeted to girls who have loved but outgrown the historical fiction of the American Girl Collection. Each of five standalone titles will feature an 11-or-12-year-old heroine who solves a mystery set in America's past.

American Girl Fiction offers contemporary novels that deal with real life issues like parents' marital problems, homelessness, and serious illness. Three titles debuted in the fall of 1999. American Girl Library will also launch five new titles of activity books.

More to Come

Asked whether the company would ever consider venturing into the young adult market, Woodburn is quick to answer 'no,' at least not under the American Girl umbrella.

"First of all, there are a number of publishers who produce YA material and do it very well. But second, I think that the older reader wouldn't be interested in reading something from American Girl. There is a point at which that whole world no longer has appeal to a girl, and I think that's as it should be."

But Pleasant Company is exploring the market for younger readers. Part of its new publishing agenda includes entering the world of acquisitions. The company has acquired the rights to Marissa Moss's line of books based on the character Amelia, who first appeared in *American Girl* 1995 and was a huge hit with readers. Amelia is the make-believe author and illustrator of *Amelia's Notebooks*. Three new notebooks and a CD-ROM were published in 1999. The company has also recently acquired the backlist and future books for a picture book character. Also under development is a new nonfiction concept. For devotees of the original American Girl books and dolls, not to worry: Two new characters are planned.

With all these projects before her, Woodburn laughs when asked to describe a typical day. "I don't think I have a typical day," she says, but the challenges clearly inspire her as she helps bring Pleasant Company into the next millennium. She has a new bookshelf waiting to be filled.

"I think the reading public, and many authors, think of us as a series publisher, which we are," she explains. "I want to broaden authors' concept of us as a publisher of many different books for many different girls."

Part 7

Idea Generation

Ideas

Idea Generators

52 Exercises for the Year 2000

By Margaret Springer

Some writers have enough ideas for several lifetimes, and are always finding more. Others are eager to write, but have nothing to write about. If only they lived somewhere else, or led more exciting lives, or enjoyed exotic vacations and interesting adventures.

For both kinds of writers—and for the rest of us in between—here are 52 idea generators for the year 2000, one for every week of the year. They are in no particular order, and each could spin off in several directions, for fiction or nonfiction.

Remember that any topic can be opened up, and made more specific and interesting, by choosing to write about it using a different setting (indoor, outdoor, region, country, culture) with a different time frame (time of day, season, past or future era) from a different viewpoint (fiction) or slant (nonfiction) for a different target age level in a different genre (mystery, how-to, profile).

"Just write what occurs to you," advises humorist Stephen Leacock. "The writing is easy. It's the occurring that's hard."

To help with that "occurring," combine this list with your own creativity and your own wonderful mind! Ask "what if?" and "why?" and "how?"—from a young person's perspective. Find the ideas below that sparkle most for you. In many cases, you won't even have to leave home.

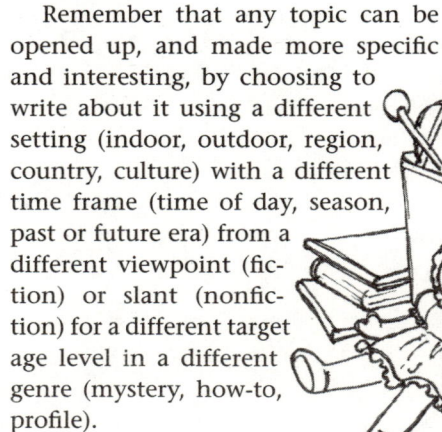

A Year of Idea Generators

Below are suggestions for each week of the year to inspire ideas. They can help with settings, characters, motivation, point of view, plot, dialogue, and more. To do each justice, use a notebook to work on each exercise over the course of a week, but space is provided here for a few initial ideas.

■ 1. Look out of your window right now. What do you see? Study that familiar scene with new eyes. Challenge yourself to use some element of that scene—setting, character, event, topic—in a new piece of writing.
....
....
....

■ 2. Brainstorm about time: calendars, clocks, sundials, computer clocks, time zones, time in space. Fill at least one page with ideas on this topic, for fiction or nonfiction.
....
....
....

■ 3. What are unusual or little-known foods in your region? Do some familiar food items have local names? Recipes for kids? Plot possibilities?
....
....
....

■ 4. What are nature's challenges where you live? Throw something you've experienced—heat, cold, tornado, blizzard, flood—at a young main character, using all five of your senses to create the scene and arouse the protagonist's emotions. Or use some aspect of this experience for an article.
....
....
....

■ 5. Pick one page at random from the *Yellow Pages*. Find something there and start writing: an occupation, topic, first or last name, setting, and so on.
....
....
....

A Year of Idea Generators

■ 6. At your local mall or shopping area, visit a store or business you have never been inside. Set a story scene here, or find a nonfiction angle.

■ 7. Study the classifieds, personal ads, and notices of auctions in a local paper. Look for unusual hobbies. Poignant sales. Hints of conflicts. Family situations.

■ 8. Visit the oldest building in your area. What is its history? Who was involved with its beginnings? What kind of story might be set there?

■ 9. Think of a skill that you enjoy, that others know you're good at. Wood carving, calligraphy, needlepoint? Write about some element of that for a young audience, or make it the hobby or job of a story character.

■ 10. What happens to stray animals in your area? Visit a humane society, wildlife sanctuary, or shelter. Find out about unusual, abandoned, or nuisance creatures, whether pets or wildlife. Fit that to a child's world.

■ 11. What is the most popular sport for kids where you live? Visit a practice, and/or a game. Take notes. Do the same for a lesser-known sport where kids are involved.

Ideas

A Year of Idea Generators

■ 12. Find out about local crime prevention and safety programs for children. Ask three kids, of different ages, what they are learning about how to cope. How is their world different, in this respect, from that of your own childhood?

....
....
....

■ 13. Spend a few hours at a bus, train, ferry, or plane terminal near you. Observe people, eavesdrop, soak up the atmosphere. Think of new beginnings—or endings—in the lives of your story characters. Consider public transportation of the future, and of the past.

....
....
....

■ 14. Imagine your home without one man-made element—plastic, for example. Now imagine homes 70 years from now, with some new element that hasn't yet been discovered.

....
....
....

■ 15. Make a list of things you fear. Transpose that into a child's world, and use a fear as the main element of conflict in a story. Or write for a teen audience.

....
....
....

■ 16. Phone or visit your local historical society. What family histories have been written in your area? What other unpublished sources can you find?

....
....
....

■ 17. Which birds migrate to or through your region? What other seasonal cycles of nature occur there? (Salmon spawning? Ice breaking up? Maple sap running?) Use this in a new piece of writing.

....
....
....

A Year of Idea Generators

■ 18. Talk to a children's librarian (public or school library). What are the favorite fiction and nonfiction choices the librarian sees in different age ranges? Which gaps might you fill? Ask young people the same questions.

■ 19. Visit a local cemetery. Read the gravestones, especially the oldest ones. What stories do these tell of children and families in years gone by? Combine names from different stones and imagine a fictional family.

■ 20. Notice familiar things in your home as if for the first time. Ask questions like a curious four-year-old. How does a toilet flush? What makes a VCR work? Why do people have toes?

■ 21. What is the ethnic background of the newest residents where you live? Learn about their customs, family names, history, festivals. Let a child from that background be a natural part of your next story.

■ 22. Visit an elderly person and ask about childhood memories (ancient history for the young!). Incorporate some element of your notes into a story or article.

■ 23. List the character traits of three adults you know very well, both strengths and weaknesses. Imagine how these appeared in childhood. Then mix these up and create three totally different young characters. Put them into a story.

A Year of Idea Generators

■ 24. Modern families. Make a list of different family situations you personally know about. Blended families? Bitter divorces? Grandparent dating/marriage? Adopted child? Illness? Write fiction or nonfiction on some aspect of one of these, from a child's viewpoint.

....
....
....

■ 25. For one full day, write down every odor you encounter, from morning coffee through each stink or fragrance. Then list the odors you remember from childhood. Use these notes in your next writing.

....
....
....

■ 26. Talk to young people involved in charities in your area. How do they raise money? Why? Who are their role models? Look for profiles and plot ideas.

....
....
....

■ 27. What body of water, or river, is closest to your home? Where does it come from, and where does it go? Find little-known facts about the history, adventures, and disasters related to it.

....
....
....

■ 28. Visit (with permission) a kindergarten class, or young Sunday School class. Ask the children for their ideas on one subject, and write down what they say. Examples: What new invention would they invent? How do they cook their favorite foods? What are their ideas to bring about world peace?

....
....
....

A Year of Idea Generators

■ 29. Revise a holiday story from your files, changing it to take place just after or just before that holiday. Or consider lesser-known festivals and holidays, and change your story setting to one of those.

....
....
....

■ 30. Eavesdrop on teens in a mall, on a bus, or other public place. Notice what they are (and are not) wearing. Start a story with dialogue you overheard. Check the style and tone of manuscripts you've written for this age group.

....
....
....

■ 31. Read today's newspaper, and write something new based on one or more elements you find there: a plot element from real news, a composite name, a situation, an important issue, an unusual event.

....
....
....

■ 32. Talk to a family member or friend about their occupation: piano tuner? security guard? child care worker? Ask about challenges, anecdotes, stereotypes, Give this job to an adult in a story, or make it a young person's goal in life.

....
....
....

■ 33. At the library, look up the day of your birth, and find out what (else!) happened that day. In your birth year? How would these events affect a child?

....
....
....

■ 34. From your own childhood, write about an incident in which one strong "negative" emotion dominated (anger, jealousy, shame). Transform that memory into a plot for young characters today, in a totally different setting.

....
....
....

Ideas

A Year of Idea Generators

■ 35. What sports programs exist in your area for children confined to wheelchairs? Are all school programs and activities accessible? What barriers do such young people encounter?

■ 36. Think about pets you have known. What memorable incidents from their lives or deaths might work in a story or give you a new angle for nonfiction?

■ 37. Brainstorm a list of titles, using published story and article titles as models. Change part of the phrase, or give a different twist, in the same number of words. Ignoring the original content, write a new story or article from one title.

■ 38. Who can kids call, outside their families, if they are in serious trouble? Talk to a social worker, or someone involved with a telephone distress line. What issues and problems are the most common among young callers?

■ 39. Who lived before you in the physical space where your home now is? Early pioneers? Native people? Where did they come from, and how did they live? How far back can you go?

■ 40. Take a manuscript you want to revise. Incorporate an element of the performing arts—music, drama, singing, dance, theater, etc.—past or present, popular or classical.

A Year of Idea Generators

■ 41. Who are the local heroes, male or female, where you live? Local villains? Why? Create young heroes and villains partly based on these models.

....
....
....

■ 42. Look in your food cupboard. How many countries are represented there? Which items traveled the farthest to get to you? How might children be involved in, or affected by, the production of those items?

....
....
....

■ 43. What is the smallest denomination or faith group where you live? Imagine a child whose family are members. How might those beliefs affect a young character at home, with friends, at school?

....
....
....

■ 44. Ask a science teacher about experiments and science fair projects: best and worst; cleverest and funniest; anecdotes and incidents. Attend a science fair, and/or talk to the young participants.

....
....
....

■ 45. Think of adults you know who are peacemakers, and those who are troublemakers. What makes them so? What messages do children get from the adult world about dealing with conflict?

....
....
....

■ 46. Visit an industry or workplace near you that is on the cutting edge of technology. Visit a place where things are deliberately made by hand, or in some other "old-fashioned" way. Mine both places for story and article ideas.

....
....
....

A Year of Idea Generators

■ 47. Food banks and poverty. How many children in your area go to bed hungry? What programs exist to help? Imagine a homeless and/or hungry child as your next protagonist.

....
....
....

■ 48. Make a list of all the textile applications you can think of beyond fashion and home decorating: in medicine, sports, engineering, space, etc. Find article ideas, or incorporate one of these applications as an element in a story.

....
....
....

■ 49. Visit an unusual educational or training program in your area. A literacy program for elderly learners? Children's classes in a specific culture/language? Training animals for the hearing-impaired? Use that experience in your writing.

....
....
....

■ 50. People live in many different kinds of homes: houses, apartments, trailers, tents, houseboats, vans. In a new story, or one being revised, set your fictional family in a home environment you have never used before.

....
....
....

■ 51. If you can, surf the Internet for children's sites. Explore their cyberspace world, and the controls that exist there. What might interest a young person, and what adventures might occur, intentionally or unintentionally?

....
....
....

A Year of Idea Generators

■ 52. Seek out a local event you would not otherwise attend: a boat show, if you know nothing about boats; a rock concert, if you prefer classical music (or vice versa); an ethnic festival you're unfamiliar with. Find characters, conflicts, angles, settings.

....
....
....

And always, keep your notebook handy!

Ideas Online

Alive with Inspiration

By Donna Freedman

Lisa Wroble, author of the Kids Through History series, was headed for a book festival. She wanted to do something fun for kids, so she decided to teach some old-time games. First stop: the Internet. Wroble found an abundance of information on the games of goose, senet, hopscotch, and other historical pastimes. She made up brochures teaching kids how to play, and brochures for teachers as well. She thought she was finished, but she wasn't. "My mind would not stop generating games and ideas for classroom history activities," says Wroble, a writer from Michigan. Her next project, she says, will be a book of historical games and activities.

Wroble did not go online in search of a book topic, but she found one anyway. That is not surprising, really: The Internet is alive with inspiration. Part research library and part town meeting, the Internet can take you anywhere in the world with just a few mouse clicks. You can roam the Library of Congress, search historical archives, page through government documents, find interviewable experts on everything from agate to zebras, and "overhear" slices of life that can provide valuable details for your works-in-progress—or even a brand-new idea, as an online search did for Wroble.

Surfing Serendipity

Ideas can happen anywhere and at any time, even if you're not looking for children's material at all; the byword of the Internet for writers may just be *serendipity*. Idaho-based author Karma Wilson was once "surfing along, studying gardening," when she noticed how many cat-named plants exist. "This generated an idea for a nonfiction picture book," she says.

Rambling or researching, you may notice an unfilled need, an unanswered question. Wroble, a part-time library aide, subscribes to two library-related listservs. She noticed many postings from parents about children and library research. Wroble wrote and sold a magazine article explaining "what librarians will and will not do to help children with research."

Sites designed for children, or created and maintained by children, provide wonderfully inspirational and ever-changing glimpses of what kids are doing, thinking, and saying. "I have found potential ideas from visiting sites intended for children, such as the Franklin Institute or FreeZone, and from reading newsgroup messages or bulletin boards," says Wroble.

Alaskan writer Debby Edwardson likes to keep tabs on certain children's sites, especially teen-oriented ones, "to keep in touch with how contemporary young people think about the issues dear to them." One of her best recent finds was a list of high school newspapers with web pages that, she says, have been "goldmines of ideas."

A particularly valuable online resource is historical archives. Author Kathiann Kowalski, of Ohio, wanted to write about the Battle of Vicksburg. During her online research, she read a soldier's letter that mentioned an intriguing fact: During the oppressive noon heat, both sides called a halt to fighting and would instead read, write letters, or play a card game called *euchre*. "It turns out that euchre is making a comeback," says Kowalski. "I proposed an activity for kids to learn how to play the game and got a go-ahead." The resulting article appeared in *Cobblestone*.

Collegial Idea Gathering

Another treasure to be mined online is the connection to be made with other writers. The Internet is full of writers' groups, how-to sites, and bulletin boards that let you post advice, celebrate a sale, or vent your dismay over the latest rejection slip. Wilson says that her online writers' group is an invaluable resource. Her picture book, *Bear Snores On*, came about as the result of an online chat. It will be published in fall 2001 by Simon & Schuster's Margaret McElderry imprint.

Wilson has floated magazine ideas to her chat buddies, too; their responses help her determine whether an idea "might be too regional to sell to a broader audience." She believes that the biggest advantage of the Internet is its ability to connect people. "I've gotten hooked up with a great online writing critique group, received several freelancing jobs, made wonderful writing friends, found an agent, and sold a book. None would have been possible without the Internet," Wilson says.

Other writers are also likely to have information or experiences on subjects that stump you. Terry Miller Shannon, a writer from Oregon, asks her e-mail pals questions about their kids: "things like, 'Would a junior high hold a dance during the daytime that a 12-year-old would go to?' and 'Do you let your 12-year-old girl shop in the mall without a parent?' This is invaluable to me."

Joanne Keating visits a chat room called Canadian Parents Online. As parents share stories of their everyday family lives, she sometimes takes notes. "Then, at some future point, the story starts to write itself when I review my notes," says Keating, a writer from British Columbia. "The best stories to write for kids are stories about kids. Life is always stranger than fiction."

Marsha Skrypuch also found inspiration from other writers. While perusing Compuserve's Litforum, on writing, she noticed a question about spider folktales. It started something spinning, so to speak, in her brain. The result was *Silver Threads*, a picture book from Penguin

Internet Interviews

One of writer Lisa Wroble's interview techniques is to e-mail people from the library listservs. E-mail is another extremely useful aspect of the Internet. Writers can make initial contact, set up times and dates for interviews, and even "interview" by e-mail, with or without follow-up telephone calls.

"When an expert responds by e-mail, it saves me substantial time and out-of-pocket expense," says author Kathiann Kowalski. "Even if an expert prefers to talk by phone, I still save time and money by avoiding fruitless rounds of phone tag."

Author Karma Wilson prefers to interview mostly by e-mail. "I'm horrible on the phone—very nervous," she admits. "Through e-mail, I can compose my questions with more tact. Sometimes I'll call to verify or clarify."

Wroble prefers the human touch. "Relying solely on e-mail interviews removes the emotion portrayed through voice inflection," she says. "When I'm trying to complete a big project, such as a book or long article, the enthusiasm of my interviewee helps me maintain my enthusiasm for the project. This can be lost when you rely only on e-mail interviewing."

Even those who prefer to do only phone interviews may find it useful to e-mail their questions in advance. That gives interviewees a chance to collect their thoughts and/or check facts ahead of time.

Canada. "I don't specifically look for kid-related themes" online, says Skrypuch, who lives in Ontario, "but I find them by serendipity."

Formal Finds

If you use intelligent research habits in a more traditional way, and at more formal sites, you'll also find astounding sources of information and ideas.

First and foremost, the Internet can help you determine whether your idea has already been done, or overdone. "I use Amazon.com like I'd use *Books in Print,* to see what's available on a given subject," says Edwardson. The same might be done at other online bookstores, such as barnesandnoble.com and borders.com. You may find out that 50 books about dinosaur nostrils have been written in the last 5 years. On the other hand, your search might come up empty.

"When I don't find what I am seeking, it may be an indication that there is a dearth of information available on the topic," says writer Hope Marston, who lives in upstate New York.

As your idea firms up, or when an article is assigned to you, the Internet is an extraordinary research tool. A couple of keystrokes will take you to universities, historical archives, chambers of commerce, newspapers and magazines, professional societies, and city, state, and local governments.

"I read newspapers from areas I will write about, investigate all official websites I can find, make contacts with people in the area," says Alaskan author Donna Walsh Shepherd. For a book about South Dakota, Shepherd e-mailed the state's website and set up interviews in advance of her visit. She expects to do the same on her next project, a book about New Zealand. "I have made very valuable contacts with people I would not even know existed otherwise," Shepherd says.

Online contacts have led Kowalski to experts in fields as varied as luminescence dating, bat sonar, lasers, geology, meteorology, and encryption. "Their valuable insights not only help me understand a wide range of complex issues better, but they help make different subjects come alive for the 10- to-16-year-olds reading my articles," says Kowalski.

The Internet's broad reach can be especially helpful when writers face tough deadlines or mountains of research. For example, Marston was given three weeks to outline a book on manta rays. Trouble was, she'd never heard of manta rays. She "rushed the 'Net," and found, among other things, a man who dives with manta rays four times a week, year-round. "Truly a godsend," says Marston, whose book, *Wings in the Water, The Story of a Manta Ray*, was published by Soundprints/Smithsonian.

Jennifer Drewry was assigned a quick-turnaround article on African-American cowboys. During her Internet research, she read about a woman named "Stagecoach Mary" Fields. She looked up Mary's hometown online, and searched for numbers for the town's library and Chamber of Commerce. As a result, she was able to interview a 95-year-old man who remembered Stagecoach Mary.

Another kind of "expert" opinion can be found through personal home pages. Not every writer trusts these, however. Shepherd sometimes consults home pages, but she checks out all recommendations personally, and "would not trust a personal site for facts." Shannon reads home pages, but with "a boulder-sized grain of salt." As she points out, "Anyone can set up a page and say anything on it. It certainly doesn't mean it's correct."

Certainly, any purported facts found on a home page should be verified. But feelings are another matter, according to Wilson. "Personal websites provide something organizations cannot—a human interest angle," she says. "People love to share a story, and contacting websites and asking for interviews or specific opinions allows people the opportunity to share their expertise."

No Cyberhermits Please

While the Internet can be a tremendous resource, it is not without its drawbacks. Writers say it is dangerous to rely on it too heavily, either for inspiration or research.

"It's good for getting basic information, but it's got to be supplemented with more serious research," Skrypuch warns. Drewry agrees. "I cannot stress the importance of reputable sites. There are many sites out there that are not worth a dime. Then there are others that have hoards of great information," she says.

Writers should not give up in-person research, Drewry adds. "Check and recheck sources no matter where they are from. Whenever possible, get the real, original info: Service records, birth/death records from town halls, old newspapers that are now on microfilm, etc." Doing so will not just confirm what you find out online; it will keep you from becoming a cyber-hermit who never leaves the keyboard.

"I look forward to receiving e-mail, to reading my listserv messages, and seeing what my critique-group members have waiting in my in-box," says Wroble. "But I'd never exchange that for meeting with my critique group at the local library, or making contacts at writing events. Even with my editors, it's great to send and receive e-mail messages, but nothing replaces those occasional telephone chats either, and I hope nothing ever will."

Possibly the worst potential problem is Internet time drain. Shannon never understood the fuss until she got online herself. "When I saw all the Internet had to offer, I wasn't only 'hooked up,' I was hooked!" she says. "Literally, I was no good for anything while I surfed the Internet for about two weeks. Now I see the Internet as a wonderful tool, as long as I don't let researching, surfing, e-mailing, and networking interfere with the writing."

Wilson has the same problem, but sees a bright side to her heavy Internet usage. "I get totally obsessed with message boards and e-mail lists. I'm constantly checking my e-mail and spend way too much time online chatting with other children's writers," she says. "But I've made many contacts this way, and I've become a far better writer and shaved years off the learning process. It's been worth it in the long run."

Ideas

Sparks for Ideas

Feasts & Celebrations

The events detailed here are a miscellany of holidays and days of recognition. They are traditional and modern, silly and serious. They are historical, corporate, literary, aesthetic, they commemorate scientific discoveries, and more. The collection of dates is here to give writers sparks. So let your brain storm and see how many queries and story concepts you can kindle.

January

Monthly Celebrations
- **National Prune Breakfast Month.**

- **National Oatmeal Month.**

Moveable Feasts and Celebrations
- **Clean Off Your Desk Day**
Second Monday in January.

- **Chinese New Year**
A lunar holiday, Chinese New Year is determined by the second new moon following the winter solstice. The holiday can fall between January 21 and February 19. Year 2000 is the Year of the Dragon. 2001 is the Year of the Serpent, and 2002 will be the Year of the Horse.

- **National School Nurse Day**
Fourth Wednesday in January
The National Association of School Nurses sponsors this day of acknowledgement.

Fixed Celebrations
- **New Year's Day**
January 1
A time for celebrations and resolutions, New Year's Day has taken on particular resonance as the new millennium has begun.

- **Trivia Day**
January 4
Trivia—random fact—is another name for the Roman goddess Diana.

- **Jackson Day**
January 8
The anniversary of the Battle of New Orleans, the last battle in the War of 1812, is named in honor of Andrew Jackson, who commanded the victorious American forces in that battle.

- **Balloon Ascension Day**
January 9
Frenchman Jen-Pierre Blanchard made his first American ascent in Philadelphia in 1793.

■ **International Thank You Day**
January 11
A time to call, write, fax, or e-mail all the people who have ever helped you to thank them.

■ **Ratification Day**
January 14
This date commemorates the 1784 ratification of the Treaty of Paris, which officially ended the American Revolutionary War.

February

Monthly Celebrations
■ **National Cat Health Month**

■ **National Snack Food Month**

Moveable Feasts and Celebrations
■ **Pay Your Bills Week**
Third week of February

Fixed Celebrations
■ **Freedom Day**
February 1
The 13th Amendment to the U.S. Constitution, which abolished slavery nationwide, was approved by President Lincoln in 1865. The amendment was ratified in December of that year.

■ **Groundhog Day**
February 2
Originally brought to the U.S. by immigrants from Great Britain and Germany, the custom of attending to the groundhog's sighting of his shadow is probably a marking of when spring arrives.

■ **St. Valentine's Day**
February 14
Geoffrey Chaucer's *Parlement of Foule*s is a poetic discourse on the medieval belief that this was the day birds chose their mates, an idea that probably had classical origins.

March

Monthly Celebrations
■ **National Noodle Month**

■ **National Peanut Month**

Moveable Feasts and Celebrations
■ **National PTA Drug and Alcohol Awareness Week**
First full week of March

■ **National Aardvark Week**
Second week of March

■ **American Chocolate Week**
Fourth week of March

Fixed Celebrations
■ **International Day of the Seal**
March 1
A day is set aside to promote awareness of the seal's peril; dangers include pollution, oil spills, driftnets, and more.

■ **National Anthem Day**
March 3
This is the date, in 1931, when President Hoover designated "The Star-Spangled Banner" as the national anthem.

■ **Alamo Day**
March 6
Mexican general Santa Anna and his troops laid siege to the fort called the

Alamo in 1836, killing 185 Texans. "Remember the Alamo" later became the battle cry for Texans in their fight for independence from Mexico.

■ **International Women's Day**
March 8
Also known as International Working Women's Day, this observance has been traced back to a female garment-worker demonstration in New York City in the mid-nineteenth century.

■ **Harriet Tubman Day**
March 10
Known as the "Moses of her people," Harriet Tubman is honored for her efforts to help hundreds of Southern slaves escape to freedom in the North via the underground railroad.

■ **Black Press Day**
March 16
The first African-American owned and edited newspaper in the U.S., *Freedom's Journal*, was published on this day in 1827 by Samuel Cornish and John B. Russwurm.

■ **World Day for Water**
March 22
The United Nations has set aside a day to promote public awareness of the importance of water resource development.

■ **Liberty Day**
March 23
This day marks the occasion of Patrick Henry's famous "Give me liberty, or give me death" speech in 1775.

April

Monthly Celebrations
■ **Mathematics Education Month**
■ **Keep America Beautiful Month**

Moveable Feasts and Celebrations
■ **National TV-free Week**
Last week of April

■ **National Volunteer Week**
Last week of April

■ **Set-Your-Clock-Forward Day**
First Sunday in April
"Spring forward" to comply with the Congress-mandated Uniform Time Act, designed as an energy conservation measure.

■ **Bird Day**
Second Friday in April
Sometimes known as Audubon Day, the date is set aside for nationwide bird appreciation.

Fixed Celebrations
■ **April Fools' Day**
April 1
The custom of playing practical jokes on this day was brought to America by early settlers.

■ **International Children's Book Day**
April 2
Designated as a day to commemorate the birthday of Hans Christian Andersen and promote children's books.

■ **World Health Day**
April 7
On the anniversary of the day the official constitution of the World Health Organization was adopted, citizens are encouraged to help promote global

health issues.

■ **Rubber Eraser Day**
April 15
This celebration of the rubber eraser, first used in the 1700s, coincides with the date when federal income tax returns must be filed.

■ **Kindergarten Day**
April 21
First developed in 1837 by Friedrich Froebel, the kindergarten was designed to serve the needs of German children in poverty or with special needs, but the early education theories behind it continue to be applied to programs for modern children.

■ **Earth Day**
April 22
Fairs and events are held nationwide to promote environmental awareness.

May

Monthly Celebrations
■ **National Physical Fitness and Sports Month**

■ **National Salad Month**

Moveable Feasts and Celebrations
■ **National Family Week**
First full week of May

■ **National Bike Week**
Third week of May

■ **Astronomy Day**
Saturday near the first quarter moon between mid-April and mid-May
Held to bring astronomy to the people, this day increases public awareness of the celestial.

■ **National Playday for Health**
Third Wednesday in May
This observance is designed to help human resource and other managers promote worksite health and wellness.

Fixed Celebrations
■ **May Day**
May 1
Dating back many centuries, May Day was especially celebrated in Elizabethan England to revel in the rebirth of spring, fertility, and natural beauty.

■ **Save the Rhino Day**
May 1
This day raises awareness of the efforts to save the endangered rhinoceros.

■ **World Red Cross Day**
May 8
Founded by Swiss humanitarian Jean-Henri Dunant, the Red Cross provides assistance during natural disasters or wartime.

■ **National Bike to Work Day**
May 16
Designed to focus on the need to cut down on traffic and pollution, National Bike to Work Day also encourages safe bicycling.

■ **International Museum Day**
May 18
A day acknowledging the role of museums boosts cultural awareness of the many extraordinary art collections in museums around the world.

■ **National Waitresses/Waiters Day**
May 21
A day of respect and appreciation was established for table-servers, who perform diverse duties.

■ **National Maritime Day**
May 22
The anniversary of the first steamship to cross the Atlantic in 1819 is celebrated on this day each year.

June

Monthly Celebrations
■ **National Fresh Fruit and Vegetable Month**

■ **Cancer in the Sun Month**

Moveable Feasts and Celebrations
■ **Hug Holiday Week**
Third week

■ **National Forgiveness Day**
Fourth Sunday in June
A day to settle unresolved problems: Forgive and forget.

Fixed Celebrations
■ **World Environment Day**
June 5
The United Nations designated a day to deepen "public awareness of the need for the preservation and enhancement of the environment."

■ **Boone Day**
June 7
This is the anniversary of the day in 1769 Daniel Boone first set eyes on Kentucky.

■ **Onset of World War I**
June 28
The Great War, which lasted from 1914 to 1918, began and ended on June 28.

July

Monthly Celebrations
■ **Anti-Boredom Month**

■ **National Hot Dog Month**

■ **National Ice Cream Month**

Moveable Feasts and Celebrations
■ **Dog Days**
July 3-15
"Dog days" is a term originated in ancient times when the hottest period coincided with the time of the year when Sirius, the Dog Star, rose just before the sun. Today, a similar period in August is designated the Dog Days of August.

Fixed Celebrations
■ **Independence Day**
July 4
Celebrated in commemoration of the formal adoption of the Declaration of Independence by Congress on July 4, 1776.

■ **Moon Day**
July 20
Astronauts Neil Armstrong and Edwin Aldrin, Jr. landed on the Moon on this day in 1969 and walked around its surface for 2 hours and 15 minutes.

August

Monthly Celebrations
■ **National Catfish Month**

Moveable Feasts and Celebrations

■ **International Clown Week**
First week of August

Fixed Celebrations
■ **Coast Guard Day**
August 4
The U.S. Coast Guard was founded on this date in 1790 to police harbors and enforce federal customs and smuggling laws.

■ **National Homeless Animals Day**
August 20
The International Society for Animal Rights, along with animal advocacy organizations, promotes responsible pet ownership.

■ **Be Kind to Humankind Week**
August 25-31
Sponsor Lorraine Jara came up with the idea in 1988 to promote a week of goodness after reading a newspaper article about people's inhumane treatment towards others.

■ **Women's Equality Day**
August 26
Celebrated as a day of achievement for women nationwide, this observance recognizes the Nineteenth Amendment to the Constitution, which gave women the right to vote.

September

Monthly Celebrations
■ **National Honey Month**

■ **National Literacy Month**

Moveable Feasts and Celebrations

■ **Banned Books Week**
Last week of September
Banned Books Week honors the freedom to read.

■ **Federal Lands Cleanup Day**
First Saturday after Labor Day
A day named to encourage volunteers to work with federal lands managers in cleanup projects.

■ **International Day of Peace**
Third Tuesday in September
The United Nations commemorates the ideal of peace among all nations and people.

■ **National Good Neighbor Day**
Fourth Sunday in September
A designated day to be a good neighbor is an incentive for community get-togethers or clean-up projects.

Fixed Celebrations
■ **Be Late for Something Day**
September 5
The Procrastinators' Club of America sponsors this day and suggests celebrating a day or two late.

■ **Mayflower Day**
September 16
On September 16, 1620, the three-masted, 100-foot Mayflower set sail from Plymouth, England, for the New World.

■ **World Gratitude Day**
September 21
Sponsors of this day encourage people to take stock, turn their thoughts inward, reflect, and be grateful.

October

Monthly Celebrations
- **National Popcorn Poppin' Month**

- **National Pizza Month**

Moveable Feasts and Celebrations
- **World Habitat Day**
First Monday in October
The United Nations promotes a different theme each year in awareness of human settlements.

- **Get Organized Week**
First week in October

- **Fire Prevention Week**
Second week in October

- **Change-Your-Clock-Back Day**
Last Sunday in October
Time to "fall back" to standard time: Get that extra hour of sleep.

Fixed Celebrations
- **World Farm Animals Day**
October 2
Held on the birthday of Mahatma Gandhi, this day was proclaimed in 1983 to "memorialize the suffering and death of billions of animals in factory farms, stockyards, and slaughterhouses."

- **Peace Corps Birthday**
October 14
The concept of the Peace Corps was advanced by John F. Kennedy on October 14, 1960, to promote the progress of other countries by helping to improve living standards.

- **Dictionary Day**
October 16
The birthday of Noah Webster, the American lexicographer and writer, Dictionary Day honors his compilation of one of the first widely respected reference books of definitions.

- **Black Poetry Day**
October 17
New York slave Jupiter Hammon, born on October 17, 1711, was the first black poet to publish his own verse. This day recognizes his contributions to American life and culture, as well as the contributions of other African Americans.

- **National Magic Day**
October 31
Magic Day is celebrated in honor of Harry Houdini, the magician, illusionist, and escape artist who died on October 31, 1926.

November

Monthly Celebrations
- **Peanut Butter Lover's Month**

- **Great American Smokeout Month**

Moveable Feasts and Celebrations
- **National Split Pea Soup Week.**
Second week in November

- **National Children's Book Week**
Third week in November

- **Great American Smokeout**
Third Thursday in November
The American Cancer Society encourages smokers to quit for one day to realize the benefits of living without smoking.

Fixed Celebrations
■ **All Saints Day**
November 1
This is a day to honor all the Christian saints, especially the more obscure saints who are known, and all the sainted deceased who are not known by name.

■ **Sandwich Day**
November 3
This food-oriented day is celebrated on the birthday of John Montague, England's fourth Earl of Sandwich, who is credited as the inventor of the sandwich.

■ **Mickey Mouse's Birthday**
November 18
Mickey was "born" on this day in 1928 when he made his debut as the star of the first synchronized sound cartoon.

■ **National Stop the Violence Day**
November 22
The anniversary of the assassination of President John F. Kennedy was chosen for observance of this day, which fosters a commitment to peace and hope.

December

Moveable Feasts and Celebrations
■ **MADD International Candlelight Vigil of Remembrance and Hope**
Early December
More than 400 nationwide chapters of Mothers Against Drunk Driving hold candlelight vigils to "remember the victims of drunk-driving crashes, to support their families, to alert the public about the reality of drunk driving, and to express hope for a less violent future."

Fixed Celebrations
■ **International Day of Disabled Persons**
December 3
The United Nations sponsors this day to raise awareness and enact measures to improve the situation of people with disabilities.

■ **Nobel Prize Day**
December 10
The first Nobel Prizes were awarded on December 10, 1901, the fifth anniversary of the death of Swedish chemist and dynamite inventor Alfred Nobel, who left more than $9 million in a fund to be distributed yearly to people who had most helped humankind.

■ **Poinsettia Day**
December 12
The popular Christmas-season tropical shrub was introduced to the U.S. by American diplomat Joel Roberts Poinsett, who died on December 12, 1851.

■ **Boston Tea Party**
December 16
On this day in 1773, enraged Americans protested against "taxation without representation" by dumping two shiploads of English tea into Boston harbor.

■ **Winter Solstice**
December 22
This is the shortest day of the year and the beginning of winter.

Sparks for Ideas

Anniversaries in History, Science, Culture

2001

5th Anniversary: 1996

History & Politics
- At the Vatican, Pope John Paul II meets for the first time with Cuban leader Fidel Castro and accepts an invitation to visit Cuba in 1997.
- Madeleine Albright is named Secretary of State by President Clinton, the first woman to hold that office.
- A subcommittee of the House Ethics Committee finds that House Speaker Newt Gingrich violated House ethics rules and brought discredit to the House.
- Peruvian rebels seize 600 hostages at the Japanese ambassador's residence.
- Senator Robert Dole resigns his Senate seat to campaign for the presidency.
- Congress approves a compromise bill that revamps the nation's welfare system.
- The U.S. government is shut down for 21 days, the longest shutdown in U.S. history, due to a budget impasse between President Clinton and Congress.
- The minimum wage is raised from $4.25 to $4.75.

Science & Technology
- In an attempt to rid the country of the so-called *mad cow disease*, Britain proposes to slaughter hundreds of thousands of cows.
- Scientists at the U.S. National Institute of Allergy and Infectious Diseases find a protein whose presence is necessary to allow the AIDS virus to enter the human immune system cells.
- The United Nations reports that 21.8 million people are infected with AIDS and the disease is spreading more quickly among women.
- Scientists find evidence of a primitive form of microscopic life on Mars.
- Olestra, a fat substitute that is free of calories, is approved by the U.S. Food and Drug Administration.

Arts & Society
- The Army investigates a large number of complaints of sexual harassment of women soldiers by higher-ranking male soldiers.
- John F. Kennedy, Jr., marries Carolyn Bessette in a private, unannounced ceremony on Cumberland Island, Georgia.
- During the summer Olympic Games in Atlanta, a homemade pipe bomb explodes in a downtown park, killing one and injuring 100.
- Jessica Dubroff, a seven-year-old girl trying to become the youngest person to pilot a plane across the U.S., is killed

when her plane crashes.
- Prince Charles and Princess Diana announce they will divorce, ending their 15-year marriage.
- An auction of 5,900 items owned by former First Lady Jacqueline Kennedy Onassis brings $34 million.
- The Oakland, California, school board recognizes black English, Ebonics, as a distinct language, setting off a controversy among American educators.
- Evander Holyfield defeats champion Mike Tyson to gain the World Boxing Association heavyweight title.
- Stock prices continue to surge; the stock market closes up 26 percent for the year.

10th Anniversary: 1991

History & Politics
- The U.S. and Allies declare war on Iraq following the Iraqi takeover of Kuwait.
- The Warsaw Pact is dissolved.
- The widow of Mao Tse-tung, Jian Qing, commits suicide.
- Boris Yeltsin is inaugurated as the first freely elected president of the Russian Republic.
- The three Baltic republics, Lithuania, Estonia, and Latvia, win independence and are recognized by the new Soviet ruling council.
- The Senate confirms Judge Clarence Thomas for the U.S. Supreme Court, following stormy hearings in which Anita Hill accuses Thomas of sexual harassment.
- The Soviet Union breaks up, following President Gorbachev's resignation; the constituent republics form the Commonwealth of Independent States.

20th Anniversary: 1981

History & Politics
- Pope John Paul II is shot twice by Mehmet Ali Agca in St. Peter's Square.
- John Hinckley shoots President Reagan, White House Press Secretary Jim Brady, and two others outside the Washington Hilton hotel.
- A leading Baptist 'creationist', Kelly Segraves, argues in a California court against the teaching of evolution in state schools.
- Twelve-year-old Walter Polovchak, who remained in the U.S. after his parents returned to the U.S.S.R., is granted political asylum against the wishes of his parents.
- Egyptian President Anwar Sadat is assassinated by soldiers at a military parade and is succeeded by Vice President Hosni Mubarak.
- After 444 days in captivity, the 52 Americans held hostage in the American Embassy in Iran are freed.
- The widow of chairman Mao Tse-tung, Jiang Qing, is sentenced to death for her role during the Cultural Revolution in China. The sentence is later commuted to life imprisonment.

Science & Technology
- Scientists identify the Acquired Immune Deficiency Syndrome (AIDS).
- The French TGV, the world's fastest train, enters service between Paris and Lyons.
- Chinese scientists are the first to clone a fish, a golden carp, successfully.
- I.B.M. launches its *home* or *personal* computer, the P.C.
- University of Denver surgeons insert a valve into the skull of an unborn

baby to drain off excess fluid from the brain and prevent hydrocephalus.
■ Two unusual meteorites found in the Antarctic may have originated from Mars, according to NASA scientists.

Arts & Society
■ *Cats*, a new musical based on poems by T.S. Eliot, becomes a surprise success on the London stage.
■ Walter Cronkite retires from regular television broadcasting.
■ Picasso's *Guernica* is donated to the Prado Museum in Spain by the Museum of Modern Art in New York.
■ Susan Hurley is elected a Fellow of All Souls College, Oxford, the first woman in 542 years.
■ A new translation of the Koran is printed in China.
■ Major league baseball players in the U.S. strike from June 12 to August 9.
■ Prince Charles and Lady Diana Spencer announce their engagement in February and are married in London on July 29.
■ *Dynasty* makes its television debut.

25th Anniversary: 1976

History & Politics
■ A treaty limiting the size of underground nuclear explosions set off for peaceful purposes is signed by the U.S. and U.S.S.R. For the first time, some on-site inspection compliance is included.
■ For the first time in 67 years, the U.S. copyright laws are revised.
■ Pope Paul VI suspends French Archbishop Marcel Lefebvre for rejecting the reforms by the Second Vatican Council in the saying of Mass. Lefebvre continues to celebrate the banned traditional Latin Mass.
■ Mao Tse-tung, leader of the People's Republic of China and founder of the Chinese Communist Party, dies.
■ South African blacks battle armed policemen as rioting and violence against apartheid and government policies spread from Soweto to Johannesburg and Cape Town in black townships and white areas.
■ A new break-away church is founded when U.S. Lutherans split over interpretation of the Bible and synod administration.
■ The Massachusetts Supreme Judicial Court overturns the manslaughter conviction of Dr. Kenneth C. Edelin in an abortion case.
■ Former U.S. President Richard Nixon testifies that he ordered wiretapping in 1969 and that Henry Kissinger selected those to be tapped.
■ The Dow Jones industrial stock average passes the 1,000 mark.
■ The death penalty does not violate the Constitution's prohibition of "cruel and unusual" punishment decides the U.S. Supreme Court.

Science & Technology
■ U.S.S.R.'s Soyuz spacecraft docks successfully with the orbiting Salyut space station.
■ The viral cause of multiple sclerosis is discovered.
■ The U.S. Food and Drug Administration bans Red Dye No. 2 in foods, drugs, and cosmetics after it is linked to cancer in laboratory animals.
■ Meteorites fall in northeastern China, with the largest fragment weighing about 3,900 pounds.

Arts & Society
- The U.S. National symbol of fire prevention, Smokey the Bear, dies at the National Zoo in Washington, D.C.
- Alex Haley publishes his nonfiction book *Roots*.
- *A Chorus Line*, a musical by Michael Bennett, wins both the Pulitzer Prize for drama and the Tony award.
- Sarah Caldwell becomes the first woman to conduct at New York's Metropolitan Opera.
- CBS television news correspondent Daniel Schorr is suspended for disclosing a secret report of the House Select Committee on Intelligence.

50th Anniversary - 1951

History & Politics
- Julius and Ethel Rosenberg are sentenced to death for espionage against the U.S.
- The peace treaty with Japan is signed in San Francisco.
- British diplomats Burgess and Maclean, who have been spying for the Russians, escape to the U.S.S.R.
- A New York City ordinance requiring police permits for preachers to hold religious services on city streets is declared invalid by the U.S. Supreme Court.
- Temple Beth Israel of Meridian, Mississippi, becomes the first Jewish congregation to allow women to perform the functions of a rabbi.
- Shah Mohammad Riza Pahlavi of Iran orders all land he inherited from his father sold to peasants, on favorable terms.
- Alfred Krupp and 32 other former Nazis are released from prison by the U.S.; death sentences of 21 others are commuted.

Science & Technology
- Charles F. Blair flies solo over the North Pole.
- Max Theiler is awarded the Nobel Prize for Medicine and Physiology for his work on a yellow fever vaccine.
- The Nobel Prize for Chemistry goes to Edwin M. McMillan and Glenn T. Seaborg for discovering plutonium.
- The U.S. Public Health Service reports that fluoride added to public water supplies decreases the occurrence of tooth decay by two-thirds.

Arts & Society
- British Film Censors introduce the X certificate classification.
- Carl Sandburg's *Complete Poems* wins the Pulitzer Prize for poetry.
- Gian Carlo Menotti writes his opera *Amahl and the Night Visitors* on commission for NBC-TV.
- Rodgers and Hammerstein's musical *The King and I* premieres on Broadway.
- J.D. Salinger's novel *The Catcher in the Rye* is published.
- The oldest and last remaining all-black unit, the 24th Infantry Regiment, is disbanded by the U.S. Army.

75th Anniversary: 1926

History & Politics
- Reforms in Turkey include prohibition of the fez, abolition of polygamy, and modernization of female dress.
- Fascist youth organizations Ballilla, in Italy, and Hitlerjugend, in Germany, are founded.
- The future Queen Elizabeth II of England is born.
- Sarah Lawrence College is founded in Bronxville, NY.

Science & Technology
- A new electric recording technique, the electrola, is developed.
- Robert H. Goddard fires the first liquid rocket fuel.
- Vitamin B in pure form is isolated by B.C.P. Jansen and W.F. Donath.
- Rear Admiral Richard Byrd of the U.S. Navy and Floyd Bennett complete the first flight over the North Pole.

Arts & Society
- The popular bear of little brain, Winnie the Pooh, is introduced by A.A. Milne.
- Sinclair Lewis turns down the $1,000 Pulitzer Prize for *Arrowsmith*.
- Renowned film director Ernst Lubitsch leaves Berlin for Hollywood.
- After completing the film *The Son of the Sheik*, movie idol Rudolph Valentino dies.
- The first recordings of Duke Ellington appear.
- A cushioned cork-centered baseball is introduced.
- U.S. swimmer Gertrude Ederle becomes the first woman to swim the English Channel.

100th Anniversary: 1901

History & Politics
- The first Prime Minister of the Commonwealth of Australia, Edmund Barton, is inaugurated.
- W.H. Taft is named Governor-General of the Philippines.
- A treaty agreement is reached on building the Panama Canal under U.S. supervision.
- J.P. Morgan organizes the U.S. Steel Corporation.
- After the longest reign of any British monarch, 63 years and 7 months, Queen Victoria of Great Britain dies and is succeeded by her son Edward VII.
- The U.S. Congress adopts the Platt Amendment, establishing a U.S. protectorate over Cuba.

Science & Technology
- The hormone adrenalin is isolated.
- The railway between Mombasa and Lake Victoria is completed.
- The first British submarine launches.
- The third law of thermodynamics is postulated by W. H. Nernst.
- Spindletop, the first great Texas oil strike, is made.

Arts & Society
- Film producer Walt Disney is born.
- Rudyard Kipling publishes *Kim*.
- Edvard Munch completes *Girls on the Bridge*.
- Rachmaninoff's *Piano concerto No. 2* debuts.
- The first municipal crematorium is opened at Hull in England.
- Anton Chekhov's *Three Sisters* premieres at the Moscow Art Theater.
- The Army Nurse Corps is organized as a branch of the U.S. Army.

200th Anniversary: 1801

History & Politics
- The English enter Cairo and French troops leave Egypt.
- The Act of Union of Great Britain and Ireland comes into force.
- The Union Jack becomes the official flag of the United Kingdom of Great Britain and Ireland.
- The War of the Oranges breaks out

between Spain and Portugal.
- The Holy Roman Empire ends when the Peace of Luneville is signed between France and Austria.

Arts & Society
- Haydn completes his oratorio, *The Seasons*.

250th Anniversary: 1751
History & Politics
- England joins the Austro-Russian alliance of June 1746 against Prussia.
- Frederick, Prince of Wales, son of George II of Great Britain dies, leaving a son who will become George III.

Arts & Society
- Tiepolo paints the ceiling of the Wurzburg Residenz.

- Europe's most fashionable dance is the minuet.
- Paris is divided into pro-Italian and pro-French music lovers by the "War of the Operas."
- The first English newspaper in Canada, *Halifax Gazette,* is published.

500th Anniversary: 1501
History & Politics
- French troops enter Rome and the Pope declares Louis XII King of Naples.
- Henry VII of England declines the Pope's request to lead the crusade against the Turks.
- Rodrigo de Bastides explores the coast of Panama.

2002

5th Anniversary: 1997

History & Politics
- After more than 150 years as a British colony, Hong Kong is restored to Chinese rule on July 1.
- Timothy McVeigh is convicted and sentenced to death for his role in the 1995 bombing of the Federal Building in Oklahoma that killed 168.
- Former college professor Theodore Kaczynski is seized by federal agents and suspected of being the Unabomber.
- President Clinton apologizes for the *Tuskegee Study of Untreated Syphilis in the Negro Male*, which was conducted between 1932 and 1972 under the auspices of the U.S. Public Health Service.
- A Presidential committee fails to resolve the mystery surrounding the Gulf War Syndrome.

Science & Technology
- IBM's Deep Blue computer defeats world chess champion Garry Kasparov in a six-game chess match.
- A federally funded study finds that cockroaches are the leading cause of asthma in children living in inner cities.
- The Hale-Bopp comet, discovered in 1995, sweeps across the sky. Its unusually large size makes it visible even in large cities.
- A camera mounted on the Hubble Space Telescope finds one of the most massive stars known behind a dense dust cloud in the Milky Way.
- A sheep named Dolly is the first mammal successfully cloned from a cell from an adult animal.

Arts & Society
- Billions of people mourn the death of Princess Diana.
- In what was an apparent mass suicide, 39 members of Heaven's Gate religious cult are found dead at an estate in California. Their leader, Marshall Applewhite, is among the dead.
- At age 14, Tara Lipinski becomes the youngest U.S. Figure Skating Champion.
- American millionaire Steve Fossett fails in his attempt to be the first to circumnavigate the globe in a hot air balloon but sets a record of 9,672 miles.
- The Medal of Honor, the highest U.S. Award for bravery, is awarded to seven black soldiers for their courage in action in World War II—the first time the Medal has been given to black World War II servicemen.
- Tiger Woods becomes the youngest person to win the Masters Tournament at age 21.
- Roman Catholic nun Mother Teresa dies in Calcutta at age 87.
- The Women's National Basketball Association completes its first season.
- Challenger Mike Tyson bites Evander Holyfield's ear during a championship boxing match. Tyson's license to fight in Nevada is revoked for one year.

10th Anniversary: 1992

History & Politics
- Presidents Bush and Yeltsin declare a formal end to the Cold War.
- Four Los Angeles police officers are acquitted in the beating of Rodney King and Los Angeles erupts in violence.
- The last of the Western hostages are

freed in Lebanon.
- The U.S. Supreme Court reaffirms the right to abortion.
- U.S. forces leave the Philippines, ending nearly a century of American military presence.
- President Bush pardons former Reagan Administration officials involved in the Iran-contra affair.

20th Anniversary: 1982

History & Politics
- The Vietnam Veterans' War Memorial is dedicated in Washington, D.C. The names of more than 58,000 dead are engraved on the black granite memorial.
- The U.S. Justice Dept. and broadcasters end restraints on the length and frequency of television commercials.
- Convicted murderer Charlie Brooks is executed by lethal injection in Texas; this is the first time this method has been used.
- Great Britain establishes full diplomatic relations with the Vatican.
- U.S. Senator Harrison Williams becomes the first Senator to resign his Senate seat in over 60 years as a result of his being charged with misconduct.
- The Sinai, captured by Israel in 1967, is returned to Egypt as part of the 1979 Camp David agreement.

Science & Technology
- Dolphins are found to have the first magnetized tissues discovered in mammals. It is believed that this may assist in navigation.
- Genetic engineering produces the first commercial product: Human insulin is produced by bacteria.
- The U.N. Law of the Sea Conference adopts an international convention to supervise the exploitation of the world's sea beds as the "common heritage of mankind," but the U.S. and the U.K. do not sign.
- U.S. space probe Voyager II transmits photographs that reveal four to six previously undiscovered moons orbiting Saturn.
- A human skeleton 60-80,000 years old is discovered in Egypt, and declared a significant link in the study of human evolution.
- British explorers Charles Burton and Sir Ranulph Fiennes become the first to cross both poles in a single journey around the earth.

Arts & Society
- By the end of 1982, 28 million U.S. households have cable television.
- N.F.L. football players go on strike for more money in September.
- New Zealander Neoli Fairhall wins the gold medal for archery at the 12th Commonwealth Games and becomes the first paraplegic to do so.
- The fourth television channel in the U.K. begins to broadcast, its aim to cater to minorities.
- Thomas Keneally wins the Booker Prize for *Schindler's List*.

25th Anniversary: 1977

History & Politics
- The first American male saint, John Neopomucene Neumann, is canonized.
- French is adopted as the official language of Quebec.
- The energy crisis in America could bring on a "national catastrophe" warns

President Jimmy Carter, and Americans must respond with the moral equivalent of war by making profound changes in their oil consumption.
- Jacqueline Means becomes the first woman ordained as a priest in the Episcopal Church in America.
- The London Court of Appeals rules that the mere possession of cannabis leaves is not an offense under English law.
- Gary Gilmore is executed at Utah State Prison, reinstating the use of capital punishment in the U.S.
- Lake Erie freezes from bank to bank for the first time in modern history.
- President Gerald Ford pardons Iva Toguri D'Aquino, known as Tokyo Rose to servicemen during World War II.
- President Carter issues a pardon for U.S. draft evaders.
- The U.S. House of Representatives approves a stringent code of ethics on itself.
- In an unprecedented two-hour radio broadcast, President Jimmy Carter speaks over the telephone with 42 callers from 26 states.
- U.S. Secretary of Health, Education, and Welfare Joseph Califano signs regulations prohibiting discrimination against the handicapped in institutions receiving federal support.
- The U.S. Supreme Court rules capital punishment for rape unconstitutional.

Science & Technology
- The U.S. National Institute of Health reports that, for the first time, a life-threatening viral infection, herpes encephalitis, has been successfully treated with a drug.
- British scientists report that they have determined for the first time the complete genetic structure of a living organism.
- The possible detection of a quark, a fundamental electric charge one-third that of the electron charge, is reported by American scientists.
- The 2,300-year-old tomb of King Philip II of Macedon, father of Alexander the Great, is discovered in northern Greece.
- A hitherto unknown bacterium is identified as the cause of Legionnaires Disease.
- Radio astronomers at the Max Planck Institute in West Germany report the discovery of water molecules outside the earth's galaxy.

Arts & Society
- Martin Charnin's musical *Annie* wins the New York Drama Critics and Tony awards for best musical.
- The widow of Britain's wartime leader Sir Winston Churchill begins selling items of great sentimental value, citing serious financial difficulties.
- Kenya issues a ban on big-game hunting.

50th Anniversary: 1952

History & Politics
- Winston Churchill announces that Britain has produced an atomic bomb.
- U.S. President Harry Truman announces H-bomb tests in the Pacific.
- The Nobel Peace Prize goes to Albert Schweitzer.
- The last London trams are retired.
- Vincent Massey becomes the first Canadian-born Governor-General of Canada.

- The peace treaty restoring Japanese sovereignty is ratified, ending the American occupation of Japan.

Science & Technology
- The U.S. explodes the first hydrogen bomb at Eniwetok Atoll in the Pacific.
- A contraceptive pill of phosphorated hesperidin is produced.

Arts & Society
- The Revised Standard Version of the Bible, prepared by 32 scholars over 15 years, is published for Protestants.
- Agatha Christie's play *The Mousetrap* opens in London; it will celebrate its 22nd year onstage in 1974.
- Ernest Hemingway publishes *The Old Man and the Sea,* which wins the 1953 Pulitzer Prize.
- Police drama *Dragnet* makes its television debut.
- John Huston's film *The African Queen,* starring Katharine Hepburn and Humphrey Bogart, opens in New York.

75th Anniversary: 1927

History & Politics
- The German economy collapses in a day known as Black Friday.
- Sacco and Vanzetti are executed.

Science & Technology
- George Whipple conducts experiments on pernicious anemia and tuberculosis.
- Ford produces its 15-millionth Model "T."
- The Great Moffat Tunnel through the Rocky Mountains opens.
- Transatlantic telephone service begins between New York and London.

Arts & Society
- Ernest Hemingway publishes his short stories, *Men Without Women.*
- Aaron Copland's *Concerto for Piano and Orchestra* has its premiere performance with the Boston Symphony Orchestra.
- African-American performer Josephine Baker becomes the toast of Paris.
- The Academy of Motion Picture Arts and Sciences is founded.
- The rush for the Grosfontein diamond field in South Africa opens with about 25,000 runners participating.

100th Anniversary: 1902

History & Politics
- The British Order of Merit, limited to 24 British subjects at any one time, is established by King Edward VII.
- The Treaty of Vereeniging ends the Boer War. The Orange Free State becomes a British Crown Colony.
- Leon Trotsky escapes from a Siberian prison and settles in London.
- Arthur Balfour becomes the British Prime Minister.
- King Edward VII of Great Britain is proclaimed Emperor of India.
- A permanent U.S. Bureau of the Census is established.

Science & Technology
- H.W. Cushing, an American neurological surgeon, begins his study of the pituitary body.
- Anaphylaxis, and abnormal sensitivity to a serum treatment, is discovered by French physician Charles Richet.
- The Aswan Dam opens.
- French scientists Pierre and Marie Curie succeed in isolating pure radium.

Arts & Culture
- British composer Edward Elgar composes the first of the *Pomp and Circumstance* marches.
- The famous *Tales of Peter Rabbit* are published by Beatrix Potter.
- Mystery writer Arthur Conan Doyle completes *The Hound of the Baskervilles*.
- The first Rose Bowl football game is played at Pasadena, California.

200th Anniversary: 1802

History & Politics
- The French suppress a "Negro rebellion" in Santo Domingo led by Toussaint-L'Ouverture.

Science & Technology
- The term *biology* is coined by German naturalist Gottfried Treviranus.
- William Herschel discovers binary stars.

Arts & Society
- Beethoven completes his *Symphony No. 2 in D major, Op. 36*.
- The Health and Morals of Apprentices Act for the protection of labor in factories passes in Britain.

250th Anniversary: 1752

History & Politics
- The first fire insurance company in colonial America, Philadelphia Contributionship, is established.

500th Anniversary: 1502

History & Politics
- Vasco da Gama founds a Portuguese colony at Cochin, India.
- Margaret, daughter of Henry VII of England, marries James IV of Scotland.

Science & Technology
- The first watch, the Nuremberg Egg, is constucted by Peter Henlein of Nuremberg.

Arts & Society
- Frederick, Elector of Saxony, founds the University of Wittenberg.
- The Church of St. Mary's at Danzig, begun in 1400, is completed.

Ideas

2003

5th Anniversary: 1998

History & Politics
- Indonesian President Suharto resigns under pressure after an economic crisis and increasing student protests.
- President Clinton visits China, the first U.S. President to do so in a decade.
- In a sharp reversal, the U. S. House of Representatives votes to approve $98 million for the National Endowment for the Arts.
- The House of Representatives votes 258 to 176 to approve an inquiry into whether President Clinton's cover-up of the Monica Lewinsky affair is grounds for impeachment.
- Two U.S. embassies in Africa are bombed. 190 are killed, including eight Americans.
- Pope John Paul II visits Cuba for five days. He calls for the release of political prisoners and criticizes the U.S. embargo.
- For the first time in 30 years, the U.S. has a balanced budget with the possibility of a budget surplus after 5 years.
- In an "act of repentance," the Vatican admits the failure of the Roman Catholic Church to deter mass killings of Jews during World War II.

Science & Technology
- The space shuttle *Discovery* brings back the last American after his four and one-half months in orbit aboard the Russian space station Mir.

Arts & Society
- The Dow Jones average breaks 9000 for the first time.
- Art thieves tie up guards at the National Gallery of Modern Art in Rome and escape with two paintings by Van Gogh and one by Cezanne.
- Swiss commercial banks and Holocaust survivors agree on $1.25 billion payment of reparations over three years.
- Texas executes Karla Faye Tucker, the first woman executed since the Civil War.
- A low-flying Marine Corps aircraft cuts a ski cable in Italy, killing 20.
- Two boys, ages 13 and 11, kill four girls and one teacher and wound 11 at a Jonesboro, Arkansas, middle school.
- The U.S. begins an antitrust case against Microsoft.

10th Anniversary: 1993

History & Politics
- President Clinton agrees to a compromise on the military's ban on homosexuals: A "don't ask, don't tell" policy.
- Federal agents besiege the Texas Branch Davidian religious cult headquarters; 72 cult members are killed when the cult standoff ends with a federal assault.
- Senior White House lawyer Vincent W. Foster, Jr. commits suicide.
- Canada's opposition Liberal Party regains power in a landslide. Jean Chretien is sworn in as Canada's twentieth Prime Minister.
- Congress approves the North American Free Trade Agreement.
- President Clinton signs the Brady Bill regulating firearms purchases.

20th Anniversary: 1983

History & Politics
- President Reagan calls the U.S.S.R. the "Evil Empire" and proposes a revolutionary new antimissile defense system that is nicknamed Star Wars.
- Jesse Jackson is the first black man to address the Alabama legislature.
- Leading German magazine *Der Stern* announces the discovery and purchase of Hilter's personal diaries, but they are later discovered to be forgeries.
- Sweden and the Vatican resume diplomatic relations after a break of 450 years.
- Peterhouse, the oldest college in Cambridge, England, votes to admit female undergraduates.
- A Congressional Committee formally condemns the internment of Japanese-Americans during World War II.
- A South Korean airliner is shot down over the U.S.S.R. in a flight from New York to Seoul. All 269 on board die.
- Times Beach, Missouri, is evacuated and declared a federal disaster area after fall floods spread dangerous amounts of the toxic chemical dioxin.
- The U.S. Department of Justice seeks a court order to force Westinghouse Electric Corporation to clean up two chemically contaminated Indiana sites in the first use of the law that comes to be called Superfund.

Science & Technology
- The compact disc is launched.
- Barney Clark is the first person to receive an artificial heart; he dies after 112 days.
- An ancient skull, Pakicetus, from a creature who lived approximately 50 million years ago, is discovered in Pakistan and may be the missing link between whales and land animals.
- The world's first artificially made chromosome is created at Harvard University and grafted onto yeast cells.
- U.S. Space Shuttle Challenger has its maiden flight and completes three missions in 1983.
- The Orphan Drug Bill, which encourages pharmaceutical companies to produce drugs for unusual illnesses with limited markets, is signed into law.
- Swiss physicists discover a new subatomic particle, the W particle.
- Babcock & Wilson Co. agrees to rebate $37 million as a settlement for the nuclear reactor accident at Three Mile Island in Pennsylvania.
- AT&T inaugurates a laser fiber-optics system between New York and Washington, D.C., the first of its kind linking two major cities.

Arts & Culture
- A previously unknown chamber symphony manuscript written by Mozart when he was nine is discovered in Odense, Denmark.
- Rudolf Nureyev is named the Director of the Paris Opera Ballet.
- George Meegan of the U.K. reaches north Alaska after walking a world record 19,000 miles from Tierra del Fuego, South America.
- Willem De Kooning's *Two Women* sells for $1,200,000, a record price for a living artist's work.
- *The Color Purple,* by Alice Walker, wins the Pulitzer Prize for fiction.
- Unemployment in the U.S. rises above 12 million, the highest figure since 1941.

- The NBA and team owners agree on a four-year labor contract which introduces revenue sharing for players for the first time in professional sports.

25th Anniversary: 1978

History & Politics
- Israeli Prime Minister Menahem Begin and Egyptian President Anwar Sadat receive the Nobel Peace Prize.
- Pope Paul VI dies and his successor Cardinal Albino Luciana, Pope John Paul I, dies soon after. Cardinal Karol Wojtyla is named to succeed him and takes the name John Paul II. He is the first non-Italian to be elected Pope in 456 years and the first Pole.
- At the Peoples Temple commune in Guyana, 917 members of a religious cult, including leader Jim Jones, commit murder-suicide following the shooting deaths of U.S. Representative Leo J. Ryan and four other Americans.
- The U.S. Supreme Court upholds a lower court decision requiring the University of California Medical School to admit Allan P. Bakke, who claimed the school's minority admissions plan was "reverse discrimination."
- Supertanker *Amoco Cadiz* breaks in two off the Brittany coast in France, resulting in one of the worst oil spills in history and dumping more than 1.3 million barrels of crude oil into the sea.
- President Jimmy Carter signs into law legislation that raises the mandatory retirement age from 65 to 70 for private industry and eliminates it for most federal workers.

Science & Technology
- Lesley Brown gives birth to the first test-tube baby, a girl, in England. Louise Brown is the first human baby conceived outside a woman's body.
- Japanese explorer Naomi Uemura becomes the first to complete a solo journey to the North Pole.
- Scientists discover that there is a moon orbiting Pluto.

Arts & Culture
- At an auction in New York, a Gutenberg Bible sells for $2 million, the highest price ever paid for a printed book.
- Brigadier General Margaret A. Brewer is appointed the first female general in the U.S. Marine Corps.
- An investigation into alleged corruption in the opera world leads to the arrest of 29 Italian opera house managers, art directors, and agents.
- Naomi James of England becomes the first woman to sail around the world alone.
- The first transatlantic balloon crossing is completed by Americans Max Anderson, Ben Abruzzo, and Larry Newman.
- Austrian climber Franz Oppurg makes the first successful solo ascent of Mount Everest.
- *Dallas* makes its television debut.

50th Anniversary: 1953

History & Politics
- Joseph Stalin dies and is succeeded by G.M. Malenkov.
- Queen Elizabeth II is crowned.
- The first fatal jetliner accident occurs when a Canadian plane crashes in Karachi, Pakistan.

Science & Technology
- Sir Edmund Hillary and Tenzing become the first to climb Mount Everest.
- Alfred Kinsey releases his report *Sexual Behavior in the Human Female*.
- Lung cancer is reported attributable to cigarette smoking.
- DNA structure is first presented in a British publication in an article by U.S. scientist James Dewey Watson and British geneticist Francis H.C. Crick.

Arts & Culture
- The Nobel Prize for Literature is awarded to Winston Churchill.
- Clare Boothe Luce becomes the U.S. ambassador to Italy. It is the first time a woman is appointed to a major diplomatic post.
- The first Phi Beta Kappa chapter at a black college is organized at Fisk Academy.

75th Anniversary: 1928

History & Politics
- The first Five-Year Plan begins in the Soviet Union.
- Britain reduces the age for women's suffrage from 30 to 21.

Science & Technology
- George Eastman exhibits the first color motion pictures.
- Alexander Fleming discovers penicillin.
- J.L. Baird demonstrates color TV.

Arts & Society
- *John Brown's Body,* Stephen Vincent Benet's novel in verse is published; it wins the Pulitzer Prize in 1929.
- *Lady Chatterly's Lover,* by D.H. Lawrence, appears.
- The first Mickey Mouse films are released by Disney.
- The New York Philharmonic Symphony Orchestra names Arturo Toscanini conductor.
- Amelia Earhart is the first woman to fly across the Atlantic.
- Women participate for the first time in the Olympic Games, in Amsterdam.

100th Anniversary: 1903

History & Politics
- The Alaskan frontier is first settled.
- The Ford Motor Company is founded by Henry Ford with capital of $100,000.

Science & Technology
- Orville and Wilbur Wright successfully fly a powered airplane.
- The electrocardiograph is invented by Wilhelm Einthoven.

Arts & Society
- The longest film to date, *The Great Train Robbery,* runs 12 minutes.
- Jack London publishes *The Call of the Wild.*
- The first recording of an opera, Giuseppe Verdi's *Ernani,* is released.
- A 20-mile-per-hour speed limit is imposed on motor cars in Britain.
- The first coast-to-coast crossing of the American continent by car takes 65 days.
- The first post-season baseball series is held.

200th Anniversary: 1803

History & Politics

- Ohio becomes a state.
- The U.S. purchases a large tract of land, extending from the Gulf of Mexico to the northwest, from the French. It becomes known as the Louisiana Purchase.

Science & Technology
- Robert Fulton propels a boat by steam power.

Arts & Culture
- Beethoven completes his *Sonata for violin and piano, Op. 47.*

250th Anniversary: 1753

History & Politics
- French troops from Canada seize the Ohio Valley.
- An Act of Parliament in England permits the naturalization of Jews.

Science & Technology
- A royal foundation charter is granted to the British Museum of London.

Arts & Culture
- William Hogarth completes his essay, "The Analysis of Beauty."
- Britain's Jockey Club establishes a permanent racetrack at Newmarket.

500th Anniversary: 1503

Arts & Culture
- Begun in 1070, Canterbury Cathedral is finished.
- Leonardo Da Vinci paints the *Mona Lisa.*
- The pocket handkerchief comes into use.

Part 8

Award, Contest, & Conference Listings

Listings

Writers' Contests & Awards

Jane Addams Children's Book Award
Jane Addams Peace Association, Inc.
Ginny Moore Kruse
1708 Regent Street
Madison, WI 53705

The Jane Addams Children's Book Award has been presented since 1953, by the Jane Addams Peace Association and the Women's International League for Peace and Freedom, for a book that most effectively promotes the cause of peace, social justice, world community, and the equality of all sexes and all races. Honor books may also be chosen.

Books may be submitted by the publishers, or requested by the committee. Books for preschool through high school ages are eligible. Entries may be translations or published in English in other countries.
Deadline: April 1.
Representative Winners: *Growing Up in Coal Country*, Susan Campbell Bartoletti; *Second Daughter: The Story of a Slave Girl*, Mildred Pitts Walter.
Announcements: Winners announced on September 6, Jane Addams's birth date, for a book published in the previous year.
Award: The award-winning author receives a hand-illuminated scroll; silver seals are placed on the book jacket by the publisher. Honor scrolls are awarded to books that merit recognition.

***AIM Magazine* Short Story Contest**
AIM, America's Intercultural Magazine
P.O. Box 1174
Maywood, IL 60153

Open to new writers, this contest looks for work demonstrating that people are more alike than they are different. It calls for short story entries and seeks to "purge racism from the human bloodstream by way of the written word" through this annual contest.

Submissions should be well-written, unpublished stories of up to 4,000 words. Multiple submissions are not accepted; no entry fee. Send an SASE for contest guidelines.
Deadline: August 15.
Announcements: Winners are announced in the fall issue of *AIM*.
Representative Winners: Fall 1998: *Miss Mae*, Robert A. Thomas.
Award: First prize, $100; Second Prize, $75, and both receive publication in *AIM Magazine*.

Alcuin Society Citation Awards
The Alcuin Society
Richard Hopkins, Director
P.O. Box 3216
Vancouver, BC V6B 3X8
Canada

The Alcuin Society recognizes the work of Canadian book designers and publishers through the Alcuin Citations, awarded for excellence in book design and production. It offers awards in four categories: general trade, limited editions, text and reference, and juveniles.

Participants may submit as many books in any or all categories as they wish. The entries are judged by a panel of experts that consider a sound marriage of design and content, appropriate cover design, page layout, typography, and where applicable, the balance of illustration and text. Entry fee, $10.
Deadline: March 31.
Announcements: Contest announced in January; winners announced at the annual meeting in May.
Representative Winners: *The Stone Angel*, Sari Ginsberg (McClelland & Stewart); *What the Crow Said*, Alan Brownoff (University of Alberta Press).
Award: An awards certificate is presented at the annual meeting.

America and Me Essay Contest
Farm Bureau Insurance
Lisa Fedewa, Contest Coordinator
7373 W. Saginaw Hwy., Box 30400
Lansing, MI 48909
www.farmbureauinsurance-mi.com/pages/events

Now in its thirty-first year, this annual contest encourages eighth-grade students in Michigan to explore their roles in America's future. The contest centers on a different theme each year; the 1999 topic was "My American Hero for the Twenty-First Century."

Submissions should have author's name, home address, school, and school address at the top of each page. Entries may be up to 500 words. Send an SASE for theme list and complete guidelines.
Deadline: November 22.
Announcements: Winners are announced in April.
Representative Winners: Nicole Nastanski, Adam Greenbaum, Colleen Shellenbarger, Jennifer Lentz.
Award: Prizes include certificates, plaques, medallions, U.S. savings bonds valued from $250 to $500 and cash prizes of $250 to $500.

American Association of University Women Award in Juvenile Literature
North Carolina Literary and Historical Association
Dr. Jerry C. Cashion, Awards Coordinator
Room 305, 109 East Jones Street
Raleigh, NC 27601-2807

The purpose of this award is to recognize and reward the writing of literature for young people. The award is open only to North Carolina residents (a three-year residency is required). Relevance to North Carolina, creative and imaginative quality, and excellence of style are the criteria on which winners are selected.

Only books published during the 12

months ending June 30 of the year for which the award is given are eligible. Three copies of each entry should be submitted. There is no entry fee; three entries maximum per participant.
Deadline: July 15.
Announcements: Contest announced every January. Winners announced in November at the Association's annual meeting.
Representative Winner: *The Juke Box Man,* Jacqueline K. Ogburn (1998).
Award: Winner receives a presentation at an awards ceremony during the annual meeting; winning title and author are inscribed on a plaque.

Américas Award for Children's and Young Adult Literature
Consortium of Latin American
 Studies Programs c/o Center for
 Latin America
Julie Kline, Contest Coordinator
University of Wisconsin-Milwaukee
P.O. Box 413
Milwaukee, WI 53201

The rationale for the Américas Award is to encourage and commend young authors, illustrators, and publishers who produce quality children's and young adult books that portray Latin America, the Carribean, or Latinos in the United States. This contest offers two awards, for primary and secondary reading levels, that are given in recognition of U.S. published works of fiction, poetry, folklore, or selected nonfiction published in English or Spanish. The intent is to reach beyond geographic borders, as well as multicultural boundaries, focusing instead on cultural heritages in the hemisphere.

Only books published in the year preceding the contest are eligible. Authors must be nominated; nominations may be submitted by anyone with an interest in literature for children and young adults. A review copy of the book should be sent to each of the seven committee members; the contest coordinator should receive a copy of the nominating letter, and a review copy of the book.
Deadline: January 15.
Announcements: Winners announced in the spring. Formal awards presentation in the summer.
Representative Winners: *Barrio: Jose's Neighborhood,* George Ancona (Harcourt Brace, 1998); *Mama and Papa Have a Store,* Amelia Lau Carling (Dial, 1998).
Award: Letter of citation to author and publisher and a cash prize of $200 for the author. Presentation held at the Library of Congress.

Hans Christian Andersen Award
International Board on Books for
 Young People
Leena Maissen, Executive Director
Nonnenweg 12,
Postfach, CH-4003
Switzerland

Named after Denmark's famous storyteller, the Hans Christian Andersen Award is presented every other year to an author and illustrator who by the outstanding value of their work are judged to have made an important and lasting contribution to children's literature. A distinguished international jury of 10 children's literature specialists chooses the winners according to

artistic and literary criteria.
Deadline: Entries must be received by August 15.
Announcements: Winners are announced at the Children's Book Fair in Bologna, Italy.
Representative Winners: 1998 winner: Katherine Paterson (USA); 1996 winner: Uri Orlev (Israel).
Award: Winners receive a gold medal and a diploma at an awards dinner.

Atlantic Writing Competition
Writers' Federation of Nova Scotia
Suite 901, 1809 Barrington Street
Halifax, Nova Scotia B3J 3K8
Canada
website: www.reseau.chebucto.ns.ca/Culture/WFNS/competitions/html

---

Sponsored by the Writers' Federation of Nova Scotia, this competition is unique in offering constructive feedback to every participant. The contest is open to writers living in Canada's Atlantic Provinces. Awards are in several categories, including three for published authors.

Contestants may send only one entry per category; entry fee, $10 for Writers' Federation members, seniors citizens, and students; $15 for non-members. Send an SASE for complete guidelines and categories.
Deadline: August 1.
Announcements: Contest announced in February; winners announced at the Federation's gala, held the following February.
Representative Winners: Harry Thurston, Harry Bruce, Shree Ghatage.
Award: Cash prizes from $50 to $150 are awarded at the annual gala.

Arizona's Young Reader's Award
Arizona Library Association
14449 North 73rd Street
Scottsdale, AZ 85260-3133
website: www.azinfo.maricopa.gov/azla

This award is given annually to familiarize young readers with high-quality, recently published books and their authors. Young readers in Arizona vote on their favorite picture book, chapter book, and middle school/YA book.

After receiving nominations, the Arizona's Young Reader's Award Committee prepares a master voting list of 10 titles for each category. The list is sent back to schools and libraries for the children's votes.

Eligible books must have been published in English, within the last five years and still be in print. Nominations can be made by students, teachers, and librarians. Each teacher or librarian may submit a total of five nominations.
Deadline: March 15.
Announcements: Winners announced at the annual conference.
Representative Winners: *Stephanie's Ponytail,* Robert Munsch; *Drive-By,* Lynne Ewing.
Award: Winning authors receive their awards at the Arizona's Young Reader's Award luncheon.

ARTS Award
National Foundation for
  Advancement in the Arts
Laura Padron, Programs Director
Suite 500, 800 Brickell Avenue
Miami, FL 33131

The Arts Recognition and Talent Search (ARTS) Award is a national program designed to identify, recognize, and encourage talented high school seniors and other 17- and 18-year-olds who take part in photography, dance, voice, visual arts, writing, jazz, and music.

In the writing category, short stories, short nonfiction, books, and poetry are eligible for consideration. Originality, language, and imagination, as well as overall excellence, are considered by the judges. Entry fee: $25 for entries received by June 1; $35 for entries received between June 2 and October 1. Include an SASE when you request guidelines and applicant packet.
Deadline: June 1 or October 1.
Announcements: Competition announced in May and September.
Award: Cash awards ranging from $100 to $3,000 and an opportunity to be named a Presidential Scholar in the Arts.

Baker's Plays High School Play Writing Contest
P.O. Box 699222
Quincy, MA 02269-9222

Baker's Plays High School Playwriting Contest is open to any high school student. The play should be about the high school experience, but can be about any subject, especially the millennium, as long as the play can be reasonably produced on the high school stage. Plays may be any length.

Entries must be accompanied by the signature of a sponsoring high school English or drama teacher, and it is strongly recommended "that the play receive a production or a public reading prior to the submission." Multiple submissions and co-authored scripts are acceptable. Teachers may *not* submit a student's work. Send copies only and enclose an SASE with correct postage or the manuscript will not be returned. Awards are based on merit; if no submission warrants an award, no prizes will be given.
Deadline: All plays must be postmarked by January 30.
Announcements: Playwrights will be notified in May.
Award: First Place: $500 and the play will be published by Baker's Plays. Second Place: $250 and an Honorable Mention. Third Place: $100 and an Honorable Mention.

Bay Area Book Reviewers Association
BABRA
Poetry Flash
1450 Fourth Street #4
Berkeley, CA 94710

Formed to honor the work of local writers, the Bay Area Book Reviewers Association presents the Fred Cody Award to the best of Northern California fiction, poetry, nonfiction, and children's literature that is committed to bettering the community. Books published in the preceding year are eligible for consideration. No entry fees; no entry form. Send three copies of each title. Send an SASE for guidelines.
Deadline: December 1.
Announcements: Winners announced at an awards ceremony.
Representative Winners: Josephine Miles, Robert Duncan, Wright Morris, M.F.K. Fisher.
Award: $100 presented at an awards ceremony.

The John and Patricia Beatty Award
California Library Association
Jane Dyer Cook, Coordinator
717 K Street, Suite 300
Sacramento, CA 95814-3477

This award, sponsored by the California Library Association, honors Professor John Beatty and his wife Patricia, who co-authored 11 young adult novels that focused on historical events in the British Isles from 1600 to 1754.

Any children's or young adult book set in California and published in the U.S. during the preceding calendar year is eligible. The California setting must be an integral focus for the book. Complete reprints of previously published works are not accepted. The books should be well-written and appropriate for their intended audience.

Deadline: Write for 2000 deadline.
Announcements: Contest announced during National Library Week in April, and awards are presented at the CLA Annual Conference in November.
Representative Winner: 1999 winner: *Bandit's Moon,* Sid Fleischman.
Award: A $500 cash prize and an engraved plaque are presented to the winner at the Beatty Award Breakfast, during the CLA Annual Conference.

The Geoffrey Bilson Award for Historical Fiction
The Canadian Children's Book Center
35 Spadina Road
Toronto, ON M5R 2S9
Canada

The purpose of this contest is to reward excellence in the writing of an outstanding work of historical fiction for young people by a Canadian author. It looks for books in which history informs the reader in a significant way and is historically authentic.

All entries must be written by Canadian citizens, published in the year preceding the contest, and have been included in the Our Choice catalogue produced by the center. Winners are chosen by a jury appointed by the centre, with a member of the Our Choice Committee acting as chairman.

Deadline: May 15.
Announcements: Winners are announced in November.
Award: $1,000 and a certificate will be presented to the winner.

Irma Simonton and James H. Black Award for Excellence in Children's Literature
Bank Street College of Education
Linda Greengrass, Coordinator of School Services
610 West 112 Street
New York, NY 10025

Honoring an outstanding book for young children in which text and illustration together produce a singular whole, this award is presented each spring. A select group of writers, librarians, and educators choose about 35 books that they consider to be the best candidates for the award. The final judging is done by second-, third-, and fourth-grade classes on the East Coast.

Authors should ask their publishers to submit one copy of their books. Multiple submissions are permitted; no entry fee.

Deadline: Books should be received no later than the beginning of January.

Announcements: Winners are announced in May.
Representative Winners: *Heckedy Peg,* Audrey and Don Wood; *Gorky Rises,* William Steig.
Award: A scroll with the recipient's name and a gold seal designed by Maurice Sendak will be given to the winners at a Harvard Club Breakfast.

Waldo M. and Grace C. Bonderman National Youth Theatre Playwriting Development Competition
Indiana University-Purdue University at Indianapolis
Priscilla Jackson, Assistant to the Chair
Suite 309, 425 University Boulevard
Indianapolis, IN 46202

The purpose of this competition is to encourage writers to create artistic scripts for young audiences and provide a forum through which each winning playwright receives constructive criticism. Plays should be intended for young audiences in grades 3 through 12. Author must suggest appropriate age category on the entry form.

Plays should run about 45 minutes, and scripts should not be committed to publication at the time of submission. Musicals are not accepted. No simultaneous submissions; no entry fee.
Deadline: Sept 1, 2000.
Announcements: Competition announced in the spring of even years; winners announced the following January.
Award: Top four winners receive $1,000 each and staged readings.

Book Publishers of Texas Award
Texas Institute of Letters
Center for the Study of the Southwest
Flowers Hall 327
Southwest Texas State University
San Marcos, TX 78666
website: www.english.swt.edu/CSS/TIL/Rules.htm

Honoring the best book for children or young people by a Texan, this award is sponsored by the Texas Institute of Letters. Each entry should be accompanied by a statement of the entrant's eligibility: birth in Texas or two years of consecutive residence in the state at some time. A book that has a subject matter substantially concerning Texas is also eligible. All works entered must have been published in the year preceding the contest.

Entries should be sent directly to the judges; send an SASE for judges' names and addresses; or visit the website.
Deadline: January.
Announcements: Finalists will be notified in March; winners announced at the April banquet.
Awards: Winner receives $250 at an award presentation.

The *Boston Globe/Horn Book* Awards

The Horn Book, Inc.
56 Roland Street, Suite 200
Boston, MA 02129
website: www.hbook.com

Since 1967, the *Boston Globe* and the *Horn Book* have cosponsored these awards for excellence in literature for children and young adults. The awards are considered among the most prestigious in the nation.

A committee of three professionals involved in the field of children's literature evaluates thousands of submissions from United States publishers to select winners in the three categories: picture book, fiction, and nonfiction. The judges may also name several honor books in each category. Eligible books must be published during the year preceding the contest, in the United States, though they may be written or illustrated by citizens of any country. Books must be submitted by publishers only. A copy of the submission must be sent to all three judges. Send an SASE for further details.

Deadline: May 15.
Announcements: Contest announced in February; winners announced in October at the New England Library Association's annual conference.
Representative Winners: *Red-Eyed Tree Frog,* Joy Cowley; *Holes,* Louis Sachar; *The Top of the World: Climbing Mount Everest,* Steve Jenkins.
Award: Winners receive $500 and an engraved silver bowl. Honor recipients receive an engraved silver plate.

Ann Connor Brimer Award

Nova Scotia Library Association
Linda Hogins, Youth Services
    Coordinator
P.O. Box 36036
Halifax, NS B3J 3S9
Canada

Given to an author of a children's book who resides in Atlantic Canada, the Ann Connor Brimer Award recognizes excellence in writing for children up to the age of 15. Fiction and nonfiction published in Canada between May of the preceding year and April 30 of the contest are eligible.

Deadline: April 30.
Announcements: Winner is announced in September.
Representative Winner: *The House of Wooden Santas,* Kevin Major.
Award: Winner receives $1,000 at an award ceremony in November at the Maritime Museum of the Atlantic.

Buckeye Children's Book Award

State Library of Ohio
Ruth Metcalf, Secretary
65 South Front Street
Columbus, OH 43215-4163
website: www.wpl.lib.oh.us/buckeyebook/

The Buckeye Children's Book Award Program was established in 1981 through a collaborative effort of the Ohio Council International Reading Association, Ohio Council of Teachers of English Language Arts, Ohio Educational Library Media Association, Ohio Library Council, and State Library of Ohio. The awards are presented in three categories: kindergarten to grade two, grades three to five, and grades six to eight. The award is determined in a two-year process, with the first year devoted to the nomination process and the second year to actual voting.

Nominated books must have been written by a U.S. citizen and originally copyrighted in the U.S. within the last three years preceding the contest. Nominations can be made by children in public and private elementary and middle/junior high school and by public libraries in Ohio. Nominations can be made in both fiction and nonfiction in all of the three categories. Send an SASE for further information on this program.

Deadline: February 2001.
Announcements: Winners announced in February or March of the contest year.
Representative Winners: *Verdi*, Janell Cannon; *Wayside School Gets a Little Stranger*, Louis Sachar; *Seedfolks*, Paul Fleischman.
Award: Winning books become part of the Buckeye Children's Book Hall of Fame, housed in the Columbus Metropolitan Library.

ByLine Magazine Contests
Contests, ByLine Magazine
P.O. Box 130596
Edmond, OK 73013
website: www.bylinemag.com/contests/htm

ByLine Magazine holds monthly contests to inspire and challenge writers. The monthly contests are open to all writers. Categories change each month and have included feature articles, inspirational poems, flash fiction, and personal experience articles. In addition, the *ByLine* Literary Awards are offered to subscribers only.

All contest entries must be unpublished; multiple entries are permitted. Entry fees must accompany each submission, and range from $3 to $5. Name, address, phone number, and contest category should be listed on the front page of manuscript (no cover sheet).

Send an SASE for contest categories and deadlines, or these may be obtained from the website.
Deadlines: Monthly contests; deadlines vary. *ByLine* Literary Awards have a deadline of November 1.
Announcements: Contest winners are announced three months after the contest deadline; winners receive cash prizes and possible publication.

Randolph Caldecott Medal
American Library Association
50 E. Huron
Chicago, IL 60611
website: www.ala.org/alsc/caldecott.html

Named in honor of nineteenth-century English illustrator Randolph Caldecott, this medal is awarded annually by the Association for Library Service to Children, a division of the American Library Association, to the artist of the most distinguished American picture book for children.

Illustrations must be original work, and the contest is open to all U.S. citizens. Necessary criteria include excellence in execution of the artistic technique and of pictorial interpretation of the story, theme, or concept and illustration style; send an SASE for guidelines.
Deadline: December 31.
Announcements: Competition is an-

nounced annually; winners are announced at the ALA Mid-Winter Meeting.
Representative Winner: *Snowflake Bentley,* illustrated by Mary Azarian; text by Jacqueline Briggs Martin.
Award: The Caldecott Medal is presented at an awards banquet.

California Book Awards
The Commonwealth Club of
   California
595 Market Street
San Francisco, CA 94105
website: www.commonwealthclub.org

Authors and publishers are invited to submit an entry to the Annual California Book Awards of The Commonwealth Club of California. Awards are presented to books of exceptional literary merit in 9 categories, including: fiction or nonfiction for children up to age 10; fiction or nonfiction for children ages 11 to 16; and fiction or nonfiction relating to the state of California.

Three copies of each book must be provided along with the entry form, which may be obtained by sending an SASE. Entries are restricted to books published in the year preceding the contest. Author must have been a legal resident of California at the time the manuscript was accepted for publication.
Deadline: January 31.
Announcements: Competition announced in the fall; winners announced in June or July.
Representative Winners: *King Leopold's Ghost,* Adam Hochschild; *Hunger,* Lan Samantha Chang.
Award: A plaque is presented to winners at a ceremony.

California Young Playwrights
   Contest
Playwrights Project
Deborah Salzer, Executive Director
450 B Street, Suite 1020
San Diego, CA 92101-8002

Open to California residents under the age of 19, the California Young Playwrights Contest seeks to encourage playwriting by young people. Entries are read and judged by theatre professionals. All scripts must be original, and written in play format, but style and form are up to you. Plays previously submitted are not accepted; no entry fees required.

Entries must be stapled and include a title page with name, address, telephone number and date of birth. Submit two copies; entries will not be returned. Include a brief letter about yourself and how you came to write your play.
Deadline: April 1.
Announcements: Competition announced in January.
Award: $100 and professional production at Old Globe Theatre in San Diego.

***Calliope* Fiction Contest**
Calliope
Sandy Raschke, Fiction Editor
P.O. Box 466
Moraga, CA 94556-0466

Sponsored by the Writers' Special Interest Group (SIG) of American Mensa, this award's purpose is to create a fun writing experience for members, subscribers, and entrants. It seeks to promote quality writing; contest theme changes yearly. Members and non-members of SIG are eligible.

Entries should be unpublished fiction that does not exceed 2,500 words. Works containing violence, horror, or erotic fiction will not be accepted. Please include a cover sheet with the author's name, address, phone number, and title of story. Each writer is allowed a maximum of five entries. SIG members receive one free entry and pay $2 for each additional entry; fee for non-members is $2 per entry. Guidelines and theme list available with an SASE.

Deadline: April.
Announcements: Winners announced in September.
Representative Winner: *Under the Light of the Web,* Owen Williams.
Award: Prizes are determined from the entry fees received, with the minimum being $10 for first place, $7.50 for second place, and $5 for third place. Winners and honorable mentions receive certificates; the winning entry is published in *Calliope*.

Canadian Authors Association Awards

Canadian Authors Association
Alec McEachern, Administrator
Box 419
Cambellford, Ontario K0L 1L0
Canada
website: www.canauthors.org

The CAA Vicky Metcalf Awards, "honoring writing inspirational to Canadian youth," were created in 1963 by the Toronto librarian whose name they bear. There are two separate categories in this award: The Body of Work Award and the Short Story Award.

The Body of Work Award is presented to a Canadian author who has published a minimum of four books that are inspirational to young people. The books can be fiction, nonfiction and/or poetry. This award may only be won one time per author. The nomination should be in letter form, listing the published works or the nominee along with the biography of the author.

The Short Story Award is for a Canadian author of a short story in English that is published in a periodical or anthology. Four tearsheets or photocopies of the published work must be submitted along with a biography of the writer, and the name of the editor.

Nominations may be made by an individual person, publisher, or association. Send an SASE or visit the website for further details.

Deadline: December 31.
Announcements: Winners announced in April.
Representative Winners: Joan Clark and Anne Carter.
Award: Body of Work Award winners receive $10,000; Short Story Award winners receive $3,000.

Canadian Library Association Book Awards

CLA Membership Services
Chairperson, Book of the Year
  Children's Award Committee
200 Elgin Street, Suite 602
Ottawa, Ontario K2P 1L5
Canada

The Book of the Year Award is given to the author of an outstanding children's book that was published in Canada during the previous calendar year. The

book must be suitable for children up to age 14, and can consist of fiction, poetry, re-tellings of traditional literature. Anthologies and collections are also eligible. Authors must be Canadian citizens or permanent residents of Canada. Contact CLA for contest guidelines.
Deadline: December 31.
Announcements: Call for nominations begins in October. Winners are announced in June at the annual conference.
Award: A handsome medal is presented to the winning author at the CLA annual conference.

Canadian Library Awards Young Adult Canadian Book Award
CLA Membership Services
Chairperson, Young Adults Canadian Book Award
200 Elgin Street, Suite 602
Ottawa, Ontario K2P 1L5
Canada

This annual award was established in 1980 by the Young Adult Caucus of the Saskatchewan Library Association. It looks to recognize an author of an outstanding English language, Canadian book that is appealing to young adults between the ages of 13 to 18. All entries must have been published in the year preceding the contest.

Entries must be a work of fiction, either short story or novel; the title must be a Canadian publication either in hardcover or paperback; and the author must be a citizen of Canada or landed immigrant.
Deadline: December 31.
Announcements: Call for nominations begins in October. Winners are announced in June at the annual CLA conference.
Representative Winner: *Janey's Girl*, Gayle Friesen.
Award: The winner receives a leather bound book with the award seal on the cover.

Raymond Carver Short Story Contest
Humboldt State University, English Department
Barbara Curiel
Arcata, CA 95221

This annual contest was put in place to honor Raymond Carver and his connection to the Humboldt State University English department. It is open to all U.S. citizens, and all entries must be previously unpublished.

Rights to the winning story will revert back to the author after publication in *TOYON*. Send two double-spaced, stapled copies of each story. Include a cover sheet with story title, name, address, phone number and e-mail address. Author's name must not appear anywhere on the manuscript. Entry fee, $10 per story.
Deadline: December 1.
Announcements: Winners will be announced in June.
Representative Winners: 1999: 1st place, "Waiting on Mavis Staples," Andrea-Michelle Smith; 2nd place, "The End of Something," Krandall Kraus; 3rd place, "San Lazaro," Jose Luis Dorado.
Awards: First place: $500 and publication in *TOYON;* second place: $250 and honorable mention in *TOYON*; third place: honorable mention.

Rebecca Caudill Young Readers' Book Award
Illinois Reading Council
Bonita Slovinski
P.O. Box 6536
Naperville, IL 60567-6536

Given in honor of Illinois author Rebecca Caudill, this award seeks to develop a statewide awareness of outstanding children's and young adult literature and a desire for literacy. The Illinois Reading Council encourages children and young adults to read for personal satisfaction.

The award is presented to the book voted most outstanding by readers in grades four to eight from participating Illinois schools. Students, teachers, librarians, and media specialists nominate titles from a master list of 20 books, finalized by the Awards Committee. To be nominated, books must be currently in print, published in the U.S. during the last five years and can be fiction, nonfiction, or poetry. Textbooks, anthologies, and translations are not eligible.
Deadline: Nominations must be submitted by May 15; ballots returned by November 28.
Announcements: Competition announced in March.
Representative Winner: Andrew Clements.
Award: Winners receive a monetary honorarium presented at an awards breakfast during the ISLMA annual conference.

Children's Writer **Contests**
95 Long Ridge Road
West Redding, Ct 06896-1124

The publishers of *Children's Writer* hold three annual contests for previously unpublished nonfiction and fiction. Entries are judged by the faculty and editorial staff of the Institute of Children's Literature. Judges look for originality, characterization, plot, quality of writing, and adherence to age range.

Contest themes and age ranges vary for each contest. Submission lengths range from 350 to 1,500 words. No entry fee for subscribers to *Children's Writer*; nonsubscribers pay a $10 reading fee for each submission, which also entitles them to an eight-month trial subscription. Guidelines and theme list available with an SASE.
Deadlines: February, June and October.
Announcements: Winners are announced in *Children's Writer*; Grand-prize winner receives publication in the newsletter.
Representative Winners: *Nature Warm-Ups and Cool-Downs,* Joan Brennan; *Run Like the Wind,* Kristen Hoel.
Award: Cash prizes of $250–$1,000; publication in *Children's Writer.*

Children's Writers Fiction Contest
Goodwin Williams, Goodwin Literary Associates
V.R. Williams, Coordinator
P.O. Box 8863
Springfield, MO 65801-8863

Open to all writers, this contest promotes writing for children by encouraging authors and giving them an opportunity to submit their work in competition. Submissions are judged on clarity, punctuation, grammar, imagery, content, and suitability for children. Stories should be about 1,000 words

and unpublished. First-time rights are acquired when a writer submits a piece. Entry fee, $5 for first piece, $2.50 each additional submission. Send for complete guidelines.
Deadline: July 31.
Announcements: Competition is announced in February.
Representative Winners: *That Little Kid*, Marjorie Ellert Berg; *The Honey King*, Marianne Walker; *Lucy Tucy and the Tooth Fairy*, Eli Estreicher.
Award: Winner receives a cash award of $150 and publication in the newsletter and/or in *HodgePodge*, along with a certificate.

Mr. Christie's Book Award Program
Marlene Yustin, Program Coordinator
2150 Lakeshore Boulevard West
Toronto, ON M8V 1A3
Canada

The purpose of this awards program is to honor excellence in the writing and illustration of Canadian children's literature and to encourage the development and publishing of high-quality children's books that promote a love of reading. All entries must be published in Canada during the calendar year prior to the contest. Translations are not accepted.

There are two judging panels, one for books written in English and one for those written in French. Each panel consists of five judges. Submissions must be sent to each. Send an SASE for complete contest guidelines and list of judges.
Deadline: January 31.
Announcements: Winners announced in May.

Award: A $7,500 cash prize is awarded to the winner.

Christopher Award
The Christophers
Judith Trojan, Coordinator
12 East 48th Street
New York, NY 10017

The Christopher Awards are presented in several categories including: juvenile books, motion pictures, books, and television specials. To be eligible, books must be original titles published in the year preceding the contest. There are no application forms or entry fees. Send four copies of each title with a press kit, press release, or catalogue copy.

Submissions are reviewed year-round. Send an SASE for complete list of categories and guidelines.
Deadlines: November 24.
Announcements: Winners announced in February in the *New York Times*.
Representative Winners: *Raising Dragons*, Jerdine Nolen; *The Summer My Father was Ten*, Pat Brisson; *Mary of Horseback*, Rosemary Wells.
Award: Bronze medallions are presented to winners at an awards ceremony in February.

CNW/FFWA Florida State Writing Competition
Florida Freelance Writer's Association
Dana K. Cassell, Executive Director
P.O. Box A
North Stratford, NH 03590
website: www.writers-editors.com

Open to all writers, this competition gives awards in 11 categories, including, nonfiction, fiction, and children's literature. Submissions are judged on presentation, suitability for intended age groups, and structure.

All entries must be previously unpublished, with the exception of one adult category for published material. There are no length limitations, but submissions should adhere to typical type and age guidelines to be judged favorably. Multiple submissions are accepted. Fees for entries over 3,000 words are $10 for members and $20 for non-members; for entries under 3,000 words or 1 to 3 poems, $5 for members and $10 for nonmembers. Send an SASE for complete guidelines.
Deadline: March 15.
Announcements: Announcements made by May 31.
Representative Winners: Denise Tiller, Julie Melear, Ruth Weitz, Claire Carr, Joanna Norris, Betty Welch.
Award: $24 to $75 and certificate.

Colorado Blue Spruce Young Adult Book Award
Dave Benson, Committee Chair
P.O. Box 27072
Denver, CO 80227

Held annually, this award is unique in that only students nominate titles and vote for their favorites, as an encouragement to read. Any student who reads three titles from the current year's nominated list of books is eligible to vote. All nominated books must have been written by an American author and been published and in the past five years. Send $2 for this year's nominated titles. Voting is limited to students in Colorado.
Deadline: Students vote throughout the school year.

Announcements: Winners announced in mid-March.
Representative Winners: *Chicken Soup for the Teenage Soul,* Jack Canfield; *Jurassic Park,* Stephen King.
Award: Winning author receives an awards presentation.

Colorado Book Awards
Colorado Center for the Book
Megan Maguire, Program Director
2123 Downing Street
Denver, CO 80205

Honoring authors living in Colorado who exemplify the best writing in the state, this contest offers awards in eight different categories for children and young adult books. Awards are based on the quality of writing, and are judged by librarians throughout the state.

Any book with a 2000 publication date, or certification that it was published in November or December of 1999, is eligible for submission. Authors must have been a Colorado resident for 3 of the last 12 months prior to December 31, 2000. Multiple entries are permitted; entry fee, $40. All entries should include six copies of the book, and will not be returned.
Deadline: December 1.
Announcements: Winners are announced in the spring.
Award: $500.

Marguerite de Angeli Contest
Bantam Doubleday Dell BFYR
1540 Broadway
New York, NY 10036

This contest was established to honor children's book author and illustrator

Marguerite de Angeli and to encourage the writing of contemporary and historical children's fiction set in North America. A standard book contract, advance, and royalty are offered to the winner.

Submissions should be for readers 7 to 10, between 40 and 144 pages in length, and include a brief plot summary with a cover letter. A maximum of two entries may be submitted by U.S. and Canadian writers who have not previously published a novel for middle-grade readers. While under consideration at Bantam Doubleday Dell, manuscripts submitted for this contest should not be sent to any other publisher. Enclose an SASE if you want your manuscript returned—no manuscript boxes, please.

Deadline: Manuscripts must be postmarked after April 1 and no later than June 30.

Announcements: Contest results will be announced no later than October 31 in *School Library Journal, Book Links, Publishers Weekly,* and other trade publications.

Representative Winner: *A Letter to Mrs. Roosevelt,* Carmine de Young.

Award: Contracts for hardcover and paperback editions of work; $1,500 in cash and a $3,500 cash advance against royalties.

Delacorte Press Prize for a First Young Adult Novel
Bantam Doubleday Dell BFYR
1540 Broadway
New York, NY 10036

The purpose of this annual contest is to stimulate the writing of contemporary young adult fiction. It is open to U.S. and Canadian writers who have not previously published a young adult novel.

Submissions should consist of a book-length manuscript with a contemporary setting that is suitable for readers ages 12 to 18. Authors may not submit more than two entries per competition. Send an SASE for guidelines.

Deadline: Entries must be postmarked between October 1 and December 31.

Announcements: Contest results will be announced no later than April 30 in *Publishers Weekly, School Library Journal, Book Links,* and other trade publications.

Award: Winner receives a book contract for hardcover and paperback edition, a cash award of $1,500, and a $6,000 advance against royalties.

Arthur Ellis Award
Crime Writers of Canada
3007 Kingston Road Box 113
Scarborough, ON M1M 1P1
Canada

This award is presented by the Crime Writers of Canada to honor the best works published by Canadian authors during the previous year. Established in 1984, it gives awards to the best in the following categories: novel, first novel, short story, juvenile, and true crime.

At the discretion of the president of Crime Writers, the Derrick Murdoch Award, named in honor of Canada's premier crime fiction reviewer, for a lifetime achievement or outstanding contribution to the genre, may be awarded; the award is not necessarily presented each year.

Authors must be residents of

Canada or Canadian citizens living in other countries. Send an SASE for complete guidelines.
Deadline: January 31.
Announcements: Winners announced in May.
Representative Winner: Best juvenile mystery: *The Body in the Basement*, Norah McClintock.
Award: Winner receives an Arthur statuette.

Emphasis on Reading Children's Choice Book Award
Dr. Jane Brady Smith, Education Administrator
Alabama State Department of Education
50 North Ripley Street, Room 5351
Montgomery, AL 36130
website: www.alsde.edu

The purpose of this children's choice award program is to encourage students to read good books and engage them in the excitement of an election to determine winners. There are three grade-grouped categories: kindergarten to grade two, grades three to five, and grades six to eight. Students are not restricted to reading and voting on books only in the category that corresponds to their grade level.

Books are chosen from the starred reviews in the *School Library Journal*. Books by Alabama authors that do not appear in the journal can also be nominated for voting. Contest guidelines available with an SASE.
Deadline: Voting for the winning books takes place in March.
Announcements: Winners are announced in April.

Award: The winner in each category receives a paperweight bearing the Emphasis on Reading logo.

Empire State Award
Shawn Bromar, Youth Services
252 Hudson Street
Albany, NY 12210
website: www.nyla.org.yss/empire.html

Nominated by librarians, the Empire State Award honors a body of work that represents excellence in literature for children and young adults. Since 1990, it has been presented annually to a New York author or illustrator who has made a significant contribution to literature for young people.
Deadline: November 30.
Announcements: Winners are announced in May.
Representative Winner: Vera B. Williams, Jean Craighead George, Nancy Willard.
Award: Winner receives an engraved medallion at the spring conference of the New York Library Association.

Shubert Fendrich Memorial Playwriting Contest
Pioneer Drama Service
Beth Somers, Assistant Editor
P.O. Box 4267
Englewood, CO 80155-4267
website: www.pioneerdrama.com

The purpose of this annual contest is to encourage quality theatrical works for amateurs. The contest is open to authors not currently published by Pioneer Drama Service. Unpublished plays on any subject are accepted. They must have a running time of 20 to 90 min-

utes and must have been produced at least once. The subject matter should be suitable for family-oriented amateur theater groups, such as schools and community theaters. Send an SASE for complete guidelines.
Deadline: March 1, 2001.
Announcements: Winners are announced June 1.
Representative Winners: *The Mirror of Dori Gray,* John Mattera; *Big Boys Don't Cry,* Vern Harden; *Bigger Than Life,* Cynthia Mercati.
Award: Winner receives $1,000 royalty advance in addition to publication.

Dorothy Canfield Fisher Children's Book Award
DCF Committee
Grace Greene
Northeast Regional Library
R.D. 2, Box 244
St. Johnsbury, VT 05819

Sponsored by the Vermont Department of Libraries and Vermont PTA, this child-selected program is designed to encourage Vermont children to become enthusiastic and discriminating readers by providing them with books of good quality. Children read books from a master list of 30 titles that were selected by the awards committee, and then choose their favorite. Books must be written by a citizen of the United States, and be published in the preceding calendar year. Send an SASE for contest guidelines. Contact Grace Greene at ggreene@dol.state.vt.us with questions.
Deadline: Entries must be received by October 29.
Announcements: Winners are announced in the spring.
Award: Winner receives a scroll illustrated by a Vermont artist; presented at an awards ceremony in May or June.

The Norma Fleck Award
The Canadian Children's Book Centre
35 Spadina Road
Toronto, Ontario M5R 2S9
Canada

The Norma Fleck Award is administered by the Canadian Children's Book Centre, a national nonprofit organization that supports, promotes, and encourages the reading, writing, and illustrating of Canadian children's books. Nonfiction books in the following categories are eligible: cultural/arts, concept, science, biography, history, geography, reference, sports, and activities and pastimes.

Exceptional quality, informative and captivating presentation, and breadth and depth of information are key criteria. Books must be written by Canadian citizens and must be nominated by the publisher. Send an SASE for complete guidelines.
Deadline: April 30.
Announcements: Announcements are made in May; winners announced in November.
Award: A $10,000 award will be presented to the winner.

FOCAL Award
Friends of Children and Literature
Renny Day, President
Los Angeles Public Library
630 West Fifth Street
Los Angeles, CA 90071

The FOCAL Award is presented to an

author and/or illustrator for a creative work that enriches a child's appreciation for and knowledge of California. Books can be fiction or nonfiction and must meet the highest standards of excellence. All submissions must be in print at the time of the award. Work should be age-appropriate for the Children's Literature Department of the Los Angeles Public Library.

Submissions are judged on: literary and/or artistic merit; interest and readability; universality; and California enrichment content.

Deadline: December 31.
Announcements: Winner announced in mid-January.
Representative Winner: *Calling the Doves: El Canto de las Palomas,* Juan Felipe Herrea.
Award: Winner is invited to an award luncheon in Los Angeles; a puppet resembling a main character in the book is presented to winning author.

Foster City Writers' Contest

Foster City Art and Culture
   Committee
Ted Lance, Contest Chairman
650 Shell Blvd.
Foster City, CA 94404

Looking to recognize new writers of fiction, humor, children's stories, rhymed verse, and blank verse, the Foster City Writers' Contest is offered annually.

Entries may be fiction, to 3,000 words; children's stories, to 2,000 words; and rhymed verse and blank verse that does not exceed two double-spaced pages. One piece per entry fee, $10. All entries must be previously unpublished and written in English. Do not include your name on the title page or any sheet of your entry, instead please attach a 3"x5" card with your name, address, and phone number, manuscript title, and category. Entries will not be returned.

Deadline: October 31.
Announcements: Winners will be announced early in the following year.
Award: First-place winner receives $250, honorable mentions receive $125.

H. E. Francis Award Short Story Competition

English Department
University of Alabama, Huntsville
Huntsville, AL 35899
website: www.uah.edu/colleges/liberal/english/whatnewcontest.html

---

This contest is sponsored by the Ruth Hindman Foundation and the University of Alabama at Huntsville, English Department. A panel of recognized, award-winning authors, directors of creative writing programs, and editors of literary journals judges the submissions.

Manuscripts must be unpublished, and not exceed 500 words in length. Multiple submissions are accepted; entry fee, $15 per submission. Include three copies of each manuscript. All submissions must include a cover sheet with the title of the story, the author's name and address, and the approximate word count. The author's name should not appear anywhere on the manuscript. Send an SASE for complete guidelines.

Deadline: December 31.
Announcements: Winners announced in March.
Award: Winner receives a $1000 prize.

Don Freeman Memorial Grant-In-Aid
Society of Children's Book Writers
 and Illustrators
Suite 296, 345 North Maple Drive
Beverly Hills, CA 90210
website: www.scbwi.org/grants.htm

The Don Freeman Memorial Grant-In-Aid was established by the Society of Children's Book Writers and Illustrators (SCBWI) to enable picture book artists to further their understanding, training, and work in the picture book genre.

This grant is available to full and associate members of SCBWI, who, as artists, seriously intend to make picture books their chief contribution to the field of children's literature. Applicants are required to submit artwork: either a rough book dummy accompanied by two finished illustrations or 10 finished illustrations suitable for picture book portfolio presentation.

Deadline: Applications available beginning June 1 and accepted between January 10 and February 10.
Announcements: Winners announced in June.
Representative Winner: Sheryl Daane Chest.
Award: Winner receives grant of $1,000; runner-up receives a grant of $500.

Georgia Children's Book Award and Georgia Children's Picture Storybook Award
Department of Language Education
125 Aderhold Hall
University of Georgia
Athens, GA 30602
www.coe.uga.edu/gachildlit/awards/index.html

These awards are held to promote reading for pleasure. After receiving nominations, a committee of teachers and librarians prepares a list of 20 titles for each award. This list is sent to children in the primary grades whose classroom teachers have agreed to take part in promoting the program.

Titles nominated should be appropriate for students in grades four to eight, and those nominated for the picture storybook category should appeal to students in kindergarten to grade four. Authors must be residents of the U.S. or Canada.
Deadline: December.
Announcements: Winners are announced in May.
Representative Winners: Ann M. Martin, Emily Arnold McCully, Dav Pilkey.
Awards: $1,000 and a plaque presented at the University of Georgia Children's Literature Conference.

Golden Archer Award
Wisconsin Educational Media
 Association
Annette Smith, Contest Coordinator
1300 Industrial Drive
Fennimore, WI 53809-9702

Founded by Marion Fuller Archer, the Golden Archer Awards seek to encourage young readers to become better acquainted with quality literature written expressly for them, to broaden students' awareness of reading and literature as a lifelong pleasure, and to honor favorite books and their authors.

Winners are selected by students in elementary through junior high in three categories: Primary, Intermediate, and Middle/Junior High. All titles pub-

lished in the previous five years are eligible. Send an SASE for guidelines.
Deadline: Nominations due October 15; ballots due March 15.
Announcements: Winners announced in April.
Award: Bronze medals and certificates are awarded to competition winners.

Golden Kite Awards
Society of Children's Book Writers and Illustrators (SCBWI)
Mercedes Coats, Contest Coordinator
8271 Beverly Boulevard
Los Angeles, CA 90048
website: www.scbwi.org

This annual contest, offered to members of SCBWI, awards prizes in four categories: fiction, nonfiction, picture book text, and picture illustration. Any book by a SCBWI member is eligible during the year of its publication.

Books may be submitted between February 1 and December 15. Authors should make a note of the category they are entering on the book. Send one book to each of the three judges in each category, and one copy to the SCBWI office. If you are submitting a book to both the picture book text and picture book illustration categories, send one book to each judge in both categories and one to the SCBWI office.
Deadline: December 25.
Announcements: Winners announced in April.
Representative Winners: *Rules of the Road*, Joan Bauer; *Martha Graham: A Dancer's Life*, Russell Freedman.
Award: Statuette or plaques presented at SCBWI events.

Gold Medallion Book Awards
Evangelical Christian Publishers Association
Doug Ross, President
1969 East Broadway Road, Suite 2
Tempe, AZ 85282

In recognition of excellence in evangelical Christian literature, the Evangelical Christian Publishers Association annually presents this award. To be eligible, books must have explicit Christian content or a distinctly Christian worldview. Judges evaluate submissions on content, literary quality, design, and significance of contribution. It offers awards in 22 categories including: fiction, preschool children, youth, elementary children, and marriage. Send an SASE for complete list of categories and guidelines.

Books should be submitted by publishers; entry fee $125 per title for ECPA members; $275 for nonmembers.
Deadline: December 2.
Announcements: Contest entry forms are mailed October 9; winners announced at the annual Gold Medallion Book Awards Banquet.
Representative Winners: Preschool Children: *The Parable Series*, Liz Curtis Higgs and Tommy Nelson; Youth: *It's Time to Be Bold*, Michael W. Smith.
Award: Plaques are awarded at the Gold Medallion Book Awards Banquet.

Governor General's Literary Awards
The Canada Council for the Arts
350 Albert Street
P.O. Box 1047
Ottawa, ON K1P 5V8
Canada

The Governor's General Literary Awards are given annually to the best English-language and best French-language work in the categories of fiction, nonfiction, poetry, drama, children's literature (text), and children's literature (illustration) and translation. All entries must be first-edition trade books that have been written or translated by a Canadian citizen or permanent resident of Canada. Books must have been published in the 13 months prior to the contest, and must be at least 48 pages, except for picture books, which have a minimum of 24 pages. Books with more than one author/illustrator are not eligible.

Send four copies of all eligible titles submitted in a category. Publishers must complete a registration form. Send an SASE for complete guidelines.
Deadline: Books published between September 1 and April 30 of the award year have a May 15 deadline. Books published between May 1 and September 30 of the award year must be submitted by October 15.
Announcements: The list of nominated books is announced in October, and winners in mid-November.
Representative Winners: *Forms of Devotion;* Diane Schoemperlen; *Harlem Duet,* Djanet Sears; *The Hollow Tree,* Janet Lunn.
Award: Each winner is presented with $10,000 and a specially bound copy of their book. They are honored with a reception and dinner.

Hackney Literary Awards
Birmingham-Southern College
P.O. Box 549003
Birmingham, AL 35254

Sponsored by Birmingham-Southern College, the Hackney Literary Awards offer cash prizes for original, unpublished manuscripts. The competition recognizes excellence in writing in three categories: short story (to 5,000 words), poetry (to 50 lines), and novels (no length requirement). Each entry must have two cover sheets listing title of entry, author's name, address, phone number, and category; author's name must not appear on manuscript. Entries can be judged in either the national category or the state category. Submissions from Alabama are placed in the state category unless otherwise specified. Entry fees: novels, $25; short stories and poetry, $10 per entry. Manuscripts are not returned. Send an SASE for guidelines.
Deadline: Novel, September 30; Short story and poetry, December 31.
Announcements: Winners announced at the Birmingham-Southern College Writing Today Conference in March.
Award: $5,000, novel; $250–$600 for short story and poetry.

Highlights for Children Fiction Contest
Highlights for Children
803 Church Street
Honesdale, PA 18431

Designating a new theme each year, this contest introduces *Highlights* to the talent of new writers and gives them a chance to reward writers of fine children's stories. The most recent theme was humorous stories. New writers are encouraged to submit unpublished material to 900 words. Stories for beginning readers should not exceed 500

words. Submissions should be clearly marked for Fiction Contest, as those not so marked will be considered as regular submissions to *Highlights*. All entries have a chance of being published in *Highlights for Children*. Enclose an SASE with each entry; no entry fee.
Deadline: Entries must be postmarked between January 1 and February 28.
Announcements: Contest announced in September; winners notified by phone in June.
Award: Three winners will receive a cash prize of $1,000 each. Their stories become the property of *Highlights for Children*, and will be published in the magazine.

IBBY Honour List
International Board on Books for
   Young People
Leena Maissen, Executive Director
Nonnenweg 12,
Postfach, CH-4003 Basel
Switzerland

The IBBY Honour List is a biennial selection of outstanding recently published books. The list honors writers, illustrators, and translators from IBBY member countries. Books that are chosen should be representative of the best in children's literature from each country, and are recommended as suitable for publication throughout the world, thus furthering the IBBY objective of promoting international understanding and world peace through children's books and to provide children everywhere with the access to books of high literary standards.

Entries are selected by the national selections of IBBY, and each member country can submit three entries, one each for excellence in writing, illustration, and translation. Books must have been published within three years prior to the awards being presented
Deadline: October 15.
Announcements: Winners are announced every other September.
Representative Winner: *A Girl Named Disaster*, Nancy Farmer.
Award: Diplomas will be presented at the biennial Congress of IBBY.

INSIGHT Writing Contest
INSIGHT Magazine
Lori Peckham, Editor
55 W. Oak Ridge Drive
Hagerstown, MA 21740
website: www.insightmagazine.com

INSIGHT Magazine sponsors this annual contest honoring previously unpublished nonfiction, written with a distinct spiritual angle. Stories must be written with a teen audience in mind, and deal with issues of concern to teenagers today. Prizes are offered in three categories: student short story, general short story, and student poetry. Authors must be under the age of 21 to enter the student categories.

Grammar, structure, and storytelling elements are judged such as showing versus telling, description, and dialogue. Points are awarded and totaled to determine the winner. Stories, 500 to 1,500 words; poetry, to 250 words; no entry fee. All entries must be typed. Submissions may be made on computer printouts, photocopies, or via email at: insight@rhpa.org. *INSIGHT Magazine* retains first rights to publish the winning entry. Guidelines and cover

sheet forms available; send an SASE.
Deadline: June 1.
Announcements: Competition announced in February issue. Winners announced in a special winners' issue of *INSIGHT*.
Representative Winners: *Deadly Dare*, Laura Mae Chen; *Acts of Kindness*, Nancy Bonneau.
Award: Winners receive cash prizes of $50–$250 and publication.

Inspirational Writers Alive! Writing Competition
Martha Rogers, Coordinator
6038 Greenmont
Houston, TX 77092

Held annually to encourage both published and unpublished writers, the Inspirational Writers Alive! Writing Competition looks for submissions that have an inspirational appeal and a Christian perspective. Writers may submit their entries to the following categories: short story fiction, nonfiction article, devotional poetry, children's and teens' short story, and book proposals.

One entry per category is allowed. Submissions must be unpublished; the author's name should not appear on the manuscript. Include a cover sheet with name, address, phone, and title of submission. Manuscripts are not returned. Send an SASE for guidelines.
Deadlines: May 15.
Announcements: Contest announced in winter; winners announced at the Texas Christian Writers Forum.
Representative Winners: Linda Caradek, Frieda Chrisman.
Award: Cash prizes to top winners, and award certificates to all winners.

Jefferson Cup Award
Virginia Library Association
Sherry Inabinet, Chair
P.O. Box 8, Cricket Hill Road
Hudgins, VA 23076
website: www.vla.org

Initiated in 1962, the Jefferson Cup Award seeks to honor books written for young people in the areas of United States history, historical fiction, and biography, and promote the reading of books that illustrate America's past.

Original short nonfiction, books, and collections published in the year preceding the contest are eligible. All submissions must be suitable for young people. Multiple submissions are accepted. All submissions must be about U.S. history, an American from 1492 to present, or fiction that highlights the U.S. past.
Deadline: March 1.
Announcements: Contest announced in August or September; winner announced in June.
Representative Winner: *Soldier's Heart: Being the Story of the Enlistment and Due Service of the Boy Charlie Goddard in the First Minnesota Volunteers*, Gary Paulsen.
Award: $500 presented at the fall Virginia Library Association.

Barbara Karlin Grant
Society of Children's Book Writers
  and Illustrators (SBWI)
Suite 296, 345 North Maple Drive
Beverly Hills, CA 90210
website: www.scbwi.org/grants

This grant was established by the Society of Children's Book Writers and Illustrators to recognize and encourage the work of aspiring picture book writers. It is available to writers who are both full and associate members of SCBWI that have never had a picture book published. It is not available for a picture book text on which there is already a contract.

One picture book manuscript per applicant may be submitted. The text may be an original story, work of nonfiction, or a retelling or adaptation of a fairy tale, folktale or legend. Send an SASE for application forms and further guidelines.

Deadline: Complete applications and accompanying materials are accepted beginning April 1 and must be received no later than May 15.
Announcements: Requests for applications are made beginning October 1 of each year.
Representative Winner: 1998 winner: Brenda Jozaiatis; runner-up: K. G. Stiles.
Award: A grant of $1,000 is awarded annually.

Keats/Kerlan Fellowship

The Ezra Jack Keats/Kerlan Collection
   Memorial Fellowship
Karen Nelson Hoyle, Coordinator
109 Walter Library
117 Pleasant Street S.E.
Minneapolis, MN 55455

The Ezra Jack Keats Foundation provides $1,500 to a "talented writer and/or illustrator of children's books who wishes to use the Kerlan Collection for the furtherance of his or her artistic development. Special consideration will be given to someone who would find it difficult to finance the visit to the Kerlan Collection."

The competition is open to all published authors and illustrators. Send an SASE for guidelines and application.
Deadline: May 1.
Announcements: Contest is announced in the fall *Kerlan Newsletter*. Winners announced in May or June.
Representative Winners: Beth Royalty, David Pelletier, Paula Nourse-Ragland.
Award: Winner receives a $1,500 travel grant.

Kentucky Bluegrass Award

Northern Kentucky University and
   Kentucky Reading Association
Jennifer Smith
W. Frank Steely Library
Highland Heights, KY 41099
website: www.nku.edu/~smithjen/kba/

The Kentucky Bluegrass Award's primary goal is to encourage children to read and enjoy a variety of books and to select their favorite from a list of recently published books. There are two divisions for this award. The first includes books frequently used in Kindergarten through grade three, such as short picture books for beginning readers. The second division includes junior and young adult novels or lengthy picture books that are used in grades four to eight.

Any adult may nominate a book for the Kentucky Bluegrass Award Master List. All Kentucky schools are eligible to participate in this program. No participation fee required. In late April, a packet of materials is sent to participating schools that includes the current Master List of books, sample ballots, and a tally sheet. Children then complete one ballot for each book they read from the Master List. Responses are recorded on the tally sheet and returned to KBA. For more complete guidelines, send an SASE to Jennifer Smith.

Deadline: May 1.

Announcements: Competition is announced in April; winners are announced at the Kentucky Reading Association's annual conference.

Representative Winners: *A Perfect Pork Stew*, Paul B. Johnson; *Christopher Changes His Name*, Itah Sadu.

Award: An award is presented at the annual Kentucky Bluegrass Award Conference on Children's Literature.

Kerlan Award
Kerlan Friends
109 Walter Library
117 Pleasant Street S.E.
Minneapolis, MN 55455

The Kerlan Award is given "in recognition of singular attainments in the creation of children's literature and in appreciation for a generous donation of unique resources to the Kerlan Collection for the study of children's literature." The contest is open to children's authors and illustrators who have donated to the collection of the University of Minnesota's Kerlan Library. It was created to honor the contribution to children's literature and in appreciation of the donation of resources to the collection.

Deadline: November 1.

Announcements: Winners announced in the winter issue of the *Kerlan Newsletter*.

Representative Winners: Marie Hall Ets, Elizabeth Coatsworth, Marguerite Henry, and Roger Duvoisin.

Award: Certificate presented at an awards dinner.

Magazine Merit Awards
Society of Children's Book Writers and Illustrators
Dorothy Leon, Contest Coordinator
8271 Beverly Blvd.
Los Angeles, CA 90048

Established to recognize excellence in original magazine work for young readers, the Magazine Merit Awards offers awards in four categories: fiction, nonfiction, illustration, and poetry. All SCBWI members are welcome to submit magazine articles published in the current year for this annual contest.

Proof of publication showing the name of the magazine and date of the issue, as well as cover sheets containing the member's name as listed by the SCBWI, mailing address, phone number, title of entry, and category must be included. Submit four complete copies of your entry. Send an SASE for further guidelines.

Deadline: Between January 31 and December 15.

Announcements: Winners announced in April.

Representative Winners: 1998 winners: Fiction: Anna Olswanger, *Young Judean;* nonfiction: Sneed B. Collard III, *Spider;* illustration: Brian Lies, *Ladybug;* poetry: Lisa Harkrader, *Story Friends*.

Award: Winners receive a plaque at an awards dinner; honor certificates awarded in each category.

Majestic Books' Writing Contest
Majestic Books
Cindy MacDonald, Publisher
P.O. Box 19097
Johnston, RI 02919

This contest looks to spark an interest in writing and encourage students to write. It is open to Rhode Island school children in grades 1 to 12. Stories will be judged by the publisher against others from the same age group.

Submissions must include an entry form. Stories under 10 pages are preferred, but not required. The first page of the story must include the student's name, age, and the name of the school. All works submitted must have a title. Multiple submissions are not accepted. Stories submitted by children in grades 6 to 12 should be typed.
Deadline: December 31.
Announcements: Contests are announced in November; winners announced in February.
Representative Winner: Christine Lally, Kelly Harrington, and Molly Little.
Award: Winning entries are published in an anthology. Complimentary copies are presented to each winner at an awards ceremony.

David McCord Children's Literature Citation
Framingham State College
100 State Street, P.O. Box 9101
Framingham, MA 01701-9101

Sponsored by Framingham College and the Nobscot Reading Council of the International Reading, this award was established to recognize David McCord's long and enduring contribution to children and their literature. It seeks to honor an author or illustrator whose body of work has made a significant contribution to excellence in the field of children's literature.

A committee of four professional librarians and teachers select the annual winner. Send an SASE for further information.
Deadline: A committee selects the award recipient 18 months in advance of the announcement.
Announcements: Winners are announced in November.
Representative Winner: Kevin Henkes.
Award: Winner is honored at the David McCord Children's Literature Festival, held in November at Framingham State College.

Milkweed Editions Prize for Children's Literature
Milkweed Editions
430 First Avenue North, Suite 400
Minneapolis, MN 55401-1743

This writing competition for quality children's novels intended for readers in the 8 to 13 age group, is part of Milkweed's children's book publishing program for middle-graders. Its purpose is to encourage writers to turn their attention to creating books for this discriminating and important group of readers.

Picture books and collections of stories are not eligible, nor is the retelling of a legend or folktale. Submissions must be unpublished; no entry fee.
Deadlines: Ongoing.
Announcements: Winner announced upon publication.
Representative Winners: *The Ocean*

Within, V.M. Caldwell; *The Dog with Golden Eyes,* Frances Wilbur.
Award: Winners receive publication and a $2000 advance on royalties.

Milkweed National Fiction Prize
Milkweed Editions
430 First Avenue North, Suite 400
Minneapolis, MN 55401-1743

Awarded each year, the Milkweed National Fiction Prize is looking for manuscripts of high literary quality that embody humane values and contribute to cultural understanding. Submission directly to the contest is no longer necessary, as the winners will now be chosen from manuscripts submitted to Milkweed during the year.

Manuscripts should be novels, collections of short stories, one or more novellas, or a combination of short stories. Work previously published as a book in the U.S. is not eligible, but individual stories previously published in anthologies or magazines are accepted.
Deadline: Ongoing.
Announcements: Winner announced upon publication.
Representative Winners: *Falling Dark,* Tim Tharp; *Tivolem,* Victor Rangel-Ribeiro; *The Tree of Stars,* Tessa Bridal.
Award: Winners receive publication and a $5,000 cash advance on royalties.

Minnesota Book Awards
Minnesota Center for the Book
2324 University Ave. W, Suite 116
St. Paul, MN 55114
website: www.mnbooks.org

This contest looks to recognize books published by Minnesota authors. It accepts entries in the following categories: picture book author; picture book illustrator; children's nonfiction; young people's fiction; information, help, and guidance; nonfiction; creative nonfiction; nature; illustrated book; history; biography; collected works; fantasy and science fiction; memoir; mystery; novels and short stories; poetry; and fine press. The Minnesota Book Awards also offers the Flanagan Prize for excellence in the literature and culture of the Midwest and the Kay Sexton Award for Outstanding Contributions to the Minnesota Community of the Book.

This contest is open to those who have lived a significant part of their life in Minnesota. All entries must be published within the preceding year. Complete guidelines available; send an SASE.
Deadline: December 31.
Announcements: Winners announced during National Library Week in April.
Representative Winners: Children's Nonfiction: *Gloria Steinem, Feminist Extraordinaire,* Caroline Evensen Lazo; Young People's Fiction: *Sooner,* Patricia Calvert; Creative Nonfiction: *The Cold-and-Hunger Dance,* Diane Glancy.
Award: Winners are honored at an awards ceremony and presentation.

Mountains and Plains Booksellers Association Regional Book Awards
Mountains and Plains Booksellers Association
19 Old Town Square, Suite 238
Fort Collins, CO 80524

The purpose of these annual awards is to honor outstanding books that are set in the mountains and plains region, which includes: Colorado, Wyoming, Utah, New Mexico, South Dakota, Idaho, Kansas, Montana, Arizona, and Nebraska. Books submitted to the contest must have been published within the year under consideration.

Publishers, as well as booksellers are welcome to nominate books throughout the year by sending a letter to MPBA. Prizes are awarded to one children's book and to three adult books.

Deadline: November 1.
Announcements: Winners are announced in January.
Representative Winners: *The Serpent's Tongue,* Nancy Wood; *The Sky, The Stars, The Wilderness,* Jim Fergus; *Legends of the American Desert,* Alex Shoumatoff.
Award: Each winning author will receive a $500 cash award and a framed copy of the Regional Book Awards poster. Winning books will also be featured on the back of the Mountains and Plains Booksellers Association's Holiday Book Guide.

Mythopoeic Fantasy Awards

David Bratman, Awards Administrator
P.O. Box 6707
Altadena, CA 91003
website: www.mythsoc.org/awards.html

Presented annually by the Mythopoeic Society, a nonprofit organization devoted to the study, discussion, and enjoyment of myth and fantasy literature, these awards are offered in the categories of children's literature and adult literature. All nominations and winners are chosen by the Mythopoeic Society. Send an SASE for guidelines.
Deadline: February 28.

Announcements: Competition announced in December; winners announced at the annual Mythopoeic Conference in July or August.
Representative Winners: *Dark Lord of Derkholm,* Diana Wynne Jones; *Stardust,* Neil Gaiman; *A Century of Welsh Myth in Children's Literature,* Donna R. White.
Award: Winners are presented with a statuette of a seated lion, intended to evoke Aslan from C.S. Lewis's *Chronicles of Narnia.*

National Association of Parenting Publications Awards

L.A. Parent Magazine
433 E. Irving Drive
Burbank, CA 91504

The purpose of NAPPA is to assist parents in choosing children's products—books, software, video, audio, and toys—that best represent a genuine intent to enrich the educational and entertainment experiences of young people. It is the largest children's media awards program for consumers.

Award winners are selected by a distinguished panel of judges committed to matching the developmental needs of kids with the most innovative children's products on the market. Books awarded are divided into four categories: preschool; picture books; nonfiction; and folklore, poetry, and song. The entry fee is $60 to $80, depending on the number of entries. Send an SASE for contest guidelines and entry form.
Deadline: July 31.
Announcements: Competition is announced in May. Winners are notified in September.

Representative Winners: *Completely Yours,* Paula Pund & friends; *It's Not My Turn to Look for Grandma,* April Halprin Wayland.

National Book Award for Young People's Literature
Sherrie Young, Program Associate
The National Book Foundation
Room 904, 260 Fifth Avenue
New York, NY 10001
website: wwwbookwire.com/NBF

Since 1950, the National Book Foundation has offered awards to enhance the public's awareness of exceptional books written by Americans and to increase the popularity of reading. Awards are given for fiction, nonfiction, poetry, and young people's literature.

Books published in the U.S. should be submitted by the publishers; all genres of children's literature are accepted. Authors must be U.S. citizens. Translations and anthologies are not accepted. Entry fee, $100. Send an SASE or visit the website for complete guidelines.
Deadline: July 13.
Announcements: The competition is announced in June, finalists in October, and winners in November.
Representative Winners: *Charming Billy,* Alice McDermott; *Slaves in the Family,* Edward Bell; *Holes,* Louis Sachar.
Award: $10,000. Other finalists receive $1,000.

National Children's Theatre Festival
Actors' Playhouse Playwriting
   Competition
280 Miracle Mile
Coral Gables, FL 33134

Actors' Playhouse, a leading producer of professional theater for young audiences, invites the submission of original musicals for judging. Only unpublished scripts will be considered, however, submission of works that have received *limited* production exposure, workshops, or staged readings are encouraged.

Musicals that appeal to adults as well as to children are at an advantage, and contemporary relevance is preferred over topicality. The script should have a 45- to 60-minute running time with a target audience of children ages 5 to 12. All entries must have a maximum cast size of eight adult actors to play any number of roles. Bilingual scripts and operettas will also be considered. New adaptations of traditional, public domain titles, as well as new stories will be accepted. Send an SASE for complete guidelines and official entry form.
Deadline: August 1.
Announcements: Winners will be notified by November 1.
Representative Winners: 1999: *Beauty and the Beast,* script by Mark A. Pence; music and lyrics by Omar D. Brancato. 1998: *The Not-So-Brave-Prince,* by Bill Overton.
Award: First-place musical receives a $1,000 cash award; second-place musical receives a $100 honorarium.

National Radio Script Contest
Midwest Radio Theatre Workshop
   (MRTW)
Sue Zizza, Coordinator
915 E. Broadway
Columbia, MO 65201
website: www.mrtw.org

Each year, MRTW sponsors this national contest to solicit radio scripts from both established and emerging writers. The preferred length of manuscripts is 25 minutes, but longer scripts of up to 30 minutes may be submitted. Each writer must submit three copies of their original radio play. No stage plays, monologues, short stories or screenplays will be reviewed.

MRTW will arrange for the rights to produce the scripts for the MRTW Live Performance with the author, however, MRTW makes no commitment to produce any script.

Multiple submissions are not accepted; entry fee, $15. Enclose an SASE if you would like your entry returned.

Deadline: November 15.

Announcements: Competition is announced in the brochure for the annual workshop and on the website; winners announced in March.

Representative Winners: *Attention Flight 153*, Laurel Dewey; *Blooming*, Sheila Daughtry; *The Contestant*, Bill Hollenbach.

Award: Winners receive $800 split among two to four authors, and free workshop production participation. Prize winners and Honorable Mentions will be published in the annual MRTW Scriptbook.

The National Written and Illustrated By ... Awards Contest for Students
Landmark Editions, Inc.
Traci Melton, Contest Director
P.O. Box 270169
Kansas City, MO 64127

The purpose of this annual contest is to encourage and celebrate creativity. Books may be entered in one of three age categories: 6-to-9-years-old; 10-to-13-years-old; or 14-to-19-years-old. The text and illustrations should run no less than 16 pages and no more than 24 pages.

All genres are acceptable—fiction, nonfiction, biography, autobiography, mystery, humor, science fiction, etc. Text may be written in prose or poetry. Books are judged on the merits of originality and the writing and illustrating skills displayed. A $2 fee is required with each entry, and the entry form (available with contest guidelines) must be signed by a teacher or librarian. Send an SASE for contest information.

Deadline: May 1.

Announcements: Winners will be notified by October 15.

Award: A publishing contract is awarded to the winning writers.

John Newbery Medal
Association for Library Service to
    Children
American Library Association (ALA)
50 East Huron Street
Chicago, IL 60611
website: www.ala.org/alsc.nmedal.html

The Newbery Medal, named for eighteenth-century British bookseller John Newbery, is awarded annually by the American Library Association to the most distinguished American children's book published in the previous year. Its purpose is "to encourage original creative work in the field of books for children; to emphasize to the public that contributions to the literature for children deserve similar recognition to poetry, plays, or novels; to give those librarians, who make it their life work to serve children's reading interests, an opportunity to encourage good writing in this field." The ALA also awards the title "Newbery Honor Book" to the runners-up.

The contest is open to U.S. residents, and only published works are eligible. Authors may submit an unlimited amount of published work; no entry fee required. All forms of writing are considered, but reprints and compilations are not eligible.

Deadline: December 31.
Announcements: Winners are announced at the ALA mid-winter meeting in January or February.
Representative Winners: 1999 winner: *Holes,* Louis Sachar; 1998 winner: *Out of the Dust,* Karen Hesse; 1997 winner, *The View from Saturday,* E. L. Konigsburg.
Award: The Newbery medal is presented at an awards banquet.

New England Book Awards
New England Booksellers Association
Nan Sorensen, Assistant Director
847 Massachusetts Avenue
Cambridge, MA 02139

Established in 1990 by the New England Booksellers Association, the largest regional bookselling organization nationwide, these awards honor excellence in fiction, nonfiction, children's, and publishing. Their purpose is to promote New England authors and publishers who have produced a body of work that represents a significant contribution to New England's culture.

Nominations are requested from more than 800 New England bookstores and publishers. The winners are selected by a committee of booksellers that are appointed by the New England Booksellers Association. Previous winners are not eligible for this competition.

Deadline: October 31.
Announcements: Winners announced in January.
Representative Winner: 1999 children's literature winner: Karen Hesse.
Award: In April, winners are honored at a Boston Public Library ceremony.

Scott O'Dell Award
1700 East 56th Street
Chicago, IL 60637

This award was put in place to honor quality writing in historical fiction. Entries must be written by an American citizen, published in the United States during the previous year, and have a setting in North, South, or Central America. Entries are usually submitted by publishers, although authors may submit their own work. Send an SASE for complete list of guidelines, entry form, and further information.

Deadline: December 31.
Representative Winner: *Forty Acres and Maybe a Mule,* Harriette Gilem Robinet; *Out of the Dust,* Karen Hesse.
Award: Winners receive a cash prize of $5,000.

Ohioana Award &
the Alice Wood Memorial Award
Ohioana Library Association
Linda Hengst, Director
65 South Front Street, Suite 1105
Columbus, OH 43215-4163

The Ohioana Award provides recognition and encouragement for Ohio authors, poets, musicians, artists, and performers. It is presented annually to the author of an outstanding published book; one of the eligible categories is juvenile books. The Alice Wood Memorial Award is given to an author of children's literature to recognize a body of work, or a lifetime of contributions to children's literature.

Authors should submit their works. They must have been born in Ohio or lived in the state for five years to be eligible for either award. Guidelines available; send an SASE.
Deadline: December 31.
Announcements: Winners announced in late summer.
Representative Winners: Alice Wood Award: Tracey Dils; Ohioana Book Award, juvenile: Michael J. Rosen.
Award: Alice Wood Award recipients receive $1,000 cash award; Ohioana Book Award recipients receive glass artwork and a certificate.

Oklahoma Book Award
Oklahoma Center for the Book
Glenda Carlile, Executive Director
200 N.E. Eighteenth Street
Oklahoma City, OK 73105-3298

This award honors and promotes Oklahoma authors and books about the state. Awards are given for fiction, nonfiction, children's/young adult, poetry, and design/illustration.

In the children's/young adult category, fiction, nonfiction, and poetry are considered. Work submitted must have been written by an author who resides or has resided in Oklahoma, or must have an Oklahoma theme. Books must have been published in the year preceding the contest to be eligible. Send an SASE for further guidelines.
Deadlines: January 5.
Announcements: Winners announced at an award dinner in mid-March.
Representative Winner: *Broken Chords*, Barbara Snow Gilbert.
Award: Medal presented at an awards ceremony.

Once Upon a World Book Award
Museum of Tolerance
Adaire Klein, Coordinator
9760 W. Pico Boulevard
Los Angeles, CA 90035-4792
website: www.tst.wiesenthal.com

This award is presented annually for outstanding children's literature with themes of tolerance and diversity. Books should reinforce mutual understanding and illustrate the effects of stereotyping and intolerance, allowing the child to sympathize with the victim and the underdog.

All submissions must be written in English and must have been published in the year prior to the award. The book should be for children ages 6 to 10 and may be fiction, nonfiction, or poetry. Books are judged on the relevance to the themes of tolerance, social justice, dignity, and the equality of all people. Send an SASE or visit the website for guidelines.
Deadline: March.
Announcements: Winners announced in October.
Representative Winners: *So Far from the Sea*, Eve Bunting.
Award: Winners receive $1,000.

Orbis Pictus Award for Outstanding Nonfiction for Children
National Council of Teachers of English (NCTE)
64 Juniper Hill Road
White Plains, NY 10607

The National Council of Teachers of English established this award in 1989 to commemorate the work of John Comenius's, *Orbis Pictus: The World in Pictures*. The contest seeks to promote and recognize excellence in nonfiction for children.

Nominations of individual titles may come from the membership of NCTE and from the educational community at large. Any nonfiction book of informational literature that has as its central purpose the sharing of information and that was published in the year preceding the contest may be nominated. Each nomination should meet the following criteria: accuracy; organization; attractive design; interesting style; and should be written with enthusiasm. All material must be useful in classroom teaching for kindergarten to grade eight and should encourage thinking and more reading.

Send nominations to the committee chair and include the author's name, book title, publisher, copyright date, and a short explanation of why you liked the book.

Deadline: November 30.
Announcements: Winners are announced in March or April.
Representative Winners: 1999 winner: *Shipwreck at the Bottom of the World: The Extraordinary True Story of Shackleton and the Endurance*, Jennifer Armstrong; Honorable Mention: *Black Whiteness: Admiral Byrd Alone in the Antarctic*, Robert Burleigh.
Award: Winners receive a plaque presented in November during the Books for Children Luncheon at the Annual NCTE Convention. Five Honor books also receive certificates of recognition.

Pacific Northwest Library Association's Young Reader's Choice Award
Marshall Public Library
Betty J. Holbrook, Chair
113 S. Garfield
Pocatello, ID 83204

The Pacific Northwest Library Association's Young Reader's Choice Award is the oldest Children's Choice Award in the U.S. and Canada. Children, teachers, parents, and librarians from the Pacific Northwest (Washington, Oregon, Alaska, Idaho, Montana, British Columbia, and Alberta) submit annual nominations. Students in grades 4 through 12 from the Pacific Northwest are eligible to vote. No unsolicited titles are accepted for this award.

Deadline: Nominations are due by February 1.
Announcements: Winners are announced April 15.
Award: $150 and a silver medal presented at an annual meeting and banquet.

Paterson Prize for Books for Young People
Poetry Center, Passaic County Community College
Maria Muzziotti Gillan, Director
One College Boulevard
Paterson, NJ 07505-1179

This annual prize was established to recognize outstanding children's books that are considered the best books for young people published in the preceding year. Collections, short stories, short nonfiction, books, and poetry are considered. One book is selected in each of the three categories: pre-K to grade 3, grades 4 to 6, and grades 7 to 12.

The publisher must submit three copies of each entry with an official entry form. Books will not be returned; they are donated to the Poetry Center Library at Passaic County College. Include an SASE for the list of winners.
Deadline: March 15.
Announcements: Winners are announced in September in *Poets and Writers Magazine*.
Representative Winners: *The King of the Dragons,* Carol Venner; *The Silence in the Mountains,* Liz Rosenberg.
Award: $500 in each age category.

PEN Center USA West Literary Award in Children's Literature
PEN Center USA West
Christina Apeles, Awards Coordinator
672 S. Lafayette Park Place, Suite 41
Los Angeles, CA 90057

Since 1982, PEN Center USA West has sponsored a unique regional literary awards competition to recognize outstanding works published or produced by writers who live west of the Mississippi River. A panel of judges comprised of writers, editors, critics, and booksellers, selects winners in 10 categories including fiction, nonfiction, children's literature, poetry, and translation.

Only books published in the previous year are eligible. Submit entry form, four copies of the submission, and $20 entry fee for each submission. Multiple entries are accepted. Send an SASE for guidelines.
Deadlines: December 31.
Announcements: Winners are announced in May.
Representative Winners: *James Printer: A Novel of Rebellion,* Paul Samuel Jacobs; *Small Steps: The Year I Got Polio,* Peg Kegret.
Award: Each winner receives a $1,000 cash prize and is honored at a ceremony in Los Angeles.

PEN/Norma Klein Award for Children's Fiction
Pen American Center
568 Broadway, Room 401
New York, NY 10012-3225

This biennial contest was established in 1990 in memory of Norma Klein, the distinguished children's author. The award recognizes an emerging voice of literary merit among American writers of children's fiction. Candidates for this award are new authors whose books for elementary school to young adult readers demonstrate the adventurous and innovative spirit that characterizes the best children's literature and emulates the work of Norma Klein.

The books are judged by a panel of three distinguished children's book authors. Candidates may not nominate themselves. The judges welcome all nominations from authors and editors of children's books, to be considered in addition to their own nominations. Nominating letters should describe the author's work in some detail—how it promises to enrich American literature

for children—and include a list of the candidate's publications Please do not send books with nominations; judges may request them later..
Deadline: December 15.
Announced: The competition is announced in September; winners are announced in May.
Representative Winners: Valerie Hobbs, Cynthia Grant, Graham Salisbury, Angela Johnson, and Rita Williams-Garcia.
Award: A cash award of $3,000 presented at the Annual Literary Awards Presentations.

Pennsylvania Young Reader's Choice Awards Program
Pennsylvania School Librarians
  Association (PSLA)
Jean B. Bellavance, Contest
  Coordinator
148 S. Bethlehem Pike
Ambler, PA 19002-5822

The purpose of the Pennsylvania Young Reader's Choice Award Program is to promote the reading of quality books by young people in the Commonwealth of Pennsylvania. The program also looks to promote teacher and librarian involvement in the area of children's literature, and to honor the authors whose work has been recognized by the children of Pennsylvania.

Participation in the program is open to all students who are attending public or private schools. It is suggested that the school library/media specialist be the sponsor of the awards program within the school, however, any teacher or administrator may act as the sponsor. Students read and select the winner from a master list of published books.

To be eligible, the author must be a current resident of the United States, and the books must have been written for readers in kindergarten through eighth grade. Books must have been published within five years of the awards presentation. Parents, students, teachers, and librarians nominate the books for the master list. Send an SASE for guidelines.
Deadline: September 1.
Announcements: The program begins as soon as school starts in the fall. Ballots are provided to the students in March; winners are announced in April or May.
Representative Winners: Grades K to 3: *Buz,* Richard Egielski; grades 3 to 6: *The Best School Year Ever,* Barbara Robinson; grades 6 to 8: *Spying on Miss Muller,* Eve Bunting.
Award: Certificate presented at PSLA conference in Hershey, PA.

Edgar Allan Poe Awards
Mystery Writers of America
Priscilla Ridgway, Executive Director
17 E. 47th Street, 6th Floor
New York, NY 10017
website: www.mysterywriters.com

Honoring works of mystery published in the year preceding the contest, the Edgar Allan Poe Awards offers prizes in 12 categories: Best Novel; Best Fact Crime; Best Young Adult Mystery; Best Motion Picture; Best Short Story; Best Television Feature; Best Episode in a Television Series; Best Paperback Original; Best Critical Biography; Best Children's Mystery; Best First Novel; and

Best Play. The contest looks to enhance the visibility of the mystery genre, the author, and Edgar Allan Poe.

Each entry may only be submitted to one category. Submit a copy of the entry to each member of the appropriate judging committee. Official entry form is required. Send an SASE for contest guidelines and official entry form.
Deadline: Varies for each category.
Announcements: Competition announced in the spring; winners announced in April.
Representative Winners: *Mr. White's Confession,* Robert Clark; *Cold Day in Paradise,* Steve Hamilton.

Pockets Fiction Writing Contest
Upper Room/Pockets Magazine
Lynn W. Gilliam
P.O. 189
1908 Grand Avenue
Nashville, TN 37202-0189

This contest, sponsored by *Pockets Magazine,* is a way to discover new writing talent for publication. There are no preselected fiction themes, but historical fiction will not be accepted.

Submissions should be between 1,000 to 6,000 words. All submissions should include a cover sheet with name, address, Social Security number, title of piece, word count, and the words "Fiction Contest." Entries are only returned with an SASE. All submissions should be previously unpublished; no entry fee.
Deadline: Submissions must be postmarked between March 1 and August 15.
Announcements: Competition announced in January; winners announced November 1.

Representative Winners: Ann Behan, Pamela Beres.
Award: Winner receives $1,000 and publication in *Pockets.*

The Prism Awards
The Kids Network
Sheila Hansen, Competition
 Coordinator
40 90 Venice Crescent
Thornhill, Ontario L4J 7T1
Canada
website: www.thekidsnetwork.com

Young Canadians are given the opportunity to express their life perspectives in story form when they participate in this annual awards program. Short stories, short nonfiction, and plays/dramas are the types of material considered. Within each category, awards are presented to two age groups; 7 to 10 and 11 to 14.

Eligible entrants are Canadian children 7 to 14. Manuscripts may be 1,000 to 6,400 words. Story categories may change yearly so please request current guidelines and an official entry form.
Deadline: January 26.
Announcements: Winners are announced in June and July of every year.
Award: $500 and a Prism Award Trophy.

Quill & Scroll International
 Writing/Photography Contest
Quill and Scroll Society
School of Journalism and Mass
 Communication
The University of Iowa
Iowa City, IA 52242
website: www.uiowa.edu/
~quill-sc/contests/

Currently enrolled high school students are invited to enter this contest, which recognizes and rewards student journalists for their writing, reporting, and photojournalism skills. Awards are given in 12 divisions, including editorial, news story, feature story, editorial cartoon, advertisement, and sports story.

Entries must have been published in a high school or professional newspaper. Each participating school is allowed two entries for each division. The fee is $2 fee per entry, to a maximum of $40.
Deadline: Early February.
Announcements: Competition announced in early December; winners' list is sent to the journalism advisors at participating schools in mid-March.
Award: Winners receive a National Award Gold Key and, if seniors, are eligible to apply for one of the $500 Edward J. Nell Memorial Scholarships.

Ayn Rand Institute's Annual Essay Contest
Ayn Rand Institute
4640 Admiralty Way, Suite 406
Marina del Rey, CA 90312
website: www.aynrand.org/contests

The Ayn Rand Institute sponsors three awards with the purpose of encouraging high school students to develop analytical thinking and excellence in writing, and to expose students to the philosophical thinking of Ayn Rand.

Awards are offered to three age groups; *The Anthem* Essay Contest, open to ninth- and tenth-grade students, requires an essay of 600 to 1,200 words; *The Fountainhead* Essay contest, open to eleventh- and twelfth-graders, requires a length of 800 to 1,600 words; and *The Atlas Shrugged* Essay Contest, open to graduate and undergraduate business students, requires 1,000 to 1,200.
Deadlines: *Anthem*, April 1; *Fountainhead*, April 15; and *Atlas*, February 15.
Announcements: Winners notified in May and June.
Representative Winners: Marc Davis, Jayne A. Garver, and Vincent P. Frank II.
Award: Winners receive cash prizes from $100 to $10,000.

Pleasant T. Rowland Prize for Fiction for Girls
Pleasant Company Publications
8400 Fairway Place
Middleton, WI 53562

This competition rewards literature appealing to girls ages 8 to 12. Its mission is to honor authors who successfully capture the spirit of contemporary American girls and show how girls' lives are touched by the issues and events shaping the United States today. The competition is sponsored by the Pleasant Company Publications.

All submissions must be previously unpublished, and feature a female protagonist between the ages of 8 and 12, in a present day setting. Character development should be an important part of the story. Historical fiction and collections of short stories or poetry are not accepted. Submission to Pleasant Company Publications may not be submitted to other publishers while under consideration for the Pleasant T. Rowland Prize. Authors must be residents of the U.S.
Deadline: Send for contest deadlines.
Announcements: Winners announced in January.

Representative Winner: *A Ceiling of Stars,* Ann Creel.
Award: A $10,000 cash advance and publication are awarded to the winner.

SCBWI Work-In-Progress Grants
Society of Children's Book Writers
  and Illustrators
345 Maple Drive, Suite 296
Beverly Hills, CA 90210

To assist and support those working in the children's book field, the SCBWI offers work-in-progress grants to full and associate SCBWI members. Grants are not available for projects for which contracts already exist.

The grants are offered in four categories: general work-in-progress, contemporary novel for young people, nonfiction research, and a work whose author has never had a book published. Runner-up grants are also awarded. Send an SASE for application and complete guidelines.
Deadline: Completed applications accepted between February 1 and March 1.
Announcements: Requests for applications are made in October; winners announced in the following September.
Representative Winners: Jackie Davies, Kristen Hoel, Gregory Daigle, and Mary Bahr Fritts.
Award: Winners in each category receive a grant of $1,000; runners-up receive a grant for $500.

Seventeen Magazine Fiction Contest
Seventeen Magazine
Melanie Mannarino
850 Third Avenue
New York, NY 10022

Sponsored by Sally Hansen, this annual fiction contest is looking for exceptional, original works of fiction. Contestants must be between the ages of 13 and 21, and all submissions must be previously unpublished. Multiple submissions are accepted. Include your name, address, telephone number, date of birth, and signature in the top right-hand corner of the first page of each entry.

Contestants are judged by the editors of *Seventeen*. Manuscripts will not be returned. Send an SASE for guidelines.
Deadline: Write for 2000 deadline.
Announcements: Announcements are made through *Seventeen Magazine;* winners notified late in the year.
Representative Winners: Sylvia Plath, Lorrie Moore.
Award: Grand-prize winner receives publication and $1,000. Other winning entries receive cash prizes from $50 to $1,000.

Skipping Stones Honor Awards
Skipping Stones Magazine
Arun Toké, Editor
P.O. Box 3939
Eugene, OR 97403-0939

Seeking to promote exceptional contributions in multicultural and international understanding, nature and ecology awareness, peace, justice, and nonviolence, *Skipping Stones Magazine* offers this annual contest. Judges looks for authenticity, presentation, and quality of illustrations, if any. Violent submissions are not accepted.

Entries must be previously published and may be short stories, short nonfiction, books, poetry, plays, collections, and videos. Entry fee, $50.

Send an SASE for entry form and additional guidelines.
Deadline: January 15.
Announcements: Competition announced in August; winners announced in April.
Representative Winners: *Aruna's Journeys,* Jyotsna Sreenivasan; *A Rainbow at Night,* Bruce Hucko; *Grandaddy's Gift,* Margaree King Mitchell; *Tomás and the Library Lady,* Pat Mora.
Award: Honor award certificates and award seals for books are given to winners, and the books are reviewed in *Skipping Stones.*

Skipping Stones Youth Honor Awards
Skipping Stones Magazine
Arun Toké, Editor
P.O. Box 3939
Eugene, OR 97403

This annual award was established to promote and honor creativity and cultural diversity; appreciation of ecology and nature; social responsibility and community building; and peace and nonviolence.

The competition is open to ages 7 to 17 years old in two categories: writing and artwork. Essays, interviews, plays, short stories, songs, travelogues, etc., are limited to 750 words; poems to 30 lines. Non-English or bilingual writings are welcome. Drawings, cartoons, paintings, or photoessays are limited to 8 frames. All work must be previously unpublished. Send an SASE for guidelines.
Deadline: June 20.
Announcements: Winners are announced in late August of each year in the fall issue of *Skipping Stones.*
Award: Ten winning entries will be published in the autumn issue. The winners receive an honor award certificate, five multicultural or nature books, and a subscription to *Skipping Stones.*

Kay Snow Writing Contest
Willamette Writers
Liam Callen, Contest Coordinator
9045 SW Barbur Blvd. #5A
Portland, OR 97210

The contest seeks to encourage new writers reach professional goals in a broad range of categories, and to honor the memory of Kay Snow, founder of the Willamette Writers Group. The six categories are adult fiction, adult nonfiction, juvenile fiction or nonfiction, poetry, scriptwriting, and student writing. Winners receive monetary awards and publication in the newsletter; first time rights required.

Entries must be typed double-spaced on white paper. The author's name should not appear on the manuscript. Each entry must be accompanied by a 3"x5" card with the author's name, address, phone number, title of entry, and category. Place the cards in a plain white, sealed envelope, labeled with the category and title. Each entry must be accompanied by a registration form and fee ranging from $10 to $15. Write for complete guidelines and registration forms.
Deadline: May 15.
Announcements: Contest is announced in January; finalists are notified by mail prior to the annual conference. Winners announced in July.
Representative Winners: *Yardsticks,* Debra Murphy; *Drifting Toward the*

Event Horizon, Robin Suttles; *A Million Starts,* Candace Mulligan.
Award: An award ranging from $50 to $200 is presented at a banquet; publication in the newsletter.

Society of Midland Authors Awards
P.O. Box 10419
Chicago, IL 60610-0419
website: www.midlandauthors.com

Sponsored by the Society of Midland Authors, this competition offers awards in adult fiction, adult nonfiction, biography, poetry, juvenile fiction, and juvenile nonfiction. The competition is open to all published authors living in the Midwest, and honors their literary achievement.

Books should be at least 2,000 words. Multiple submissions are accepted. No entry fee. Send an SASE for complete guidelines.
Deadline: January 30.
Announcements: Winners will be announced at the Society of Midland Authors Annual Banquet in May.
Representative Winners: Juvenile Fiction: *Susannah,* Janet Hickman; Juvenile Nonfiction: *Pioneer Girl: Growing Up on the Prairie,* Andrea Warren.
Awards: Winners receive cash prizes at the awards dinner in May.

South Carolina Book Awards
South Carolina Association of School
 Librarians
P.O. Box 2442
Columbia, SC 29202
website: www.lib.sc.edu/scas/

Sponsored by the South Carolina Association of School Librarians, this contest encourages South Carolina students to read quality contemporary literature, and honors the authors whose books students elect as favorites. The awards are given for children's books, junior books, and young adult books.

Each year, an awards committee must read 100 to 150 books, chosen from reliable review sources, and present a list of 20 finalists that are read by students across the state. The students then make their selections on the books they liked the best. All books that are reviewed have been published in the year preceding the contest.
Deadline: Ongoing.
Announcements: Winners are announced in the spring.
Representative Winners: 1999 Children's Book: *Tornado,* Betsy Byars; Junior Book: *Crash,* Jerry Spinelli; Young Adult: *Slam!,* Dean Myers.
Award: Winners of these book awards receive publication and are presented with a medal at the award's dinner at the SCASC annual conference.

South Dakota Prairie Pasque Children's Book Award
Siouxland Libraries
Monique Christensen
201 N. Main Avenue
Sioux Falls, SD 57104

The Prairie Pasque Award was established by the Public Library Section of the South Dakota Library Association. The recipient is determined by South Dakota children in grades four to six, who vote for their favorite book in school and public libraries. The Book Award Committee formulates a master list of 20 titles from the books suggested.

The books, by living American authors only, must have been published two to three years before the voting year competition and remain in print; they must be appropriate for children in grades four to six and must not be television or movie tie-ins.
Deadline: Ongoing.
Announcements: Competition commences in November. Voting is held at the end of March and local contest results are submitted to the book award committee by April 1.
Representative Winners: *Frindle,* Andrew Clements; *Devil's Bridge,* Cynthia DeFelice; *Shiloh,* Phillis Reynolds Naylor.
Award: Winner is announced in April during National Library Week. The author of the winning book is invited to the South Dakota Library Association's annual conference the following fall.

Southern California Council on Literature for Children Awards

Southern California Council on
  Literature for Children and
  Young People
Anne Connor, Committee Chair
630 W. 5th Street
Los Angeles, CA 90071

This competition seeks to reward the writing or illustration of a Southern California resident. Entries must be published and may be fiction, nonfiction, plays, poetry, and collections.

Submissions are read and judged by an awards committee. Multiple submissions are accepted; no entry fee. Send an SASE for further information.
Deadline: Ongoing.
Announcements: Winners are announced in June and September.
Representative Winners: *Frontier Merchants,* Jerry Stanley; *No, David!,* David Shannon; *Riding Freedom,* Pam Munoz Ryan; *Old Elm Speak,* Kristine O'Connell George.
Awards: Winners are recognized at an awards dinner and given a one-year membership in the organization.

South Jackson Civic Center Playwriting Competition

South Jackson Civic Center
Community Playhouse
P.O. Box 326
Tullahoma, TN 37388

South Jackson Civic Center presents this themed playwriting competition. This year's theme is "fairy tale theater." All plays should be based on traditional fairy tales or have fairy tale elements, such as princesses and magic spells.

Plays should be from 45 to 75 minutes long. Musicals are accepted, but stories should not be dependent on the songs for plot development, since they may be cut for time purposes. Plays are to be written for school-aged children, so language and situational content must be G-rated. Plays that have been produced before, but not yet published are accepted; entry fee, $5. Plays must be typed; handwritten manuscripts will be returned unread. Playwright's name should appear on cover sheet only. Send an SASE for complete guidelines and next theme.
Deadline: March 15, 2000.
Award: First prize is $500 and production of the play. SJCC and the Community Playhouse reserve the right to edit the play as needed. All rights revert to the author after production.

Southwest Writers Workshop Contest
Southwest Writers Workshop
1338-B Wyoming Blvd. N.E.
Albuquerque, NM 87112
website: http://southwestwriters.org

Encouraging new writers and honoring excellence are the main goals of this contest. Novel submissions should be 20 pages or fewer, including a prologue and/or first chapter and a synopsis of no more than 3 pages. Middle-grade or young adult fiction may be mainstream, mystery, romance, science fiction, or historical works. Short story entries should be no more than 25 pages of science fiction, mainstream, or mystery, for children or young adults. A third category encompasses nonfiction articles or essays of 300 to 3,000 words and nonfiction books. For book submissions, send the first 20 pages or fewer with a query of no more than 2 pages. Indicate age ranges. Send an SASE for a category list, guidelines, and entry form.

Multiple submissions are accepted; include an entry form with each and mail them under separate cover. Submit two copies of each entry, and number each page.
Deadline: May 1.
Announcements: Winners are notified by mail, but not told of their ranking, which is announced at the annual conference in August.
Representative Winners: *In Evita's Shadow,* Anita Crocus; *The Sun Queen,* Annette Germon; *Song of the Beast,* Carol Berg.
Award: Prizes range from $50 to $200. The Best of Show receives The Storyteller Award and $500.

Spur Award
Western Writers of America, Inc.
W.C. Jameson, Contest Coordinator
60 Sandpiper
Conway, AR 72032

This annual award was created to honor excellence in literature. It recognizes the best book-length juvenile fiction and nonfiction, novels for adult readers, and a special category called the Storyteller Award, which honors the year's best picture book. Entries must have settings in either territory west of the Mississippi River or in the early frontier.

To be eligible, the works must have been published prior to submission to the award committee. There is no limit on the number of pieces that may be submitted, provided that they are from different publishers. Send an SASE for guidelines and entry form.
Deadline: December 31.
Announcements: Contest announced in July, winners between March and June.
Award: Plaque presented to the winner in each category at a ceremony at the annual convention.

The Stanley Drama Award
Wagner College
Department of Theatre and Speech
631 Howard Avenue
Staten Island, NY 10301

All original full-length plays, musicals, or one-act plays that have not been professionally produced or published in trade book form are eligible for this award. Writers should submit music on audiocassettes, as well as book and lyrics.

Only one submission per playwright will be considered. Previously entered

plays may not be resubmitted. Former Stanley Award winners are not eligible. A reading fee of $20 must accompany manuscripts. Please enclose an SASE for an application form and complete submission guidelines.
Deadline: October 1.
Announcements: Winners announced in April.
Award: Winner receives $2,000.

George C. Stone Center for Children's Books Recognition of Merit
Stone Center
Claremont Graduate School
131 East 10th Street
Claremont, CA 91711-6188

This contest recognizes books of superior artistic quality that have been used effectively and extensively in the classroom. An author and/or illustrator may be honored for a single title or body of work, and any genre of children's or young adult literature from any period or country is eligible.

Entrants must be published writers. The awards committee considers recommendations from students, elementary and secondary schoolteachers, teachers of children's literature, and librarians. Multiple submissions are permitted. Send an SASE for guidelines.
Deadline: July 1.
Announcements: Winners announced at Claremont Reading Conference in March.
Representative Winners: *Good Luck Gold* and *A Suitcase of Seaweed*, Janet S. Wong.
Award: Winners receive a framed calligraphy scroll at the annual conference.

STORY's Short Short Story Competition
STORY Magazine
1507 Dana Avenue
Cincinnati, OH 45207

Looking for short works of fiction that are both bold and brilliant, this competition accepts entries up to 1,500 words in length. Any entry above the word limitation will be disqualified. All entries submitted for the competition will also be considered for publication in *STORY Magazine*.

Submission must be unpublished, original material that has not been submitted elsewhere until the winners are announced. Manuscripts will not be returned. Multiple submissions are accepted as long as each has a $10 entry fee. Send an SASE for complete list of guidelines and entry form.
Deadline: October 31.
Announcements: Competition is announced in the summer issue of *STORY*; winners announced in the spring issue.
Representative Winners: 1999 First-place winner: *Clud Chambers*, Holly Woodward; Second-place: *Devil's Workshop*, David Griffith.
Award: Winners receive cash prizes from $100 to $1,500.

The Sugarman Family Award for Jewish Children's Literature
District of Columbia Jewish Community Center
Rabbi Tamara Miller, Director of Jewish Learning and Living
1529 Sixteenth Street NW
Washington, D.C. 20036

The purpose of this biennial award is to enrich children's appreciation of literature and culture, and to inspire and encourage other writers and illustrators of Jewish literature for children. Books published in the previous calendar year are eligible.

Submissions may include picture books, fiction, and nonfiction categories and should be geared for use by children 3 to 16 years of age. The writing must "accurately reflect Jewish concepts, trends and traditions" and should present a Judaic perspective. Applicants need not be of the Jewish faith. **Deadline:** December 31, 2002.
Announcements: Winners are announced at a spring awards ceremony.
Representative Winner: *Masada*, Gloria Miklowitz.
Award: Winners will receive a cash award of $750, presented at Washington, D.C. awards ceremony.

Sydney Taylor Manuscript Competition
Association of Jewish Libraries
1327 Wyntercreek Lane
Dunwoody, GA 30338

Hoping to launch many fine writers on their new careers, and to encourage outstanding books with Jewish themes, this contest is presented by the Association of Jewish Libraries. It invites the submission of work in the realm of Jewish children's literature. All submissions should be fictional, written in English, and have universal appeal of Jewish content for readers 8 to 11. Material should serve to deepen the understanding of Judaism for all children, and reveal positive aspects of Jewish life. Short stories or collections are not eligible.

Entries should be a minimum of 64 pages and a maximum of 200 pages long, double-spaced. Author's name should only appear on cover sheet. Send two copies of each manuscript. Writers must be previously unpublished. Multiple submissions are not accepted; no entry fee. Manuscripts will not be read without an accompanying release form. Write for full contest guidelines and release form.
Deadline: January 15. Applicants should not submit elsewhere until May 15.
Announcements: Competition is announced in September; winners announced in June.
Representative Winners: 1999: *Zayda Was a Cowboy,* June Nislick; 1998: *Devorah,* Linda Press Wulf; 1997 winner: *All Star Brothers,* Tovah S. Yaniv.
Award: Winner receives $1,000 cash prize.

Texas Bluebonnet Award
Texas Library Association
Annette Nall, Coordinator
3355 Bee Cave Road, Suite 401
Austin, TX 78746

The Texas Bluebonnet Award encourages Texas children to read more books, to explore a variety of current books, to develop powers of discrimination, and to identify their favorite books through the voting process. Students in grades 3 to 5 are encouraged to read books from a master list of titles chosen by school and public librarians throughout Texas. Those children who read five or more books from the list are eligible to vote for their favorite title.

The committee considers literary quality, favorable reviews, and reading level. Authors must be a living U.S. citizens and the book must have been published in the U.S. in the previous three years. Fiction and nonfiction are eligible.
Deadline: August 1.
Announcements: Contest announced in April; master list sent out in January. Winners announced on March 1.
Award: Engraved medallion presented to the winner at an annual award luncheon in April.

Treasure State Award
Missoula Public Library and Missoula County Schools
Bette Ammon, Director
Carole Monlux, Media Coordinator
301 E. Main
Missoula, MT 59802

The Treasure State Award was established in 1990 for the purpose of "fostering reading for pleasure, encouraging critical reading skills, and exposing readers and listeners to a variety of authors and illustrators." The winner of this statewide children's choice picture book award is selected from a ballot of five nominated picture books. Children in kindergarten through third grade select the winner.

Nonfiction and fiction picture books published in the preceding five years and still in print are eligible. Send an SASE for guidelines.
Deadlines: March 20.
Announcements: Winners announced in April.
Representative Winners: *A Bad Case of Stripes*, David Shannon.
Award: Varies.

Rip Van Winkle Award
School Library Media Specialists of Southeastern New York
Lynn Cordy, Coordinator
29 Queen Anne Lane
Wappingers Falls, NY 12590

The Rip Van Winkle Award is presented annually by the School Library Media Specialists of Southeastern New York to an author or illustrator who has made outstanding contributions to the field of children's literature.

Nominees must live in the seven-county area that includes Ulster, Rockland, Dutchess, Orange, Putnam, Westchester, and Sullivan counties. Send an SASE for complete guidelines and further information.
Deadline: Ongoing.
Announcements: Winners are announced in the spring at the annual conference.
Representative Winner: 1999 winner: James Howe; 1998 winner: Jerry Pinkney: 1997 winner: Lee Bennett Hopkins.
Award: Winners receive silver-plated engraved bowl presented at the spring conference.

Vegetarian Essay Contest
The Vegetarian Resource Group
P.O. Box 1463
Baltimore, MD 21203

This annual essay contest is designed to encourage young people to express their opinions about vegetarianism. It is open to children ages 8 to 18 and entrants need not be vegetarians.

Any aspect of vegetarianism, such as culture, health, ethics, or the environment, should be discussed in a two- to

three-page essay that is based on interviews, research, and/or personal opinion. There are three categories of entries: 8 years and under, 9 to 13, and 14 to 18.
Deadline: May 1.
Announcements: Winners are announced in late summer/early fall.
Award: Winning essays are published in *Vegetarian Journal* and a $50 savings bond is awarded.

Volunteer State Book Award
Curriculum Library
Sue Thetford, Coordinator
P.O. Box 150
Middle Tennessee State University
Murfreesboro, TN 37132

The purpose of the Volunteer State Book Award is to promote awareness, interest, and enjoyment of good new children's and young adult literature. The award also hopes to promote literacy and lifelong reading habits by encouraging students to read quality contemporary literature, which broadens understanding of the human experience and provides accurate, factual information. This award will honor the outstanding books chosen annually by Tennessee students.

Books of fiction and nonfiction are chosen by librarians and educators who work with children in kindergarten to grade 12. The committees welcome nominations from participating schools. Books must be written by authors residing in the United States. Any student who has read a minimum of three of the books is eligible to vote.
Deadline: Tally sheets must be returned by April 1.
Announcements: Winners announced at the spring conference.
Representative Winners: *Martha Callin*, Susan Meddaugh; *Shiloh Season*, Phyllis Reynolds Naylor; *Tears of a Tiger*, Sharon Draper.
Award: Winners are honored at an awards banquet.

Stella Wade Children's Story Award
AMELIA Magazine
Fredrick A. Raborg, Editor
329 "E" Street
Bakersfield, CA 93304-2031

AMELIA Magazine presents their annual contest in order to reward the efforts of those producing quality children's fiction.

Entries should be up to 1,500 words and accompanied by the $7.50 entry fee for each submission. Winners receive publication in *AMELIA*; first North American serial rights required.
Deadline: August 15.
Announcements: This contest is announced continually in *AMELIA*; winners receive notification by mail within 12 weeks.
Award: Publication and $125.

Western Heritage Awards
National Cowboy Hall of Fame
M. J. Van Deventer, Publications
   Director
1700 N.E. 63rd Street
Oklahoma Cty, OK 73111

Honoring authors who contribute to the preservation of Western heritage, the National Cowboy Hall of Fame sponsors this annual award. All submissions must relate to the American West or Western experience and can be written as a novel, nonfiction book, art book, juvenile book, magazine article, poetry, or short story. This competition also give awards in the areas of television or film and music.

Submissions are judged by a panel of three separate and independent qualified judges who are not affiliated with the National Cowboy Hall of Fame. Entries are judged on quality of writing, originality, organization, and faithfulness to the facts. Send an SASE for full guidelines.

Deadline: November 30.
Announcements: Competition is announced in January. Winners are announced by phone and mail.
Award: Wrangler trophies (original bronze sculptures) are given to winners during a ceremony at the National Cowboy Hall of Fame in Oklahoma City.

Jackie White Memorial National Children's Playwriting Contest
Columbia Entertainment Co.
Betsy Phillips, Director
309 Parkade Blvd.
Columbia, MO 65202-1447

The primary goal of this contest is to encourage the writing of large cast plays suitable for production by the Columbia Entertainment Company's Children's Theatre School. Entrants should submit original, unpublished plays ranging from one to one-and-a-half hours in length. Plays should have speaking roles for 20 to 30 characters, with at least 10 characters developed in some detail. Plays should be for all audiences, especially for middle-school students and up. Previously produced plays are accepted.

Deadline: June 1.
Announced: Contest announced in January; winners notified in August.
Representative Winners: 1999 First-Place: *Operation Ollie,* John Urquart; Second-Place: *The Somewhat True Tale of Robin Hood,* Mary Lynn Dobson.
Award: $250 and the play's production.

Laura Ingalls Wilder Award
American Library Association
50 East Huron Street
Chicago, IL 60611
website: www.ala.org/alsc/awards.html

Recognizing an author or illustrator whose books, published in the United States, have over a period of years made a substantial and lasting contribution to literature for children. It is awarded every other year. Nominees must have books that have been available to children for at least 10 years.

Members of ALA present their nominations to the award committee. Books are judged on literary and artistic merit. They must be exceptionally notable, and leading examples of a particular genre.
Deadline: Ongoing.
Announcements: The 2001 contest will be announced this year.
Representative Winner: Russell Freedman
Award: Winner receives a medal at an award presentation.

Thomas Wolfe Fiction Prize
North Carolina Writers' Network
3501 Hwy, 54 West, Studio C
Chapel Hill, NC 27516
website: www.newriters.org/twpf.htm

This annual fiction contest honors the

internationally acclaimed North Carolina author Thomas Wolfe. It looks for unpublished works of fiction that may include a novel excerpt or short story.

Submit two copies of each entry. Include a cover sheet with name, address, phone number, and title. Name should not appear on manuscript itself. Submissions should not exceed 12 double-spaced pages. Include an SASE for a list of winners; manuscripts will not be returned. Multiple submissions are accepted; $7 per entry.
Deadline: August 31.
Announcements: Winners are announced in December.
Award: Winner receives $1,000 cash award and possible publication.

Women in the Arts Annual Writing Contest
Women in the Arts
Linda Hutton, Vice-President
P.O. Box 2907
Decatur, IL 62524

To encourage beginning writers, especially in the field of children's literature, Women in the Arts sponsor this contest. Entries may be short stories, to 1,500 words, or poetry, to 32 lines. Manuscripts should have quality presentation. Multiple entries are accepted; no entry fee. Send an SASE for complete guidelines.
Deadline: November 15.
Announcements: Competition is announced year-round.
Representative Winners: *Worst Sport,* Kathryn Lay; *Spelldown,* Becky Mushko.
Award: Monetary awards are presented to first-, second-, and third-prize winners ranging from $15 to $30.

Carter G. Woodson Book Award
National Council for the Social Studies
Manager of Awards and Special
    Projects
3501 Newark Street NW
Washington, D.C. 20016
website: www.ncss.org/awards/writing.html

Presented by the National Council for the Social Studies, this award seeks to encourage the writing, publishing, and dissemination of outstanding, sensitive, and accurate social science books for young readers on topics related to ethnic minorities and relations.

All submissions must have been published in the United States, in the year prior to the contest. A copy of each nominated title must be provided to the full Carter G. Woodson Book Award Subcommittee, which ranges from 14 to 20 members.
Deadline: February.
Announcements: Competition is announced in January; winners announced in the spring.
Representative Winners: *Leon's Story,* Leon Walter Tillage; *Buffalo Days,* Diane Hoyt-Goldsmith; *I Am Rosa Parks,* Rosa Parks with Jim Haskins.
Award: Certificates are presented to winners at the annual NCCS conference in November.

***Writer's Block* Literary Contest**
Writer's Block Magazine
Shaun Donnelly, Editor
Box 32, 9944 - 33 Avenue
Edmonton, AB T6N 1E8
Canada

Writer's Block Magazine sponsors this

biannual contest, which looks for well-written pieces of horror, mystery, science fiction, fantasy, romance, and Western novels.

Submissions should be typed and authors should try not to exceed 5,000 words. Includes an SASE and a short bio with your entry. Up to 3 submission per person are permitted so long as each has the $5 entry fee.

Deadline: Contest deadlines are March 30 and September 30.

Announcements: Contest is announced in *Writer's Block Magazine*.

Representative Winners: *Edges*, Doretta Lau; *The Heart Is on Fire*, Joy Hewitt Mann.

Award: Winners receive cash awards ranging from $5 to $150 and publication in *Writer's Block Magazine*, along with assorted books in their chosen genre.

Writer's Digest Writing Competition

Writer's Digest
Terri Boes, Promotion Associate
1507 Dana Avenue
Cincinnati, OH 45307
website: www.writersdigest.com

This competition offers prizes in each of its six categories: Memoirs/Personal Essay and Feature Article, to 2,500 words; Mainstream/Literary Short Story and Genre Short Story, to 4,000 words; Inspirational Writing, to 2,500 words; Children's Fiction, to 2,000 words; Poetry, to 32 lines; and Stage Play Script, send first 15 pages.

Entries must be accompanied by an official entry form and $10 entry fee per submission. All entries must be unpublished, and not currently accepted for publication elsewhere. Market or audience specifications must be listed on the manuscript. Entries exceeding the word or page limits will be disqualified. Type exact word count on the first page of entry. Send for official entry form and complete list of guidelines.

Deadline: June 7.

Announcements: Contest announced in January; winners announced in the November issue of *Writer's Digest*.

Representative Winners: *The Keepsake Thief*, Maureen Mayer; *Lost But Not Forgotten*, Stephen Wallenfels; *Sincerely Yours*, Gila Moldoff-Reinstein.

Awards: The Grand-Prize winner receives a $1,500 cash award and a trip to New York City to meet with four editors or agents; other prizes include cash awards to certificates honoring their accomplishment.

Writers' International Forum Writing Competition

Writers' International Forum
Sandra Haven, Editor
P.O. Box 516
Tracyton, WA 98393

Sponsored by the Writers' International Forum, this contest is held twice a year, looking to encourage traditional short story writing, especially positive messages. It offers awards in four categories: fiction, essays, Christian fiction, and manuscripts written for children (clearly marked with designated age group). Manuscripts containing derogatory language, violence or horror will not be accepted.

All entries should include a brief letter stating the manuscript's intended

audience and a short biography on yourself. Entries must be previously unpublished, and not under consideration elsewhere. Writing must be original, and free of distasteful or derogatory language. Submissions should be typed and double-spaced, and 2,500 words maximum. A $3 entry fee and 9x12 SASE is required with each submission. Multiple entries are accepted. Top winners will receive publication on the Internet; First Electronic Rights required.
Deadline: January 15 and July 31.
Announcements: Winners notified one month after competition closes.
Representative Winners: *Requiem for an 8-year-Old,* Mike Lipstock; *Mystery Guest,* Anna Bentley.
Award: Winners receive $250 and publication on the Internet, as well as magazine subscriptions and other merchandise.

Writers' Union of Canada's Writing for Children Competition
Writers' Union of Canada
24 Ryerson Ave.
Toronto, ON M5T 2P3
Canada
website: www.swifty.com/twuc/wfcc.htm
―――――
The Writers' Union of Canada sponsors this contest for Canadian citizens or landed immigrants who have not been published in book format, and do not have a contract with a publisher.

Fiction and nonfiction prose for children that is up to 1,500 words and written in English will be accepted. Submissions should include a separate cover letter with full name, address, phone number, title of entry, number of pages, and whether the entry is fiction or nonfiction. Author's name should not appear anywhere on manuscript. Submissions will only be returned if an SASE is included. The entry fee is $15.00.
Deadline: April 23, 2000.
Announcements: Winners will be announced on Canada Day.
Award: Winner receives a $1,500 cash prize and along with 11 other finalists will have his work submitted to a Canadian publisher of children's books.

The Writing Conference, Inc. Writing Contest
The Writing Conference, Inc.
John Bushman, Director
P.O. Box 27288
Shawnee Mission, KS 66225-7288
website: www.writingconference.com
―――――
The Writing Conference, Inc. sponsors these writing contests to increase the writing of elementary, middle, and high school students. Students may submit one original poem, narrative, or essay that is previously unpublished.

Winning entries are published in *The Writers' Slate.* The contest topic changes yearly, so please send an SASE for guidelines and an entry form, or they may be obtained through the website. Photocopies, computer printouts, and Microsoft Word disk submissions are accepted. Students should not put their name on the submission itself, only on the entry form.
Deadline: January 6.
Announcements: Competition announced in the fall; winners announced at the end of February.
Representative Winners: Marie Brauk-

mann, Alison Koppe, Elizabeth Belden.
Award: Winning entries are published in *The Writers' Slate*, and, along with their parents, will be guests at the annual Conference on Writing and Literature. Second- and third- place winners in each category will receive certificates and will have their work published in *The Writers' Slate*.

Young Hoosier Award
Association for Indiana Media
　Educators
Wenda Clement, General Chair
1908 E. 64th Street, South Drive
Indianapolis, IN 46220-2186

This award looks to honor good writing for children aged kindergarten through eighth grade, and illustration for kindergarten through third grade. Authors must be living in the U.S. and nominated books must have been published within the last five years.

Any school serving students in grades K-8 is eligible to participate in the Young Hoosier Book Award Program by enrolling with the YHBA chairperson. Children read the nominated books and vote on the winners. Send an SASE for complete guidelines.
Deadline: New schools may enroll in the program up until December 1. Voting results are due in April.
Announcements: Winners announced in April.
Award: Winners receive an engraved award and are asked to speak at an awards dinner.

Young Reader's Choice Award
Young Reader's Choice Award
　Committee, Marshall Public
　Library
Betty Holbrook, Chair
113 S. Garfield
Pocatello, ID 83204

Honoring books that reflect quality children's literature, this annual award is the oldest children's choice award in the U.S. and Canada, and is the only regional award that is selected by children of both countries.

Nominations are taken only from children, teachers, parents, and librarians from the Pacific Northwest: Washington, Oregon, Alaska, Montana, British Columbia, and Alberta. Nominated titles must have been published three years prior to the voting year, and the target reading age for the two divisions of the award is grades 4 to 8 (junior division), and grades 9 to 12 (senior division). Send an SASE for further information.
Deadline: Book nominations must be received by February 1. Tallied votes for nominated titles are due by March 15.
Announcements: Winners are announced in April.
Representative Winners: *S.O.S. Titanic,* Eve Bunting; *Frindle,* Andrew Clements.
Award: Winners are presented with an award made of Idaho silver in the image of the YRCA logo.

Writers' Conferences

Conferences Devoted to Writing for Children
General Conferences

Celebration of Children's Literature
Montgomery College Continuing Education
51 Mannakee Street
Rockville, MD 20850

In its tenth year, this annual contest honors the past and looks to create a new future for children's literature. The one-day event is open to librarians, teachers, writers, booksellers, artists, parents, and readers. It also offers continuing education credits.
Date: April 29, 2000.
Subjects: Some of last year's conference themes were: "The Art of the Picture Book"; "The Art of the Tale; the Craft of the Story."
Speakers: Featured speakers at the 1999 conference were Valerie Tripp, Linda Krauss Melmed, and Michael Cooper.
Location: Montgomery College, Germantown Campus, MD.
Costs: $60 for Maryland residents; $84 for out-of-state attendees.
Contact: Sandra Sonner, Senior Program Director, or visit the website at www.mc.cc.md.us.

IBBY Conferences
International Board on Books for Young People
Nonneweg 12, Postfach, CH-4003
Basel, Switzerland

Bringing together children's literature specialists from around the world, IBBY sponsors many regional and international writers' conferences. The congresses are an opportunity for IBBY members and others involved in children's books and reading development to make contacts, exchange ideas, and open horizons.
Dates: Contact IBBY at the above address for information on dates.
Subjects: Themes have included "Literacy through Literature," "Children's Literature and the New Media," and "Peace through Children's Books."
Location: Past conferences have been held in India, Norway, and throughout the United States.
Costs: Workshop costs vary. Contact IBBY for fees.
Contact: Leena Maissen, Executive Director, +4161 272 29 17, or visit the website at www.ibby.org.

In Celebration of Children's Literature
University of Southern Maine
College Avenue
Gorham, ME 04038

In Celebration of Children's Literature 2000 is a conference for preschool to high school teachers, librarians, consultants, curriculum directors, media specialists, principals, and parents. The conference aims to immerse participants into the world of children's literature. The faculty consists of authors, illustrators, poets, storytellers, librarians, and teachers that give valuable insight into the market for children's literature during this three-day conference. For more information visit the website at www.usm.maine.edu/~coe/pdc/cele.htm.
Date: July 12-14, 2000.
Subjects: 1999 topics included "Exploring Diversity through Children's Literature," "Behind the Scenes of a Nonfiction Nature Book," and "Global Awareness through Poetry and Art."
Speakers: In 1999, featured speakers included Newbery medal winner Sharon Creech; Janet Stevens, Anita Silvey, and Bill Harley.
Location: University of Southern Maine.
Costs: $180 for the three-day program including snacks and lunch.
Contact: Joyce Martin, Director, 207-780-5326.

Highlights Foundation Writers Workshop
Highlights Foundation
814 Court Street
Honesdale, PA 18431

This workshop is a week-long immersion in writing for children for seasoned authors and novice writers. It covers both fiction and nonfiction writing for children. Each participant receives two manuscript-critique sessions with a mentor.
Date: Third week in July.
Subjects: 1999 topics included basic writing skills, writing for young children, and market topics.
Speakers: Jane Yolen, James Cross Giblin, and Sarah Stewart were among last year's faculty.
Location: Chautauqua Institution, Chautauqua, New York.
Costs: 1999 costs: First time attendees, $1,485; Others, $1,900.
Contact: Kent L. Brown, Executive Director, 570-253-1192.

Institute of Publishing and Writing: Children's Books in the Marketplace
Vassar College
124 Raymond Avenue
Poughkeepsie, NY 12604

This six-day conference is directed this year by Jean Marzollo. The goal of the conference is to help writers and illustrators publish their writing for children and young adults. Anyone with an interest in children's literature is eligible to participate. Participants can also submit their work to be critiqued.
Date: June 11-16, 2000.
Subjects: This year's topics include: "High Point in Middle-Grade Fiction," "Picture Books 2000," "Rejection and Success," and "How Writers and Editors Work Separately and Together."
Speakers: Gail Carson Levine, Jean Van Leeuwen, Emily Arnold McColly, and David Reuther.

Location: Vassar College, Poughkeepsie, New York.
Costs: 1999 costs: $800, including room and board; student rate, $750.
Contact: Maryann Bruno, Program Coordinator.

Ohio Kentucky Indiana Children's Literature Conference

The Greater Cincinnati Library Consortium
2181 Victory Parkway
Suite 214
Cincinnati, OH 45206-2855

This annual one-day conference is an opportunity to share information and ideas about children, books, and reading. In addition to keynote speakers, there is a variety of writers' workshops.
Date: November 4, 2000.
Subjects: Topics presented at the 1999 conference included "Trends in Children's Literature," and "Nancy Drew with Attitude."
Speakers: To be announced. Jerry Handorf, Charlotte Decker, and Margaret Rieger were among last year's faculty.
Location: Xavier University.
Costs: Conference fee is $35, including continental breakfast, lunch, information packet, and a directory of TriState Authors & Illustrators of Children's Books.
Contact: Martha McDonald, Executive Director, 513-751-4422.

Robert Quackenbush's Children's Book Writing & Illustrating Workshop

Robert Quackenbush Studios
460 East 79th Street
New York, NY 10021

These workshops for both beginning and professional writers are sponsored by the Robert Quackenbush Studios in order to prepare authors to create a work from start to finish that is ready to submit to publishers. The goal of this workshop, whose focus is on picture books, is to learn how to create children's books from start to finish. Workshops are limited to 10 participants and cover writing and/or illustrating picture books, chapter books, and easy-to-read books for young readers. Send an SASE to Robert Quackenbush Studios, or visit the website at www.rquackenbush.com.
Dates: July 10–14, 2000.
Subjects: Some of the topics include: how to create a picture book dummy and/or manuscript; and new directions and outlets for children's books.
Speakers: Robert Quackenbush.
Locations: New York.
Costs: $650; $100, non-refundable deposit. College credits on request.
Contact: Robert Quackenbush, Director, 212-744-3822.

Spoleto Workshop on Writing for Children

Spoleto Arts
760 West End Ave. #3-A
New York, NY 10025

This eight-day workshop is held in Spoleto, Italy, and provides writers with the opportunity to explore their talents in writing literature for children. The conference covers all aspects of writing for children including picture books, fantasy, nonfiction, young adult novels, and story books. Basic techniques and problems common to this writing

genre will be addressed.
Date: To be announced.
Subjects: All aspects of children's literature will be covered.
Speakers: Workshops are led by author, Elizabeth Isele.
Location: Spoleto, Italy.
Costs: Costs range from $1,150 to $1,400. Fees include daily breakfast.
Contact: Clinton Everett, Executive Director, 212-663-4440.

Conferences Devoted to Writing for Children
Society of Children's Book Writers & Illustrators

Alabama
Spring Mingle 2000!
SCBWI, Southern Breeze Chapter
P.O. Box 26282
Birmingham, AL 35260

Held annually in Alabama, Georgia, or Mississippi since 1993, this conference offers a professional focus for writers and illustrators of children's books and encourages the production of quality children's literature. Writers and illustrators from all levels of professional experience benefit from these group sessions. The conference will feature guest speakers, workshops, an autograph party, and a forum for book sales.
Date: March 17–19, 2000.
Subject: "Promotion with Pizzazz" will be the featured topic.
Speaker: Evelyn Gallardo, author of *How to Promote Your Children's Book*, will be the conference speaker, and will lead all workshops.
Location: Atlanta, Georgia.
Costs: SCBWI members, $80–$100; non-members, $100–$125.
Contact: Joan Broerman, Regional Advisor, or visit the website at http://hometown.aol.com/southbrez/.

Writing and Illustrating for Kids
SCBWI, Southern Breeze Chapter
P.O. Box 26282
Birmingham, AL 35260

With a purpose of supporting the production of quality children's literature, the Southern Breeze Chapter of the Society of Children's Book Writers & Illustrators hosts this conference for writers and illustrators of all levels. The conference also offers manuscript critiques and portfolio reviews.
Date: October.
Subjects: Topics covered will be the basic information necessary in a competitive field; picture books through young adult novels; fantasy characterization; and research techniques.
Speakers: Past faculty members include Charles Ghigna, Cheryl Zach, Han Nolan, and Ted Rand.
Location: Birmingham, Alabama.
Cost: SCBWI members, $50–$60; non-members, $65–$75. Critiques and portfolio reviews are extra.
Contact: Joan Broerman, Regional Advisor, or visit the website at http://hometown.aol.com/southbrez/

Arkansas
Writing for Children Conference
SCBWI Arkansas Chapter
Sandy Fox, Regional Advisor
P.O. Box 474
Mountain Home, AR 72654

The Arkansas chapter of the Society of Children's Book Writers & Illustrators will hold its eighth annual "Writing for Children" conference this year. The conference will provide manuscript and portfolio critiques, along with lectures from authors and editors.
Date: April 7–8, 2000.
Subject: The annual topic is "Writing for Children."
Speakers: This year's speakers include Newbery Award winner Sid Fleishman;

-387-

senior editor at Scholastic Press, Lauren Thompson; and McIntosh & Otis agent Tracey Adams.
Location: Hendrix College, Conway, Arkansas.
Cost: Registration. $65–$70; manuscript critiques, $25 extra.
Contact: Sandy Fox, Regional Advisor; e-mail: sfox@mtnhome.com.

California
Mid-Year National Conference
SCBWI Executive Offices
8271 Beverly Boulevard
Los Angeles, CA 90048

The year 2000 sees the first ever national conference held outside California by the SCBWI. Its location is New York City. The one-and-a-half-day conference features six panel presentations with prominent editors, agents, art directors, and marketing and promotion executives from children's publishing. It provides an intensive look at various aspects of children's publishing, with sessions designed for both professional authors and new writers.
Date: February 5–6, 2000.
Subjects: Topics include "The Art of Promotion and Publicity," "Creating Quality Books for the Mass Market," and "The Making of a Picture Book."
Speakers: Keynote speakers for this conference are children's book editor Margaret K. McElderry, and author and humorist, Dan Greenburg.
Location: The Roosevelt Hotel, Manhattan, New York.
Cost: Full conference enrollment, $150.
Contact: Nancy D. Lewis, 718-937-6810, or write to the SCBWI Executive Offices.

Writing and Illustrating for Children
Membership Office
Suite 296
345 North Maple Drive
Beverly Hills, CA 90210

Accomplished children's book authors and illustrators host workshops and give lectures throughout this national SCBWI six-day conference. In its twenty-seventh year, it is designed to inspire and educate writers and illustrators about children's literature. The Golden Kite Awards are presented during the conference.
Date: August.
Subjects: Last year's topics included "Opportunities for Writers and Illustrators in Multimedia Development," "Collaboration: How Do People Work Together and Stay Friends," and "Ways to a Successful Mid-Grade Novel."
Speakers: Last year's speakers included Ashley Bryan, Paul Aiken, Jeanine Manfro, and Russell Freedman.
Location: Century Plaza Hotel, Los Angeles, California.
Costs: Members and early registration, $310; after July 10, $335 for members; $355 for nonmembers. Critiques and consultations on manuscripts received by July 15, $40.
Contact: Lin Oliver, Conference Director, 818-888-8760.

Canada
Canada Conference
130 Wren St. RR#1
Dunrobin, ON K0A 1T0
Canada

The Society of Children's Book Writers & Illustrators presents this annual con-

ference entitled, "Honing Your Craft." Editors are on-hand to provide insight and writing tips on how to get published. The conference also features portfolio critiques, panel discussions, and book sales.
Date: September 23, 2000.
Subject: "First and Best Steps" is a sample workshop.
Speakers: This year's faculty includes Kathryn Cole, publisher and chief operating officer of Stoddart Kids.
Location: Wyndham Garden Hotel, Dallas, Texas.
Cost: To be announced.
Contact: Noreen Violetta, Regional Advisor, 613-832-1288.

**New England
Spring Conference**
SCBWI New England
106 Goodwin Road
Eliot, ME 03903

Designed to meet the needs of the working writer and illustrator, this conference is set in a different New England state each year. The conference is open to all writers, and will also feature panel discussions. Each participant will have the opportunity to meet in a small group with an editor or art director.
Date: May 6, 2000.
Subjects: Workshops this year include "Developing Picture Book Perspectives," "How to Push Your Book Without Being Too Pushy," and "Is It a Magazine Piece?"
Speaker: Keynote speaker for the 2000 conference is Karen Voight.
Location: Marriott Hotel, Portland, Maine.
Cost: To be announced.

Contact: Patty Schremmer, or see the New England SCBWI website at http://members.aol.com/nescbwi/

Writers Retreat
SCBWI New England
106 Goodwin Road
Eliot, ME 03903

This three-day retreat for the serious writer offers the chance to work intimately with professionals in an idyllic setting. On Friday evening, participants may network with each other before a dinner with the mentors. Saturday and Sunday are devoted to a mixture of one-on-one and group critiques. Participants have the chance to meet with a mentor for a half-hour session. The retreat also offers workshops and a book sale.
Date: February 18-20, 2000.
Subject: A workshop from this year's retreat will involve sharing rejection letters and learning how they can be used to hone a manuscript for publication.
Speakers: The 2000 Retreat speakers will be Jackie French Koller, Phoebe Yeh, Barbara Garrison.
Location: Whispering Pines Conference Center, West Greenwich, Rhode Island.
Cost: To be announced.
Contact: Patty Schremmer, or see the New England SCBWI website at http://members.aol.com/nescbwi/

**New York
Hofstra University Summer
    Writers' Conference**
UCCE
Hofstra University
Hempstead, NY 11549

The Children's Literature Conference provides an ideal venue for both published and aspiring writers and illustrators to gather with librarians, educators, editors, booksellers, and all others who wish to create or share good children's books. Students receive individual feedback on manuscripts from mentoring authors. Graduate and undergraduate credit is available.
Date: April 15, 2000.
Subjects: Workshop topics include picture books, illustrating books, fiction, nonfiction, and poetry.
Speakers: 2000 Workshop leaders include Judith Caseley and Cecilia Yung.
Location: Hofstra University.
Costs: SCBWI members, $66; non-members $72.
Contact: Lewis Shena, Assistant Dean, UCCE, 516-463-5016; or e-mail to dcekah@hofstra.edu.

North Carolina
Carolinas Annual Conference
104 Barnhill Place
Chapel Hill, NC 27514

This conference is informational and encouraging to aspiring authors and illustrators of children's books and magazines. It is open to writers, illustrators, librarians, and all others interested in children's literature. Participants are invited to attend a social on the night preceding the conference. The presentation of the SCBWI-Carolinas Service Award, a book sale, and an illustrator's display are other activities offered to participants.
Date: To be announced.
Subjects: Conference usually covers the following topics: picture books, middle-grade and young adult novels, fiction and nonfiction, and marketing and publishing.
Speakers: To be announced. Barbara Seuling and Marileta Robinson were among last year's presenters.
Location: To be announced. Last year's conference was held in Greensboro, North Carolina.
Costs: Members, about $60; non-members, about $70. Manuscript critique, approximately $30.
Contact: Frances A. Davis, Regional Advisor.

Wisconsin
Wisconsin Retreat
Route 1, Box 137
Gays Mills, WI 54631

Since 1990, the Wisconsin chapter of SCBWI has sponsored this retreat for Wisconsin writers. Although the specific topics vary from year to year, the retreat covers information on writing for all age groups. It looks to provide advice on the writing process and to connect with writers and editors from both coasts and the larger community.
Dates: October 13-15, 2000.
Subjects: Past subjects covered have been picture books, chapter books, magazines, and young adult novels.
Speakers: This year's speakers include Harold Underdown, of Charlesbridge Publishing, and Ron McCutchan, of Cricket Books.
Location: St. Norbert Abbey Ministries and Life Center, Greenbay, Wisconsin.
Cost: Approximately $230, including accommodations and all meals.
Contact: Patty Pfitsch, Co-regional advisor, 608-735-4707.

Conferences with Sessions on Writing for Children
University or Regional Conferences

Arkansas Writing Conference
17 Red Maple Court
Little Rock, AR 72211

In its sixth year, this annual conference was founded by Arkansas Pen Women and offers writers' workshops for beginning and experienced writers. The two-day conference also features a variety of literary awards and an awards banquet. Write for submission details.
Date: August.
Subjects: 1999 topics included "Writing the Romance," "Writers and the Internet," and "The Short Story."
Speakers: Last year's featured speaker was Louise Munro Foley, author of 29 books ranging from picture books to young adult novels.
Location: Little Rock, Arkansas.
Costs: 1999 costs: $10, two-day conference; $5, one-day conference.
Contact: Barbara Longstreth Mulkey, Director, 501-312-1747.

California Writers' Club Conference at Asilomar
3975 Kim Court
Sebastopol, CA 95472

This annual conference has changed its program this year and is adding focus on works-in-progress during intensive seminars on advanced fiction, mystery, children's novels, poetry, and nonfiction. Seminars are limited to 25 participants each, although participants can enjoy the other conference activities. Other workshops are also offered for those not choosing a seminar.
Date: To be announced.
Subjects: Last year's topics include: "Telling Your Own Crazy Mixed-Up Story," and "Constructing Your Own Do-It-Yourself Press Kit."
Speakers: Some of the speakers from the 1999 conference were: Greg Sarris, Sheree Petree, and Linda Allen.
Costs: To be announced.
Contact: Susan Edwards, Registrar.

Cape Cod Writers' Summer Conference
Cape Cod Writers' Center
P.O. Box 186
Barnstable, MA 02630

Since 1963, many distinguished authors have led workshops or given evening talks at this annual conference. The Cape Cod Writers' Center seeks to act as a resource for schools and anyone committed to the craft of writing. Scholarship courses are provided at this conference for young adults, 12 to 16. Guest authors, who are also teachers, conduct classes in nonfiction, writing for children, fiction, poetry, and young adults. The conference also features an agent- and editor-in-residence. Yearly membership with the center provides benefits at the conference, although you need not be a member to attend.
Date: To be announced.
Subjects: Workshops cover a wide range of topics including fiction, nonfiction, writing for children, and screenwriting.
Speakers: Speakers at the 1999 conference

included Wes McNair, Ellen Clooney, Deirdre Callanan, and Steve Swinburne.
Location: Craigville Beach Conference Center, Cape Cod, MA.
Costs: Registration: $50, members; $60, non-members; one-day course, $30; 30-minute manuscript evaluation, $30.
Contact: Don Ellis, President, 508-375-0516, or e-mail to ccwc@capecod.net.

Colorado Magazine Writers Institute Conference
Colorado Magazine Writers Institute
P.O. Box 4424
Boulder, CO 80306

The second annual conference of the *Colorado Magazine* Writers Institute is sponsored by the Rocky Mountain Chapter of the American Society of Journalists and Authors, and the University of Colorado School of Journalism and Mass Communication. It offers an opportunity to hear from editors of five national magazines describing their editorial needs, what they look for in nonfiction ideas, and their readership and policies. The conference also gives writers a chance to make contacts by meeting and sharing with other freelance writers.
Date: To be announced.
Subjects: 1999 panel discussions included "Anatomy of an Article," and "Ask the Editors."
Speakers: Last year's faculty included: Editor in Chief of *Parents Magazine*, Sally Lee; Executive Editor of *Health*, Bruce Kelley, and Deputy Editor of *Woman's Day*, Maureen McFadden.
Location: Boulder, Colorado.
Cost: Early-bird registration (prior to September 15): ASJA members, $95; nonmembers, $115. Normal registration: $150.
Contact: Catherine Dodd, 303-543-2390, or e-mail: ASJARocky@aol.com.

The Columbus Conference
P.O. Box 20548
Columbus, Ohio 43220

This conference offers a range of presentations on topics from writing advice to children's books genres. The two-day event features editors, agents, and authors as workshop leaders and lecturers, with good opportunities for networking.
Date: September, 2000.
Subjects: 1999 topics included "Writing and Marketing the Nonfiction Book," "Bones of Writing a Children's Book," and "How to Write the Perfect Book Proposal."
Speakers: Among the 1999 faculty were Jeff Herman, Doris S. Michaels, and Laurie Lazzaro Knowlton.
Location: Columbus, Ohio.
Cost: $134 for early-bird registration, $150 for regular registration.
Contact: Angela Palazzolo, 614-451-3075.

DownEast Maine Writer's Workshops
P.O. Box 446
Stockton Springs, ME 04981

These three-day workshops are ideal for all aspiring writers. They provide invaluable "inside the industry" information and multi-perspective insights. The workshops include interactive and experiential writing exercises, and demonstrate the how-tos of focusing and organizing your material. Work-

shops are limited to 12 participants in order to maintain individualized attention. Questionnaires are sent to the participants prior to the workshop, so that the workshop can be constructed from the individual responses.
Date: Workshops offered in the summer, dates to be announced in January on website: www.maineweb.com/writers.
Subjects: 1999 workshops included "Writing for a Children's Market," and "How to Get Your Writing Published."
Speakers: Workshops are led by Janet J. Barron, a 30-year professional author, editor, publisher, and writing teacher.
Location: Stockton Springs, Maine.
Cost: Full three-day tuition is $295 (10% discount offered if two people are registering together); accommodations not included, they range from $50 and up.
Contact: Janet J. Barron, 207-567-4317, or e-mail redbaron@agate.net.

Florida Suncoast Writers' Conference
University of South Florida
Department of English CPR 107
Tampa, FL 33620

Attendees of this conference have in the past been impressed by the variety of topics covered including children's writing, fiction, nonfiction, and inspirational. The three-day event offers manuscript critiques, keynote speakers, lectures, writing sessions, and contests.
Subjects: Workshops from past conferences include "The Business of Being a Writer," "Getting Started," and "Techniques of Fiction."
Speakers: Speakers from past conferences include Claudia Johnson, Bret Lott, and Stewart Nan.
Location: University of South Florida.
Cost: Early registration and students, $110. Regular Registration, $125.
Contact: Steve Rubin, Director, 813-974-1711.

The Golden Triangle Writers Guild
4245 Calder Avenue
Beaumont, TX

GTWG has the reputation for offering some of the highest quality conferences in the nation. The Guild, in cooperation with the Beaumont Visitors Bureau and South East Texas Arts Council, works hard to present a conference for both new and experienced writers.
Date: To be announced.
Subjects: Workshops from the 1999 conference include "Once Upon a Time No More—Contemporary Children's Books" and "Avoid Embarrassment—Do Your Research."
Speakers: Among last year's faculty were Rita Clay Estrada and Jessica Jones.
Location: Beaumont, Texas.
Cost: Last year's conference costs ranged from $120 to $260.
Contact: Becky Blanchard, Conference Coordinator.

The Heights Writer's Conference
Writer's World Press
P.O. Box 24684
Cleveland, OH 44124

This conference is sponsored by Writer's World Press, whose motto is "Dedicated to helping writers and publishers succeed." The conference is open to all writers interested in learning the craft of the writing business. It

covers a variety of genres including children's writing. The conference is limited to 25 participants.
Date: To be announced.
Subjects: Some of the workshops covered in the conference are "Children's Literature," "Fiction," "The Basics of Getting Started," and "Working with Publishers and Editors."
Speaker: One of last year's speakers was Tracey Dils.
Location: Beachwood, Ohio.
Costs: Pre-registration, $85; $95 for registration at the door.
Contact: Lavern Hall, 330-562-6667

Houston Writers Conference
P.O. Box 742683
Houston, TX 77274-2683

The 2000 Houston Writers Conference offers workshops to help writers develop their own styles. Workshops range from basic to advanced techniques. This conference provides an opportunity to meet with authors, experts, teachers, agents, and editors, and learn about today's ever changing publishing world. Registration includes up to three individual 10-minute agent/editor interviews, book signing events, and an awards banquet.
Date: March 16–19, 2000.
Subjects: Topics include contracts, tax tips, as well as writing subjects.
Speakers: This year's faculty includes Christopher Vogler, Nancy Robinson Masters, Wendell Mayo, and Sara Freeman Smith.
Location: Houston Marriott Westside, Houston, Texas.
Cost: Full registration, $255.
Contact: Write to address above, or visit the website at www.houstonwrites.com.

Manhattanville's Summer Writers' Week
Manhattanville College
2900 Purchase Street
Purchase, NY 10577

Since 1983, this conference has been an intensive, week-long experience featuring distinguished published authors. Workshops include the genres of fiction, children's/young adult literature, creative nonfiction, and poetry. The conference is open to both beginning and experienced writers.
Date: June 26–30, 2000.
Subjects: Sample workshops include: The Writer's Craft (for beginners), Short Fiction, Young Adult Literature, and Script Writing.
Speakers: This year's speakers include: Alice Elliott Dark, Phillip Lopate, Marie Howe, and Richard Peck.
Location: Manhattanville College, Purchase, New York.
Costs: $560 for the week. Graduate credits available at an additional cost.
Contact: Ruth Dowd, Dean of Adult & Special Programs, 914-694-3425.

Maritime Writers Workshop
University of New Brunswick
Dept. of Extension & Summer Session
P.O. Box 4400
Fredericton, NB E3B 5A3
Canada

The annual Maritime Writers' Workshop is a practical, wide-ranging program designed to help writers develop and refine their creative writing skills. Workshop groups will consist of a maximum of 10 writers each in the topics of children's writing, fiction, nonfic-

tion, and poetry. This workshop has provided counsel, encouragement, and direction for hundreds of developing writers. Participants are urged to register early, as space is limited in the workshop groups.
Dates: July 9-15, 2000.
Subjects: Workshop activities include lectures, discussions, special events, and public readings.
Speakers: Among the speakers at the 1999 conference were Paul Kropp, Pamela Donoghue, and David Helwig.
Location: University of New Brunswick.
Costs: In 1999, the tuition consisted of a $25 application fee that was applied to the workshop balance of $350, if accepted; financial assistance may be available.
Contact: Rhona Sawlor, 506-474-1144, or e-mail to K4JC@unb.ca.

Maui Writers Conference
P.O. Box 1118
Kihei, HI 96753

Since 1993, the Maui Writers Foundation, a non-profit organization, has offered this annual writing contest. It features celebrity authors, and offers the Rupet Hughes Prose Writing Competition to all conference attendees. One-on-one consultations with over 70 editors, agents, and screenwriting professionals.
Date: To be announced.
Subjects: Among the 1999 workshops were "Crafting Captivating Stories," and "What Editors Are Acquiring for the 21st Century."
Speakers: Last year's faculty included Pulitzer Prize-winning columnist Dave Barry; best-selling author, James McBride; and screenwriter, Jeff Arch.
Location: Maui, Hawaii.
Costs: In 1999, $395 for early-bird registration, $595 for regular registration.
Contact: Shannon Tullis, Executive Director, 808-879-0061, or e-mail to: writers@maui.net.

Mendocino Coast Writers Conference
College of the Redwoods
1211 Del Mar Drive
Fort Bragg, CA 95437

In its eleventh year, this conference offers workshops and lectures on a variety of writing topics. The three-day event, has a limit of 95 participants and has such activities as one-on-one, private consultations with faculty, intensive workshops, writing sessions, lecture sessions, and new this year, the editor/agent/publisher chat rooms, where participants have the opportunity to ask questions in a small informal setting. The conference also sponsors a writing contest.
Date: June 1–3, 2000.
Subjects: This year's intensive workshop topics include: "Visualizing Your Children's Story," and "Playwriting—Creating the Visual." Lecture topics include, "If We Can Do It, So Can You: How It Happened," and "Every Word Costs Money—How to Value Yours."
Speakers: Among the 2000 faculty are Maxine Scur, Lynne Barrett, and Kathy Dawson.
Location: Mendocino, California.
Cost: Early-bird registration (prior to April 20): $245; regular registration: $295. Two-day conference options also

available; write for costs.
Contact: Suzanne Byerley or Ginny Rorby, Co-chairs, 707-961-6248.

Michigan Working Writers' and Illustrators Retreat
SCBWI - Michigan
5859 124th Ave.
Fennville, MI 49408

In its third year, this retreat is for writers and illustrators to help them hone their craft. It focuses on writing workshops and critique groups to demonstrate writing and illustration techniques. Participants will establish new contacts, and be encouraged to nurture the creativity within themselves. Retreat is limited to 50 people.
Dates: October, 2000.
Subject: All subjects related to children's books.
Speakers: 1999 speakers included Elaine Marie Alphin and John Allen.
Location: Gull Lake Conference Center in Kalamazoo, MI.
Costs: 1999 retreat costs, $160; early-bird discounts offered. Critiques, $30.
Contact: Anna Celenza, Co-Chair; Celenzaa@pilot.msu.edu.

National Writers Association Summer Conference
National Writers Foundation
3140 S. Peoria Street, #295
Aurora, CO 80014

This annual conference strives to put writers of all genres in contact with publishing and writing professionals. The National Writers Foundation offers scholarships to talented young writers and servicers of the writing community. The three-day event features best-selling authors of young adult and children's books, and covers the areas of mass-market and series writing. Critiquing services are also available through the conference.
Date: June.
Subjects: This year's conference will feature the topics of young adult writing, film and books, magazine writing, and self-promotion.
Speakers: This years speakers include: Coleman Stokes and Ken Bark.
Location: Denver, Colorado.
Costs: $195 for NWA members.
Contact: Sandy Whelchel, Executive Director, 303-841-0246.

North Carolina Writers' Network Fall Conference
P.O. Box 954
Carrboro, NC 27510

This annual conference, sponsored by the North Carolina Writers' Network, has writers' workshops that are geared toward beginner, intermediate, advanced, and professional levels. Workshops are offered on fiction, children's literature, and poetry.
Date: November 10–12, 2000.
Subjects: Some topics covered in previous workshops were: "Writing for Kids" and "Writing for Children in the Middle Years."
Speakers: This year's faculty includes Doris Buchanan Smith and Ellen Bridgers.
Location: Raleigh, North Carolina.
Costs: Prices range from $175–$190.
Contact: Bobbie Collins-Perry, Program and Services; 919-967-9540.

North Carolina Writers' Network Spring Conference

North Carolina Writers' Network
P.O. Box 954
Carrboro, NC 27510

Held in different forms, this annual conference features readings, workshops, and access to information pertinent to writers. It encourages networking among writers, and looks to build audiences for literature and highlight resources for writers. The North Carolina Writer's Network mission is to serve, support, and connect writers.
Date: June 3, 2000.
Subjects: Screenwriting, playwriting, and book reviews will be covered at this year's conference.
Speakers: This year's faculty includes Jason Shinder, Thulani Davis, and David Perkins.
Location: Chapel Hill, North Carolina.
Costs: NCWN members, $50; Non-members, $65.
Contact: Bobbie Collins-Perry, Programs and Services Director, 919-967-9540; ncwn@sunsite.unc.edu

Oklahoma Fall Arts Institute

P.O. Box 18154
Oklahoma City, OK 73154

The Oklahoma Fall Arts Institute holds workshops over four days for amateur and professional artists, and teachers from elementary school to university instructors. Most workshops are limited to 20 participants to ensure a close working relationship between participant and faculty artist.
Date: Writing workshops are held from October 20-24.
Subjects: Workshops cover writing; music, and the visual arts.
Speakers: Some of last year's workshop leaders were: Stephen Dunn, Alice Lovelace, and Rilla Askew.
Location: Quartz Mountain Arts and Conference Center.
Costs: $450 (tuition, meals, lodging, meals, and processing fee).
Contact: Christina Newendorp, Assistant Director of Programs, 405-319-9019; www.okartinst.org.

Pennwriters Conference 2000

492 Letort Road
Millersville, PA 17551-9660

Pennwriters, Inc., a multi-genre writers organization of 400+ residents of Pennsylvania and other states, sponsors this annual writers' conference. A staff of agents, authors, and editors are on hand to perform manuscript critiques, lectures, workshops, and social events. The three-day program is open to anyone interested in writing; all genres will be covered.
Dates: May 19–21, 2000.
Subjects: Sample topics from previous workshops include "The Who, What & Why's of E-Pubbing," and "First-time Book Authors Panel."
Speakers: The 2000 conference faculty includes mystery author Keith Snyder; publisher of *Romantic Times,* Kathryn Faulk, and Pat Lobrutto of Random House.
Location: Harrisburg, Pennsylvania.
Cost: Pennwriter members, $100–140; non-members, $140–165.
Contact: Elizabeth Darrach, Conference Coordinator, 717-871-9712, or www.pennwriters.org.

Pima Writers' Workshop
2202 W. Anklam Road
Tucson, AZ 85709-0295

The Pima Writers' Workshop is open to anyone interested in writing. It offers opportunities to meet with other writers and agents and have manuscripts critiqued. Manuscripts must be sent prior to the conference.
Date: To be announced.
Subjects: Last year's workshops presented at the 1999 conference were "How to Get There from Here," and "Rising Above the Slush: Why You Need an Agent and How to Get One."
Speakers: Among the 1999 faculty were Julie Bennet, David Citino, and Karla Kuban.
Location: Pima Community College.
Costs: $65. College credits also available, write for fees.
Contact: Meg Files, Director, 520-206-7974; e-mail: mfiles@pimacc.

Sandhills Writers' Conference
Dept. of Languages, Lit. & Comm.
2500 Walton Way
Augusta, Georgia

In its twenty-fifth year, the Sandhills Writers' Conference is sponsored by Augusta State University. The three-day event is open to all writers and covers such topics as fiction, children's literature, nonfiction, poetry, and song lyrics.

Full conference registration includes attendance at all literary events, a manuscript submission in one category, and an individual consultation.
Date: March 23–25, 2000.
Subjects: Talks on the writers' craft, and other workshops will be offered.
Speakers: Among the 2000 faculty are Pulitzer-Prize winner Robert Butler; and Iowa Short Fiction Award winner Starkey Flythe.
Location: Augusta State University, Augusta, Georgia.
Cost: Prior to February 4, full conference registration, $156; student rate, $76. Conference only (no manuscript critiques), $110. Write for rates after February 4.
Contact: Anthony Kellman, 706-737-1500; e-mail: lkelman@aug.edu.

Skyline Writers' Conference
Skyline Writers' Club
P.O. Box 33343
North Royalton, OH 44133

The Skyline Writers' Club hosts this annual conference featuring such topics as writing for children and writing for the inspiration market. Participants are eligible to participate in the club's literary contest and may submit manuscripts in two of the following categories: Fiction, Nonfiction, Poetry, and Children's Literature. Additional manuscripts may be submitted for a fee of $5 each. Professional writers will critique all entries. Winners are announced at the conference luncheon.
Date: August 5, 2000.
Subjects: Writer's survival guide; fiction, writing for children, poetry, and inspirational writing.
Speakers: To be announced.
Location: North Royalton.
Costs: 1999 fees: Skyline members, $40; non-members, $50; half-day attendance, $35.
Contact: Lilie Kilburn, Program Coordinator, 440-234-0763.

Southwest Writers Workshop
8200 Mountain Road NE, Suite 106
Albuquerque, NM 87110

The SWW Conference offers to writers of all levels a great opportunity to improve their craft and make valuable contacts. The three-day workshop covers plotting for children's books, dialogue and descriptions, and picture books. Attendees may register for a 10-minute session with a featured editor or agent.
Date: To be announced.
Subjects: Some of the subjects from the 1999 conference included: "What Children Love to Read and Why," "The Role of the Editor in Modern Day Publishing," and "Writing Humor."
Speakers: Last year's faculty included Elmer Kelton, Max Evans, Elizabeth Law, and Deborah Vetter.
Location: Albuquerque, New Mexico.
Costs: Last year's tuition costs were approximately $80 per night.
Contact: Carol Bruce-Fritz, Executive Director, 505-293-0303 or visit the website at www.southwestwriters.org.

Taos Institute of the Arts Workshops
Taos Institute of the Arts
P.O. Box 5280 NDCBU
Taos, NM 87571

Now in its eleventh year, the Taos Institute of Arts offers workshops set to recognize and nurture individual creativity by establishing programs which utilize the physical, intercultural and spiritual environment of Northern New Mexico. Many of its workshops deal specifically with the arts of the Southwest; they have added eight classes in various forms of writing, including one on writing and illustrating children's books. Workshops are generally 3 to 5 days. Continuing education credits are available.
Date: Spring and summer.
Subjects: Some of the writing workshops include: Dynamics of Fiction; The Land, The Culture, The Word; Travel for Free: Get Paid to Write; Growing Short Stories.
Speakers: Pierre Delattre and Sean W. Murphy are among this year's faculty.
Location: Taos, New Mexico.
Costs: Vary; call for workshop prices.
Contact: Judith Krull, Instruction Coordinator, 505-758-2793.

Trenton State College Writers' Conference
Department of English
Hillwood Lakes CN 4700
Trenton, NJ 08650-4700

This annual one-day conference brings authors, agents, and editors together with writers and readers. The conference also offers writing and poetry contest for participants.
Date: April 4, 2000.
Subjects: Some of this year's workshops will be "Memoir Writing," and "Literature for the Young."
Speaker: One of the 1999 speakers was Nancy Sicoe from Crown Books for Young Readers.
Location: Trenton State College.
Costs: Day of presentations, $40; Trenton State College staff, $20, students $10. Workshops, $10 each.
Contact: Jean Hollander, Director, 609-771-3254.

Winter Poetry & Prose Getaway
18 N. Richards Avenue
Ventnor, New Jersey 08406

This writing conference is well-known for its challenging, yet supportive atmosphere which encourages imaginative risk-taking and promotes freedom and transformation in participants' creative work. Activities include consultations with faculty, readings, social events, workshops, and writing sessions. Workshops cover all genres of writing.
Date: January 14–17, 2000.
Subjects: Workshops include "Turning Memory into Memoir," "Finishing Your Novel," and "Story Telling."
Speakers: Among this year's faculty are Peter E. Murphy, Renée Ashley, and Stephen Dunn.
Location: Cape May, New Jersey.
Costs: $355 for double-room; $455 for single room. Cost includes three nights hotel, breakfast, lunch, pool, and other amenities.
Contact: Peter Murphy, Founder/Director, 609-823-5076.

Writers Retreat Workshop
P.O. Box 139
South Lancaster, MA 01561

This 10-day workshop offers in-depth classes, diagnostic sessions, readings, one-on-one time with a WRW instructor, and continuous feedback. It labels itself as "an intensive learning experience for small groups of serious-minded writers who are committed to improving and completing their novels for submission." Workshops are taught in Gary Provost's step-by-step course for crafting your novel for publication. The first few days of the workshop focus on story structure and then move to diagnosing strengths and weaknesses.
Date: May 26–June 4, 2000.
Subjects: Consultations, lectures, and writing sessions are all part of this workshop.
Speakers: Among the 1999 faculty were Gail Provost Stockwell, Dr. Keith Wilson, and Donald Maass.
Location: Marydale Retreat Center, Northern Kentucky.
Cost: $1620, which includes all meals, room, classes, and materials.
Contact: Gail Provost Stockwell, Director, 800-642-2494, or visit the website at www.channel1.com/wisi.

Conferences with Sessions on Writing for Children
Religious Writing Conferences

American Christian Writers
P. O. Box 110390
Nashville, TN 37222

This conference covers all aspects of Christian literature from writing for children to the adult market. There are 30 conferences in cities nationwide including: Orlando, Seattle, Baton Rouge, and Houston. In November, ACW hosts a "Writer's Cruise" that sails to the Grand Cayman and Jamaica while offering writers' workshops. Usually there is an awards ceremony during the conference.
Dates: Conferences are held several times throughout the year; the Writer's Cruise will be from November 27–December 1, 2000.
Subjects: All conferences have at least one workshop on children's writing.
Speakers: The year's cruise speakers included Mark Littleton, Dr. Dennis Hensly, and Jeannette Gardner Littleton.
Location: 30 conferences in cities across the United States.
Costs: Conference costs are approximately $149, with room accommodations being extra; the Writer's Cruise is $999 per person including accommodations, meals, and ship-board activities.
Contact: Reg A. Forder, Director.

Catholic Library Association Convention
Catholic Library Association
100 North Street, Suite 224
Pittsfield, MA 01201-5109

This convention offers members an opportunity to participate in a variety of programs and view an extensive exhibit of educational and library materials. The convention spans three days and includes an awards luncheon where the Regina Medal is presented.
Date: To be announced.
Subjects: Among the topics at the 1999 convention were "Storytelling: Southern Style," "Just How Adult Is the Adult Book?," and "Teaching Online Strategies: A Complete Teaching Unit for Librarians and Classroom Teachers."
Speakers: Last year's faculty included 1999 Regina Medal recipient Eric Carle, Sara Baron, and Lester Sullivan.
Location: New Orleans, Louisiana.
Contact: Jean R. Bostley, SSJ, Executive Director, 413-443-2252.

Montrose Christian Writers' Conference
5 Locust Street
Montrose, PA 18801

The Montrose Christian Writers' Conference is a "hands-on" seminar where the workshop format encourages participation and interaction to develop practical expertise in a chosen area. The conference also offers two full drama productions. Professional critiques with editors and in critique groups, an autograph party, and writers' theater are available.
Date: July 23–28, 2000.
Subjects: Topics from previous conferences include "Book Proposals that Sell," "Online Opportunities," and "Understanding the Christian Market."

Speakers: Among the past speakers were Elizabeth Sherrill, Dr. James Schaap, and Connie Bretz.
Location: Montrose, Pennsylvania.
Cost: To be announced. Last year's rates: early-bird tuition, $90. After June 30, $100. Room and board ranges from $38–$57 per day and $170–$255 per week. RV grounds also available.
Contact: Patti Souder, Director.

Mount Hermon Christian Writers Conference
Mount Hermon Christian Conference Center
P.O. Box 413
Mount Hermon, CA 95041

The purpose of this annual conference is to expose writers to the Christian publishing world and to equip participants with the information they need to communicate in print. The conference offers over 50 workshops covering every genre of Christian writing including children's literature, nonfiction, fiction, and article writing. Individual meetings with editors and manuscript critiques are also offered at no extra charge.
Date: To be announced; usually Palm Sunday weekend.
Subjects: This year's workshops include, writing for beginners; writing for children; writing fiction books; and professional writers' advanced track.
Speakers: Among this year's faculty are Gary Richardson, Roger C. Palms, Lee Roddy, and Ethel Herr.
Location: Mount Hermon, California.
Cost: Tuition: $315. Tuition including meals, $490–$730.
Contact: David Talbott, Director, 831-335-4466.

Texas Christian Forum
Inspirational Writers Alive!
6038 Greenmont
Houston, TX 77092

For nine years, this forum has been a way for inspirational writers in the Texas area to meet and talk with Christian authors. The main purpose of the conference is to encourage Christian writers and to give them the opportunity to improve their writing. The conference covers all areas of writing.
Dates: First Saturday in August.
Subjects: The topics of creating stories for children, conflict and character in children's stories, and marketing will be covered in this conference.
Speakers: This year's faculty will include Susan Titus Osborn and Anita Higman.
Location: Houston, Texas.
Costs: To be announced.
Contact: Martha Rogers, State Board President, 713-686-7209.

Part 9

Index

Index

A

ABC-CLIO, 106
ABC television, 40
Abraham Lincoln's World, 118
Harry N. Abrams, 41, 42
Accidental Lily, 66
Acquisitions *(See Mergers and acquisitions.)*
Action fiction, books, 41
Activities
 books, 16, 40, 282, 283
 preschool, 45
 teachers, 16
Adoff, Arnold, 75
Adventure books, 59
Advertising, 25, 30, 255, 260, 261
African-American
 black English, 120, 121
 magazine, 149-151
 research, 216
African-American Poets, 75
Africa World Press, 21
Agents, 137, 139, 171, 183-191
Aladdin, 11
Albert, Lou, 39
Alice and Greta: A Tale of Two Witches, 13
Alice in Wonderland, 190
All Alone in the Universe, 64
Allen, Dave, 40
Allen, John, 128, 130, 133
Allen, Lorrie, 161, 162, 164
Alphabet books, 10, 53
Amazon.com, 8, 15, 191, 224, 301
Amelia's Notebooks, 283
American Academy of Physicians, 29
American Association of Publishers, 23
American Association of Retired Persons (AARP), 181
American Association of University Women (AAUW), 181
American Baby, 29
American Baby Group, 29
American Booksellers Association (ABA), 35, 55
American Booksellers for Children, 155

American Booksellers Foundation for Free Expression, 35
American Cowboy, 93
American Family Publisher, 162
American Girl, 15, 16, 281
 American Girl, 16, 246, 281, 282
 American Girl Collection, 15, 16, 283
 American Girl Fiction, 15, 16, 41, 283
 American Girl Library, 283
 History Mysteries, 15, 16, 41, 283
American Library Association (ALA), 35, 38, 40, 142
 Young Adult Library Services, (YALSA), 42, 185
Americans for Financial Security, 178
America Online (AOL), 215, 224
Amy Love's Real Sports, 26
Ancona, George, 93
Andersen, Bethanne, 38
Anderson, Margaret, 250
Anderson, Marilyn 79, 80, 81, 97
And If the Moon Could Talk, 250
Andres, Lori, 29
Angel, 18
Angell, Jenefer, 61, 64, 66
Angels in the Outfield, 213
Animals, Black and White, 55
Animals and nature, 44, 53, 56, 70, 81
Animorphs, 39
Anthologies, poetry, 69, 70, 74-75, 214
Applebaum, Irwyn, 40
Apple Island, 65
Appleseeds, 82, 83, 149
archaeology's dig, 26, 29, 43
Armstrong, Jennifer, 63
Armstrong, William, 46, 121
Art, picture books, 20
Arthur series, 11
Ashe, Arthur, 216
The Ashwater Experiment, 64
Associated Press, 224, 229
Association for Library Collections & Technical Services, 23

Association of American Publishers (AAP), 35
Associations, and book marketing, 162, 163
Atheneum Books, 37, 61, 62, 66, 74, 113
Athletic Shorts, 214
At-risk children, 42, 61
Auch, Herm, 65
Auch, Mary Jane, 63, 65
Audience, 127, 131, 146
Audio books, 39
Authors,
    and illustrators, 10
    new, 9, 13
    visits, 139, 142
An Author's Guide to Children's Book Promotion, 169
Authors Guild, 181
Avalon Books, 21
Avisson Press, 21
Avon Books, 8, 9, 11, 39, 41, 42
Awards and prizes, 38
    Jane Addams Award, 38
    Aesop Prize, 38
    Boston Globe-Horn Book Award, 38, 272
    British Book Award, 14
    Caldecott Medal, 38, 42, 239, 241, 263, 265
    Christopher Award, 38
    contests, awards, grants, 329-382
    Lee Bennett Hopkins Award, 38
    Coretta Scott King Award, 38
    NAACP Image Award, 38
    National Book Award, 38, 185, 251, 252, 272
    Newbery Medal, 19, 38, 42, 43, 46, 65, 70, 251, 252, 272
    Scott O'Dell Award, 38
    Michael L. Printz Award, 42, 185
    Pleasant T. Rowland Prize, 16
    Carl Sandburg Literary Award, 38
    Smarties Prize, 14
    Spur Award, 38
    Charlotte Zolotow Award, 38
Axelrad, Nancy, 46, 127, 131, 132
Azarian, Mary, 38, 239-242, 265

B

Babe: The Life and Legend of Babe Didrickson Zaharias, 219
Baboon, 250
Baby Animals, Black and White, 55
Babybug, 51, 56
Baby Magazine Infant Care Guide, 29
Baby Publishing Group, 29

Baby Sitter's Club, 66
Backlists, 9, 170
Bailey, Sandy, 26
Baker, Charles, 149, 150, 151
Baker & Taylor, 157, 158
The Ballot Box Battle, 114
A Band of Angels, 115, 116
Banks, Joan, 82, 92
Banks, Kate, 250
Bantam Doubleday Dell, 8, 11, 40, 112
Barefoot Books, 52, 53, 54, 56
    Barefoot Beginners, 52
    Barefoot Collections, 53
    Barefoot Poetry Collections, 53
Bare Hands, 61
Barn Cat, 240, 241
Barnes & Noble, 13, 25, 39, 40, 143, 224, 246
Barnyard Song, 74
The Baseball Encyclopedia, 218
Baseball's Hall of Fame, 219
Bat 6, 213, 214, 217
BB, 32
Beachfront Publishing, 34
"A Bear's Gift," 100
Bear Snores On, 300
Becoming a Nation of Readers, 52
Beech Tree, 11, 39
Been to Yesterdays, 72
Belindy Girl, 70
Bemelmans, Ludwig, 37
Berinstein, Paula, 232
Berkower, Amy, 183, 184, 185, 186, 187, 188, 189, 190
Bertelsmann AG, 8, 11, 43
Best-sellers, 10, 11, 13, 185
    Harry Potter books, 14, 187, 188, 267
    picture books, 9
Best's Key Rating Guide, 180
Better Homes & Gardens, 33, 34
Bettmann Archive, 233
Beyond the Mango Tree, 63
The BFG, 20
Bibliography, 80, 81, 84, 87, 91
Biography, 53, 84, 85, 104, 109-118
Bishop, Gerald, 30
Bizzy Bones and the Lost Quilt, 265
Black English, 120, 121
Blackstone, Margaret, 211, 214, 217
Blackwood, Gary, 178
Blake, Quentin, 38
The Blue Butterfly: A Stroy About Claude Monet, 163

-406-

Bluejean, 47
Blue's Clues series, 11
Blue Sky Marketing, 21
Blume, Judy, 13
Board books, 13, 22, 39, 51, 53, 184
Bogacki, Tomek, 250
Bond, Michael, 37
Book fairs and clubs, 169-175
    Book-of-the-Month Club, teen, 42
    online, 44
    preschool, 54
Book Industry Study Group, 7
Book Kansas!, 157
Book quality, 9, 10, 13
Book Marketing Update, 161, 164
The Bookmen, 156, 158, 159
Book publishers, 7-23
    electronic, 44, 45
    list development, 9, 13
    new imprints, 13, 15, 16, 22, 41, 282
    size, 11
Books Are Fun (BAF), 172-175
Bookselling and bookstores, 7, 11, 183 *(See also Amazon.com, Barnes & Noble, Borders.)*
    bookseller ideas, 19
    brand names, 18
    chains, 156
    distribution, 153, 155, 157, 159
    Harry Potter books, 14-15
    independent, 159, 188
    marketing strategies, 18, 19, 22
    online, 7, 45
    poetry, 69, 70
    religious, online, 44
    school and library, 7, 9
    special markets, 161, 165
    teens, 19
    television tie-ins, 18
    writer networking, 141, 143
Books in Print, 157, 224, 301
BOP, 32
Borders, 25, 42
Bortz, Fred, 127, 128, 130, 132
Bowker, 157
Boyds Mills Press, 55, 70, 71, 153
Boyko, Alan, 170, 171
Boyles, Andy, 127, 130, 132, 146
Boys' Life, 80, 83, 96
Boys' Quest, 86, 131, 243, 244, 245, 246
The Boy Who Lost His Face, 272, 273, 274
Brackett, Ginger Roberts, 84, 85, 104, 106

Brimner, Larry Dane, 212, 213, 215, 217, 218, 219, 220, 221
British Library, 195, 198-200
Broerman, Joan, 223
Bronson, Rebecca, 81, 90
Brotherhood of Magicians, 243
Brother's Keeper program, 179
Brown, Andrea, 183, 186, 188, 190
Browndeer Press, 47
Brown, Helen Gurley, 33
Brown, Julie, 229, 230, 231
Brown, Lynn Michael, 255, 256
Brown, Marc, 11
Brown, Margaret Wise, 10, 37
Bubblemania: The Chewy History of Bubble Gum, 137
Buffy the Vampire Slayer, 18
Bulletin (SCBWI), 169
Bunnicula, 37
Bunnicula Strikes Again, 66
Bureau of the Census, 51
Burton, Virginia Lee, 37
Bush, Barbara, 52
Bush, Timothy, 74
The Busy World of Richard Scarry, 163
Button, Bucket Sky, 263, 265

C

Cabot, Tammy, 163, 164, 165, 166
Caldecott Medal *(See Awards and Prizes.)*
California Chronicles, 149
California Eagle, 216, 217
Calliope, 93, 149
Calvert, Patricia, 84, 103
Cameron, Ann, 250, 252
Campus Life, 145, 147-149
Canadian Parents Online, 300
Candlewick Press, 46, 187
Capstone Press, 131
Captain Underpants, 171
The Care Bears Help Chase Colds, 163
Carle, Eric, 11
Carolrhoda, 131
Carpenter, Stella, 265
Carroll, Lewis, 190
Cartwheel Books, 42, 53, 54, 56
Carus Publishing *(See Cricket Magazine Group.)*
Cascardi, Andrea, 59, 60, 66, 67
Cash, Mary, 60, 64, 65
Catalanotto, Peter, 52
Catalogues, 162, 167
The Cat Ate My Gymsuit, 37

Cat Running, 109
Cayleff, Susan E., 219
Cecka, Melanie, 53, 54, 162, 165, 167
Celebrating the Powwow, 93
Celebrities, magazines, 43
Censorship, 35, 40, 42, 272
Cerro, Ana, 70, 73, 74
Chaosium, 21
Chapter
   books, 65, 184
   nonfiction focus, 128
Characters
   agent and editor needs, 188
   biography, 109-118
   character education, books, 13
   development, 16, 251
   historical fiction, 109-118
   middle-grade books, 67
   real life, in fiction, 109-118
   sports, 213
Charlesbridge Publishing, 10, 13, 37, 39, 53, 54, 55, 56
Charlotte's Web, 14
Charlie and the Chocolate Factory, 249
The Charlotte Years, series, 41
Charmed, 18
Charts and graphs
   fantasy, 17
   parenting magazines, 28
   preschool books, 12
   sports magazines, 27
   young adults, small presses & special interest, 21
Cheshire, Marc, 46
Chicago Defender, 217
Child development
   middle-grade, 64
   preschool, 56, 72
   reading needs, 131, 132
Child Labor, A Global Crisis, 129
Children of Summer, 250
Children's Better Health Institute (CBHI), 56, 57, 131
Children's Book Council, 142
Children's Defense Act, 35
Children's Online Protection Act (COPA), 35, 40, 41
Children's Television Workshop, 47
Children's Writer, 92
Chinaberry Book Service, 162
Choices, 83
"Choosing the Right Camp for Your Child," 99

Christian Brotherhood Newsletter, 178
Christian Ed. Publishers, 93
A Christmas Tree in the White House, 109
Chronicle Books, 42
Chronicles of Narnia, 268
Church Educator, 93
City Parent Magazine, 99
Clarion Books, 71
Clark, Christine, 145, 146
I.E. Clark Publications, 21
Classroom at the End of the Hall, 65
Classroom Connect, 45
Classrooms
   magazines, 43
   poetry, 70
Cleary, Beverly, 11
Clements, Andrew, 11
Click, 56, 57
CNN, 224
Cobblestone, 149, 229, 300
Cobblestone Publishing, 82, 149, 150, 151, 229, 261
Coffman, Suzanne, 122, 123
Cohen, Ruth, 183, 186, 188, 189, 190
Collins, Timothy, 32
Colonial Williamsburg Press, 122, 123
The Color Purple, 219
Concept books, 53
Conferences, writers', 383-402
   religious, 401-402
   SCBWI, 387-390
   university or regional, 391-400
Conflict, 113
Consolidated Omnibus Budget Reconciliation Act (COBRA), 177
Consolidation, 8
Contemporary Drama, 21
Contemporary fiction, 16, 41
Contests, writing, 329-382
Contracts, 171, 188, 189, 190
Cook, Nick, 128, 130, 131
Cooperative Children's Book Center, 110
Cooper, Barbara, 156, 158, 159
The Copper Elephant, 63
Copyright, 189 *(See also Rights.)*
Corbis, photo stock house, 231, 233
Corduroy, 22
Cornelius, 250
Corporate book premiums, 161, 163
Cosmo-girl!, 33, 43
Cosmopolitan, 33, 43
Costello, Claire, 103

Joanna Cotler Books, 8, 11, 39
Counting books, 53
Cover letter *(See Queries and cover letters.)*
Cowboy with a Camera: Erwin E. Smith, Cowboy Photographer, 38
Cowley, Joy, 38
Cox, Judy, 65
Crafts, 16 *(See also Activities.)*
Crayola Kids, 26, 33, 259-261
The Crazy Horse Electric Game, 220
Creative Minds series, 131
Cricket, 98, 128, 130, 246, 264
Cricket Magazine Group, 54, 56, 98, 261
Crosshaven Books, 52
Crossway Books, 22, 23
Crown Books, 8, 11, 59, 63, 66, 67, 70, 71, 257
Crum, Robert, 93
Crutcher, Chris, 211, 213, 214, 217, 218, 219, 220
Cullinan, Bernice, 70, 71, 72, 75
Cultural authenticity, 120
Cultures, 52
Cunningham, Carolyn, 88
Curriculum materials, 41
Curtis Brown, 183
Curtis, Christopher Paul, 11
Curtis, Jamie Lee, 9, 11
Cuyler, Margery, 46

D

Dabalos, Deborah, 94
The Daddy Poems, 75
Dads & Daughters, 257
Dahl, Roald, 249, 250, 268
Daily, Elise, 172
Dalgliesh, Alice, 249
The Dance, 11
Dangerous Skies, 250
Danny, Champion of the World, 250
Danziger, Paula, 37
Daughters, 43
Davis, Rebecca, 46
Davis, Terry, 218, 219
Dawson's Creek, 18
Daycare markets, 54
DEAL WITH IT: A Whole New Approach to Your Body, Brain and Life as a gURL, 18
Dean, Tanya, 127, 130, 132
Dear America, 19, 39, 186
Deford, Frank, 219
Dell/Delacorte, 40
Demographics, 7, 18, 20

Detzner, Georgiane, 100, 101
Developmental skills,
    middle-grade, 64
    preschool, 56, 72
Dial Books, 11, 46, 62, 64
Dialect, 119, 120, 121, 122-124
Diana: The Life of a Princess, 93
Diaries, 19
Michael di Capua Books, 8, 11, 39
Dickens, Charles, 66
"A Different Kind of Pet," 90
Dillon, Ann, 149
Dingwall, Cindy, 85, 108
Discovery Channel, 41
Discovery Kids, 41
Walt Disney Company, 20, 40, 44, 46
    Disney's Animal Kingdom, 33, 44
    Mouseworks, 46
Distribution, book, 153-160, 164
    small press, 156, 157, 159
    writer's role, 154, 155
Dlouhy, Caitlyn, 61, 62
Dogs Don't Tell Jokes, 273
Donovan, Melanie, 8, 9, 19, 20, 22
Dork in Disguise, 65
Dorling Kindersley, 45, 60
    DK, 40, 62, 66
Dotlich, Rebecca Kai, 55, 56
Dovey Coe, 61
Dowell, Frances O'Roark, 61
The Dreams of Mairhe Mehan, 63
Drewry, Jennifer, 302
Duffy's Rocks, 16
Duncan, Virginia, 63, 64, 265
Durston, Linda Moore, 129, 132
Dutton Books, 11, 41, 46

E

Eagle Drum: On the Powwow Trail with a Young Grass Dancer, 93
Eakin Press, 122
Early readers, 42
Earth Shattering Poems, 70
E-books, 44, 189, 190
Echoes of the Elders: The Stories and Paintings of Chief Lelooska, 38
Editors,
    freelance, 138, 249
    and marketing, 183, 186, 187
    networking, 137, 138, 139
Edmiston, Jim, 52
EdPress, 260

Educational publishing
   book markets, 9, 10, 16
   curriculum, 41, 45
   geography, 41
   magazines, 26, 31, 32, 33, 43, 149, 150, 258, 277
   online, 44
   poetry, 70
   preK, 54
   science, 26, 41
   social studies, 41
   submissions, 85, 108
   trade books in the classroom, 16
   whole language, 10, 13
   young adults, 31
Edwards, Marilyn, 86, 98, 131, 243-247
Edwards, Patricia, 51
Edwardson, Debby, 300, 301
Ella Enchanted, 9, 11
Electronic media, 30 *(See also Websites.)*
   book publishers, 44
   online hazards, 35
   electronic publishing, 189, 190
   electronic rights, 189, 190, 191
Element Books, 161, 164
Eliot, T.S., 73
Elisabeth, 250
Eloise, 41
Eloise in Paris, 11
E-Map, 47
Emerging readers, 53
The Emperor Who Hated Yellow, 52
Encyclopedia Britannica, 45
End, Hedy, 32, 33
Engh, Rohn, 232
The Enormous Crocodile, 250
Enslow Publishers, 75, 128
Entertainmenteen, 32-33, 43
Epstein, Ari, 26
Eshensen, Barbara, 75
Eskildsen, Alison, 230, 231, 234
Evans, Don and Jane, 243
Evans, Douglas, 65
Evans, Richard Paul, 11
Expert sources, 220, 302
Explorations, 26, 29
An Extraordinary Egg, 250
Extreme Elvin, 63
Eyewitness Travel Guides series, 45

F

Faces, 149

A Fairy Called Hilary, 63
Fairy tales and folktales, 39, 188
Family,
   magazines, 96
   middle-graders, 59, 60, 61, 65
   preschool, 52
Family Christian Stores, 44
Family Fun, 26
Family Life, 29
Family publishing, 26, 28, 29, 31
A Family Trait, 65
Fantasy
   books, 14-15, 44, 59
   chart, 17
   Harry Potter books, 14-15, 59, 188
   middle-grade, 59, 65
Faraway Summer, 239
A Farmer's Alphabet, 239, 241
Farrar, Straus & Giroux, 8, 38, 272, 275
Fearless, book series, 41
Federal Trade Commission (FTC), 39
Feldman, Thea, 47
Fenton, Edward, 16
J.G. Ferguson, 21
Ferocious Girls, Steamroller Boys and Other Poems in Between, 69, 74
Fiction *(See also Characters; Story.)*
   action, 41
   books, 13
   classic, 16
   contemporary, 16, 41
   fantasy, 17
   historical, 15, 16, 41, 42, 59, 84, 103
   inspirational, 81
   life issues, 61, 188
   literary, 188
   middle-grade, 14-15, 41, 59-68, 84, 98, 103
   multicultural, 83, 98
   mysteries, 15, 16
   niche, 83, 84, 99
   and nonfiction, division, 46
   paperbacks, 41
   picture book-like stories, 13
   regional, 16
   series, 59
   serious fiction, 13
   sports, 212, 220
   stories and character education, 13
   submissions, 83-84, 98, 100, 101, 102, 103, 104
   young adult, 18, 21, 41
Figel, Christina, 162, 165, 166

Filler, 224
Filtering devices, Internet, 40
Finding Images Online: Online User's Guide to Image Searching in Cyberspace, 232
First Book, 42
First Moments, 29
Fisher, Cynthia, 65
The 5000 Hours of Baseball, 213
Flannigan, Jennifer, 16
Flare, 41
Fletcher, Susan, 62
The Flicker, 47
The Flunking of Joshua T. Bates, 67
Fly Girl and Other Poems, 70
Fogelman, Phyliss, 13, 14, 15
Footsteps, 145, 149-151
Ford, Bernette, 53, 54
Forecasts Club, 42
Form and formats,
  experimental, 60
  poetry, 73
Fort Ticonderoga Museum, 229
Forty Acres and Maybe a Mule, 38
Foster, Frances, and Frances Foster Books, 38, 249-254, 273, 275
Foster, Genevieve, 118
Fourth Grade Weirdo, 63
FPG, photo stock house, 229
First Amendment, 35
Franklin Watts, 214
Freedman, Russell, 118
Freeman, Martha, 63
Free speech, 35, 40
Free Willy, 129
Friedman, Andrew, 34
Frindle, 11
Fritz, Jean, 118
From College to the Real World, 163
Frontlists, 170, 173
Front Street, 61, 62, 63, 65
Fryxell, David, 130
Funding, schools and libraries, 7
Futech Interactive Products, 39

G

Gaber, Susan, 265
Gale, David, 119, 122, 124
Galleazzi, Amy, 32
Gallo, Dan, 214
GAME BOY, 60
A Gardener's Alphabet, 241
Garretson, Jerri, 157

Garten, Keith, 31
Gates, Tracy, 70, 71
Gay, Kathlyn, 127, 128, 129, 130, 132
G Ball, 26, 43
Genesis, 125
Geography texts, 41
George and Martha, 22
George, Jean Craighead, 163
George, Kristine O'Connell, 71
George Shrinks, 22
George Washington's World, 118
Geringer, Laura, 8, 11, 39
Gerstein, Mordicai, 250
GetNetWise.org, 35
Getty Research Institute, 195, 200-202
Ghosts of the 20th Century, 177
Giblin, James Cross, 230, 231, 233
Gib Rides Home, 110, 111, 112
Gilligan, Carol, 255, 256
Gillman, Alec, 265
A Giraffe and a Half, 37
Girls, 16, 18, 26, 43, 44, 64, 212, 221, 255-259
The Giving Tree, 37
Glisson, Michele, 233, 234
Global Children's Books, 46
Golden Books, 11, 40, 47
Golden Triangle Books, 16, 42
Goodman, Joan, 109, 110, 111, 117, 118
Good News Publishing, 22
Good Times on Grandfather Mountain, 265
Goosebumps, 66
Goosebumps Thrillogy, 163
Gorman, Carol, 65
Gould, Betsy, 46
Grace's Letter to Lincoln, 110, 116, 117
Gramataky, Hardie, 37
Grandmother Bryant's Pocket, 263, 265
The Grandparent Poems, 75
The Grand Rapids Press, 216
Graves, Robert, 9
The Great Frog Race, 71
Greenburg, Hank, 219
Green, Rhonda Gowler, 74
The Green Truck Garden Giveaway, A Neighborhood Story and Almanac, 263, 265
Greenwillow Books, 8, 11, 39, 63, 64, 74
Grolier, 8
Grosset & Dunlap, 11, 37, 163
Grossman, Bill, 71, 72, 74
Growing Tree, 55, 70, 72
Gruner + Jahr, 29

Gruver, Nancy, 255-258
Guare, John, 143
Guess How Much I Love You, 187
Guide, 93
Guideposts for Kids, 46, 93, 224, 229, 230, 231
Guideposts for Teens, 127, 130, 224, 229, 230, 231
Gunning, Monica, 71
Gutman, Dan, 212, 218, 219

H

Haas, Jesse, 63
Habibi, 38
Hachette Filipacchi, 29
Halberstam, David, 219
Hall, Donald, 241
Hallensleben, Georg, 250
Halloween Hoots & Howls, 72
Hamilton, Virginia, 272
Hammett Company, 45
Hamm, Mia, 26
Hand-selling, 157
"Hangin', Just Us Two," 73
Hanks, Stephen, 29
Harcourt, Inc., 47, 162, 164, 165
Hardcover books, 13, 19, 67
A Hard Road to Glory, 216
Hardy Boys, 163
Harkrader, Lisa, 127, 131, 132
Harness, Cheryl, 177
Harper, Bob, 56
HarperCollins, 7, 8, 9, 10, 11, 23, 37, 39, 41, 46, 55, 60, 64, 65, 66, 70, 159, 185
    HarperFestival, 8, 11, 39
    HarperTrophy, 8, 11, 39
Harris, Joel Chandler, 119
Harry Potter books, 14, 15, 19, 20, 41, 59, 187, 188, 267, 268
    Harry Potter and the Chamber of Secrets, 14, 44, 59, 267
    Harry Potter and the Prisoner of Azkaban, 14, 15, 267
    Harry Potter and the Sorcerer's Stone, 14, 20, 44, 59, 267, 269
Harshman, Terry, 56, 57
Harvey Potter's Balloon Farm, 20
Hasbro, 44
Have You Been to the Beach Lately, 74
Health, fitness, nutrition, 26, 43, 131
Healthy Kids, 29
Hearne, Betsy, 38
Hearst Corporation, 11, 33, 39

Heaton, Mary, 259-261
Heaven, 38
Henkes, Kevin, 63
Hesse, Karen, 70, 72
Heyman Films, 44
"Hey Ma, Something's Under My Bed," 72
Hicklebee's Bookstore, 155
Higgins Bend Song and Dance, 265
Highlights for Children, 30, 127, 128, 130, 145-147, 246, 260
Highsmith Press, 21, 108
Hildebrandt, Tim, 174
Hill, Donna, 38
Hinman, Bill, 180
Hippocrene Books, 41
Hippocrene Children's Illustrated Foreign Language Dictionaries, 41
Hirschman, Susan, 74
"His Hand Is Quicker Than Your Eye" 96
Hispanic markets, 44
Historical fiction, 15, 16, 19, 41, 42, 59, 84, 103, 109-118, 119, 120, 122, 123
History, 109-118, 130, 213
History Mysteries, 15, 16, 41, 283
History of Woman Suffrage, 114
Hodge, Alicia, 148, 149
Holes, 19, 38, 42, 65, 251, 252, 272, 273, 274, 275
Holiday House, 60, 63, 65
Holm, Jennifer, 63
Holohan, Maureen, 211, 212, 218, 219, 221
Henry Holt, 8, 69, 72, 75, 164, 165, 277
Holton, Lisa, 46
Homeless Bird, 64
Honus & Me, 212
Hope's Crossing, 110, 111
Hopkins, Lee Bennet, 72, 75
Hopkinson, Deborah, 112, 113, 114, 115, 116
Hopscotch, 83, 98, 131, 243, 244, 245, 246
Horn Book, 52, 272
Horowitz, Ellen, 80, 81, 88
Horten, Edith, 214
Horton, Joan, 72, 73
Houghton Mifflin, 37, 42, 240, 265
"How the Animals Came to Earth," 121
Howard, Ginger, 186
Howe, James, 37, 66
How the Grinch Stole Christmas, 20, 42
How I Saved Hanukkah, 65
How to Be a Successful Self-Publisher, 218
How to Talk to Your Cat, 163
How to Write Fast (While Writing Well), 130

Hues, 257
Hughes, Dean, 212, 217, 219, 221
Human Kinetics, 21
Humor, 59, 65, 67
Hurwitz, Johanna, 241
Hyde, Henry, 35
Hyperion, 40, 46

I

I, Claudius, 9
Ideas,
    development, 287-325
    Internet, 299-303
    sports, 213
If That Breathes Fire, We're Toast, 65
If You Give a Pig a Pancake, 9
I Hate You! I Like You!, 250
Illustrators, 10, 20, 22, 239-242
The Important Book, 37
Imprints, new, 13, 15, 16, 22, 41, 282
Ingram Book Group, 39, 154, 158, 159
Inspirational
    fiction, 81
    magazines, 130
Insurance, freelancers, 177-181
    Aetna/US Healthcare, 181
    Americans for Financial Security, 178
    Best's Key Rating Guide, 180
    Brother's Keeper program, 179
    Christian Brotherhood Newsletter, 178
    coinsurance, copayments, 178
    college alumni associations, 181
    Consolidated Omnibus Budget Reconciliation Act (COBRA), 177
    deductible, 178
    drug card, 178
    group coverage, 180
    health maintenance organization (HMO), 178, 180
    individual policy, 180
    Manufacturers Life Insurance Company, 181
    Medicare, 181
    Mega Life and Health, 178
    Mutual of Omaha, 177, 181
    preferred provider organization (PPO), 178, 180
Interactive books, 51, 52
International Reading Association, 52, 70
Internet, 19 *(See also World Wide Web.)*
    best sites for writers, 225-228
    book printing, 43, 45
    children's sites, 299, 300
    Compuserve's Litforum, 300
    digital images, 233
    e-rate discounts, 40
    filtering devices, 40
    forums, 224
    historical archives, 300
    ideas, 299-303
    insurance sites, 180
    interviews, 301, 302
    listservs, 299, 301, 303
    networking contacts, 137, 142
    photo research, 229-236
    Read-Aloud with Random House, 45
    research, 195, 197, 198, 200, 202, 208, 209, 223-228
    search engines, 223, 224
    special sales, 165
    sports research, 215
    teen sites, 300
    writers' groups, 223
Interviews, 128, 301, 302
The Iron Giant, 42
Ironman, 211
I See the Rhythm, 38
Islander, 60
I Spy, 39
It's Mine, 250
I Was a Third Grade Science Project, 63, 65
Izzie, Growing Up on the Plains in the 1880s, 157

J

Jackie & Me, 212
Jackson, Kate Morgan, 46
Jackson, Richard, 11, 13
Jacobs, Michael, 14, 19
Janescko, Paul, 70
A Jar of Tiny Stars, 75
Jenkins, Dan, 219
Jensen, Malcolm, 149
Jericho Historical Museum, 240
"Jody's Triumph," 99
Johnny Kaw, The Pioneer Spirit of Kansas, 157
Johnny's in the Basement, 273
Johnson, Angela, 38
Johnson, Dinah, 70
Johnson, Donna, 56, 57
Jostens Learning, 33
Jukes, Mavis, 250, 251
Junie B. Jones series, 184
JuniorNet, 30
Jupiter Communications, 30

Just Us Two, Poems About Animal Dads, 69, 70, 73

K
Kaiser, Richard J., 99
Kalman, Bobbie, 93
Kane, Cindy, 46, 64, 65, 67
Kansas Originals Market, 157
Katz, Susan, 7, 9, 10, 23, 39
Kavka, Dorothy, 218
Keating, Joanne, 300
Kelly, Joe, 255-258
Kick!, 25
Kidding Around Kansas City, 127
Kids Can!, 54
Kids Discover, 277, 278, 279
A Kind of Grace: A Treasury of Sportswriting by Women, 219
King-Smith, Dick, 11
Kleinsasser, Lois, 178
Knight, Hilary, 41
Alfred A. Knopf Books, 8, 11, 59, 63, 66, 67, 69, 70, 71, 249, 252, 273
Knowlton, Ginger, 183, 184, 185, 187, 189, 190, 191
Koss, Amy Goldman, 64, 65
Kouts, Barbara, 183, 184, 185, 186, 187, 189
Kowalski, Kathiann, 300, 301
Kremer, John 161, 162, 164, 165, 167
Kruse, Ginny Moore, 110, 118
Kundiger, Marion, 157
Kuskin, Karla, 75
Kwan, Nancy, 42

L
Lacanski, June, 51, 52
Ladybug, 51, 56, 73
The Lamp, the Ice and the Boat Called Fish, 264
Language,
 dialect, slang, accents, 119-126
 preschool, 55
Lardner, Ring, 219
Larios, Julie, 63
Larson, Jeannette, 165, 166
Latingirl, 44
Launches,
 book imprints, 13, 15, 16, 22
 magazines, 25, 26, 30
Lax Mag, 25
Lazard Frères, 32
Leacock, Stephen, 287
Learning Company, 40, 41

Lee & Low Books, 42
LeFay, Alexandra, 122
Leftover Lily, 66
Leisure Concepts, 40
Lelooska, Chief, 38
Lemonade Sun and Other Summer Poems, 55
Lerner Publishing, 127, 131
LeRoy, Yolanda, 53, 54, 57
Lester, Julius, 119, 120, 121, 124, 125
Let My People Go, 38
Levin, Judy, 265
Levine, Arthur 269
Levine, Gail Carson, 9, 11
Levine, Mark, 277
Lewis, Catherine, 62
Lewis, C.S., 268
Lewis, Tommi, 47
Lewis, Valerie, 155, 159
Libraries and librarians *(See also Education; Research, Schools and libraries.)*
 book fairs and clubs, 172
 budgets, 23
 encouraging reading, 19
 poetry, 69
 prek books, 51, 53
 resources, 16
 technology, 40
 writer networking, 139, 143
Library of Congress, 195, 204-209, 231
Licensing, photos, 232, 234
Lieurance, Suzanne, 129, 130, 131
Lift-the-flap books, 22
Like Jake and Me, 250
Lindstrom, Elizabeth, 90
Lion Books, 21
Lionni, Leo, 250, 251, 253
Listen, 81, 89
Listening Library, 39
Literacy, 51, 52
Literary Marketplace, 269
Little Bill series, 42
Little, Brown, 240
Little, Christopher, 269
Little Hands, 54
Little House series, 41
Little Simon, 11
Little Tiger, 39
Little Toot, 37
Little Women, 44
Living, 81, 97
Livingston, Myra Cohn, 71
Logan, Don, 26

Logan, Harriet, 175
Loganberry Books, 175
Lombardi, Robert, 162, 163, 165, 166, 167
A Long Way from Chicago, 65
Lothrop, Lee & Shepard, 8, 11, 39
Lotz, Karen, 46
Love from Your Friend Hannah, 66
Lugara, Rebecca, 84, 102
Lunchbox Mail, 70
Lurie, Stephanie, 46, 164, 165
Lutes, Christopher, 148, 149
Lynch, Chris, 63
Lyon, George Ella, 52

M

Macmillan, 8, 9, 69
Macy, Sue, 212, 215, 216, 217, 218, 219, 221
Madeline, 37
Magazine Publishers of America, 25
Magic Attic Press, 46
The Magic School Bus, 186
Magalog, 44
Magazine Publishers of America, 25
Magazines
    advertising, 25
    brand names, 30
    celebrity, 32, 33
    consumer spending, 25
    editorial development and production, 145-151
    educational, 26, 31, 32, 33, 43, 149, 150
    electronic, 30
    new niches, 25, 31
    parenting and family, 28, 29, 31
    pictures and text, 278
    preschool, 45, 51, 52
    religious, 147-49
    science, 26, 27, 29
    service, 32
    special interest, 32, 33, 34
    sports, 25, 26
    vertical titles, 31
    young adults, 31, 32-33
The Mailbox Teacher, 47
Making Up Megaboy, 67
Malinchak, James, 163
Malk, Steve, 183, 187, 188, 191
Maloney, Cynthia, 171
The Man Who Lived Alone, 241
Marcello, Patricia Cronin, 82, 93
Marcus, Barbara, 46
Maria's Comet, 112, 113, 114

Markets and marketing
    age groups, books, 184
    catalogues, 162
    daycare, 54
    demographics, 7, 18
    discount stores and price clubs, 9
    educational, 9, 10, 16, 26, 31, 32
    elementary, 26, 31, 32
    encouraging readers, 22
    fairs and clubs, 169-175
    Internet, special markets, 165
    K-12, 54
    library, 53, 54
    middle school, 31
    museums, 163
    niche or special, 161-168
    online, 7
    premium sales, 162
    preschool, 53, 54, 55
    publicity, 161, 162, 165
    research, 55
    resources, 168
    retail, 9
    sales forces, 166
    schools and libraries, 7, 9, 10, 108, 258
    segments, 9
    special markets, 9, 10
    teens, 18, 19
    trade, 10, 31
    writer's role, 166, 167, 169, 170
Marshall, James, 9
"Marshmallows, a Medicine?" 86, 87
Marston, Hope, 301, 302
Martin, Jacqueline Briggs, 38, 110, 239, 263-265
Martin, Mary, 119, 120, 125
Martin, Terri, 65
Marvin Redpost books, 273
Mary Geddy's Day: A Colonial Girl in Williamsburg, 122, 123
Massey, May, 249
Mass-market books, 9, 66
Masters Press, 21
MATH, 83
Mathers, Petra, 265
Math Made Easy series, 45
Mattel, 40, 41
Matthew's Dream, 250
Mayes, Walter, 153, 154, 155
Max and Ruby books, 13
McCaffrey, Janet, 147
McCallum, Jack, 219

McCord, David, 75
McCully, Emily Arnold, 114, 115
McElderry, Margaret K., 11, 71, 300
McEntire, Reba, 42
McGraw-Hill, 41
M.C. Higgins, The Great, 272
McKissack, Patricia and Fredrick, 38
McMullan, Kate, 72
Meadowbrook Press, 73
Micklos, John, 75
Media specialists *(See Librarians.)*
Media tie-ins, 18, 19, 190
Meers, Bill, 173
Meeting at the Crossroads, 255
Meier, Manuela, 149
Memories of the Mick, 219
The Meow Mix Guide to Cat Talk, 163
Merchandising, 8-9
Meredith Corporation, 33, 260
Mergers and acquisitions, 39, 252
   books, 8, 9, 184, 186, 191
   magazines, 29, 32, 33
Middle-grades, 14, 15, 19, 20, 41, 184, 185, 187
   developmental issues, 64
   family, 59, 60, 61, 84, 98, 103
   fiction, 59-69
   life issues, 61
   nonfiction, 88, 96
   readers, 64
Midnight in the Garden of Good and Evil, 186
Mike Mulligan and His Steam Shovel, 37
Miles of Smiles, 73
The Millbrook Press, 40, 70
Millen, C.M., 241
Milwaukee Magazine, 281
Minnesota Historical Society, 233
Missouri Historical Society, 233
Miss Spider's Tea Party, 261
Mitchell, Viola, 218
Modern Curriculum Press, 46
Moeyart, Bart, 61
Molthop, Susan, 223, 224
The Mommy Poems, 75
Money, teen magazine, 43
Monkey Soup, 273
Monohon, Louise, 84, 100
Moore, Mary Alice, 46
Pierpont Morgan Museum Library, 195, 202-204
Morgan Reynolds, 21
William Morrow, and Morrow Junior Books, 8, 9, 11, 39, 41, 185
Morrow, Paula, 51, 57
Moss, Marissa, 283
The Most Beautiful Place in the World, 250
Motivation, 113
Mountain Biking, 212
A Mouse Called Wolf, 11
"Mouse Haiku," 73
The Mouse of Amherst, 250
Mouseworks, 46
Movies, and books, 19, 20, 42, 44
Mulberry, 11, 39
Multicultural fiction, 83
Murphy, Steven, 40
Museums, 163
My Little Sister Ate One Hare, 72
My Little Sister Hugged an Ape, 72
Mysteries, 15, 16, 20

N

Nancy Drew books, 16, 163
Narrative,
   nonfiction, 56
   verse, 72
National Children's Poetry Week, 69
National Directory of Magazines, 25
National Geographic Society, 41
   National Geographic, 230
   National Geographic World, 92, 230, 231
National Poetry Month, 69
National Runaway Switchboard, 94
National Teen Read Week, 42
National Wildlife Federation, 44, 56, 162
National Writers Union, 181
Natural history, 41
The Nature Conservancy, 92
Naylor, Phyllis Reynolds, 37, 64, 66
Newspapers *(See Research.)*
Networking, 137-144
   author visits, 139, 140, 142
   bookstores, 141
   libraries, 139, 143
   schools, 138, 139, 141
   tips, 140-41, 142
   writers' conferences, 137
   writers' groups, 137, 138
Networking at Writers' Conferences, From Contacts to Contracts, 139, 141
New Age books, 191
Newbery Medal *(See Awards and Prizes.)*
Newman, Aline, 224
New Moon, 255-258

New Moon Books, 257
New Moon Network, 257
Newsmagazines, 43
New York Times Company, 43
New York Times, 15, 59, 218
New York Times Upfront, 31, 43
Niche publishing
  magazines, 25, 31
  small presses, 10, 21
  special interest, 21, 25
Nickelodeon, 45
  Nick Jr., 45
  Nick Jr. Noodle, 45
Nintendo, 40
Nivola, Claire, 250
Noise, 43
Nolan, Jim, 177, 181
Nonfiction *(See also Biography; History; Science; and other nonfiction topics.)*
  creative nonfiction, 186
  focus, 127-133
  magazines, 54, 56, 57, 258, 282
  middle-grade, 88, 96
  narrative, 56
  picture books, 53
  preschool, 51, 52, 53
  sales, 129, 130, 131
  sports, 27, 212, 220
  storytelling, 56, 186
  submissions, 79-81, 84-96, 104-106
  v. fiction, 56, 129
  young adult, 18, 21, 90, 96
No, No, Jo, 69, 72
Nordstrom, Ursula, 10, 191, 249
North-South Books, 41, 46
Not a Copper Penny in Me House, 71
Novelty books, 53
Numeroff, Laura Joffe, 9
Nye, Naomi Shihab, 38

O

O'Brien, Kim, 219
Occult, and censorship, 42
Odyssea, 277
Odyssey, 81, 90, 149
The Official Major League Baseball Fact Book, 218
Old Possum's Book of Cats, 73
Old, Wendi, 128, 129
Olive, the Other Reindeer, 42
On-demand printing, 43
Ondracek, Brian, 22, 23

101 Ways to Bug Your Parents, 137
Online sales, 7
On the Stairs, 63
Open Horizons, 161, 164
Ophelia Speaks: Adolescent Girls Write About Their Search for Self, 11
Orchard Books, 8, 46, 70, 73, 74
Ormai, Stella, 265
The Other Side: Shorter Poems, 38
Ottaviano, Christy, 69, 70, 75, 164, 165
Our Only Mae Amelia, 63
Outlines, 80, 81, 85, 87, 91, 95, 130
Out of the Dust, 70
Orgel, Doris, 186
Outside Images, 219
The Oxford English Dictionary (OED), 123

P

Pack-O-Fun, 100
Paddington, 37
Palotta, Jerry, 10
Pantheon, 249
Paperbacks, 9, 42, 67
Parents
  online book club, 44
  encouraging reading, 19
  low-income, and reading, 52
  magazines, parenting, 28, 29, 31
  middle-grade, 60
  preschool, 45, 51, 54
  purchases, 14
  resources, 16
  safe websites, 35
Parents, 29
Parents as Partners in Reading: A Family Literacy Training Program, 52
Parenting, 29
Park, Barbara, 184
Partners, 156, 158, 159
Pattison, Darcy, 173
Paul, Ann Whitford, 71
Paulsen, Gary, 13
"Paying the Price," 89
Payne, Allison, 224
PBS, 257
Peck, Richard, 65
"The Pecking Order," 102
Peerson, Marie, 52
Penguin Canada, 300
Penguin Putnam, 8, 11, 13, 159, 162
J.C. Penney, 43
The Perfect Storm, 186

-417-

Perkins, Lynn Rae, 64
Personal experience, 211
Petersen Publishing, 34, 47
Peterson, Linda, 22
The Philadelphia Inquirer, 219
Philadelphia Tribune, 217
Philomel Books, 11
Photographs, 219, 220
    budgeting for, 231
    Center for Disease Control (CDC), 231
    digital images, 233
    Library of Congress, 231
    licensing, 232, 234
    NASA, 231
    royalties, 232
    stock agencies, 229, 230, 231
    Web research, 229-236
Photo Stock Notes, 232
"Piano Panic," 97
Picture books, 9, 10, 13, 14, 19, 22, 39, 41, 263, 264
    art, 20
    dummies, 240
    heart of book lists, 20
    middle-grade, 62
    movies, 20
    nonfiction, 53
    poetry, 70, 72
    preschool, 53, 187
    religious, 23
    sales, 9
Pilkey, Dav, 170
Pines, Nancy, 18, 19
Pink and Say, 120
Pinkney, Jerry, 13
Pinkney, Myles, 70
Pittsburgh Courier, 217
Play Like a Girl, 212
Pleasant Company, 15, 41, 43, 281, 282 *(See also American Girl.)*
Plot, 112, 274
Pocket Pulse, 11, 41, 42
Pocket Books, 41
Poems That Sing to You, 75
Poetry, 69-76, 187, 188
    form, 73
    narrative, 72
    older readers, 70
    picture books, 70, 72
    preschool, 70
    rhyme, 57, 70, 71, 72, 73, 74, 188
    rhythm, 70, 71

school market, 70
teens, 72
themed, 75
verse play, 84, 100, 101
voice, 72, 73
Point of view, 275
Pokémon, 40
Polacco, Patricia, 120
"Polly and the Three Bears," 100, 101
Pool, Deborah, 57
Population, 51
Postcards to Father Abraham, 62
Pow-Wow, 93
Prelutsky, Jack, 69, 74, 75
Preschool, 51-57
    books, 12, 14, 20
    developmental skills, 56
    magazines, 43, 45
    poetry, 70
    research, 56, 57
    verse play, 84
Price, Oliver, 16
Primedia, 29, 32, 34, 43
Princeton University, 216, 217
Profiles, 96
Project Headstart, 52
Promotion, book, 161-169, 187
Proposal, book, 84, 85, 103
Publicists and publicity, 161, 162, 165
Publisher's Clearinghouse, 162
Publishers Weekly, 11, 13, 69
Puffin Books, 11, 37
"Put the Brolly in the Boot and Let's Go," 98
G.P. Putnam & Sons, 11, 138

Q

Queries and cover letters, 79-108
    fiction, 83, 84, 97, 98, 99, 100
    nonfiction, 80, 86, 88, 89, 92, 93
    photos, 224

R

Raab, Susan Salzman and Raab Associates, 161, 164, 165, 166, 169
The Rainbow Hand, 71
Raising Teens, 33
Ramona's World, 11
Random House, 8, 11, 39, 44, 45, 69, 74, 159, 162, 163, 165, 252
The Random House Book of Poetry for Children, 74
Ranger Rick, 30, 56, 57, 82, 92
Rapoport, Ken, 219

Rapp, Adam, 63
Rapunzel, 38
Ravenstone Press, 157
Read-Aloud with Random House, 45
Readers
    age needs, 131, 132
    becoming readers, 22
    early, 53
    emerging, 53
    girls, 16
    literacy, 51, 52
    middle-grade, 14, 20, 64
    9-14 years, 15, 16
    "older" children, 15, 23
    preschool, 14, 20
    promoting, 42, 45
    religious publishing, 23, 130
    reluctant, 212
    second-to-sixth-grade, 23
    12-13 years, reading drop, 19
    young adults, 18, 19, 20, 42
Reader's Digest, 162
The Readers Guide to Periodical Literature, 218
Reading aloud, 52, 72
Reading Rainbow, 40
Reba's First Book Club, 42
Redenbaugh, Vicki Jo, 265
Red-Eyed Tree Frog, 38
Reeves, Howard, 42
References, 39, 45, 84, 85
Regional fiction, 16
Relatively Speaking, 74
Religious publishing, 22, 23
    board and lift-the-flap books, 22
    bookselling online, 44
    magazine, 147-49
    picture books, 22, 23
    quality in books, 22
    readers, 130
    series, 23
    spirituality, 191
    submissions, 81
    technology, 22, 23
Reluctant readers, 212
Reorganizations, 8, 31, 32, 39
Research, 195-235
    audience, 56
    British Library, 195, 198-200
    children's sites, 299
    electronic resources, 195, 197, 198, 200, 202, 208, 209
    experts, 220, 302
    Getty Research Institute, 195, 200-202
    historical archives, 300
    Internet, 223-228
    interviews, 301, 302
    IRIS, 195
    language, 123, 124
    Library of Congress, 195, 204-234
    listservs, 299, 301, 303
    newspapers, 216, 217, 301, 303
    nonfiction focus, 128
    Pierpont Morgan Museum Library, 195, 202-204
    OPAC, 195
    organization, 217, 218
    photos, Web, 229-236
    preschool nonfiction, 57
    special collections, 195
    sports, 211-221
    teen sites, 300
    university and research libraries, 195-210
    University of Chicago, 195, 196-197
    websites, 235
Retailers
    magazines, 44
    new media, 45
Returns, book, 158
Reuther, David, 41, 46
Reviews, books, 153
Reynolds, Christi, 81, 89
Rhythm, 70, 71, 123, 124
Rhyme, 57, 70, 71, 72, 73, 74, 188
Rich, Susan, 60, 66, 67, 68
Richter, Rick, 7, 9, 13, 18, 19
Rider, Ann, 265
Rights, 189, 190, 191
Ripplewood Holdings, 32
The River Dragon, 173
Roberts, Melissa, 122, 124
Robinet, Hariette Gillem, 38
Robinson, Marileta, 145, 146
Rock Climbing, 212
Rocket Books, 190
Roller Coasters, or I Had So Much Fun I Almost Puked, 128, 130
Rolling . . . In-line!, 219
Romero, Emily, 54
Roome, Hugh, 32, 39
Roop, Peter and Connie, 110, 116
Rosenberg, Liz, 70
Ross, Catherine, 83, 99
Roswell, 42
Roswell High series, 42

Rothenberg, Alan, 30
Roundtable Press, 46
Roussan Publishers, 21
Rowland, Pleasant T., 281, 282
Rowling, J.K., 14, 19, 42, 187, 267-269
Roxburgh, Stephen, 61, 62, 63, 64, 65
Royalties, photos, 232
Running Loose, 211
Russenberger, Susie, 154, 158, 159
Russo, Camille, 29
Ryan, Mary, 80, 83, 96
Rylant, Cynthia, 60

S

Sabia, Mary Ann, 10, 13
Sachar, Emily, 92
Sachar, Louis, 19, 38, 42, 65, 250, 251, 252, 271-275
Sager, Donald J., 108
Sales
   book publishers, 11, 14
   demographics, 7, 18, 10
   hand-selling, 19
   hardcovers, 19
   Harry Potter books, 14-15
   online, 7, 15
   poetry, 69, 70
   teens, 18, 19
Sammy Keyes and the Hotel Thief, 63
Sand, Sea and Surf, 75
Sands, Stella, 277-279
Sarah Morton's Day: A Day in the Life of a Pilgrim Girl, 124
Satchmo's Blues, 117
Saul, Carol P., 241
Sawicki, Norma Jean, 265
Scarpa, Julie, 171, 172
Schaefer, Carole Lexa, 72
Schaffer, David, 83, 94
Schertle, Alice, 71
Schlessinger, Dr. Laura, 9
Schmitt, Donna, 80, 86
Scholastic, 14-15, 19, 39, 42, 43, 44, 46, 53, 59, 83, 92, 122, 169, 170-171, 173, 174, 186, 187, 267, 269, 277
Scholastic Choices, 94, 95
Scholastic Magazine Group, 31
Scholastic MATH, 94
Scholastic Update, 31, 43
School Library Journal, 74
Schools and libraries *(See also Educational publishing.)*

funding, 7, 183
markets, 7, 9, 29, 70
school and library markets, 258
writer networking, 138, 139, 140, 141
Schroeder, Alan, 117
Schroeder, Pat, 35
Schulman, Janet, 69, 74, 75
Schwartz, Anne and Anne Schwartz Books, 112, 113, 114, 116
Science,
   books, 26, 41
   focus, 128, 129, 130
   magazines, 26, 27, 29
   preschool, 53, 56
Science fiction, 190
Science at Home, 29
Scientific American, 26
Scieszka, Jon, 66, 188
Scope Systems, 224
Scrappers series, 212, 218
Charles Scribner's Sons, 103, 249
Sea Gifts, 239, 241
The Secret Life of Amanda K. Woods, 250
Segal, Lore, 250
Seibold, J. Otto, 42
Self-publishing, 156, 189
Senate Commerce Committee, 40
Sendak, Maurice, 9, 10
Series fiction, 59, 67
A Series of Unfortunate Events, 66
Sesame Street, 52
Seuss, Dr., 69, 74, 163
Seven Brave Women, 38
Seventeen, 32, 33
Sideways Arithmetic from Wayside School, 273
Sideways Stories from Wayside School, 271, 272, 273
Shabanu: Daughter of the Wind, 250
Shadow Spinner, 62
The Shakespeare Stealer, 178
Shandler, Sara, 11
Shannon, George, 241
Shannon, Terry Miller, 300, 303
Sheldon, Ken, 229
Shepherd, Donna Walsh, 301, 302
Shields, Amy, 70, 72, 73
Shiloh 2: Shiloh Season, 42
Shipwreck Season, 38
Shriek!, 22
Shriver, Maria, 11
Shulevitz, Uri, 38
Sidman, Joyce, 70, 73

Silverstein, Shel, 10, 37, 69
Silver Threads, 300
Silver Whistle, 124
Simmonds, Steve, 13
Simon & Schuster, 7, 8, 9, 11, 13, 40, 41, 42, 46, 61, 119, 153, 154, 159, 164, 165, 177, 300
Simon Spotlight, 11
Simpson, Cleary, 26
Sis, Peter, 38, 250, 252
Six Degrees of Separation, 143
16 magazine, 32
16 Superstars, 32
Sixth Grade Secrets, 273
Skechers USA, 44
Skolsky, Mindy Warshaw, 66
Skrypuch, Marsha, 300, 302
Skurzynski, Gloria, 62
Slang, 119, 120, 124, 125
Slant *(See Nonfiction, focus.)*
Slattery, Kathryn, 83, 98
Smagler, Alan, 153, 154
Small presses, 10, 20, 184
　distribution, 156, 157, 159
　young adult, chart, 21
A Small Tall Tale from the Far Far North, 250
Smith, Hope Anita, 70
Smith, Ken, 219
Smith, Lane, 188
Smithmark Publishers, 46
Sneed, Brad, 265
Snicket, Lemony, 66
Snyder, Zilpha Keatley, 109, 110, 111, 112
Snow, 38
Snowflake Bentley, 38, 110, 239, 240, 263-265
Snowflake Bentley, Man of Science, Man of God, 264
Society of Children's Book Writers and Illustrators (SCBWI), 142, 169
　insurance, 181
　research, 223
　writers' conferences, 387
Softball for Girls, 218
SoftBook Press, 44
Softbook Reader, 44
Someday Angeline, 273
Songs from Home, 109
Sort of Forever, 63
Souder, Eugene K., 97
Sounder, 46, 121
Soundprints, 39, 302
Sowienski, Richard, 34

Special interest magazines, 32, 33, 34
Special markets, 161-168
Spratt, Lee and Steven, 139, 141
Spider, 98
Spider's Voice, 62
Spinelli, Jerry, 9
Spires, Elizabeth, 250
Sports
　chart, magazine nonfiction, 27
　girls', 212, 218, 221
　experts, 220
　magazines, 25, 26, 43
　references, 218
　research, 211-221
　women's, 212
　young adults', 211
Sports Illustrated, 219
Sports Illustrated For Kids, 26, 30, 37, 246
Sports Illustrated For Women, 26, 43
The Stable Where Jesus was Born, 74
Staples, Suzanne Fisher, 250, 251, 252
Stark, Jayson, 219
Starr, Nancy, 46
Starry Messenger, 250
Star Wars, 11
Staying Fat for Sarah Barns, 211, 212
Stein, Ellen, 70, 72
Stevenson, Dinah, 265
Stewart, Jennifer, J., 65
The Stinky Cheese Man, 22
Stoddard, Gloria May, 264
Stoll, Don, 260
Tony Stone, photo stock house, 229
The Stories Julian Tells, 250
Story, 18, 113, 120
　nonfiction, 56, 128, 186
　sports, 213
Storybook Birthday Parties, 85, 108
Storybooks, 39, 40
The Story of Mrs. Lovewright and Purrless Her Cat, 250
Strauss, Linda Leopold, 63
Strickland, Michael, 75
Strickland, Tessa, 52
Straight, 84, 102
Structure, 128
Stuart Little, 20, 42
Style, middle-grade fiction, 60
Submissions, 79-108
Subtext, 32
Sun & Spoon, 63
SuperScience, 82, 92

Superteen, 32
Surfing, 212, 217, 220
Sweet Dreams of the Wild, 55
Sweet and Sour Lily, 66
Sweet Valley series, 45
Swine Lake, 9
Symphony for the Sheep, 239, 241

T

The Tale of John Barleycorn: Or from Barley to Beer, 241
Talewinds, 13
The Tales of Uncle Remus, 121
Talking to Angels, 163
Target, 44
Tarshis, Lauren, 94
Taxi Dog, 20
Taylor, Mildred, 13
Teachers, (See also Education; Schools and libraries; Textbooks.)
   encouraging reading, 19
   online book club, 44
   preschool, 54
   resources, 16
   safe websites, 35
   training materials, 39
Technology
   books, 41
   censorship, 40
   publishing technology, 22, 23, 189
Teen, 32, 33, 47
Teen Beat, 32
Teen Beat Allstars, 32
Teen Machine, 32
Teen Newsweek, 31, 43
Teen People, 32, 33
Teen Read Week, 42
Teens (See Young Adults.)
Teen 'Zine, 44
Telander, Rick, 219
Television,
   ABC, 40
   and books, 18, 19, 20, 22, 41, 42
   and magazines, 45
   newsmagazine for girls, 257
   PBS, 40
   Reading Rainbow, 40
Tell Me Something Happy Before I Go to Sleep, 167
Tempest Books, 8, 11, 39, 41
Textbooks, 10, 13
Theme, 127, 258

There's A Boy in the Girls' Bathroom, 250, 251, 252, 273
The Things They Carry, 219
Thompson, Kay, 11, 41
Three Golden Rivers, 16
Tibet: Through the Red Box, 38, 250
Tichnor & Fields Children's Books, 265
Tiger Beat, 32
Tiger Press, 39
Tildes, Phyllis, 55
Time, 31
Time For Kids, 31
Time, Inc., 26, 29, 31
The Time Machine, 44
Titanic Crossing, 67
Today, I Feel Silly and Other Moods That Make My Day, 9, 11
To Kill a Mockingbird, 61
Tolin, Rosanne, 46
Tomey, Sasha, 143
The Top of the World: Climbing Mount Everest, 38
Topspin, 47
Tor Books, 21
Torstar Corporation, 39
Trails 'N' Treasures, 47
Travel, 26
Traversy, Nancy, 52
Troll, 39, 169, 171-172
Trudy Corp., 39
The True Story of the Three Little Pigs, 188
Tucker, Charlotte, 41
Turtle, 56, 57
20th-Century Children's Poetry Treasure, 75
20,000 Leagues Under the Sea, 44
The Twits, 250

U

Unbroken, 63
Uncle Remus stories, 119, 124
University of Chicago, 195, 196-197
University of Pittsburgh Press, 16, 42
University of South Florida, 141
University of Wisconsin-Madison, 52, 110
Upfront, 31
USA Today, 30
U*S*Kids, 46, 127

V

Valerie and Walter's Best Books for Children: A Lively, Opinionated Guide, 153, 154, 156
van Draanen, Wendelin, 63

Van Leeuwen, Jean, 13
Verlaggesbruppe Georg von Hotzbrinck, 8
Veronis, Suhler & Associates, 25
Verse play, 84, 100
The Very Clumsy Click Beetle, 11
Viacom, 40
Victor, 250
Video games, 40
Viking Children's Books, 53, 54, 162, 165
Violence,
    books, 61
    free speech, 35
Virtually Perfect, 212
Vision Quest, 218
Vogel, Kate, 173
Voice, 18, 72, 188, 256, 275

W

Waldmen, Brett, 156, 158, 159
Walker, Alice, 219
Walker's Crossing, 37, 64
Wallace, Heather, 102
Wallace, Rich, 145, 146
Walsh, Vivian, 42
Walter, Virginia, 67
Wardlaw, Lee, 137, 138
Warner Brothers, 44
Warner, Sally, 63, 66
Waryncia, Lou, 149, 150, 151
Washing the Willow Tree Loon, 264, 265
The Wasteland, 73
Waters, Kate, 122, 123, 124
Watson, Esther, 163
The Watsons Go to Birmingham—1963, 11
Wayside School is Falling Down, 273
Wayside School Gets a Little Stranger, 273
Weaver, Will, 219
Weekly Reader, 30, 127
Weekly Reader Corporation, 31, 32
We Goddesses, 186
Wells, Rosemary, 13
West, Diana, 178, 179
Whelan, Gloria, 64
When the Wilderness Beckons, 99
Wild Outdoor World, 81, 88
Wild West, 93
What's Heaven, 11
When the Beginning Began, 124, 125
Where the Sidewalk Ends, 37
Where the Wild Things Are, 22
Whispering Coyote Press, 39
White, E.B., 14

Whitehead, Jenny, 70
Albert Whitman, 37
Who Came Down This Road, 52
Whole language, 10, 13
Wholesalers, 153-160
Why Do You Love Me?, 9
Wild Baby Animals, 43, 56, 57
The Wild Boy, 250
Wilder, Laura Ingalls, 41
Williams, Robin, 20
Williams, Sherley Anne, 46
Williamson Publishing, 53, 54, 56
Williamson, Susan, 53, 54
Willis Stein & Partners, 39
Wilson, Karma, 299, 301, 302
Wings in the Water, The Story of a Manta Ray, 302
Winning Ways: A Photohistory of American Women in Sports, 212, 216
Winslow Press, 46
Winters, Clay, 153
Wiseman, Paula, 124, 125
Wizards of the Coast, 44
Wojtyla, Karen, 112, 117
Wolff, Virginia Euwer, 213, 214, 218, 219
Women in Sports and Events (WISE), 218
Women's Sports Foundation, 218
"The Wonderful Tar Baby," 119
Wong, Janet, 71
Wood, Kim Marie, 128, 128
Wood, Michelle, 38
Woodburn, Judith, 15, 16, 281-283
Worcester, Don, 38
Wordsong, 70, 71, 72, 75
Wordware Publishing, 21
The World Series Encyclopedia, 219
World Wide Web
    about.com, 223
    alloy.com, 45
    amazon.com, 301
    alta Vista, 223
    ask Jeeves, 231
    authors, 165
    barnesandnoble.com, 40, 301
    best sites for writers, 225-228
    book fairs and clubs, 44, 172, 174
    bookselling, 45
    borders.com, 301
    britannica.com, 45
    broadcasts, 45
    broadcast.com, 44
    Delphi, 224

digital images, 233
e-books, 44
e-rate discounts, 40
forums, 224
Franklin Institute, 299
FreeZone, 299
frontstreetbooks.com, 63
GetNetWise.org, 35
gettingit.com, 45
girls, 18
gurl.com, 45
ibelieve.com, 44
insurance sites, 180
JuniorNet, 30
Kansas Originals Market, 157
logan.com/loganberry, 175
magazines, 30
networking contacts, 137, 142
newmoon.org, 258
online writing groups, 143
parent, teacher, library resources, 16
photo research, 229-236
preschool nonfiction, 56
research, 195, 197, 198, 200, 202, 208, 209, 215, 216, 235, 223-228
retailers, 45
safety, 35, 40
search engines, 223
sports, 215, 216
sweetvalley.com, 45
teens, 45, 300
teensatrandom.com, 45
teenreads.com, 45
writers' groups, 142, 223
Worth, Valerie, 75
The Wright Group, 119
Wringer, 9
Writers' conferences, 137, 139, 383-402
 book distribution, 154
 religious, 401-402
 SCBWI, 387-390
 university or regional, 391-400
Writers' Contests, 329-382
Writer's Exchange Guide, 223
Writers' groups, 137, 138
 online, 143, 223
Writers House, 183
Wroble, Lisa, 299, 300, 301, 303

X
Xerox Corporation, 43

Y
Yahoo! Broadcast Services, 44
YALSA *(See American Library Association.)*
The Year of the Sawdust Man, 122
YM, 32
Young Adult Library Services, (YALSA), 42
Young adults
 adolescence, 255, 256, 272
 biography, 104, 105
 "bleak book," 19
 book awards, 42
 book needs, 62
 Book-of-the-Month club, 42
 celebrities, 43
 e-books, 190
 education, 31
 fiction, 18, 39, 41, 84, 99, 102, 103
 Internet, 45, 300
 magazines, 31, 32-33, 43, 44
 marketing to, 18, 19
 nonfiction, 18, 94, 95, 96, 104, 105, 106, 107,
 poetry, 72
 promoting reading, 42
 religious magazine, 147-149
 series, 41
 small presses, 21
 special interest markets, 21
 sports, 211, 214
 teen culture, 18
Young & Alive, 99
Young Authors workshop, 141
Young Equestrian, 47
Young Money, 44
Your Big Backyard, 56, 57

Z
Zany Brainy, 45
Zelinsky, Paul, 38
Zemlicka, Shannon, 127, 131
Zemser, Amy Bronwen, 63
Zillions, 30
Zinny Weston, 65
Zonderkidz, 22
Zondervan Publishing, 22